GOOD READING

GOOD READING

A Guide for Serious Readers
21st Edition

J. Sherwood Weber, Editor

Ruth Ulman, Ethel Ashworth Crockford,
Arthur Waldhorn, Olga S. Weber, Arthur Zeiger,
Assistant Editors

R. R. BOWKER COMPANY
New York & London, 1978

Published by R. R. Bowker Company
1180 Avenue of the Americas, New York, N.Y. 10036
Copyright © 1978 by The Committee on College Reading
All rights reserved
Printed and bound in the United States of America

Library of Congress Cataloging in Publication Data
Main entry under title:

Good reading.

Includes index.
1. Bibliography—Best Books.   I. Weber, John
Sherwood, 1918-   II. Ulman, Ruth.
Z1035.G63   011   78-2424
ISBN 0-8352-1063-4

Contributors to *Good Reading*

OSWALDO ARANA, *California State University at Fullerton*
WILLIAM RAY ARNEY, *Dartmouth College*
JOSEPH A. BYRNES, *New York University*
ETHEL ASHWORTH CROCKFORD, *H. W. Wilson Company*
SUSAN E. CROCKFORD, *Yale University*
JAMES T. CROWN, *New York University*
DANIEL GERZOG, *Pratt Institute*
GLENDERLYN JOHNSON, *The Schomburg Center for Research in Black Culture*
HERMAN Y. KRINSKY, *Pratt Institute*
DANIEL McKINLEY, *State University of New York at Albany*
JACK MINKOFF, *Pratt Institute*
PAUL C. OBLER, *California State University at Fullerton*
PAUL OPPENHEIMER, *The City College of the City University of New York*
PHILIP RODDMAN, *Pratt Institute*
MARK SCHULMAN, *Antioch College*
JOAN SCHULZ, *State University of New York at Albany*
DONALD A. SEARS, *California State University at Fullerton*
OSCAR SHAFTEL, *Queens College of the City University of New York and Pratt Institute*
PAUL SHEPARD, *Pitzer College*
RUTH ULMAN, *H. W. Wilson Company*
AUSTIN L. VENABLE, *University of Alabama*
ARTHUR WALDHORN, *The City College of the City University of New York*
KENNETH G. WALLACE, *Pratt Institute*
ELIZABETH WEATHERFORD, *School of Visual Arts*
BERNERD C. WEBER, *University of Alabama*
J. SHERWOOD WEBER, *Pratt Institute*
OLGA S. WEBER, *R. R. Bowker Company*
JULES A. WEIN, *Pratt Institute*
ARTHUR ZEIGER, *The City College of the City University of New York*

Contents

HUMANITIES, SOCIAL SCIENCES, AND SCIENCES

SPECIAL SECTION

To the Reader

J. Sherwood Weber

For half a century, through twenty previous revisions and expansions, *Good Reading* has directed serious readers of all ages to books that inform and delight the mind. Published first in 1932 as a pamphlet, *Good Reading* then served as a guide to supplementary reading for college students. It was subsequently expanded in size and comprehensiveness every few years. In 1947 it appeared as a full-sized paperbound book. Periodically since then, *Good Reading* has been thoroughly revised. Two previous editions, including the most recent in 1969, were published also in hardcover editions primarily for libraries. Today, as an R. R. Bowker Company publication, this extensive revision attempts to touch upon all major fields of knowledge in which high school and college students, teachers on all levels, and the ever-growing audience of self-directed adult readers need and seek guidance.

This 1978 edition makes its predecessors obsolete. More than half of its chapters have been prepared by new editors, and many have new or substantially revised introductions; all its annotated book lists have been updated, and several have been expanded; data about authors, books, editions, and translations are current as of January 1978; a few chapters appear as self-contained entities for the first time.

The reader might be interested in several problems encountered in the course of preparing this revision. The first grew out of our observation that many traditionally distinct disciplines, particularly in the sciences and social sciences, are no longer clearly distinct. Interdisciplinary titles—for example, Edward Wilson's *Sociobiology*—were in the original book lists of three chapter editors; numerous other such books were cited by two or three editors. It is dramatically evident that modern research and thought span various disciplines, hence giving rise to departments of interdisciplinary studies in colleges and universities. This growing awareness of the complexity of our world, of the interrelatedness and interdependence of various entities, makes traditional classification difficult. We have tried to resolve this problem through the use of cross-references.

Second, we have found it inexpedient to represent in separate chapters truly interdisciplinary subjects, such as women's and minority studies. The reader will find numerous books on such subjects in many of the chapters, located according to the focus of the specific book involved. For example, books about the status of women during the Middle Ages are in "The Middle Ages"; books about minority employment are in "Economics" or "Sociology." Finally, we have endeavored to eliminate sexist and racist diction.

Despite the extensive changes in this 21st edition, the editorial goals remain constant: to provide the adult reader with an acute and compact companion for personal reading; the serious student with an experienced guide to the best in the vast world of books; the teacher with an informed aid for preparing reading lists and directing student reading; and the librarian with a proved consultant for advising readers as well as for shaping both the general and reference collections in the small library.

TO THE READER

One tested way to start using *Good Reading* is to check through the list, or those sections of it that particularly interest you, writing in one column those books you have already read and in another those you would like to read or reread. By systematically transferring titles from one column to the other, you can keep a record of your intellectual growth.

If you are seriously determined, you will set a reading standard for yourself and stick to it. A fair minimum is one book a week (in addition to a good daily newspaper and several periodicals), but a well-read person averages significantly more than this. No matter how occupied you think you are, and despite the audiovisual explosion, you must find time for non-required reading or surrender your aspirations to a wide culture. In short, what you read both measures your intellectual level and elevates it.

Desultory reading, while often attractive, is usually not as productive as organized reading. An easy way to plan the growth of your knowledge is to follow for several months an interesting trail of your own choosing: perhaps 20th-century European fiction, or Afro-American history, or the environment. If you enjoy one novel by Mann or Proust, or one history by John Hope Franklin, or one book on ecology by Aldo Leopold, you may want to read others by the same author on the same general subject.

But do not specialize too much. From time to time check the breadth of your reading by turning the pages of this book to discover where your large gaps appear. If you find that you know very little about 20th-century painting, Latin America, anthropology, or language and communications, you will know what to do.

Always read with a purpose—or, rather, with a succession of purposes—following a broad and flexible program, without binding yourself too rigidly to any scheme or system. And gamble occasionally: try an interesting looking book you happen to see on a library shelf or that someone casually recommends or that was favorably reviewed. Give yourself the opportunity for intellectual lightning to spark your mind and soul.

ARRANGEMENT

In order to profit most from this guide, familiarity with its arrangement is necessary. *Good Reading* is a highly selective, annotated bibliography of about 2,500 books that range across the varieties of literature—"the literature of knowledge" as well as "the literature of power." Its 35 book lists have been grouped into three parts: the first part consists of 10 chapters, classified by historical and regional criteria; the second has 6 chapters (divided into 11 book lists), arranged by standard literary types; and the third part contains 13 chapters, devoted to various humanities, social sciences, and sciences. A special final chapter lists basic reference books informed readers will want to know about and use. Subject areas not explicitly covered in separate chapters are generally included in related chapters and can be found by consulting the index. For example, if you desire books on prehistory, the index will refer you to "Greece," "The Middle East," "East and South Asia," "Africa," "History," and "Anthropology"—each of which chapters includes some titles on prehistory. The key to finding what is not readily apparent is generally the index.

The complete entry for any title, with rare exceptions, appears in the earliest chapter in which it logically belongs. Although the same book may be listed in a subsequent chapter, the second (or third) listing serves only as a cross-reference to the original, fully detailed entry. For example, the complete entry for Edward Wilson's *Sociobiology* appears in "Sociology." When *Sociobiology* subsequently reappears in "Biological Sciences" and "Ecosophy and the Environment," it does so as follows: "WILSON. *Sociobiology.* See 'Sociology,' page 226."

The compact essays that introduce each chapter, though varying in length and style, outline the subject matter historically, descriptively, or analytically, or in a combination of these methods. In addition, they often suggest authors and books the reader new to the subject will find especially helpful.

The annotated book lists form the core of the book. Within each section of each list, entries are ordered alphabetically by author. Each of the approximately 2,500 book entries observes, with minor variations, the same general format: author, title, brief comment, editions in print. The reader should be aware of the bibliographical conventions employed by the editors in these lists:

AUTHOR   Authors' names appear first (editors are noted as *ed.*, translators as *trans.*), except in the case of well-known anthologies, for which a title listing seems more appropriate. Authors' dates, when known, follow their names.

TITLE   Titles usually appear in English, not in the original language when the book is a translation. The original date of publication, when known, follows the title in parentheses. For revised editions of modern expository works, only the latest edition and its date are cited. When a writer's shorter works (poems, short stories, plays, essays, criticism, etc.) exist in collections variously titled, catch-all titles but no publication dates are supplied. Multiple titles by the same author are generally ordered chronologically.

ANNOTA-   Annotations have been carefully prepared to assist
TION   readers to determine the potential interest and value of each listed book. The annotation succinctly indicates the general subject of the book, locates its thesis or encapsulates its plot, and distinguishes its special merit. When advisable, comments have been made about the level of difficulty or about preferred translations.

EDITIONS   Because of the frequency of price increases during the past two decades, our once-traditional policy of citing hardcover prices and listing paperbound price ranges has been discontinued. Following each annotation, in italics and in standard abbreviated form (see pages xvi to xviii for a list of publisher abbreviations), is listed the hardcover publisher after *H—* ; then, after a semicolon, the paperbound edition is listed after *P—* . Example: *H—Har-Row; P—Dell.* When more than several paperbound editions are in print, as with most novels that have become classics, the entry is as follows: *P—over 10 eds.* Some few titles noted as *o.p.* (out of print) are included because they are first-rate books, are widely available in libraries, and should soon be back in print.

              For paperbound editions, generally only those most widely available in larger bookstores have been listed. If a title is not in stock, it can be obtained by direct mail from the publisher or publisher's distributor.

              Up-to-date listings of paperbound editions in print and of publisher and distributor addresses may be checked in the latest *Paperbound Books in Print*, available for consultation at most bookstores and libraries. The publisher symbols cited in *Good Reading* are those used in both *Books in Print* and *Paperbound Books in Print*.

One further gloss on the organization of this volume may be helpful. Individual chapter book lists have often been divided. The basis of subdivision varies, but the headings clarify the rationale for the breakdown. Whenever a subdivision occurs, entries continue to be listed alphabetically by author, or editor, or sometimes by title.

After browsing through *Good Reading* for an hour, you will become adept at finding what you want. If, on occasion, you are seeking a book with a known author or title or on a general subject not explicit in a chapter heading, turn immediately to the index.

TO THE TEACHER AND LIBRARIAN

A great many uses have been found for *Good Reading* in colleges, schools, libraries, and homes since 1932. Teachers have turned to its book lists for a wide range of courses; it is particularly useful for Advanced Placement and independent study courses in high schools and for comprehensive college survey courses variously labeled Freshman English, Humanities, Great Books, Western Civilization, Asian Culture, African Culture, Impact of Science, etc. Many teachers, finding that the selective lists in *Good Reading* solve their collateral reading needs, require the book for their courses.

To make students aware of the primary use of *Good Reading*, a number of devices have been employed. At some small liberal arts colleges and a few preparatory schools, the new student tour of the library concludes with the presentation to each student of a copy of the paperbound edition. At others, *Good Reading* serves as the formal basis for the summer reading program. Many teachers, in both high school and college, recommend the book when advising students on their self-directed college-preparatory or postgraduate reading.

Librarians have always found *Good Reading* a valuable tool for helping readers. Some keep a copy at the circulation desk, some next to the catalogs where it can be consulted by readers looking for the best books on a given topic, some in the general or special reference rooms, some in browsing rooms. Large university libraries place copies of each new revision in various strategic locations. Finally, *Good Reading* has often served as a guide to book purchases for high school, community college, and small public libraries.

The editors hope that this 21st revision continues to lead an increasing number of people to savor the great or significant books, both those that strive to light the dark places in our understanding of our complex world and our equally complex selves, and those that aim simply to delight.

100 Significant Books

This list offers a representative selection of 100 books that many people have found rewarding to know; they are not necessarily the best or greatest works of imagination and thought. Originally compiled for the 1934 edition of *Good Reading*, the list has been revised several times, including for this edition. Revisions were made by the editors in consultation with many distinguished teachers, writers, and critics.

Ancient Times

Aeschylus—*The Oresteia*
Aesop—*Fables*
Aristophanes—*Comedies*
Aristotle—*Nicomachean Ethics*
The Bible
Confucius—*The Analects*
Euripides—*Dramas*
Homer—*Iliad* and *Odyssey*

Lao-Tzu—*The Way of Life*
Lucretius—*The Nature of Things*
Plato—*Republic* and *Symposium*
Plutarch—*Lives*
Sophocles—*The Theban Plays*
Thucydides—*The Peloponnesian Wars*
Vergil—*Aeneid*

Middle Ages and Renaissance

The Arabian Nights
Bacon—*Essays*
Boccaccio—*Decameron*
Cervantes—*Don Quixote*
Chaucer—*Canterbury Tales*
Dante—*Divine Comedy*
Machiavelli—*The Prince*
Malory—*Le Morte d'Arthur*

Mohammed—*Koran*
Montaigne—*Essays*
More—*Utopia*
Omar Khayyám—*The Rubáiyát*
Rabelais—*Gargantua and Pantagruel*
Shakespeare—*Complete Tragedies, Comedies, and Histories*

17th and 18th Centuries

Boswell—*Life of Samuel Johnson*
Bunyan—*Pilgrim's Progress*
Burns—*Poems*
Defoe—*Robinson Crusoe*
Descartes—*Discourse on Method*
Donne—*Poems*
Fielding—*Tom Jones*

Gibbon—*The Decline and Fall of the Roman Empire*
Hamilton et al.—*Federalist Papers*
Kant—*Critique of Pure Reason*
Locke—*Essay Concerning Human Understanding*
Malthus—*Principles of Population*

Milton—*Paradise Lost*
Molière—*Comedies*
Paine—*The Rights of Man*
Rousseau—*The Social Contract*
Smith—*The Wealth of Nations*

Spinoza—*Ethics*
Sterne—*Tristram Shandy*
Swift—*Gulliver's Travels*
Voltaire—*Candide*

19th Century

Austen—*Pride and Prejudice*
Balzac—*Eugénie Grandet*
Browning (Robert)—*Poems*
Byron—*Poems*
Chekhov—*Plays*
Darwin—*The Origin of Species*
Dickens—*Great Expectations*
Dickinson—*Poems*
Dostoevski—*The Brothers Karamazov*
Eliot—*Middlemarch*
Emerson—*Essays*
Flaubert—*Madame Bovary*
Goethe—*Faust*
Hardy—*Tess of the D'Urbervilles*
Hawthorne—*The Scarlet Letter*

Hugo—*Les Misérables*
Ibsen—*Dramas*
Keats—*Poems*
Marx—*Capital*
Melville—*Moby Dick*
Nietzsche—*Thus Spake Zarathustra*
Poe—*Short Stories*
Shelley—*Poems*
Stendhal—*The Red and the Black*
Thackeray—*Vanity Fair*
Thoreau—*Walden*
Tolstoi—*War and Peace*
Twain—*Huckleberry Finn*
Whitman—*Leaves of Grass*
Wordsworth—*Poems*

20th Century

Einstein—*The Meaning of Relativity*
Eliot—*Poems and Plays*
Ellison—*Invisible Man*
Faulkner—*The Sound and the Fury*
Frazer—*The Golden Bough*
Freud—*Introduction to Psychoanalysis*
Frost—*Poems*
Hemingway—*The Sun Also Rises*

Joyce—*Ulysses*
Lawrence—*Sons and Lovers*
Mann—*The Magic Mountain*
O'Neill—*Plays*
Proust—*Remembrance of Things Past*
Shaw—*Plays*
Steinbeck—*The Grapes of Wrath*
Veblen—*The Theory of the Leisure Class*
Yeats—*Poems*

Key to Publisher Symbols

The 35 *Good Reading* book lists use the following abbreviated publishers' names. These are the same symbols employed by both *Books in Print* and *Paperbound Books in Print*. The current price for any title can be secured from your bookstore or from the latest annual *Books in Print*, available in your bookstore or your public or college library. *Good Reading* no longer lists publishers' addresses—first, because experience indicates that many will change addresses during the lifetime of this revision, and second, because many publishers do not distribute their own books. Consult the latest annual *Books in Print* for the publisher's or distributor's address if you wish to order a book by mail.

The hardcover publisher for each title is listed, following the annotation, after *H—*; the paperbound publisher(s) after *P—*. Publishers cited only several times are not listed below but are given in identifiable form.

A S Barnes	A. S. Barnes & Co.
Abingdon	Abingdon Press
Abrams	Harry N. Abrams, Inc.
ACC	Appleton-Century-Crofts
Airmont	Airmont Publishing Co., Inc.
Aldine	Aldine Publishing Co.
Allyn	Allyn & Bacon, Inc.
Apollo	Apollo Editions
Arno	Arno Press
Assn Pr	Association Press
Astor-Honor	Astor-Honor, Inc.
Atheneum	Atheneum Pubs.
Avon	Avon Books
Ballantine	Ballantine Books, Inc.
B&N	Barnes & Noble, Inc.
Bantam	Bantam Books, Inc.
Barron	Barron's Educational Series, Inc.
Basic	Basic Books, Inc.
Beacon Pr	Beacon Press, Inc.

Berkley Pub	Berkley Publishing Corp.
Bobbs	Bobbs-Merrill Co., Inc.
Bowker	R. R. Bowker Co.
Braziller	George Braziller, Inc.
Cambridge U Pr	Cambridge University Press
Chandler Pub	Chandler Publishing Co.
Chilton	Chilton Book Co.
Citadel Pr	Citadel Press
Columbia U Pr	Columbia University Press
Cornell U Pr	Cornell University Press
Coward	Coward, McCann & Geoghegan, Inc.
D Van Nostrand	D. Van Nostrand Co.
Dell	Dell Publishing Co., Inc.
Devin	Devin-Adair Co., Inc.
Dial	Dial Press
Dodd	Dodd, Mead & Co.
Doubleday	Doubleday & Co., Inc.
Dover	Dover Publications, Inc.
Dufour	Dufour Editions, Inc.
Dutton	E. P. Dutton & Co., Inc.
Fawcett World	Fawcett World Library
Free Pr	Free Press
FS&G	Farrar, Straus & Giroux, Inc.
Funk & W	Funk & Wagnalls Co.
G&D	Grosset & Dunlap, Inc.
Grove	Grove Press, Inc.
Har-Row	Harper & Row Pubs., Inc.
HarBraceJ	Harcourt Brace Jovanovich, Inc.
Harvard U Pr	Harvard University Press
Hawthorn	Hawthorn Books, Inc.
Hill & Wang	Hill & Wang, Inc.
HM	Houghton Mifflin Co.
HR&W	Holt, Rinehart & Winston, Inc.
Humanities	Humanities Press, Inc.
H W Wilson	H. W. Wilson Co.
Ind U Pr	Indiana University Press
Intl Pub Co	International Pubs. Co., Inc.
Irwin	Richard D. Irwin, Inc.
Johns Hopkins	Johns Hopkins Press
Knopf	Alfred A. Knopf, Inc.
Lippincott	J. B. Lippincott Co.
Little	Little, Brown & Co.
McGraw	McGraw-Hill Book Co.
McKay	David McKay Co., Inc.
Macmillan	Macmillan Publishing Co., Inc.
MIT Pr	M. I. T. Press
Modern Lib	Modern Library, Inc.
Morrow	William Morrow & Co., Inc.
NAL	New American Library, Inc.
Nelson	Thomas Nelson, Inc.
New Directions	New Directions Publishing Corp.
Noonday	Noonday Press
Norton	W. W. Norton & Co., Inc.
NYU Pr	New York University Press
Odyssey Pr	Odyssey Press

Open Court	Open Court Publishing Co.
Oxford U Pr	Oxford University Press, Inc.
P-H	Prentice-Hall, Inc.
PB	Pocket Books, Inc.
Penguin	Penguin Books, Inc.
Peter Smith	Peter Smith
Pitman	Pitman Publishing Corp.
Popular Lib	Popular Library, Inc.
Praeger	Praeger Pubs.
Princeton U Pr	Princeton University Press
Putnam	G. P. Putnam's Sons
Pyramid Pubns	Pyramid Publications, Inc.
Rand	Rand McNally & Co.
Random	Random House, Inc.
Regnery	Henry Regnery Co.
S Ill U Pr	Southern Illinois University Press
S&S	Simon & Schuster, Inc.
Schocken	Schocken Books, Inc.
Scott F	Scott, Foresman & Co.
Scribner	Charles Scribner's Sons
St Martin	St. Martin's Press, Inc.
T Y Crowell	Thomas Y. Crowell Co.
U of Cal Pr	University of California Press
U of Chicago Pr	University of Chicago Press
U of Mich Pr	University of Michigan Press
U of Minn Pr	University of Minnesota Press
U of Notre Dame Pr	University of Notre Dame Press
U of Tex Pr	University of Texas Press
U of Wis Pr	University of Wisconsin Press
Ungar	Frederick Ungar Publishing Co., Inc.
Van Nos Reinhold	Van Nostrand Reinhold Co.
Viking Pr	Viking Press, Inc.
WH Freeman	W. H. Freeman & Co.
Wiley	John Wiley & Sons, Inc.
WSP	Washington Square Press, Inc.
Yale U Pr	Yale University Press

Historical and
Regional Cultures

1. Greece

J. Sherwood Weber

To know the mainsprings of our own 20th-century culture we must know Greece and the Hellenic world. The Greeks—an assimilative, analytical, self-expressive, and creative people—absorbed much from earlier cultures (Eastern Mediterranean, North African, and Chinese, particularly) and interpreted and adapted all they had inherited by the clear light of intellect and in relation to their experience. In almost every activity of the human mind—in architecture, art, science, medicine, philosophy, government, education, poetry, drama—and even in athletics, we are deeply indebted to the Greeks of the 5th and 4th centuries B.C. Indeed, some of their achievements we may not yet have surpassed.

The singular contribution of the Greeks to civilization was that between 900 and 300 B.C., between Homer and Epicurus, they forged a totally new conception of the purpose of human life and exhibited for the first time in the long history of humanity both the intellectual and the creative potentials of the mind. Their humanistic view of people functioning in the universe and their rational yet idealistic approach to the practical problems of living and enjoying life yielded significant results in every area of human endeavor, projecting ideas and making achievements both impressive for themselves and widely influential ever since.

The hub of Greek commercial and intellectual life was the city-state of Athens, particularly in the 5th century B.C. Athenian society had a threefold foundation: economic prosperity, democratic government (for the native males qualified to vote), and freedom of thought and inquiry. Athens dominated the sea in the Persian wars early in the century, resulting in its becoming protector of many other city-states in a maritime confederacy that brought to Athens large sums of tributes. This income was expended on impressively handsome public buildings, employing the talents of architects, sculptors, and painters and providing forums for public

3

debates and creative civic events. Other sources of wealth—a large
merchant fleet, rich silver mines, an extensive marble quarry, and
a huge slave labor force—enhanced public income and private leisure. The Athenian government stimulated pride of citizenship in
the fifth of the population that qualified as voters (women, slaves,
and resident aliens were not enfranchised), but, as Thucydides and
others clearly saw, it exhibited also, particularly in times of stress,
the faults of democracy: vacillation in policy, encouragement of
demagogues, bickering among the classes, and waste of resources.
Nevertheless, the climate of free thought promoted by prosperity
attracted to Athens intellectuals and artists from the scattered
points of the Mediterranean world, making Athens the center of
thought and art as well as of commerce.

Eventually Athens was conquered by Sparta, later by Philip of
Macedon, and finally by Rome. Paradoxically, each new conquest
resulted in a wider spread of Greek language, thought, and culture:
Alexander the Great Hellenized Egypt and the Near East; Rome
transmitted Greek culture over Western Europe, through North
Africa, and to the British Isles. Even during the many centuries of
the Roman Empire, Greek remained the first language of Eastern
Mediterranean countries and the second language of the educated
everywhere. And we should not forget that the original Greek of
the New Testament and the Septuagint translation of the Old Testament made possible the rapid rise of Christianity from a small
Hebrew sect to an international religion.

Greek philosophy, which began in the 6th century B.C. as a result
of an effort to comprehend the rational ordering of the physical
universe, was developed in the 5th century by the Sophists, itinerant scholars who accepted fees for discoursing to such students as
were willing to pay. Socrates shifted the direction of philosophy
from its concern with order in the physical universe (science) and
practical matters such as rhetoric to a preoccupation with morality,
ethics, and the search for final truth and the good life. The "Socratic
dialogues" of Plato draw upon a vast range of earlier philosophic
theories, harmonizing them, arranging them, and charting a logical course through the intricate maze. Plato founded the Academy,
"the world's first university," which lured the best minds from all
over in a systematic search for truth. One of Plato's pupils, but far
from his disciple, was Aristotle, perhaps the greatest systematizer
of all time. He also opened an intellectual center that drew scholars
and researchers as well as students. Aristotle's perception that
every subject can be better understood through rational analysis,
orderly arrangement, and reduction to first principles is perhaps
the most influential concept in the history of human knowledge in
the West.

The Greek sense of fairness and honesty, of harmony and balance, of proportion and moderation—exhibited both in Greek government and in formal thought—is equally evident in the artistic
and literary output. Greek sculpture, vases, architecture (particu-

larly the Parthenon, designed by Ictinus and adorned by Phidias) are models of simplicity, grace, and symmetry. Greek tragedy—the origins of which are obscure but seem to be located in ritual, myth, and dance—projects life steadily and whole, portraying without rancor or sentimentality the sad but ennobling workings of human fate. The extant plays of Aeschylus, Sophocles, and Euripides (only about a tenth of their combined total of 300 survive) constitute the greatest dramatic flourish in any single age. Greek comedy served both to amuse and to expose people, policies, and institutions to public ridicule. The Greek epic, widely popular, survives only in the two superb examples by Homer, the *Iliad* and the *Odyssey*, which draw upon the mytho-legendary Trojan War. Told dramatically and humanely, each epic contains a wealth of information about the everyday world of Homeric times and about the values of subsequent generations of Greeks. Greek historical writing, best illustrated in Herodotus and Thucydides, shows the Greek preoccupation with both form and fairness.

To prepare citizens to use and to enjoy freedom and to promote the general search for knowledge, the Greeks encouraged education. Realizing, too, that mind and body are inseparable, they advocated physical development and athletic skills for their own sake (winning an Olympic or regional contest) as well as for their aid to clear thinking. Many of the principles of education detailed by Plato in *The Republic* are still honored and employed—some by democratic countries, some by totalitarian states. Many "texts" compiled by Aristotle are still used in adapted form.

One need not read long, or look at many art books or museum Greek collections, before sensing the glory that was Greece.

Greek Literature

Collections

Complete Greek Tragedies (1959). Ed. by David Grene and Richmond Lattimore. Generally first-rate translations of the surviving dramas of Aeschylus, Sophocles, and Euripides, soundly edited and excellently introduced. *H—U of Chicago Pr 4 vols*. Selections from each dramatist: *P—U of Chicago Pr 3 vols*.

Poems from the Greek Anthology in English Paraphrase (1956). Ed. and trans. by Dudley Fitts. A good short introduction to Greek literature. *H & P—New Directions*.

The Portable Greek Historians (1959). Ed. by M. I. Finley. Generous selections from Herodotus, Thucydides, Xenophon, and others, with illuminating introduction and notes. *P—Viking Pr*.

The Portable Greek Reader (1948). Ed. by W. H. Auden. The best one-volume collection, containing 720 pages of entire works and excerpts plus an acute introduction, bringing together the significant high spots of Greek literature and thought from Homer to Galen. *H & P—Viking Pr*.

Ten Greek Plays in Contemporary Translations (1957). Ed. by L. R. Lind. A first-rate inexpensive collection of fresh translations of major plays presented with solid and detailed introductory material. *P—HM*.

Individual Authors

AESCHYLUS 525-456 B.C. *Tragedies*. In tense, taut, oblique verse, Aeschylus projects his stern moral view of the universe through myths fashioned into dramas. Best known is *The Oresteia*, the only surviving Greek trilogy, comprising *Agamemnon*, *Choephoroe*, and *Eumenides*, superb tragedies of bloodshed, revenge, and moral regeneration. The most readable translations are by Richmond Lattimore (*P—U of Chicago Pr*); Paul Roche (*P—NAL*); and Philip Vellacott (*P—Penguin*). *Over 30 other eds. of indiv. or coll. plays.*

AESOP c. 6th cent. B.C. *Fables*. Delightful animal stories illustrating folk morality with pointed, sometimes cynical wit. *Over 10 eds.*

ARISTOPHANES c. 448-380 B.C. *Comedies*. Lyrical, topical burlesques, combining boisterous farce with poetic beauty: on Socrates, *The Clouds*; on war and women, *Lysistrata*; on utopian schemes, *The Birds*. *Over 30 eds. of indiv. or coll. plays.*

ARISTOTLE 384-322 B.C. *Nicomachean Ethics*. A profound pioneer analysis of the modes, methods, and values of human conduct. The most encyclopedic Greek thinker carefully interprets the good life as achievement of well-being or fullest virtue, the mean between too much and too little in social relations. See also "Philosophy," page 181. *H— Harvard U Pr, Oxford U Pr; P—Bobbs, Penguin.*

_____. *Politics*. Influential analysis of the various forms and functions of government, of the human political animal. *Over 6 eds.*

DEMOSTHENES 383-322 B.C. *Orations*. The best in rhetoric and oratory. *H—Dutton, Harvard U Pr, Oxford U Pr.*

EURIPIDES c. 484-408 B.C. *Tragedies and Tragi-Comedies*. Realistic, humane, highly theatrical dramas by the most modern of the great Greek playwrights, whose favorite targets were irrationality, war, and women's rights. His best-known plays include *Hippolytus*, *Medea*, *The Suppliants*, and *The Trojan Women*. *Over 30 eds. of indiv. and coll. plays.*

HERODOTUS c. 484-425 B.C. *History*. Shrewd analysis of geopolitics in the ancient world, and lively narrative of the crucial struggle between democratic Greece and totalitarian Persia. *Over 10 eds.*

HESIOD c. 770 B.C. *Theogony. Works and Days*. Myths of the gods, fables, proverbs, social protest, moral advice, prayers, and religious chants, by a probable contemporary of Homer. *H—Harvard U Pr, Oxford U Pr; P—Bobbs.*

HOMER c. 800 B.C. *Iliad*. In moving verse, the epic develops the tragic consequences of Achilles' anger against Agamemnon over the distribution of war spoils. Through this slight incident in the Trojan War, Homer projects the total life-view and standard of values of early Greeks as well as creates many memorable characters. The most faithful verse translation is by Richmond Lattimore (*H & P—U of Chicago Pr*); the most fluent and readable, by Robert Fitzgerald (*H & P—Doubleday*). William Rouse's prose translation is vigorous and clear (*P— NAL*). *Over 12 other versions.*

_____. *Odyssey*. The exciting and varied experiences of Odysseus during his ten-year trip home from Troy demonstrate the ability to triumph over human, natural, and supernatural obstacles, and etch brilliantly the world of Odysseus. This "novel" provides a splendid introduction to Homeric myth and religion, social institutions, and cultural values. The recommended verse translations are by Robert Fitzgerald (*H & P—Doubleday*) and Richmond Lattimore (*P—Har-Row*). The preferred prose versions are by T. E. Shaw (*P—Oxford U Pr*) and William Rouse (*P—NAL*). *Over 10 other versions.*

LUCIAN c. 125-210. *Dialogues of the Dead. Dialogues of the Gods*. Pungent and witty satires with philosophic implications. *H—Harvard U Pr 8 vols*. Selections: *P—Bobbs, Norton*.

PINDAR 522-443 B.C. *Odes*. Chief writer of choral or "Pindaric" odes celebrating Olympic triumphs and special events. Richmond Lattimore's translations are excellent: *P—U of Chicago Pr*.

PLATO c. 427-347 B.C. *The Republic*. While developing in detail a definition of justice and the characteristics of a utopian state, Plato expounds his Theory of Eternal Ideas, his influential views on education, his paradoxical concept of the philosopher-king, and other fundamental aspects of his world view. The skillfully annotated abridged translation by F. M. Cornford is recommended: *P—Oxford U Pr. Over 6 unabr. eds.*

_____. *Dialogues*. See "Philosophy," page 183.

PLOTINUS 204-275. *The Enneads*. See "Philosophy," page 184.

PLUTARCH c. 46-120. *Lives*. Short biographies, paralleling the lives of famous Greeks with the careers of famous Romans. Remarkable character interpretations. *Over 10 eds.*

POLYBIUS 204-122 B.C. *Histories*. An outstanding interpretation of Rome's rise to power. *H—Greenwood 2 vols., Harvard U Pr 6 vols.*

SOPHOCLES 496-406 B.C. *Tragedies*. In the whole range of Greek tragedy, two of his "Theban Plays"—*Oedipus Rex* for plot, *Antigone* for wide-ranging moral significance—are the most widely known. The best translations of the Theban trilogy are by Theodore Banks (*P—Oxford U Pr*), Dudley Fitts and Robert Fitzgerald (*P—HarBraceJ*), and E. F. Watling (*P—Penguin*). *Over 15 other eds. of indiv. or coll. plays.*

THUCYDIDES c. 470-400 B.C. *The Peloponnesian Wars*. An acutely analytical yet stirring account of the fateful struggle for power between Athens and Sparta. A classic work of history. *Over 10 eds.*

XENOPHON 431-355 B.C. *Anabasis*. Describes the military campaigns of Cyrus of Persia and the retreat of the Greek mercenaries across the Arabian deserts to the Black Sea. *H—McKay; P—U of Mich Pr, Penguin.*

Books about Greece

AGARD, WALTER R. b. 1894. *The Greek Mind* (1957). A stimulating philosophic interpretation of the intellectual achievements of the Greeks. *H—Peter Smith*.

BOWRA, C. M. 1898-1971. *The Greek Experience* (1958). Brilliant popular analysis of Greek life, thought, and culture. *P—NAL*.

CERAM, C. W. (KURT W. MAREK) 1915-1972. *Gods, Graves, and Scholars* (rev. ed. 1967). A vivid, fluent account of archaeological discoveries and their significance, covering ancient Greece and the entire area of the Near East. *H—Knopf; P—Bantam.*

DURANT, WILL b. 1885. *The Life of Greece* (1939). Comprehensive yet eminently readable survey of Greek civilization from remote times to the Roman conquest. *H—S&S.*

FARRINGTON, BENJAMIN 1891-1974. *Greek Science* (1939). Illuminating survey of the physical and economic forces and of the speculative minds that laid the foundations for modern science. *o.p.*

FINLEY, M. I. b. 1912. *The World of Odysseus* (1954). The best popular introduction to the world and works of Homer. *P—Viking Pr.*

————. *The Ancient Greeks* (1963). A sound, readable account of ancient Greek history and culture, rich in anecdote and illuminating in assessing Greek strengths and shortcomings. *P—Viking Pr.*

FRAZER, JAMES GEORGE 1854-1941. *The Golden Bough* (1915). Monumental and provocative comparative analysis of primitive religions and ancient folklores. *H—St Martin 13 vols. Abridgments: P—Macmillan, NAL.*

GRAVES, ROBERT b. 1895. *Hercules, My Shipmate* (1945). Imaginative reconstruction of the savage, lusty, daring adventures of the Argonauts who sought the Golden Fleece. *o.p..*

————. *The Greek Myths* (1955). The complete story of the Greek gods and heroes assembled—with many fresh insights and occasional idiosyncrasies—into one continuous narrative by a poet and novelist of great learning and ability. *H—Braziller; P—Penguin 2 vols.*

HAMILTON, EDITH 1867-1963. *The Greek Way* (1930). Entertaining and stimulating study of Greek writers and their influence in ancient as well as modern times. *H—Norton; P—Avon.*

HARRISON, JANE 1850-1928. *Prolegomena to the Study of Greek Religion* (1903). Fascinating scholarly account of deities, ceremonials, sacrifices, and other elements of primitive Greek religion. *H—Arno.*

HIGHET, GILBERT 1906-1977. *The Classical Tradition* (1949). With both scholarship and charm, analyzes the major influences of Greek and Roman literature and thought on contemporary Western culture. *H & P—Oxford U Pr.*

JAEGER, WERNER 1888-1961. *Paideia* (1939). Profound, difficult, but highly rewarding study of the development of Greek thought and ideals. *H—Oxford U Pr 3 vols; P—Oxford U Pr Vol. 1 only.*

KITTO, H. D. F. b. 1897. *The Greeks* (1954). A witty, sometimes opinionated popular introduction, focusing on social conditions in ancient Greece. *P—Penguin.*

————. *Greek Tragedy* (3rd rev. ed. 1969). Informed, perceptive, unusually illuminating analysis of Greek tragedies and their backgrounds. *H & P—B&N.*

LAWRENCE, ARNOLD WALTER b. 1900. *Greek Architecture* (rev. ed. 1975). Lavishly illustrated history. *H—Penguin.*

LOUŸS, PIERRE 1870-1925. *Aphrodite* (1896). Lushly detailed tragic romance of a priestess of love in rich, corrupt Alexandria. *H—AMS Pr.*

MacKENDRICK, PAUL L. b. 1914. *The Greek Stones Speak* (rev. ed. 1962). A lively, well-illustrated survey of recent archaeological work in Greek lands. *H—St Martin; P—NAL.*

RENAULT, MARY (MARY CHALLANS) b. 1905. *The Last of the Wine* (1956). A first-rate historical novel set in Athens during the Peloponnesian Wars, featuring historical figures such as Socrates, Alcibiades, and Plato and tracing the decline of Athenian democratic ideals under the pressure of protracted war. *H—Pantheon; P—Random.*

———. *The King Must Die* (1958). Another clear, delicate evocation of ancient Greece, centering around the legendary Theseus. *H—Pantheon; P—Bantam.*

WARNER, REX b. 1905. *The Greek Philosophers* (1958). Useful as an introductory study of the major philosophers and their predecessors. *P—NAL.*

2. Rome

J. Sherwood Weber

The word *Roman* conjures up a vision of blocks of masonry—strong, massive, durable. And with reason, for many of the roads, temples, bridges, aqueducts, amphitheatres the Romans built still survive. But they made contributions to Western culture even more enduring. Their network of roads and their settlements helped give modern Europe its shape. Their language, Latin, was the main source of eight modern languages, including Italian, French, and Spanish. Their political system strongly influenced the founding fathers of America, among others. And their law is the core of one of the two major legal systems in Western civilization.

Such accomplishments of the Roman gift for social organization are important, but they leave a misleading impression. Efficiency implies hard practicality, perhaps even lack of feeling. Yet the Romans, like other Mediterranean peoples, were also emotional and excitable, as their literature abundantly reveals. Though the Romans did not match the intellectual and artistic originality of the Greeks, their literature often exhibits wit, emotional insight, and esthetic power. The uniqueness of Latin literature lies in the fusion of sophistication with the moral force and earnestness produced by a strong orientation toward public affairs and social issues.

A sampling will show the variety. The comedies of Plautus, written near the beginning of Latin literature, are full of lively humanity. His comic animation and chaotic plots stand in sharp contrast to Terence's quieter, more polished and sensitive comedies of manners.

In the literature of the first half of the 1st century B.C., the outstanding names are Cicero and Caesar in prose, Catullus and Lucretius in poetry. The orations and letters of Cicero reveal a humane politician and a consummate orator. The strong and brilliant personality of Caesar appears vividly in his accounts of the Gallic and civil wars. These two writers, political enemies, help us to know deeply a crucial period in world history when republic was yielding to empire. Catullus pictures in his lyrics the sophisticated society of poets, rakes, and beauties, using his art for the graceful expression of erotic feeling. Lucretius undertakes in *The Nature of Things* to crush superstition and ignorance with the materialistic thought of Epicureanism.

The following half century, "the Augustan age," produced equally notable work. Vergil's *Aeneid*—the most significant single Latin book to read—portrays the cultural mission of Rome with grandeur and intelligence. Horace's lyrics—sometimes delicate, sometimes weighty, usually brilliant—and his pungent satires have been relished by many readers. Ovid's *Metamorphoses* fascinates with its remarkable narrative power and prescientific conception of change. In a period memorable mainly for its poetry, Livy's epical history of Rome is a prose masterwork.

The reader will find much that seems contemporary in the social criticism of Roman decadence that permeates the best writing of the early centuries of the Christian era. The precursors of novelists, Petronius and Apuleius, wrote bawdy, satiric social romances. The materialism and immorality of Rome are the targets of Juvenal's satires. Also critical of the times are Tacitus' devastating historical analysis of the emperors, and Seneca's Stoic writings. Stoicism was the source of much social liberalism, as is shown in a Senecan letter challenging slavery: "Just remember that he whom you call your slave was born from the same seed, enjoys the same sky, and equally breathes, lives, and dies."

The continuous movement from pagan to fully Christian times is reflected in the literature from the 4th century through the 6th. Jerome, whose favorite authors were Plautus and Cicero, was primarily responsible for the great Latin translation of the Bible known as the Vulgate. Augustine's *Confessions* records his conversion to Christianity from and through classical thought. Boethius clings firmly to the rationality of pagan philosophy as a support to the faith of Christianity. So new vitality arises from old.

Literature of the Roman Era

Collections

An Anthology of Roman Drama (1960). Ed. by P. W. Harsh. Selected comedies of Plautus and Terence, tragedies of Seneca. *P—HR&W.*

Classics in Translation: Latin Literature (1952). Ed. by P. L. MacKendrick and H. M. Howe. Roman culture presented through a generous selection of complete works and excerpts, both prose and poetry, mostly in new translations. *H—U of Wis Pr.*

Latin Poetry in Verse Translation (1957). Ed. by L. R. Lind. An excellent anthology of poetry in Latin from the beginnings to the Renaissance. *P—HM.*

The Portable Roman Reader (1951). Ed. by Basil Davenport. A competent survey of Roman literature and thought, generously representing the poets, playwrights, historians, satirists, and philosophers. *H & P—Viking Pr.*

Individual Authors

APULEIUS, LUCIUS c. 160. *The Golden Ass*. The only complete surviving Latin novel, about an adventurer who is changed into an ass and doomed to fantastic experiences until the goddess Isis allows him to resume human form. *Over 6 eds.*

AUGUSTINE, SAINT 354-430. *The City of God*. The fall of the Roman Empire and the death of paganism interpreted by a Christian believing in Divine Providence. See "Philosophy," page 181.

———. *Confessions*. The odyssey of a powerful mind from materialism through Platonism to Christian belief, acutely analyzing "time" and "creation." *Over 10 eds.*

BOETHIUS 480-524. *The Consolation of Philosophy*. A moving dialogue concerning pagan philosophy and Christianity by "the last great pagan author." *H—Oxford U Pr, Scholarly; P—Bobbs, Penguin, Ungar.*

CAESAR, GAIUS JULIUS 100-44 B.C. *Commentaries*. The conqueror of Gaul and Britain and the victor in civil war gives propagandistic reports of crucial campaigns and political struggles. *Over 10 eds.*

CATULLUS, GAIUS VALERIUS 84-54 B.C. *Poems*. A hypersensitive young artist expresses intense emotion in lyrics ranging from personal feeling to contemporary life to the world of myth. *Over 10 eds.*

CICERO, MARCUS TULLIUS 106-43 B.C. *Selected Works*. Essays on philosophy and rhetoric, forceful orations, and revealing personal letters, written by a Roman active equally in politics and the arts. *Over 6 eds.*

HORACE (QUINTUS HORATIUS FLACCUS) 65-8 B.C. *Poems.* Polished lyrics, sophisticated satires, and poetic essays by one who belonged to the court circle but retained independence of mind. His name symbolizes urbanity and wit. *Over 20 eds.*

JUVENAL (DECIMUS JUNIUS JUVENALIS) c. 60-140. *Satires*. Bitter, realistic attacks on vices, abuses, and follies of imperial Rome, by an idealist driven to indignation. *Over 10 eds.*

LIVY (TITUS LIVIUS) 59 B.C.-A.D. 17. *Early History of Rome*. Picturesque account of the growth of the Roman state from the earliest times, emphasizing that the decline in moral values of the Roman world would cause its downfall. *H—Gannon; P—Penguin.*

LUCRETIUS (TITUS LUCRETIUS CARUS) c. 94-55 B.C. *On the Nature of Things*. Impressive philosophic poem presenting materialistic Epicureanism as the cure for superstition and human folly. Anticipates such modern concepts as the atomic theory, conservation, evolution, and survival of the fittest. See "Philosophy," page 183.

MARCUS AURELIUS ANTONINUS 121-180. *Meditations*. An emperor records his thoughts as he struggles for composure and order in the face of national disaster. See "Philosophy," page 183.

OVID (PUBLIUS OVIDIUS NASO) 43 B.C.-A.D. 17. *The Art of Love*. Playful, risqué verses on the devices of love, full of charm and humor. The Rolfe Humphries version is superior (*H—Peter Smith; P—Ind U Pr*). *Over 6 other eds.*

_____. *Metamorphoses*. Tales of miraculous transformations by a versatile narrative poet. Its broad coverage of Greek and Roman myth has made it an important source book. Again, the Humphries translation is preferred (*P—Ind U Pr*). Others: *H—McKay; P—NAL, Penguin*.

PETRONIUS, GAIUS d. 66. *The Satyricon*. Picaresque novel about the adventures of three rascals, incorporating both social and literary criticism. This hilarious satire provides useful information about everyday life in Rome. The William Arrowsmith translation is recommended: *H—U of Mich Pr; P—NAL*.

PLAUTUS, TITUS MACCIUS c. 251-184 B.C. *Comedies*. Rollicking farces about tricky servants, braggart soldiers, identical twins, courtesans, et al. *H—Oxford U Pr; P—Bobbs, Norton, Penguin*.

PLUTARCH. *Lives*. See "Greece," page 7.

SENECA, LUCIUS ANNAEUS c. 5 B.C.-A.D. 65. *Works*. Essays and letters applying Stoic thought to perennial human problems and conditions of Roman life; Stoic melodramas showing the destruction of reason by passion. *H—Harvard U Pr, Macmillan, Norton; P—Bobbs, Penguin*.

TACITUS, CORNELIUS c. 55-117. *Works*. History of the Roman Empire to A.D. 70 and of the Roman occupations in Britain and Gaul, written from a republican bias and exhibiting ironical insights as well as sustained literary qualities. *Over 10 eds.*

TERENCE (PUBLIUS TERENTIUS AFER) c. 195-159 B.C. *Comedies*. Polished, refined comedies of manners stressing moderation. *Over 6 eds.*

VERGIL (PUBLIUS VERGILIUS MARO) 70-19 B.C. *Aeneid*. A great national epic glorifying the Latin temperament as well as the historical tradition and the universal cultural mission of Rome. The C. Day Lewis translation is preferred: *P—Doubleday*. *Many other versions*.

_____. *Eclogues*. Ten pastoral poems blend sensitive descriptions of nature with political commentary. *H—Doubleday, St Martin*.

VITRUVIUS, POLLIO MARCUS c. 85-26 B.C. *On Architecture*. A unique record of Greek and Roman city planning, engineering, and construction of private and public buildings. *H—Peter Smith; P—Dover*.

Books about Rome

BARROW, R. H. b. 1893. *The Romans* (1949). Clear sketch of their traits, history, achievements, and contributions to modern times. *H—Aldine; P—Penguin*.

BULWER-LYTTON, EDWARD 1803-1873. *The Last Days of Pompeii* (1834). A colorful historical romance about the life that perished beneath the ashes of Vesuvius. *o.p.*

DUDLEY, DONALD R. b. 1918. *The Civilization of Rome* (1960). An up-to-date, popular account of Rome from 753 B.C. to 476 in the Christian era, including history, politics, religion, and art. *P—NAL.*

DURANT, WILL b. 1885. *Caesar and Christ* (1944). Well-informed, fluently written cultural history of Rome and Christianity from their beginnings to A.D. 325. *H—S&S.*

GIBBON, EDWARD 1737-1794. *The Decline and Fall of the Roman Empire* (1776-78). A monumental masterwork of great analytical power that has become a classic of history. *Over 6 eds.*

GRANT, MICHAEL b. 1914. *The World of Rome* (1961). Illustrated, readable interpretation of Roman history and culture and of their subsequent influence. *P—NAL.*

_____. *Myths of the Greeks and Romans* (1962). Excellent presentation of the major myths via the most important sources. Applies different theories of myth, stressing the continuing influences of the tradition. *P—NAL.*

GRAVES, ROBERT b. 1895. *I, Claudius* (1934). Fictional autobiography of a strange emperor, which makes excellent use of historical sources. *P—Random.*

HIGHET. *The Classical Tradition.* See "Greece," page 8.

MacKENDRICK, PAUL L. b. 1914. *The Roman Mind at Work* (1958). Identifies Roman attitudes and qualities and illustrates them with translated readings from Greek and Latin sources. *H—Peter Smith; P—Van Nos Reinhold.*

_____. *The Mute Stones Speak* (1960). A lively, well-illustrated account of recent archaeological work at major Roman sites. *P—Norton.*

PATER, WALTER H. 1839-1894. *Marius the Epicurean* (1885). Many-sided picture of Roman life and thought in the 2nd century A.D. as seen by a young patrician. *H—Dutton.*

RENAN, ERNEST 1823-1892. *The Life of Jesus* (1863). A moving, skeptical portrayal of the Great Teacher against the background of Roman Judea. *o.p.*

ROWELL, HENRY T. b. 1904. *Rome in the Augustine Age* (1962). An expert analysis of the factors that made classical Rome a significant world capital. *H & P—U of Okla Pr.*

WILDER, THORNTON 1897-1975. *The Ides of March* (1948). The assassination of Julius Caesar vividly told through imaginary letters and documents. *P—Avon, G&D.*

YOURCENAR, MARGUERITE b. 1903. *Hadrian's Memoirs* (1954). Brilliant novelistic re-creation of an intelligent emperor's reflections on the Roman world of his times. *H & P—FS&G.*

3. The Middle Ages

Jules A. Wein

Though most of the lights of classical civilization went out in Europe with the collapse of the western Roman Empire by A.D. 500, the half millennium that followed, while often labeled the Dark Ages, was anything but a dreary stretch of time during which society lay prostrate and unproductive. Rather, it was an age of incubation during which a complex fusion of classical, Christian, and "barbarian" cultures prepared the way for the great achievements of the later Middle Ages. Greco-Roman society was dying of its own socio-economic diseases long before alien invaders administered the *coup de grâce*. It was those vigorous and independent peoples, aided by a store of practical knowledge preserved in manor and monastery, who, by the year 1000, created a basis for social progress far beyond the capability of the ancient world. Among their accomplishments were the replacement of the international system of the Roman Empire by the international structure and ideology of the Roman Church and the development of the great vernacular languages of the West.

Some of the notable literature of the five centuries of incubation, like Boethius' *Consolation of Philosophy*, drew inspiration from the Greco-Roman past. Other major works, like the great Anglo-Saxon epic *Beowulf* and numerous Norse, Icelandic, and Teutonic sagas, embody the values of northern peoples with their characteristic cult: glorification of the warrior hero. Still others, like Bede's *Ecclesiastical History of England*, manifest the dominating intellectual force of Christianity.

But the complex historical process that led to the High Middle Ages did not occur as a peaceful blending of cultures out of the wreckage of classical civilization. Warfare was endemic both within and among the new barbarian kingdoms. And a Europe that had progressed far enough to enable an economic, political, and cultural revival under Charlemagne in the latter part of the 8th century

15

barely survived savage invasions by Vikings, Arabs, and Magyars
in the 9th and 10th. Responses to those invasions affected the
development of different parts of Europe differently. But in the
long run, military necessity, weak central governments, poor
communications, and a precarious agrarian economy produced
almost everywhere some form of the socio-economic system now
known as feudalism. In that system a relatively small nobility of
professional fighting men organized territorial military functions,
regulated their internal relationships, and kept control of the
wretched millions who tilled the soil and did the humble productive
work that kept society alive.

The third great social stratum of the medieval world was the
clergy, headed by the papal Church at Rome. Some of its members
worked with the lay world, administering the business of the Church
or serving the spiritual needs of the people. But in the early centuries most of the clergy were isolated in monasteries and convents.
At first withdrawn from secular life for the salvation of their own
souls, they came in time to be seen as surrogates serving God on be-
half of the Christian community at large. With the expansion of
monasticism, some of the greatest orders turned outward, under-
taking public works of labor, education, and charity—always inci-
dental, of course, to their basic mission of saving souls. In education,
the Church provided for many centuries the only schools Christendom knew. Apart from a theological college in most cathedral
cities, however, schools were uncommon. It is unlikely that more
than a tenth of the medieval population had any schooling at all.
Economically, the Church became the greatest landowner and one
of the wealthiest powers of the Middle Ages. Politically, it provided
a counterweight to secular authority, especially to claims of
European dominion by the emperors of Germany. A long-drawn-out
power struggle between the Church and secular governments was
in fact one of the central political conflicts of the later Middle
Ages.

After the 10th century, when invaders from all points of the
compass had been thrown back or absorbed and internal warfare
had lessened, Western Europe entered an era of tremendous creativity. Immense primeval forests were cleared and vast lowlands
wrested from the sea for agriculture and settlement. Trade revived
and expanded prodigiously, partly as a result of the Crusades,
Europe's first major experiments in overseas conquest and colonization since antiquity. Everywhere new towns sprang up, including
most of the major cities we know today. In the process they developed urban values and a money economy that transformed
Europe. At the same time, ambitious monarchs prepared the
political transformation by laying the foundations of the great
national states of the future. Universities were founded, philosophy
flourished, scientific speculation revived, architects and artists
fashioned the monumental achievements of the Romanesque and
Gothic styles.

In some ways a still more consequential development was the transformation of attitudes toward women in the socio-literary phenomenon now styled Courtly Love. After millennia of subjection and contempt, women (if only a small, aristocratic minority) were suddenly placed on pedestals and worshiped—in poetry, if not in life. If they have been struggling to climb down from the pedestal to real equality ever since, their elevation by medieval lyric poets was nonetheless one of the great revolutions in human history, the basis not only of much Western literature but also of romantic love down to our own time. The normal condition of women in the Middle Ages was one of oppression, sexual exploitation, and vilification. The more remarkable, therefore, were individuals who achieved greatly in the face of almost insuperable odds: a Marie de France in poetry; an Heloise (she of the star-crossed love for Peter Abelard) in character and intellect; an Eleanor of Aquitaine in politics and patronage of the arts; a Christine de Pisan in literature and advocacy of women's rights; a Joan of Arc in politics, battle, and spirit.

For another oppressed group, the Jews, the most brilliant medieval centuries were the most terrible: hideous with massacres by Crusaders, expropriation and expulsion from England and France, and attempts at extermination in Germany.

Like all periods in history, the Middle Ages were centuries of violent contrasts—of piety and corruption, idealism and atrocity, paternalism and oppression, pageantry and poverty, splendor and disease. Medieval literature is rich and varied, reflecting this turbulent, colorful world. Among the most moving works are the chivalric *Song of Roland*, the romantic tragedy *Tristan and Iseult*, Arthurian tales of the Knights of the Round Table and their ladies, the lyrics of the Wandering Scholars and of the poet-outlaw François Villon, and that sweetest and most charming of all love stories, *Aucassin and Nicolette*. To Christian inspiration we owe Dante's *Divine Comedy*, matchless epic of sin, love, and redemption, and Langland's dream allegory, *Piers Plowman*. In their quest for truth, love, and justice, Dante and Langland epitomize, each in his own way, the best of the Middle Ages and humanity's eternal yearning for a social order fit for human beings.

Medieval Literature

ANDREAS CAPELLANUS fl. 12th cent. *The Art of Courtly Love* (c. 1185). Fascinating formulation of the theory and practice of courtly love by the chaplain of Countess Marie of Champagne. *P—Norton.*

Arabian Nights. See "The Middle East," page 50.

AUGUSTINE. *The City of God* and *Confessions*. See "Rome," page 12, and "Philosophy," page 181.

Beowulf (8th cent.). Anglo-Saxon epic about a legendary hero's struggles for humanity in a savage world. *Over 10 trans. and eds.*

BOCCACCIO. *The Decameron*. See "The Renaissance and Reformation," page 26.

BOETHIUS. *The Consolation of Philosophy*. See "Rome," page 12.

CHAUCER, GEOFFREY 1340?-1400. *The Canterbury Tales* (1387-1400). A wonderful panorama of English life, thought, and social types of the 14th century, drawn in character sketches and stories touched with wit, pathos, common sense, and shaped through superb literary art. *Over 15 trans. and eds.*

————. *The Portable Chaucer*. Representative selections from *The Canterbury Tales, Troilus and Criseyde* ("a psychological novel in verse"), shorter poems, and selections from other long poems—all in modern translations. *H & P—Viking Pr.*

CHRÉTIEN DE TROYES fl. 12th cent. *Arthurian Romances*. Verse tales of love and chivalry that inaugurated the Arthurian vogue in literature. *H & P—Dutton.*

DANTE ALIGHIERI 1265-1321. *The Divine Comedy* (1300-21). This brilliantly imagined epic journey through Hell, Purgatory, and Paradise, by one of the world's greatest poets, synthesizes medieval religion, politics, learning, and philosophy in a timeless story of faith and love. The translation of poet John Ciardi is particularly good (*P—NAL*). *Over 12 other trans. and eds.*

English Drama before Shakespeare. Medieval miracle and mystery plays, interludes, and early 16th-century plays have been variously anthologized and titled by at least six different publishers.

FRANCIS OF ASSISI, SAINT 1182-1226. *The Little Flowers*. A series of short anecdotes giving unequaled and often beautiful glimpses of the saint and his companions. *H—Dutton, Peter Pauper; P—Doubleday.*

FROISSART, JEAN 1333?-1400? *Chronicles of England, France, and Spain* (1373-90). The classic contemporary history of the first half of the Hundred Years' War. *H—AMS Pr, W J Johnson.*

GEOFFREY OF MONMOUTH 1100?-1154. *History of the Kings of England* (c. 1136). Idealized, often imaginary history that underlies much of Arthurian romance. *H—Mediaeval Acad, Peter Smith; P—Dutton, Penguin.*

GEOFFROY DE VILLEHARDOUIN 1160?-1212? and JEAN DE JOINVILLE 1224?-1317? *Memoirs of the Crusades* (c. 1207 and 1309). Vivid and fascinating first-hand accounts of the 4th and 7th Crusades. *H—Dutton.*

GUILLAUME DE LORRIS 1215?-1278? and JEAN DE MEUN d. 1305. *The Romance of the Rose*. The most popular and influential poem of the Middle Ages, this dream allegory is really two poems, one embodying courtly love, the other satirizing it. *H—AMS Pr, Princeton U Pr; P—Dutton.*

Koran. See "The Middle East," page 51.

LANGLAND, WILLIAM 1332?-1400? *Piers Plowman*. A powerful social protest in vigorous verse. *Over 6 eds.*

Laxdaela Saga (c. 1245). A family saga and Icelandic epic whose romantic triangle and tragedy make it especially appealing to the modern reader. *H—Am Scandinavian, Dutton; P—Penguin.*

MALORY, SIR THOMAS 1430?-1471. *Le Morte d'Arthur* (1485). Sometimes lusty, sometimes idealized fiction of chivalric combat and courtly love, much of it written in prison. *Over 15 eds.*

MANDEVILLE, JOHN d. 1372. *Travels* (1371). An entertaining compound of geographical facts and legendary marvels. *Over 6 eds.*

Medieval Romances. Available in libraries in various collections variously titled, all now out of print.

Medieval Song. Trans. by James J. Wilhelm. A fine and comprehensive anthology of Western European lyrical poetry from late classical times through the Middle Ages. *P—Dutton.*

Njal Saga (c. 1280). A lust for wealth and power brings on violence, turbulence, and tragedy in this greatest of classical Icelandic epics. *H—Twayne; P—Penguin.*

OMAR KHAYYÁM. *The Rubáiyát.* See "The Middle East," page 52.

The Poem of the Cid (12th cent.). The oldest Spanish epic, a tapestry of medieval life, chivalry, and adventure, woven around the idealized exploits of the 11th-century hero, Rodrigo Diáz de Vivar. *H—B&N, Kraus Repr; P—NAL, U of Cal Pr.*

POLO, MARCO 1254?-1324? *Travels* (1300-24). Colorful autobiographical account of the adventures of a Venetian merchant who was for a time an official of the great Kublai Khan in China. *Over 6 eds.*

The Portable Medieval Reader (1949). Ed. by James B. Ross and Mary M. McLaughlin. The world of the High Middle Ages and Early Renaissance in a profusion of selections from biography, history, science, theology, politics, and poetry. *H & P—Viking Pr.*

THOMAS À KEMPIS 1380-1471. *The Imitation of Christ* (c. 1471). A famous devotional work reflecting the ideals of the medieval Church. *Over 6 eds.*

THOMAS AQUINAS, SAINT 1225?-1274. *Writings.* The greatest Catholic theologian and philosopher writes about God, humanity, and human destiny. *Over 20 eds.* See also "Philosophy," page 184.

Tristan and Iseult (c. 13th cent.). The unforgettable medieval legend of tragic love in conflict with the institutions and values of feudal society. *H—AMS Pr, Dutton, Random; P—Penguin.*

VILLON, FRANÇOIS 1431-1463? *Poems.* Compelling, powerfully charged lyrics by a 15th-century Parisian poet-outlaw. *Over 6 eds.*

Volsunga Saga (c. 1200). The national epic of the Teutonic peoples, with characters and dramatic situations familiar from Wagner's *Ring of the Niebelungen. o.p.*

Books about the Middle Ages

ADAMS, HENRY 1838-1918. *Mont-Saint-Michel and Chartres* (1904). Penetrating, sensitive analysis of the medieval spirit in architecture and literature. *H—Gordon Pr; P—Doubleday.*

The Age of Chaucer (rev. ed. 1959). Ed. by Boris Ford. Contains short essays on the literature of the period and an excellent collection of poems and short plays. *P—Penguin.*

BARBER, RICHARD. *The Knight and Chivalry* (2nd ed. 1975). A learned and witty treatment of knighthood from origin to decline and of its medieval social setting. *H—Rowman.*

BATTERBERRY, MICHAEL. *Art of the Middle Ages* (1972). Lively, informative, lavishly illustrated survey, from the catacombs to the 15th century. *H—McGraw.*

BAUTIER, ROBERT-HENRI. *The Economic Development of Medieval Europe* (1972). The best-illustrated survey available, clear and vivid. *P—HarBraceJ.*

BLOCH, MARC 1886-1944. *Feudal Society* (1960). Creates in detail a vast panorama of the social system of the Middle Ages; the single most important book on the subject. *H & P—U of Chicago Pr 2 vols.*

BOGIN, MEG b. 1950. *The Women Troubadours* (1976). This study and translation of some 20 women poets of medieval Provence, with an introduction on courtly love, is valuable both in its own right and as a corrective to the male troubadours' views of women and love. *H—Two Continents.*

BULLOUGH, DONALD. *The Age of Charlemagne* (1966). Portrays the social and religious history, the arts, and the learning of the Dark Ages, as well as the first and last ruler of a united Europe. *H—Putnam.*

COSMAN, MADELEINE P. b. 1937. *Fabulous Feasts* (1976). Delightful and definitive study of medieval cookery and ceremony, illustrated from medieval sources; includes 133 recipes. *H & P—Braziller.*

COULTON, GEORGE G. 1858-1947. *Medieval Panorama* (1947). Richly detailed survey of the English scene from the Norman Conquest to the Reformation. *P—Norton.*

DURANT, WILL b. 1885. *The Age of Faith* (1950). Encyclopedic yet lively popular history of 1,000 years of medieval civilization, with many short excerpts from documents. *H—S&S.*

GIES, JOSEPH b. 1916 and FRANCES GIES b. 1915. *Life in a Medieval Castle* (1974). Chepstow Castle in Monmouthshire and the lives of its knights and villagers, with generous quotations and illustrations from contemporary sources. *H—T Y Crowell.*

————. *Life in a Medieval City* (1969). First-rate account of the life of the burghers of the Middle Ages. *H—T Y Crowell; P—Apollo Eds.*

HEER, FRIEDRICH b. 1916. *The Medieval World* (1961). Learned, vigorous account and analysis of the people, institutions, and culture of the High Middle Ages. *P—NAL.*

HUGO, VICTOR 1802-1885. *The Hunchback of Notre Dame* (1831). The love of a hunchback for a dancer. A great historical novel set in 15th-century Paris. *Over 6 eds.*

HUIZINGA, JOHAN 1872-1945. *The Waning of the Middle Ages* (1924). Colorful and original interpretation of the psychology of the late Middle Ages in France, based on contemporary literature, art, and costume. *H—St Martin; P—Doubleday.*

KELLY, AMY b. 1878. *Eleanor of Aquitaine and the Four Kings* (1950). The life and times of one of the great women of the Middle Ages, wife of two kings and mother of two others. Biography and history that read like a novel. *H—Harvard U Pr.*

MAYER, HANS E. *The Crusades* (1972). Causes, Crusades, consequences; the best one-volume survey available. *H & P—Oxford U Pr.*

MUNTZ, HOPE b. 1907. *The Golden Warrior* (1949). A distinguished and beautiful novel about Harold, last of the Saxon kings, and his gallant, losing fight against William the Conqueror. *H—Scribner.*

OLDENBOURG, ZOÉ b. 1916. *Destiny of Fire* (1961). Compassionate and moving novel based on the 13th-century atrocity known to history as the Albigensian Crusade. *P—Avon.*

PERNOUD, RÉGINE b. 1909. *Joan of Arc* (1967). Contemporary documents—letters, chronicles, trial testimony—with connecting commentary bring the Maid of Orléans to life as a credible human being. *P—Stein & Day.*

POUILLON, FERNAND b. 1912. *The Stones of the Abbey* (1970). Re-creating the building of a 12th-century French abbey, this finely wrought short novel captures the flavor of the Middle Ages and illuminates the problems involved in the creation of medieval monasteries and cathedrals. *H—HarBraceJ.*

POWER, EILEEN 1889-1940. *Medieval People* (1924). Fine scholarship and stylistic grace re-create six medieval lives in memorable fashion. *H—B&N, Peter Smith; P—B&N.*

_____. *Medieval Women* (1975). Ed. by M. M. Poston. The author's attractive personal approach is contained in the texts of lectures given at various places and times. *H & P—Cambridge U Pr.*

READE, CHARLES 1814-1884. *The Cloister and the Hearth* (1861). Vigorous, realistic novel about Erasmus' parents, set in Flanders, France, Germany, and Italy. *H & P—Dutton.*

ROWLING, MARJORIE b. 1900. *Everyday Life in Medieval Times* (1968). A sound, sensitive, well-documented account of how all classes of people lived from the time of Charlemagne to the Renaissance. *H—Putnam.*

SCOTT, SIR WALTER 1771-1832. *Ivanhoe* (1819). Famed romance of Old England, with Richard the Lion-Hearted, Robin Hood, tournaments, robber barons, and love. *Over 10 eds.*

SHAKESPEARE. *Richard II, Henry IV (Parts 1 and 2), Henry V, Richard III, Henry VI (Parts 1, 2, and 3)*. These historical plays reflect the violence and glories of England in late feudal times. See "The Renaissance and Reformation," page 29, for editions.

TIERNEY, BRIAN b. 1922 and SIDNEY PAINTER 1902-1960. *Western Europe in the Middle Ages* (1970). Outstanding one-volume survey of the civilization from 300 to 1475. *H—Knopf.*

VALENCY, MAURICE J. b. 1903. *In Praise of Love* (1958). A brilliant, original analysis of the poetic tradition of the troubadours in its historical, social, and psychological setting. *H—Octagon.*

WADDELL, HELEN 1889-1965. *Peter Abelard* (1933). Deeply moving novel about one of the most famous true love stories of all time and about the brilliant, passionate scholar whose love for Heloise brought tragedy. *H—Peter Smith, Viking Pr; P—Penguin.*

WHITE, HELEN b. 1896. *Bird of Fire* (1958). St. Francis of Assisi and
his age come alive in a well-spun and soundly researched historical
novel. *o.p.*

WHITE, LYNN b. 1907. *Medieval Technology and Social Change*
(1966). A remarkable and convincing effort to relate profound social
developments to humble technological innovations such as the stirrup
and the heavy plow. *P—Oxford U Pr.*

4. The Renaissance and Reformation

Jules A. Wein

A complex, multiphased process varying in time from country to country, and in aspect even in individual countries, the Renaissance is not easy to comprehend as a coherent historical phenomenon. What magical formula will harmonize, for example, humanists and Inquisitors, feminists and woman haters, scientists and witch-burners, ascetics and voluptuaries, idealists and cynics? Of all attempts, Wallace K. Ferguson's seems the least assailable because it is the most illuminating. The Renaissance, he holds, "was the age in which the decisive change from a largely feudal and ecclesiastical culture to one predominantly secular, lay, urban, and national took place, and it contained elements of both types in varying proportion." That change, which marks the end of the Middle Ages and the beginning of modern civilization, occurred first in Italy, much later in northern Europe and Spain. Different dates may thus be assigned to the Renaissance in different countries and to specific developments in the arts, science, politics, religion, and so on. But the three centuries from 1300 to 1600, give or take a few decades, embrace just about all elements comfortably.

In totality, a new movement of mind and spirit, growing out of the processes and transformations of medieval society, the Renaissance found justification as well as inspiration in ancient classical conceptions congenial to its outlook—political and philosophical as well as artistic. At its most modern, that outlook was individualistic, activist, acquisitive, pragmatic, challenging, questing, affirmative of humanity, of life and joy. In all these respects it opposed the official posture if not the invariable practice of the ecclesiastical Middle Ages. Inevitably, this involved a radical rethinking of the nature of humankind, of human relationships and values of every kind, of the universe in which we live, and of the artistic response to reality newly perceived.

In business affairs and love affairs, in painting, politics, sculpture, literature, and science, the creators of the Renaissance were committed to this world; neither Boccaccio at the beginning nor Montaigne, Shakespeare, or Cervantes at the end has more than a passing word for the next. This signals not a decline of piety but a new kind of piety, as well as a reordering of priorities to which most moderns still subscribe. From artists like Masaccio (some historians would begin with Giotto), the Van Eycks, and Donatello to Da Vinci, Michelangelo, Raphael, and Titian, religious subjects are as important if not as mandatory as they were in the Middle Ages, and as deeply felt. But theirs is religion humanized, enriched by the eloquence of the human body, by the wonder of life and of nature realistically observed. In much of the greatest art of the Renaissance, as in much of its life and literature, the Word has truly become flesh, and the exploration and celebration of the earthly gifts of a beneficent divinity are the highest form of worship. "I love life and cultivate it," Montaigne testifies gratefully, "such as it has pleased God to bestow it on us."

Yet the religious tendencies of the period were as complex and contradictory as any other, embracing the fanaticism of a reformer like John Calvin (for all his humanistic training) as amply as the humanism of a pope like Pius II. The Protestant Reformation, a product of the same forces that shaped the Renaissance, remains equally elusive of final definition. Smoldering in pockets of heresy from at least the 11th century (erupting at last with Martin Luther in Germany in 1517) the Reformation fused a variety of interests— religious, nationalistic, economic, and social—that plunged Western Europe into a century of war and shattered the unity of medieval Christendom forever. The plight of Erasmus, who died (albeit in bed) out of favor with Catholics and Lutherans alike, exemplifies the dilemma of men of good will in the last century of the Renaissance. And Erasmus was lucky. The roll call of distinguished Christian martyrs to the sectarian bigotry of the age is long and cosmopolitan enough to serve as a monument to the multitudes whose names we shall never know. If the thundering Italian monk Savonarola was strangled and burned at the stake in 1498 in the full flush of the Florentine Renaissance, the saintly German Anabaptist Michael Sattler went to the flames in Austria some thirty years later. In the Lowlands in 1536, William Tyndale, greatest English translator of the Bible, paid for his talent by suffering the same fate as Savonarola. Michael Servetus, Spanish physician and theologian, escaped the Catholic Inquisition in France in 1553 only to be roasted in a slow fire by French Protestants in Switzerland before the year was out. And in 1600, to recall but one other instance of pious ferocity and public entertainment during the Renaissance, the Italian philosopher and poet Giordano Bruno was burned at the stake for heresy in Rome.

The triumphs of the Renaissance were achieved despite religious censorship and repression, such natural disasters as plague and famine, and the apparent human propensity for mass slaughter. Italy was never at peace, seething with class conflict, wars among the states, marauding mercenaries, and the march and counter-march of foreign invasion. This is the sorry background of Machiavelli's desperate patriotism and political cynicism in *The Prince*. In England, a literary renaissance, sparked by Chaucer in emulation of Boccaccio, was smothered for a century by the wastage of the Hundred Years' War and the sordid power struggle romantically misnamed the Wars of the Roses. Germany had time to produce few men of the status of Dürer and the younger Holbein before going under in civil wars precipitated by the Reformation. France suffered atrociously from the same scourge later in the 16th century, while Spain was absorbed throughout the century in a career of war in the Old World and conquest and rapine in the New.

Though its artists endlessly celebrated the beauty of young women, the Renaissance was a bad time for the old, who provided the vast majority of victims of the crazed campaign against witches that savaged Europe in the 15th and 16th centuries. For the Jews, who were able briefly to participate in creating the great intellectual and cultural movement of the Renaissance in Italy, the period of the Renaissance as a whole was no exception to the European rule of persecution, forced conversion, mass expulsion, and slaughter that began with the Crusades. Some 100,000 Jews were massacred in Spain alone toward the end of the 15th century. The year in which Columbus discovered America under the sponsorship of Ferdinand and Isabella was also the year of the spoliation and expulsion of the entire Jewish population of Spain. In the same country, in 1498, Christians as well fell under the shadow when the Spanish Inquisition began its bloody career. When one adds to this catalog of horrors evidence that Western Europe suffered prolonged economic depression in the 14th and 15th centuries, it is apparent that for most people the Renaissance was anything but a Golden Age.

Nevertheless—and this is perhaps most astonishing of all—the Renaissance remains, on balance, one of the most lavishly creative and fruitful periods in all of Western experience. As in its artistic profusion, so in science and technology. Heroic captains—Vasco da Gama, Columbus, Vespucci, Magellan—opened new horizons on earth and in the human mind. They were rapidly followed by that swarm of explorers and colonizers who annexed the Western hemisphere. Copernicus, whose majestic theoretical reconstruction of the solar system was given mathematical elaboration by Kepler and telescopic confirmation by Galileo, repudiated the doctrine of earth's centrality and thus the theological dogma of the place of humans in the universe. Da Vinci and Vesalius, pioneering the new science of anatomy, discovered the world within. Altogether, Renaissance science was magnificent in scope and profound in effect, transforming the configuration of heaven, earth, and humankind. Yet all

these discoveries, and others, might have passed largely wasted but
for one Renaissance craftsman, Johann Gutenberg, thought to have
been the first European to print from movable metal type. For most
people, without printing there would have been no books to read.
Mass education, modern democracy, and modern science would
have remained the most visionary of dreams, and the very idea of
history—like that of the cultural Renaissance itself—would have
continued to be the possession of a privileged few.

As a cultural phenomenon the Renaissance was the creation of
a small elite of artists and intellectuals favored in varying degree
by talent, will, and opportunity. To see human beings through the
eyes of a Michelangelo or a Shakespeare; to conquer uncharted seas
with Columbus; to explore the cosmos with Copernicus and Galileo;
to meet Rabelais and Cervantes face to face—this is to sample the
range, the depth, the brilliance of the Renaissance. In its creative
energies set free, we mark for the first time in history the limitless
possibilities of the modern mind. The optimism of the early Renaissance languished in confrontation with reality. In the sorrow and
the pity of Michelangelo's late elegies in stone and the gathering
darkness of Shakespeare's greatest plays, in Montaigne's skepticism and Cervantes' tragic irony, one perceives the response of
sensitive men to undiminished human cruelty and suffering.

The voice of Renaissance promise speaks in the contrast between
the graveyard of the past and the gardens of a possible future in
Boccaccio's *Decameron;* in the celebration of the body's appetites
and functions in Rabelais' *Gargantua and Pantagruel;* as well as in
Michelangelo's inexpressibly beautiful and confident *David.* If
experience tempered hope, it never destroyed it. Out of the aspiration, accomplishment, and agony of those three remarkable centuries, Miranda, in Shakespeare's final play, *The Tempest,* still
sounds for us the central credo of the Renaissance:

> *How beauteous mankind is! O brave new world*
> *That has such people in't!*

Continental Renaissance Literature

BOCCACCIO, GIOVANNI 1313-1375. *The Decameron* (c. 1350). A lusty
age and the author's radical social philosophy brilliantly delineated
in 100 tales of love, intrigue, and adventure. *Over 6 eds.*

CASTELLIO, SEBASTIAN 1515-1563. *Advice to a Desolate France*
(1562). A Christian humanist's appeal for religious toleration and freedom of conscience during the horrors of the French civil wars of
1562-1598. *H—Patmos Pr.*

CASTIGLIONE, BALDASSARE 1478-1529. *The Courtier* (1528). The
enormously influential Renaissance ideal of gentleman and lady set
forth in four evenings of supple conversation at the ducal palace of
Urbino. *Over 6 eds.*

CELLINI, BENVENUTO 1500-1571. *Autobiography* (1728). The artist as
irascible, kindly, egotistical, vindictive rogue and assassin, patronized

by popes and royalty, true to nothing but his family and his art. *P— Doubleday, Dutton, Penguin.*

CERVANTES SAAVEDRA, MIGUEL DE 1547-1616. *Don Quixote* (1505-15). Begun as a satire on arrogant, self-serving crusaders and their followers, this endlessly inventive picaresque novel ends in ironic comment on the situation of the idealist in the real world. The translation by Samuel Putnam (*P—Viking Pr*) is superior. *Many other trans. and eds.*

DA VINCI, LEONARDO 1452-1519. *The Notebooks.* While perfecting the spiritual and esthetic heritage of his time, a towering prototypical "Renaissance man" experimented toward the scientific and technological wonders of ours. *H—Peter Smith; P—Dover.*

ERASMUS, DESIDERIUS 1466-1536. *In Praise of Folly* (1512). Witty satire ridiculing monkish superstitions, theological squabbling, learned ignorance, war, and other human irrationalities, by the most influential humanist of the Northern Renaissance. *Over 6 eds.*

LEONARDO DA VINCI. See DA VINCI.

LOPE DE VEGA CARPIO, FÉLIX 1562-1635. *Five Plays* (1961). A mere sampling of the enormous output of one of the greatest figures in Spanish literature. *P—Hill & Wang.*

MACHIAVELLI, NICCOLÒ 1469-1527. *The Prince* (1513). This cynical yet patriotic little treatise on political psychology and manipulation evidences the unfettering of the Renaissance mind—and has served as a handbook for tyrants down to our own time. *Over 10 eds.*

MICHELANGELO BUONAROTTI 1475-1564. *I, Michelangelo, Sculptor* (1972). Ed. by Irving and Jean Stone. An autobiography fashioned from his letters and art. *P—NAL.*

MONTAIGNE, MICHEL DE 1533-1592. *Essays* (1580-88). In a France aflame with bigotry, irrationality, and civil war, a retired gentleman thinks aloud, dangerously but serenely, about the human condition. *Over 10 eds.*

PAINTER, WILLIAM 1540?-1594. *Palace of Pleasure* (1566-7, 1575). The popular 16th-century anthology of stories, mined for plots by Elizabethan playwrights. *H—AMS Pr 4 vols., Peter Smith 3 vols; P— Dover 3 vols.*

PETRARCH (FRANCESCO PETRARCA) 1304-1374. *Selected Sonnets, Odes, and Letters* (1966). Ed. by Thomas G. Bergin. A brief but representative selection of the work of one of the greatest lyric poets of all time. *P—AHM Pub.*

The Portable Renaissance Reader (rev. ed. 1958). Ed. by James B. Ross and Mary M. McLaughlin. The world of the Continental Renaissance in a profusion of selections from biography, history, science, theology, politics, and poetry. *H & P—Viking Pr.*

The Protestant Reformation (1968). Ed. by Hans J. Hillerbrand. An excellent documentary overview of the great movements and leaders of the Reformation. *H—Walker & Co; P—Har-Row.*

RABELAIS, FRANÇOIS 1494?-1553. *Gargantua and Pantagruel* (1533-35). Between the lines of these fantastic farces with their gigantic heroes, the exuberant young French Renaissance laughs away the old order of medieval education and morality. *H—AMS Pr 3 vols., Dutton 2 vols; P—AHM Pub, Penguin.*

Renaissance Letters (1976). Ed. by Robert J. Clements and Lorna Levant. The Renaissance brought to life in a splendid anthology of 200 letters by famous people who lived it. *H & P—NYU Pr.*

ROJAS, FERNANDO DE d. 1541? **The Celestina** (1499). A Spanish tragic novel in dramatic form, this masterly portrayal of human passion and weakness establishes its author as Cervantes' greatest forerunner. *Over 6 eds.*

Source Readings in Music History: The Renaissance (1965). Ed. by Oliver Strunk. An unusual anthology, especially enlightening to readers with some knowledge of music theory and terminology. *P—Norton.*

VASARI, GIORGIO 1511-1574. **The Lives of the Artists** (1550). A pupil of Michelangelo and Andrea del Sarto gives astute and reasonably accurate accounts of the famous Italian painters, sculptors, and architects of his day, largely from personal knowledge. *H—AMS Pr, Dutton 4 vols; P—Penguin, S&S.*

VESPASIANO DA BISTICCI, FIORENTINO 1421-1498. **Lives of Illustrious Men** (1839). Lively thumbnail biographies of the most gifted and important men of the author's time, largely from personal recollection. *H—Gannon.*

Tudor Literature

Anthology of English Drama before Shakespeare (1952). Ed. by Robert B. Heilman. A satisfying selection of early dramas, showing how the form developed before reaching a climax in Shakespeare. *H—Peter Smith; P—HR&W.*

BACON, SIR FRANCIS 1561-1626. **Essays** (1597, 1612, 1625). Shrewd, practical estimates of human life in aphoristic sentences. Macaulay estimated that these essays "moved the intellects that moved the world." *Over 6 eds.*

CAMPION, THOMAS 1567-1620. **Poems.** The lyrics of a "doctor of physick" who was also a great poet and composer. *Over 6 eds.*

DONNE, JOHN 1573-1631. **Poems.** First of the so-called metaphysical poets, still intellectually as well as emotionally challenging, Donne writes about passionate love as if it were a religion and about religion as if it were a passionate love. *Over 15 eds.*

Elizabethan and Jacobean Poets (1950) and **Medieval and Renaissance Poets** (1950). Ed. by W. H. Auden and Norman Holmes Pearson. Generous anthologies of selections and complete poems of major and minor poets. *P—Viking Pr.*

Elizabethan People: State and Society (1972). Ed. by Joel Hurstfield and Alan G. R. Smith. Very readable and informative collection of excerpts from Elizabethan historical and literary works. *P—St Martin.*

Elizabethan Plays (1945). Ed. by Hazleton Spencer. Collection of 28 plays by Shakespeare's friends, rivals, and successors, from Christopher Marlowe to James Shirley. *H—Heath.*

An Elizabethan Song Book (1955). Ed. by Noah Greenberg, W. H. Auden, and Chester Kallman. Words and music for more than 80 lute songs, madrigals, and rounds. *P—Faber & Faber, Humanities.*

HAKLUYT, RICHARD 1552-1616. *Voyages* (1598-1600). Selected reports of English voyagers and explorers, real and imaginary. A bestseller with Elizabethans and still often fascinating. *Over 6 eds.*

JONSON, BEN 1572?-1637. *Plays.* A skillful satirist who, next to Shakespeare, was the best and most interesting of Elizabethan playwrights. *Over 20 eds. of indiv. and coll. plays.*

King James Bible. See *Bible* under "Religion," page 189.

MARLOWE, CHRISTOPHER 1564-1593. *Plays.* If this gifted poet-playwright had lived longer, he might well have rivaled Shakespeare. *Over 10 eds. of indiv. and coll. plays.*

MORE, SIR THOMAS 1478-1535. *Utopia* (1516). A challenging, influential little book that envisions a good society based on economic communism and primitive Christian ethics. *Over 6 eds.*

PAINTER. *Palace of Pleasure.* See page 27.

The Portable Elizabethan Reader (1946). Ed. by Hiram Haydn. The best one-volume cross section of Elizabethan writing. *P—Viking Pr.*

SHAKESPEARE, WILLIAM 1564-1616. *Plays.* The greatest treasure of Western literature since the ancients. Of the 35 histories, comedies, and tragedies, perhaps the most popular are *Antony and Cleopatra, As You Like It, Hamlet, Henry IV, Julius Caesar, King Lear, Macbeth, A Midsummer Night's Dream, Othello, Romeo and Juliet, The Tempest,* and *Twelfth Night.* Available in countless hardcover and paperbound collections and single editions. The best of the single-play paperbound editions: *Dell, NAL, Penguin, Yale U Pr.*

————. *Sonnets* (1609). An uneven and puzzling sonnet sequence containing some of the world's best examples of the form and raising some seemingly unanswerable questions about Shakespeare and his subjects. *Over 10 eds.*

SIDNEY, SIR PHILIP 1554-1586. *Astrophel and Stella* (1591). The first sonnet sequence in English and one of the finest of the type. *H—British Bk Ctr.*

Songs from Shakespeare's Plays and Popular Songs from Shakespeare's Time (1964). Ed. by Tom Kines. Many of the superb lyrics from the plays are here set to contemporary tunes, usually those known or reputed to be those used on Shakespeare's stage. The music is arranged for modern guitar. *o.p.*

SPENSER, EDMUND 1552-1599. *Poems.* The first major English poet after Chaucer, celebrated for his great technical skill, rich imagery, and gifted imagination. *Over 6 eds.*

SURREY, HENRY HOWARD, EARL OF 1515?-1547. *Poems.* Soldier and courtly poet, Surrey apparently introduced blank verse into English poetry and invented the "Shakespearean sonnet form." *H & P—Oxford U Pr.*

WYATT, SIR THOMAS 1503-1542. *Collected Poems* (1975). Diplomat and poet, Wyatt wrote the first sonnets in English and changed the course of English poetry by importing the Italian lyrical mood of Dante and Petrarch. *H & P—Oxford U Pr.*

Books about the Continental Renaissance

ADAMCZEWSKI, JAN and EDWARD J. PISZEK. *Nicolas Copernicus and His Epoch* (1974). Sound, beautifully illustrated account of the life and times of the man who moved heaven and earth. *o.p.*

BAINTON, ROLAND H. b. 1894. *Women of the Reformation in France and England* (1973) and *Women of the Reformation in Germany and Italy* (1971). Brief but informative biographical sketches of women who played prominent roles in the religious crises of the 16th century. *H—Augsburg; P—Beacon Pr.*

BLUME, FRIEDRICH b. 1893. *Renaissance and Baroque Music* (1967). Comprehensive survey of the rich achievements of the period, especially recommended to readers with some knowledge of music theory and terminology. *H—Peter Smith; P—Norton.*

BRUCKER, GENE b. 1924. *Renaissance Florence* (1969). The society and thought of the most splendid of Renaissance cities, effectively surveyed. *P—Har-Row, Wiley.*

BURCKHARDT, JAKOB 1818-1897. *The Civilization of the Renaissance in Italy* (1860). The great work of historical synthesis which remains the point of departure for all studies of the Renaissance. *H—Peter Smith; P—Har-Row.*

CHAMBERLIN, E. R. b. 1926. *Everyday Life in Renaissance Times* (1965). Concise and lively visualization of Renaissance society in structure and action, from war to entertainment, witchcraft to science. *H & P—Putnam.*

CROMBIE, A. C. b. 1915. *Medieval and Early Modern Science*, Vol. 2 (1959). The beginnings of the scientific revolution and the foundations of modern science and technology (13th to 17th century) expertly summarized. *o.p.*

DURANT, WILL b. 1885. *The Renaissance* (1953) and *The Reformation* (1957). Encyclopedic yet lively popular histories with many short excerpts from documents. *H—S&S.*

Essays on the Renaissance. Modest collections of illuminating modern essays on various aspects of the subject include: KARL H. DANNENFELDT, ed., *The Renaissance: Basic Interpretations* (1959); WALLACE K. FERGUSON et al., *The Renaissance: Six Essays* (1953); DENYS HAY, ed., *The Renaissance Debate* (1965); J. H. PLUMB, ed., *Renaissance Profiles* (1961); ROBERT SCHWOBEL, ed., *Renaissance Men and Ideas* (1971); KENNETH A. STRAND, ed., *Essays on the Northern Renaissance* (1968); JAMES W. THOMPSON et al., *The Civilization of the Renaissance* (1929). *Various pubs.*

FERGUSON, WALLACE K. b. 1902. *Europe in Transition, 1300–1520* (1964). The best one-volume introduction to the Renaissance, integrating social, political, and economic history with the culture. *o.p.*

———. *The Renaissance.* (1940). A slim but brilliant sociological essay, still the most plausible and penetrating analysis of the Renaissance and its medieval background. *o.p.*

GILBERT, CREIGHTON b. 1924. *History of Renaissance Art* (1973). The arts, artists, and artistic centers of Western Europe from 1300 to 1600, capably surveyed and well illustrated. *H—P-H.*

HALE, J. R. b. 1923. *Renaissance Exploration* (1972). An outstanding treatment and pleasurable reading besides. *P—Norton.*

HARTT, FREDERICK b. 1914. *History of Italian Renaissance Art* (1969). The best text and the first to offer an integrated discussion of the painting, sculpture, and architecture. *H—P-H.*

HILLERBRAND, HANS J. b. 1931. *Christendom Divided: The Protestant Reformation* (1971). Excellent study of the religious reform movements and their leaders in historical context. *H—Westminster.*

KIECKHEFER, RICHARD b. 1946. *European Witch Trials* (1976). Relates the trials to their cultural setting, 1300-1500, with differential analysis of the various elements of witchcraft. *H—U of Cal Pr.*

MALLET, MICHAEL. *The Borgias* (1970). Authoritative delineation of the rise and fall of a notorious Renaissance dynasty, in historical perspective. *o.p.*

MATTHEWS, GEORGE T. b. 1917 (ed.). *The Fugger Newsletters* (1959). Business and political intelligence of the great German family of merchant-bankers. *H—Peter Smith; P—Putnam.*

MATTINGLY, GARRETT 1900-1962. *The Armada* (1959). A masterpiece of historical writing, as dramatic as a good novel, about the Spanish attempt to invade Elizabethan England. *P—HM.*

MEE, CHARLES L. b. 1938. *Lorenzo de' Medici and the Renaissance* (1969). Outstandingly illustrated, popular introduction to the Renaissance prince and the city of Florence. *H—Am Heritage.*

MORISON, SAMUEL ELIOT 1887-1976. *Admiral of the Ocean Sea* (1942). Unrivaled biography of Columbus, emphasizing his genius as navigator and seaman. Beautifully written and already a classic. *H—Little.*

PANOFSKY, ERWIN 1892-1968. *Meaning in the Visual Arts* (1955). A profound student of art and culture attractively describes the relationship between life and art in the High Middle Ages and the Renaissance. *P—Doubleday.*

PLUMB, J. H. b. 1911. *The Italian Renaissance* (1961). A fresh look at the Renaissance through the eyes of a modern historiographer. Concise and stimulating. *P—Har-Row.*

The Renaissance Philosophy of Man (1956). Ed. by Ernst Cassirer et al. Selections from the major thinkers of the early Italian Renaissance on the human condition. *H & P—U of Chicago Pr.*

ROTH, CECIL b. 1899. *The Jews in the Renaissance* (1959). A detailed account of how the Jews influenced the Italian Renaissance and of how for a brief while they benefited from it. *H—Peter Smith.*

SYMONDS, JOHN ADDINGTON 1840-1893. *The Renaissance in Italy* (1875-86). Rich, encyclopedic, intelligent, well written, and a monument of cultural history. *H—Peter Smith 3 vols.*

SYPHER, WYLIE b. 1905. *Four Stages of Renaissance Style* (1955). Integrating the fine arts and literature, the author describes and appraises their transformations from 1400 to 1700 in a profound, difficult book. *H—Peter Smith; P—Doubleday.*

WILKINS, ERNEST H. 1880-1966. *Life of Petrarch* (1961). Trustworthy, straightforward historical biography of the scholar and poet who, more than any other individual, fathered Renaissance literature and humanistic studies. *P—U of Chicago Pr.*

Books about Tudor England

BATE, JOHN. *How to Find Out about Shakespeare* (1968). Still an invaluable guide to the most important books and articles on practically everything you might want to know about the man, his world, and his works. *H & P—Pergamon.*

BRADLEY, A. C. 1851-1935. *Shakespearean Tragedy* (2nd ed. 1905). Extremely influential analyses of *Hamlet, Othello, King Lear,* and *Macbeth.* A landmark of 20th-century criticism. *H—St Martin; P—Fawcett World, St Martin.*

BROWER, REUBEN A. 1908-1975. *Hero and Saint* (1972). Explores the interaction between classical heroic tradition and Christian concepts in Shakespeare's greatest tragedies. *o.p.*

CHAMBERS, E. K. 1866-1954. *Shakespeare, a Survey* (1925). A stimulating collection of a great scholar's introductions to the plays. *o.p.*

CHUTE, MARCHETTE b. 1909. *Shakespeare of London* (1949). A brilliant research scholar and popular writer lets the facts speak for themselves in this splendid study of the bard and the world in which he lived. *H&P—Dutton.*

————. *Ben Jonson of Westminster* (1953). A first-rate account of the life and work of Shakespeare's nearest rival. *H—Dutton.*

COLERIDGE, SAMUEL TAYLOR 1772-1834. *Shakespearean Criticism.* A great Romantic poet and critic analyzes the plays and particularly the characters. *H—Dutton.*

DICKENS, ARTHUR G. b. 1910. *The English Reformation* (1964). The best general history, splendidly illustrated. *H & P—Schocken.*

DUSINBERRE, JULIET. *Shakespeare and the Nature of Women* (1975). An overdue attempt to place Shakespeare's attitudes toward women in the context of Renaissance thought and practice. *H—B&N.*

FRYE, ROLAND MUSHAT b. 1921. *Shakespeare's Life and Times: A Pictorial Record* (1967). Sparse biographical material made vivid and convincing by a magnificent selection of illustrations from Elizabethan sources. *H & P—Princeton U Pr.*

GODDARD, HAROLD CLARKE 1878-1950. *The Meaning of Shakespeare* (1951). Widely underrated but, as the *Christian Century* observed, one of the few really great books about Shakespeare. Original, radical analyses of 33 plays, full of exciting insights. *H & P—U of Chicago Pr.*

GRANVILLE-BARKER, HARLEY 1877-1946. *Prefaces to Shakespeare* (1944-47). An outstanding producer-director's shrewd and sensitive analyses of plot, character, language. *H & P—Princeton U Pr.*

HACKETT, FRANCIS 1883-1962. *Henry VIII* (1929). Rounded portrait of the lusty monarch who ran Britain as his private business and established the balance-of-power principle as the basis of English foreign policy. *H & P—Liveright.*

HARBAGE, ALFRED B. 1901-1976. *Conceptions of Shakespeare* (1966). Every age re-creates its own Shakespeare and in a sense rewrites the plays. This scholarly book makes one ponder the man behind the many conceptions. *H—Harvard U Pr; P—Schocken.*

_____. *Shakespeare's Audience* (1941). Rich in its understanding of the world of the London theater. *H—Peter Smith; P—Columbia U Pr.*

_____. *William Shakespeare: A Reader's Guide* (1963). A valuable general introduction for the beginner, with careful analyses of 14 of the plays. *H—Octagon; P—FS&G.*

HARRISON, GEORGE B. b. 1894. *Introducing Shakespeare* (1939). Still the best brief introduction to Shakespeare and to all that is involved in Shakespearean study. *H—Somerset Pub; P—Penguin.*

HOGREFE, PEARL. *Tudor Women* (1975). Englishwomen of the upper classes, 1485-1600, especially those who achieved distinction despite the obstacles of English law and tradition. *H—Iowa St U Pr.*

LACEY, ROBERT b. 1944. *Sir Walter Raleigh* (1974). Vivid, fast-paced biography of the adventurer, courtier, and poet, profusely illustrated. *H—Atheneum.*

McELROY, BERNARD. b. 1938. *Shakespeare's Mature Tragedies* (1973). A fresh and sensitive exploration of the meaning of the four great tragedies whose analysis by Bradley (see page 32) inaugurated 20th-century Shakespeare criticism. *H—Princeton U Pr.*

MATTINGLY. *The Armada*. See page 31.

PILL, DAVID H. *The English Reformation* (1973). A more popular history than the standard survey by Dickens (see page 32.) *H & P—Rowman.*

REESE, MAX M. b. 1910. *The Cease of Majesty* (1961). Insightful examination of Shakespeare's history plays against the background of Tudor thought. *H—St Martin.*

ROWSE, A. L. b. 1903. *The Elizabethan Renaissance* (1972). All levels of the society portrayed in the immediacy of their daily life and mentality. *P—Scribner.*

_____. *The England of Elizabeth* (1950). An authoritative work on the rural, urban, political, and religious complex of the age. *P—Macmillan.*

RUOFF, JAMES E. b. 1925. *Crowell's Handbook of Elizabethan and Stuart Literature* (1975). Some 500 articles of basic information on the writers and literature of the English Renaissance. A reliable guide and reference work. *H—T Y Crowell.*

SCOTT, SIR WALTER 1771-1832. *Kenilworth* (1821). A full-dress historical novel about Elizabethan times and people. *Over 6 eds.*

SMITH, LACEY BALDWIN b. 1922. *The Elizabethan World* (1967). The ideas and forces at work on the Continent as well as in England. Well written and, in the Horizon Book edition, handsomely illustrated. *H & P—HM.*

_____. *Elizabeth Tudor* (1975). A penetrating and entertaining portrait of the great queen. *H & P—Little*.

SPENCER, THEODORE 1902-1949. *Shakespeare and the Nature of Man* (2nd ed. 1949). Brilliant, influential analysis of the dramatist's presentation of the human condition. *H & P—Macmillan*.

SPURGEON, CAROLINE F. E. 1869-1942. *Shakespeare's Imagery* (1935). A basic treatment of the subject, encyclopedic in scope, highly influential, vital for any serious student of the plays. *P—Cambridge U Pr*.

TRAVERSI, DEREK A. b. 1912. *An Approach to Shakespeare* (1956). This outstanding development of Spurgeon's ideas traces the organic unity of language, images, and themes in eleven of the plays and in the sonnets. *P—Doubleday 2 vols*.

ZEEVELD, W. GORDON b. 1902. *The Temper of Shakespeare's Thought* (1974). Comprehensive, eminently readable treatment of Shakespeare's intellectual milieu and orientation. *H—Yale U Pr*.

5. The 17th Century

Joseph A. Byrnes

Between the Renaissance and the Age of Reason, prolonging one and preparing for the other, came the politically turbulent, intellectually active 17th century—the century of genius, as it has been called. In science, the age began with the new cosmology of Copernicus and Galileo and ended with Newton's law of gravitation. Along the way, it saw the experimental methods advocated by Bacon and Descartes, the founding of the English Royal Society and the French Academy of Sciences, and inventions and discoveries crucial for the future: the telescope and microscope, the calculus and logarithms, and Harvey's demonstration of the "Motion of the Heart and the Blood." In the arts, painting had distinguished practitioners: Rembrandt, Hals, Rubens, Van Dyck, Vermeer, Poussin, and Velasquez. Monteverdi, Corelli, Lulli, and Purcell (England's greatest native-born composer) developed the Baroque style in music, as polyphony yielded to harmony, madrigal to opera.

These impressive, peaceful accomplishments took place when Europe was torn by political, economic, and religious strife. During the Thirty Years' War (1618-1648), pious Catholic and zealous Protestant thoroughly devastated most of Germany. Victims of religious persecution fled; many, like the Huguenots and the Pilgrim Fathers, sought liberty of conscience in the wilderness of the New World. Spain's great empire was weakening; the French monarchy, with brilliant administrators like Richelieu and Mazarin, established its supremacy, although on an uncertain financial basis. The English, during and after their Civil War (1642-1649), modified their government—in part by killing one king, expelling another, and importing a third; and in part by applying the liberal political tenets being advocated by men like Milton and Locke. Europe's merchant classes made weapons of their wealth in their vigorous struggle for power, nowhere with more success than in

England. Energetic, practical, forward-looking, predominantly radical-Protestant, they were eventually to triumph over the conservative aristocrats.

Religion, long a source of bitter controversy, found itself harassed from a new quarter by doubts induced by the "new science." The issue of faith versus reason began increasingly to trouble speculative minds. Although the bulk of partisan religious writing is unreadable today, not all religion was acrimonious; among Englishmen, Fox, the Quaker, and Bunyan achieved serene personal approaches to God; Donne and Herbert spoke poetically for Anglican moderation.

Philosophy was concerned with its perennial problems, but especially with religion and politics. Descartes began with a complete and radical skepticism; Hobbes postulated man's inhumanity to man, advocating absolutism as the safeguard of domestic tranquillity. Locke's *Two Treatises of Government* later formed part of the liberal intellectual heritage of America's founding fathers. Spinoza geometrically reexamined the fundamentals of ethics and religion; Pascal, moralist and mathematician, paradoxically exalted faith. In educational theory, the Moravian Comenius offered an idealistic project for universal free education.

This century gave us Spain's foremost contributions to European letters: Cervantes' comic knight and the dramas of Calderón and Lope de Vega. French drama likewise found its most sublime classical formulation in Corneille and Racine, and its supreme comic vision in Molière. English literature began the century with the glory of Shakespeare and the Jacobean dramatists, and with Donne and his fellow metaphysical poets, who compressed their world into intense, striking images. Unlike the metaphysicals, the greatest Puritan literary spokesman, Milton, was deeply committed to politics as well as to his attempt to "justify the ways of God to men" on rational lines. His rejection of royal absolutism and his fervent plea in the *Areopagitica* for the free exchange of ideas unhampered by censorship are seminal propositions in the British and American view of democratic life.

In England, after years of Puritan repression, the Restoration of 1660 ushered in not only a king but the social reaction reflected in its witty, rationalistic comedies about eager gentlemen in pursuit of equally eager ladies. Life in the England of Charles II was reported with humor and frank self-revelation by the prince of diarists, Pepys. The style of verse changed, and the varied stanzas and subtle lyrics of the metaphysicals, Herrick, and the Cavaliers were replaced by Dryden's pointed, balanced, rational, "heroic" couplets. English prose, the best of it nonpolemic, developed rapidly. What the English sentence lost throughout the century in Elizabethan exuberance (and length), it gained in power, precision, and suppleness. The magnificent phrasing of the King James Bible, the cadences of Sir Thomas Browne, the devotional simplicity of Bunyan, the rational power of Dryden's critical essays—all influenced the course of our language.

During the Renaissance, Western civilization reached the threshold of the modern world and in the 17th century entered fully into it, with its conflicts and confusions—some of which still plague us today. We have inherited from that age some of the scientific and philosophic principles we still live by, as well as the enduring literary record of its agonies, delights, and accomplishments.

17th-Century Literature

AUBREY, JOHN 1626-1697. *Brief Lives* (1813). Informal, revealing sketches, with often amusing details, of a host of 17th-century persons. *H & P—U of Mich Pr.*

Authorized Version of the Bible (King James translation, 1611). "The noblest monument of English prose." See "Religion," page 189.

BACON. *Essays*. See "The Renaissance and Reformation," page 28.

BEAUMONT, FRANCIS 1584-1616 and JOHN FLETCHER 1579-1625. *Selected Plays*. Excellent theatre, violent and exotic; elegant, poetic, witty. *H—Dutton; P—Barron, U of Nebr Pr.*

BOYLE, ROBERT 1627-1691. *The Sceptical Chymist* (1661). Empirical demolition of the myths of alchemy and other pseudochemistry by an early exponent of the scientific method. *H—Dutton.*

BROWNE, SIR THOMAS 1605-1682. *Religio Medici* (1643). The style—stately, cadenced, lucid, and personal—distinguishes the reasoned liberalism of Browne's Platonist doctor's faith. *Over 6 eds.*

BUNYAN, JOHN 1628-1688. *Pilgrim's Progress* (1678). A visionary thinker's allegory of the Christian's journey to self-fulfillment; the most abiding scripture of English Puritanism, with a strong influence on later English prose style. *Over 20 eds.*

CERVANTES. *Don Quixote*. See "The Renaissance and Reformation," page 27.

Colonial American Writing (1950). Ed. by Roy H. Pearce. A wide-ranging anthology marking the New World's progress from Old England to the American Enlightenment. *H—Peter Smith.*

CONGREVE, WILLIAM 1670-1729. *Comedies*. Satire on, and for, fashionable society; brilliantly cynical situations; dialogue of amazing finish and verve. *H—Oxford U Pr, U of Chicago Pr; P—Hill & Wang.* There are also numerous collections and single volumes of Congreve and his fellow Restoration dramatists (Etherege, Wycherley, Otway, et al.).

CORNEILLE, PIERRE 1606-1684 and JEAN RACINE 1639-1699. *Plays*. These two playwrights created many of the masterpieces of France's neoclassic theatre. Theirs is a world of formal tragedy, phrased in polished verse, following the classic unities in presenting irreconcilable conflicts of reason and passion. *Many eds. of indiv. and coll. plays.*

DESCARTES. *Discourse on Method*. See "Philosophy," page 181.

DONNE. *Poems*. See "The Renaissance and Reformation," page 28.

DRYDEN, JOHN 1631-1700. *Poems*. Poet laureate and pioneering critic, a titan of 17th-century English letters in drama, translation, criticism, lyric and especially satiric poetry. *Over 10 eds.*

The Golden Age (1963). Ed. by Norris Houghton. Anthology showing how the sweepingly Romantic Spanish style of drama (Calderón, Lope de Vega) contrasts with the neoclassicism of the French (Corneille, Racine, Molière). *P—Dell.*

GRIMMELSHAUSEN, HANS JACOB CHRISTOFFEL VON 1625?-1676. *Simplicius Simplicissimus* (1669). A satiric fantasy, cast in a picaresque mold, of an innocent at large in mid-17th-century Europe, written by a veteran of the Thirty Years' War. *H—Bobbs, Ungar.*

HERRICK, ROBERT 1591-1674. *Poems.* (1648). Piquant, poignant, graceful lyrics, encompassing both religious devotion and an Epicurean feeling for life and love. *Over 6 eds.*

HOBBES. *Leviathan.* See "Philosophy," page 182.

LA FONTAINE, JEAN DE 1621-1695. *Fables* (1668-94). Traditional beast fables from Aesop and other sources adapted to the not-too-nice world of Louis XIV. *H—U Pr of Va; P—Dover.*

LA ROCHEFOUCAULD, DUC DE 1613-1680. *Maxims* (1665). Polished wit and courtly cynicism reflecting the world as it was and is rather than as theorists would have it. *P—Branden.*

LEIBNIZ, GOTTFRIED WILHELM VON 1646-1716. *Philosophical Writings.* The philosophy of rationalized optimism later to be Voltaire's target in *Candide. H & P—Rowman.*

LOCKE, JOHN 1632-1704. *Two Treatises of Civil Government* (1689). The source of much of the early political theory of America, especially Jefferson's. *Over 6 eds.*

_____. *An Essay Concerning Human Understanding.* See "Philosophy," page 183.

MARVELL, ANDREW 1621-1678. *Poems.* Puritan, politician, and poet, author of one of the greatest love poems in English ("To His Coy Mistress"). *Over 6 eds.*

Metaphysical Lyrics and Poems of the Seventeenth Century (1921). Ed. by H. J. C. Grierson. A classic anthology, with a helpful introduction to this knotty but fascinating verse. *P—Oxford U Pr.*

MILTON, JOHN 1608-1674. *The Portable Milton* (1949). Introduction by Douglas Bush. One of the best and handiest collections of the works of the poet ranked by many authorities next to Shakespeare. It contains the incomparable *Paradise Lost* and other poetry, and selected prose, including the *Areopagitica,* the most impassioned defense in English of free speech. *H & P—Viking Pr. Over 20 other eds. of indiv. and coll. works.*

MOLIÈRE (JEAN BAPTISTE POQUELIN) 1622-1673. *Comedies.* Comic genius, expert theatricalism, and classic art united in satiric portrayals of 17th-century society. Translations of Molière vary in quality; Richard Wilbur's renderings of *Tartuffe, The Misanthrope,* and *The School for Wives* are superb. *H & P—HarBraceJ. Many other trans. and eds.*

Oxford Book of Seventeenth-Century Verse (1934). Ed. by H. J. C. Grierson and G. Bullough. A standard collection representing over 100 English poets. *H—Oxford U Pr.*

PASCAL, BLAISE 1623-1662. *Pensées (Thoughts)* (1670). Reflections of a sensitive mathematician on nature, humanity, and God. *Over 6 eds.*

PEPYS, SAMUEL 1633-1703. *Diary*. Pepys reformed the Royal Navy, collected books, attended theatres, chased upper-class women (and their maids), and wrote it all down in a shorthand deciphered years later. A fascinating and frank picture of work and play in the London of the Merry Monarch, Charles II. *Over 6 eds.*

SÉVIGNÉ, MARIE, MARQUISE DE 1626-1696. *Letters*. Charming, witty, superbly styled, and natural letters which give a fine picture of the times of Louis XIV. *H—Dutton.*

SEWALL, SAMUEL 1652-1730. *The Diary of Samuel Sewall* (1973). Ed. by M. Halsey Thomas. Almost all aspects of colonial life as reported by one of Massachusetts Bay's most observant men of affairs. *H—FS&G 2 vols.*

SPINOZA. *The Ethics*. See "Philosophy," page 184.

WALTON, IZAAK 1593-1683. *The Compleat Angler* (1653). Generations of fishermen have delighted in this serene recommendation of the contemplative sport, with its interpolations on literature and life. *H—British Bk Ctr, Dutton, Oxford U Pr; P—Dutton, British Bk Ctr.*

———. *Lives* (1678). Four Anglican churchmen (including the poets Donne and Herbert) are seen as saints in "the most literary and the most readable today of the 17th-century biographies." *H—British Bk Ctr, Oxford U Pr; P—British Bk Ctr.*

Books about the 17th Century

BAZIN, GERMAIN b. 1907. *Baroque and Rococo Art* (1964). A brief but excellent and well-illustrated introduction to the visual arts of the age by the curator of the Louvre Museum. *H & P—Praeger.*

BREDVOLD, LOUIS I. 1888-1977. *The Intellectual Milieu of John Dryden* (1934). Dryden is seen as the figure around whom swirl the intellectual currents of the later decades of the century, arising from the interaction of skepticism, religion, and the "new science." *P—U of Mich Pr.*

CATHER, WILLA 1876-1947. *Shadows on the Rock* (1931). French pioneers on the Quebec frontier struggle to maintain the decorum of their homeland. *H—Knopf.*

CHUTE, MARCHETTE b. 1909. *Two Gentle Men: The Lives of George Herbert and Robert Herrick* (1959). Caroline England gracefully evoked, with enlightening details, through the lives of two great lyric poets. *H—Dutton.*

DEFOE, DANIEL 1660-1731. *A Journal of the Plague Year* (1722). A vivid *tour de force* of imaginative journalism that chills the reader with the nightmare world of the London pestilence of 1665. *Over 6 eds.*

DUMAS, ALEXANDRE 1802-1870. *The Three Musketeers* (1844). Swashbuckling adventure in the court of Louis XIII. *Over 6 eds.*

DURANT, WILL b. 1885 and ARIEL DURANT b. 1898. *The Age of Reason Begins* (1961) and *The Age of Louis XIV* (1963). A panoramic view of Western civilization during the formative years of the modern world. Engagingly written with illuminating detail. *H—S&S.*

FRASER, ANTONIA b. 1932. *Cromwell: The Lord Protector* (1973). The great Puritan leader—a complex personality and a man who wielded extensive power—portrayed sympathetically in a full and readable biography. *H—Knopf; P—Dell.*

GOOCH, G. P. 1873-1968. *English Democratic Ideas in the Seventeenth Century* (rev. 1955). An important study defining the sources of some of our most cherished political ideals. *H—Cambridge U Pr.*

GRIERSON, H. J. C. 1866-1960. *Cross Currents in Seventeenth Century English Literature* (1929). The age-old oppositions of world, flesh, and spirit, as manifested in a complex milieu. *H—Peter Smith.*

HALLER, WILLIAM 1885-1974. *The Rise of Puritanism* (1938). Even without Cromwell's New Model Army in the field, Puritanism became a force to be reckoned with. This standard study traces the movement from its humble beginnings. *P—U of Pa Pr.*

HAWTHORNE, NATHANIEL 1804-1864. *The Scarlet Letter* (1850). The classic American novel set in Puritan New England, highly dramatic and cannily symbolic, with masterly examination of the characters and their motives. *Over 30 eds.*

JOHNSON, SAMUEL 1709-1784. *The Lives of the English Poets* (1779-81). Cowley, Milton, and Dryden are among the English poets of the 17th century appraised with sturdy independence and common sense by the 18th century's great literary dictator. *Over 6 eds.*

LEWIS, WARREN H. b. 1895. *The Splendid Century* (1953). A wide-ranging view of the great and the lowly in French society during the reign of Louis XIV. *P—Morrow.*

MACAULAY, THOMAS B. 1800-1859. *The History of England* (1855). Scholarship joins dramatic imagination to present English history, with a Whig political bias. *H—Dutton 4 vols.*

————. *Essays.* Lively criticism of Bacon, Milton, Bunyan, and the drama. Much good sense, despite a dogmatic style that may at first tend to alienate the modern reader. *H—Dutton 2 vols.*

MILLON, HENRY A. b. 1927. *Baroque and Rococo Architecture* (1961). A concise and well-illustrated introduction to an era of impressive creations. *H & P—Braziller.*

ROBERTSON, ALEC b. 1892 and DENIS STEVENS b. 1922. *Renaissance and Baroque* (1964), Vol. 2 of *The Pelican History of Music.* A useful, not too technical introductory survey of the period. *P—Penguin.*

SCOTT, SIR WALTER 1771-1832. *Old Mortality* (1816), *The Fortunes of Nigel* (1822), and *Woodstock* (1826) are among Scott's novels set in the 17th century. Of these, *Old Mortality*, a tale of Presbyterian revenge, resolution, and fortitude under Royalist persecution, is the best. *H—Dutton.*

STARKEY, MARION L. b. 1901. *The Devil in Massachusetts* (1949). A vivid, horrifying, and strictly factual narrative of the delusion that seized on the good people of Salem and led to the infamous witch trials of 1692-1693. *H—Peter Smith; P—Doubleday.*

SYPHER. *Four Stages of Renaissance Style.* See "The Renaissance and Reformation," page 31.

TAWNEY, RICHARD H. 1880-1962. *Religion and the Rise of Capitalism* (1926). A now classic argument, relating the Protestant work ethic to the economic development of Western Europe. *H—Peter Smith.*

VAN LOON, HENDRIK W. 1882-1944. *Rembrandt, a Biography of the Master* (rev. ed. 1942). An imaginative presentation of a great man and artist in a great time. *H—Liveright.*

WILLEY, BASIL b. 1897. *The Seventeenth-Century Background* (1934). Primarily literary-philosophical and sometimes difficult, these essays examine English religion and poetry against contemporary climates of opinion. *H—Columbia U Pr; P—Doubleday.*

6. The 18th Century

Joseph A. Byrnes

The philosophers and scientists of the Renaissance and 17th century bequeathed to their successors of the 18th century a more or less coherent intellectual system for viewing the world. Fundamentally rational, the 18th century perhaps found its characteristic expression in the Newtonian laws that were to dominate physics for nearly 200 years. The spirit of experiment flourished and the tools of science were further refined. Things we take for granted—the exact composition of air and water, the relation of lightning to electricity, Lavoisier's chemical equations, Hutton's view that the earth has a geologic history, the Linnean classification system in biology, the refutation of the accepted view that heat was a substance—all were discovered or established and, once established, facilitated subsequent developments, both scientific and technological. Interest in practical engineering was spreading, as manifested by the illustrations of machines and industrial processes in the French *Encyclopedia*. Later in the century, the creation of canal systems and the inventions of the steam engine, textile machinery, and hard-paved roads started Europe on the way to what we know as the Industrial Revolution, the rapid growth of which left a poet like Blake lamenting "Among these dark Satanic mills."

In philosophy, thinkers from Berkeley through Hume to Condorcet, whatever their premises, based their systems on reason, and Kant's insistence on the innate logicality of the mind is still the principle behind our computers and linguistic science. Not only among philosophers was reason honored; satirists and critics like Swift and Voltaire complained in its name, and rational religion (Deism) even seemed to threaten orthodox faith. Politically, the concept of the "rights of man" had been foreshadowed by the two English revolutions in the 17th century and by Locke's argument that people create government. However, it remained for Rousseau and Paine, in France and America respectively, to promote greater and more comprehensive revolutions. In economics, Adam Smith restored to the mainstream of European thought the Platonic doctrines of trade and the division of labor. A sobering warning on the relation of population increase to food supply was issued by Malthus long before technological and medical advances generated modern population pressures.

In spite of setbacks like the financial collapse of the South Sea Bubble of 1720, European expansion continued. England and France were drawn by their conflicting economic interests onto battlefields as far-flung as Canada and India, where English victories led to the consolidation of the British Empire—that greatest of the 19th-century politico-economic powers, the collapse of which in our own time has left a vacuum still being painfully filled.

A reasonable and pragmatic age—one that could produce and admire Benjamin Franklin—did not approve of extremes of individualism or emotion, however it might at times allow itself to behave. There were dissidents, of course, the most prominent being Rousseau, whose influence helped spark not only the French Revolution but also the 19th century Romantic movement and such earlier, tentative manifestations as the cultivation of "sensibility" in England and France, and the "storm and stress" experienced by German youth in the 1770s.

The new literary form, born of the century, was the novel, specializing in the realistic portrayal of individual men and women against recognizable backgrounds. Written mostly by and for the middle class, the novel developed a great variety of styles: realism (serious and comic, respectively) in Defoe and Fielding, psychological penetration and "sentiment" in Richardson, the philosophical tale in Voltaire, free-wheeling extravagance in Sterne, even the Gothic thriller in Walpole. The drama of the age is less striking than its fiction. An 18th-century tragedy could be acted today only as a curiosity; among the comedies, however—by Goldoni in Italy, Sheridan and Goldsmith in England, Marivaux and Beaumarchais in France—there are classic examples: witty, polished, brilliantly theatrical, and perceptively satiric.

Form dominated poetry and poetic diction when the century began. In England, the heroic couplet, as perfected by Pope, was unsurpassed for pithy epigram and witty satire. Later, when literary rebels like Burns and Blake wanted to express their often unconventional feelings, they sought less confined lyric forms. Ending the century, the Romantic Wordsworth declared for simplicity, urging poets to write in "a selection of language really used by men." Among the other arts, paintings, though much cultivated, fell short of earlier achievements. Perhaps the noblest and most enduring art of the century was its music: opera developed steadily; the form for the symphony was created. Bach, Handel, Haydn, and Mozart composed music that blends elegance, precision, and order with a touch of passion under firm control.

Old certainties, like the idea of an unchanging social and political order, crumbled during these years. By 1800, after two major revolutions, that concept was no longer tenable; even faith in reason had been shaken. Serious questions had arisen: how to cope with the irrational, with industrialization, with humanity's striving for equality—for all of which the 18th century produced no definitive answers. It is not too much to say that we are still seeking them.

18th-Century Literature

ADDISON, JOSEPH 1672-1719 and SIR RICHARD STEELE 1672-1729. *The Spectator* (1711-12). Polished and witty commentary on the fashions, foibles, and fops of Queen Anne's London. *Over 6 eds.*

The Age of Enlightenment (1956). Ed. by Isaiah Berlin. Generous selections from the major philosophers of the 18th century with helpful commentary by the editor. *H—Bks for Libs; P—NAL.*

BEAUMARCHAIS, PIERRE CARON DE 1732-1799. *The Barber of Seville* (1775) and *The Marriage of Figaro* (acted 1784). Comedies satirizing class privilege, best known now in the opera versions by Rossini and Mozart. *P—AHM Pub, Penguin.*

BERKELEY, GEORGE 1685-1753. *A Treatise Concerning the Principles of Human Knowledge* (1710). Platonic idealism reworked in the light of Newtonian science. *H—British Bk Ctr; P—Bobbs, Open Court.* See also "Philosophy," page 181.

BLAKE, WILLIAM 1757-1827. *Poems.* Blake as both artist and poet was simple and original, profound, lyrical, and challengingly symbolic in his best work. *Over 10 eds.*

BOSWELL, JAMES 1740-1795. *The Life of Samuel Johnson* (1791). The sturdy common sense and literary judgments of an impressive mind, recorded by a shrewd, devoted friend in one of the greatest biographies ever written. *Over 6 eds., some abr.*

BURKE, EDMUND 1729-1797. *Reflections on the Revolution in France* (1790). A conservative defense of gradual change, opposed to the violence Burke predicted. *Over 6 eds.*

BURNS, ROBERT 1759-1796. *Poems.* Songs and meditations, mostly in Scottish dialect, that speak for the common folk and have proved enduringly popular. *Over 10 eds.*

CASANOVA DE SEINGALT, GIACOMO 1725-1798. *Memoirs* (1826-38). Most of his adventures were amorous, some doubtless exaggerated; the filler sketches very ably etch the times. *H—HarBraceJ; P—Macmillan.*

CHESTERFIELD, LORD 1694-1773. *Letters to His Son* (1774). Urbane advice on manners and morals for a worldly and aristocratic society. *H—Dutton, R. West.*

Constitution of the United States and *Declaration of Independence.* Basic American documents every citizen should know. Found in almost every history book of the United States and in most encyclopedias and almanacs. Bound together: *H—McKay; P—AHM Pub.*

CRÈVECOEUR, ST. JOHN DE 1735-1813. *Letters from an American Farmer* (1782). These letters to an imaginary friend in Europe reflect both an idealistic and a realistic view of life in young America. *H—Dutton, Peter Smith; P—Dutton.*

DEFOE, DANIEL 1660-1731. *Robinson Crusoe* (1719). The original and immortal desert island story. *Over 20 eds.*

———. *Moll Flanders* (1722). A realistic novel about one woman's life through many marriages and many crimes. *Over 6 eds.*

DIDEROT, DENIS 1713-1784. *The Encyclopedia* (1751-1772). The scholarship and judgments of the French *philosophes*. Selections: *H & P—Bobbs.*

The Enlightenment: A Comprehensive Anthology (1973). Ed. by Peter Gay. A generous collection of contemporary (and earlier) writings illustrating the development and complexity of this intellectual move-ment, with helpful editorial commentary and suggested further read-ings. *H & P—S&S.*

Federalist Papers (1787-88). Essays—excellent examples of political theory—by James Madison, Alexander Hamilton, and others, that in-fluenced the ratification of the Constitution. *Over 6 eds.*

FIELDING, HENRY 1707-1754. *Joseph Andrews* (1742). Adventures of a chaste footman and a sturdy parson, told in mockery of 18th-century sentimentalism. *Over 10 eds.*

———. *Tom Jones* (1749). The long, lusty, zestful, skillfully plotted story of an engaging hero from childhood to marriage, filled with lively characters and adventures. *Over 6 eds.*

FRANKLIN, BENJAMIN 1706-1790. *Autobiography* (1791, 1818, 1868). A great American, prototype of the pragmatic man, explains his rise to fame and fortune in aphoristic prose. *Over 10 eds.*

GAY, JOHN 1685-1732. *The Beggar's Opera* (1728). Rollicking burlesque of politics and society: thieves, highwaymen, harlots sing false senti-ments to old ballad tunes. The basis of Brecht and Weill's *Threepenny Opera. Over 6 eds.*

GIBBON. *The Decline and Fall of the Roman Empire.* See "Rome," page 14.

GOETHE, JOHANN WOLFGANG VON 1749-1832. *The Sorrows of Young Werther* (1774). An early, very "romantic" novel in which the hero kills himself for unrequited love. *H—Ungar; P—HR&W, Ungar.*

———. *Faust* (1808-32). Goethe worked for 60 years on this monumental two-part drama on the meaning of life. The Jarrell translation of Part I is recommended: *P—FS&G. Many other trans. and eds.*

GOLDONI, CARLO 1707-1793. *Comedies.* Actable and natural comedies by one of the few good dramatists of the century. *P—Theatre Arts.*

GOLDSMITH, OLIVER 1728-1774. *The Vicar of Wakefield* (1766). A novel relating the amusing tribulations of a gentle and gullible clergy-man and his family. *Over 6 eds.*

———. *She Stoops to Conquer* (1773). A comic masterpiece and one of the most actable of all plays. *Over 6 eds.*

HUME. *Enquiry Concerning Human Understanding.* See "Philoso-phy," page 182.

JEFFERSON, THOMAS 1743-1826. *Autobiographical and Political Writings.* A multitalented founding father writes clearly and elo-quently on many subjects still very much of concern to Americans. *Over 6 eds.*

JOHNSON, SAMUEL 1709-1784. *Selected Writings* (1965). Ed. by R. T. Davies. A broadly representative selection of the work of the literary dictator of his age. *H—Northwestern U Pr.*

KANT. See "Philosophy," page 182.

LACLOS, P. A. F. CHODERLOS DE 1741-1803. *Les Liaisons Dangereuses* (1782). A novel in letters describing the behavior and motives of heartless but intelligent debauchees among the French aristocracy. *P—NAL, Penguin.*

MALTHUS, THOMAS ROBERT 1766-1834. *Essay on the Principles of Population* (1798). Classic study of the relationship between population growth and means of subsistence. *Over 6 eds.*

MONTESQUIEU, CHARLES DE 1689-1755. *The Spirit of the Laws* (1748). Sometimes called the greatest French work of the century, it treats laws as the products of men and as codes that relate differently to different societies. *P—Hafner.*

PAINE, THOMAS 1737-1809. *The Rights of Man* (1791). Paine's impassioned answer to Burke's criticism of the French Revolution. *H—Dutton; P—Citadel Pr, Dutton, Penguin.*

_____. *The Age of Reason*. (1794-5). A spirited defense of Deism, the religion of 18th-century intellectuals. *P—Bobbs, Citadel Pr.*

POPE, ALEXANDER 1688-1744. *Poems*. Devastating social satire, political ridicule, philosophic optimism, some restrained emotion—all wrought into neat epigrammatic heroic couplets. *Over 20 eds.*

PRÉVOST, ANTOINE 1697-1763. *Manon Lescaut* (1731). The story of a young man fascinated and ultimately ruined by a courtesan—the source of operas by Puccini and Massenet. *P—French & Eur.*

RICHARDSON, SAMUEL 1689-1761. *Pamela* (1740). In letters that reveal the "sentiments" of the age, a maidservant tells how she resisted her young master until he offered marriage. *H—Dutton, Garland Pub; P—Dutton, HM, Norton.*

ROUSSEAU, JEAN JACQUES 1712-1778. *Émile* (1762). A didactic novel, important for developing the theory of progressive education (though not for women). *H & P—Dutton.*

_____. *The Social Contract* (1762). A document that helped bring about the French Revolution. *H—Dutton; P—Dutton, Hafner, Penguin, WSP.*

_____. *Confessions* (1781-88). Uninhibited self-revelations by a romantic egoist. *H—Dutton; P—Penguin.*

SHERIDAN, RICHARD BRINSLEY 1751-1816. *The Rivals* (1775) and *The School for Scandal* (1777). Two famous, still often played comedies, noted for wit and good humor, intricate plots, and memorable caricatures (e.g., Mrs. Malaprop). *Over 6 eds.*

SMITH, ADAM 1723-1790. *The Wealth of Nations* (1776). The classic explanation of the economic advantages of free trade and of specialization of labor. *Over 6 eds.*

The Spirit of 'Seventy-Six (Bicentennial ed., 1975). Ed. by Henry Steele Commager and Richard B. Morris. A wealth of contemporary material on the American Revolution: fascinating descriptions and opinions set down in their own words by those who made, supported, opposed, fought, won, and lost the war. *H—Har-Row.*

STERNE, LAURENCE 1713-1768. ***Tristram Shandy*** (1760-67). Comic domestic episodes in an almost bewildering assortment of styles—whimsical, digressive, extravagant. *Over 6 eds.*

SWIFT, JONATHAN 1667-1745. ***Gulliver's Travels*** (1726). Imaginary journeys that amuse children but are really first-rate, highly inventive, and unrelenting attacks on irrationality and inhumanity. *Over 20 eds. Recommended: P—HM, HR&W, NAL, Norton, Penguin.*

VOLTAIRE (FRANÇOIS MARIE AROUET) 1694-1778. ***Candide*** (1759). A short, funny, well-spiced adventure story and a masterly satire on optimism, war, religion, government, romantic love, wealth, and a host of other things by one of the greatest minds and the most versatile literary figure of the century. *Over 10 eds.*

WALPOLE, HORACE 1717-1797. ***Letters***. The activities of the civilized 18th century come to life in these charming letters to and about his friends. Selections: *H—Dutton, Yale U Pr; P—Yale U Pr.*

_____. ***The Castle of Otranto*** (1764). The first famous Gothic novel of horror and the supernatural. *P—Dover, HR&W, Macmillan, Oxford U Pr.*

Books about the 18th Century

BECKER, CARL LOTUS 1873-1945. ***The Heavenly City of the Eighteenth-Century Philosophers*** (1932). A lively, scholarly, provocative analysis of 18th-century thought. *H & P—Yale U Pr.*

BRINTON, CRANE 1898-1968 (ed.). ***The Portable Age of Reason Reader*** (1956). A good introduction by the editor, with many short excerpts on many subjects from thought to private morals. *P—Viking Pr.*

BUTTERFIELD, HERBERT b. 1900. ***The Origins of Modern Science*** (rev. ed. 1965). A classic volume on the history of science, particularly good on 18th-century developments and their effects. *P—Free Pr.*

CARLYLE, THOMAS 1795-1881. ***The French Revolution*** (1837). A long and highly dramatic account, more bedazzled with Napoleon than the facts warrant. *H—Dutton.*

CASSIRER, ERNST 1874-1945. ***The Philosophy of the Enlightenment*** (English trans. 1951). A thoughtful, balanced, illuminating corrective to Becker's *Heavenly City. H & P—Princeton U Pr.*

COBBAN, ALFRED 1901-1968. ***A History of Modern France*** (1965). Regarded as the best short history of the period. *H—Braziller; P—Penguin.*

CUNLIFFE, MARCUS b. 1922. ***George Washington*** (1958). A successful effort to re-create Washington's life as it really was rather than as legend and myth have recorded it. *H—Little; P—NAL.*

DICKENS, CHARLES 1812-1870. ***A Tale of Two Cities*** (1859). A tale of self-sacrifice during the French Revolution, famous for Sydney Carton and Madame Defarge. *Over 15 eds.*

DURANT, WILL b. 1885 and ARIEL DURANT b. 1898. *The Age of Voltaire* (1965) and *Rousseau and Romanticism* (1967). Entertainingly written, well-illustrated presentation of the historical, social, and cultural developments of the century. *H—S&S.*

FLEXNER, JAMES T. b. 1908. *Washington: the Indispensable Man* (1974). A judicious study of the father of his country, balancing virtues and faults, and stressing the cohesive effect of his presence. (For a fuller treatment, see the same author's four-volume biography.) *H & P—Little.*

GAY, PETER b. 1923. *The Enlightenment: An Interpretation* (2 vols., 1966, 1969). This well-received study (1967 National Book Award) traces the genesis, development, and effects of the movement throughout the century, ending with its involvement in the American Revolution. *H—Knopf.*

HAUSER, ARNOLD b. 1892. *The Social History of Art* (1951). Volumes II and III put the art of the period in its social setting. *P—Random.*

LACY, DAN M. b. 1914. *The Meaning of the American Revolution* (1966). An exploration of our national origins and of the significance of independence. *P—NAL.*

LEFEBVRE, GEORGES 1874-1959. *The Coming of the French Revolution* (1939). A balanced, authoritative history. *H & P—Princeton U Pr.*

MILLER, PERRY 1905-1963. *The New England Mind* (1953). A major study by the most distinguished historian of American thought. *H—Harvard U Pr; P—Beacon Pr.*

MORGAN, EDMUND S. b. 1916. *The Birth of the Republic, 1763–89* (1956). Perhaps the best short treatment of an often-handled subject. *H & P—U of Chicago Pr.*

NOCK, ALBERT J. 1872-1945. *Jefferson* (1926). A short, penetrating, and laudatory biography written out of conviction and sympathy. *H & P—Hill & Wang.*

TOCQUEVILLE, ALEXIS DE 1805-1859. *The Old Regime and the French Revolution* (1855). Shrewd observations on the subject by a wise Frenchman. *H—Peter Smith; P—Doubleday.*

7. The Middle East

J. Sherwood Weber

The vast and various Middle East—which cradled and nurtured civilization from the earliest recorded times (about 4000 B.C.) down to roughly A.D. 800—has undergone greater social, political, and economic changes during the last four decades than in the preceding thousand years. Heirs both to an illustrious remote past and a depressed modern history, shackled for centuries by the chains of their own ages-old traditions as well as by the many-faceted dominance of a succession of imperialist powers, the people of the Middle East—Arabs, Jews, Iranians, Turks—are today attempting to construct futures that will enable expression of national as well as individual aspirations.

Occupying a strategic landmass the size of the continental United States, the numerous countries of the Middle East evidence a new enthusiasm in politics and international affairs. In open conflict concerning their respective destinies, these people cry out to be understood. Understanding will not come easily. Both the problems and promise of the countries of the Middle East stagger the Western observer. Deeply rooted in a complex cultural continuum, explicable in part by anthropology, religion, philosophy, politics, and economics, the various cultures stretch so far back in time that they defy summary or synthesis.

Despite some notable exceptions, the cultures and literatures of the ancient, the modern, and even the contemporary Middle East are available to us in English mainly in secondary sources—that is, in histories. Until modern times, considerable bodies of literature produced in this area of the world have been religious, devotional, and sacred, of little appeal to Western readers; and the secular literatures, steeped in the diverse cultures and social traditions from which they grew, do not parallel genres familiar in the West and do not translate well. Hence, we have come to learn about the Middle East, often the modern and certainly the ancient, largely through books about it written by Western scholars and journalists rather than through its own voluminous creations. This situation is currently changing.

The book list that follows is shaped to foster an understanding of both the past and present of this complex and critical world region. No half-dozen books will provide a comprehensive view. Partial views are at hand. Though racially biased, *Caravan*, by an anthropologist, Carleton Coon, is an encompassing and useful account of peoples and their environments in the Middle East. H. A. R. Gibb's short, superb *Mohammedanism* places Islam in focus and makes clear the Prophet's intention that Islam be a religion and a total way of life. An excellent recent United Nations-sponsored anthology, *Jewish Society through the Ages*, contains solid and readable articles that illuminate the history of the Jews in the Middle East (and elsewhere) from oldest times to the present. And, happily, the creative writers of the Middle Eastern countries, who can help us understand the spirit, cultures, and concerns of their lands, are becoming increasingly available to Western readers through good translations.

AGNON, S. Y. (SHMUEL YOSEF CZACZKES) 1888-1970. *The Bridal Canopy* (1931). The 1966 Nobel Prize winner writes a pious picaresque tale of a Hasidic simpleton-saint and a Sancho Panza wagon-driver seeking a dowry for a marriageable daughter. *H—Schocken.*

———. *A Guest for the Night* (1937). An emigrant to Jerusalem returns for a visit to his native town after World War I and finds destruction and demoralization, the old faith gone, the growing generation apathetic. *H—Schocken.*

ALTER, ROBERT b. 1935 (ed.). *Modern Hebrew Literature* (1975). Contains representative short stories by leading contemporary Hebrew writers. *H & P—Behrman.*

ANTONIUS, GEORGE b. 1891. *The Arab Awakening* (2nd ed. 1965). A fundamental introduction to the Arab national movement in the early 20th century. *H—Gordon Pr; P—Putnam.*

Arabian Nights (8th to 15th cent.). Fascinating stories of genii and magicians, of golden palaces and lush gardens, of wonderful voyages and adventures, of intrigue and enchantment. The best translation is by Burton: *H—Modern Lib.*

BEN-SASSON, H. H. b. 1914 and S. ETTINGER (eds.). *Jewish Society Through the Ages* (1972). Contains many essays, most of high quality, on a wide range of important aspects of Jewish life from ancient to modern times. *H & P—Schocken.*

Bible. Monumental in the history of religion, literature, and the Middle East. See "Religion," page 189.

BLOCKER, JOEL (ed.). *Israeli Stories* (1975). A very good collection of nine stories by leading Israeli writers, including Agnon, Amichai, and Hazaz. *H & P—Schocken.*

BURROWS, MILLAR b. 1889. *The Dead Sea Scrolls* (1955). Scholarly, temperate account of the discovery and contents of the scrolls that have profoundly affected Biblical studies. *H—Viking Pr.*

COON, CARLETON b. 1904. *Caravan* (rev. ed. 1958). Despite its racist bias, a useful anthropological introduction to the entire Middle East written for readers and students. *H—HR&W.*

DIEHL, CHARLES 1859-1944. *Byzantium: Greatness and Decline* (1957). The classic study by the great French Byzantinist; difficult but rewarding. *P—Rutgers U Pr.*

FISHER, SYDNEY b. 1906. *The Middle East* (rev. ed. 1968). Probably the best introductory survey of Islam, the Ottoman Empire, and the modern (but not contemporary) Middle East. *H—Knopf.*

GIBB, H. A. R. 1895-1971. *Mohammedanism* (2nd ed. 1953). Superb and succinct account of Islamic religion and culture. *P—Oxford U Pr.*

———. *Arabic Literature* (2nd ed. 1974). A sound introduction to the subject, with a bibliography of Arabic literature in translation. *H & P— Oxford U Pr.*

GOITEIN, S. D. b. 1900 (ed.). *Jews and Arabs* (1975). A scholarly presentation of the social and intellectual relations of Jews and Arabs through the ages, useful for lending perspective to contemporary views of Jews and Arabs. *H & P—Schocken.*

HARARI, MAURICE b. 1923. *Government and Politics of the Middle East* (1962). A country-by-country analysis, linking the current political systems to their historical origins. Though not up to date, the most nonpartisan survey available. *o.p.*

HITTI, PHILIP KHURI b. 1886. *History of the Arabs from the Earliest Times to the Present* (10th ed. 1970). The standard text for the history of the Arab peoples down to the 16th century, but superficial on the last four centuries. *H & P—St Martin.*

———. *Capital Cities of Arab Islam* (1973). A leading Arabist writes charmingly about Mecca, Medina, Damascus, Baghdad, Cairo, and Cordova. *H—U of Minn Pr.*

JACOBSEN, T. b. 1904 with HENRI FRANKFORT b. 1897 and JOHN WILSON. *The Intellectual Adventure of Ancient Man* (1946). An indispensable book summarizing comprehensively the intellectual first principles of ancient Near Eastern thought; particularly good on Egypt and Babylonia. *H—U of Chicago Pr.*

KHADDURI, MAJID b. 1909. *Independent Iraq, 1932–1958* (2nd ed. 1960). The most thorough, objective, and complete single volume on the emergence of Iraq as an independent Arab nation. *o.p.*

KHOURI, MOUNAH A. b. 1918 and HAMID ALGAR. *An Anthology of Modern Arabic Poetry* (1974). Contains an excellent introduction, helpful notes, and fresh translations of leading modern Arabic poets. *H & P—U of Cal Pr.*

Koran. The sacred scriptures of Islam by the Prophet Muhammad (c. 570-632). The literal but highly readable translation by Mohammed Marmaduke Pickthall is recommended. *P—NAL.*

KRAMER, SAMUEL NOAH b. 1897 (ed.). *Mythologies of the Ancient World* (1961). Using new translations, ten scholars discuss the myths of individual ancient Middle East cultures in essays the general reader can comprehend and enjoy. *P—Doubleday.*

LAWRENCE, THOMAS EDWARD 1888-1935. *Seven Pillars of Wisdom* (1935). Lawrence of Arabia describes in this absorbing account his military-political activities among the Arabs in World War I. *P—Penguin*.

LEWIS, BERNARD b. 1916. *The Arabs in History* (1950). Concise, readable interpretation of the rise of the Arabs and of the broad economic movements influencing the history of the Middle East. *P—Har-Row*.

———. *The Emergence of Modern Turkey* (2nd ed. 1968). A comprehensive, well-written, scholarly history of 20th-century Turkey. *P—Oxford U Pr*.

LITTLE, TOM b. 1911. *Modern Egypt* (1967). A well-informed, well-written account of the emergence of modern Egypt, strong on politics but superficial on economics and ideology. *H—Praeger*.

MACK, JOHN E. b. 1929. *A Prince of Our Disorder* (1976). This Pulitzer Prize biography of T. E. Lawrence provides an excellent introduction to the Arab world of the 20th century. *H—Little*.

MANZALAOUI, MAHMOUD b. 1924 (ed.). *Arabic Writing Today* (1970). Contains translations of 30 short stories written by contemporary Arabs. *H—U of Cal Pr*.

MEIR, GOLDA b. 1898. *My Life* (1975). An outstanding stateswoman and former prime minister of Israel discusses her integral involvement with the Israeli struggle for independence and well-being. *H—Putnam; P—Dell*.

MOOREHEAD, ALAN b. 1910. *Gallipoli* (1956). The story of the famous campaign that might have changed the course of World War I. *H—Har-Row*.

MOSCATI, SABATINO. *The Face of the Ancient Orient* (1962). Readable summary of the more important aspects of ancient Middle East history and cultures. *P—Doubleday*.

MULLER, HERBERT J. b. 1905. *Loom of History* (1958). Stimulating studies of old civilizations in Asia Minor viewed from a humanistic position with "reverence and irony." *H—Har-Row; P—Oxford U Pr*.

NAAMANI, ISRAEL T. b. 1913. *Israel* (1972). A compressed, colorful, readable account of the past and present of Israel; particularly good on evaluation of contemporary trends and conflicts. *H—Praeger*.

NASSER, GAMAL ABDEL 1918-1970. *The Philosophy of the Revolution* (1959). A fundamental statement by the ideological leader of Arab nationalism in the 1960s. *o.p.*

OMAR KHAYYÁM d. 1123? *The Rubáiyát*. Pleasant cynicism in deft quatrains filled with vivid and traditional Oriental images and symbols. The very free but splendid poetic translation by Edward Fitzgerald is available in many editions.

OSTROGORSKY, GEORGE b. 1902. *History of the Byzantine State* (rev. ed. 1969). An uncommonly clear one-volume history. *H—Rutgers U Pr*.

PARKES, JAMES b. 1896. *Whose Land?* (rev. ed. 1970). A sound, eminently readable short history of Palestine; understanding of the Arab point of view despite a pro-Zionist bias. *P—Penguin*.

PATAI, RAPHAEL b. 1910. *The Kingdom of Jordan* (1958). The history of a political and economic anomaly. *H—Princeton U Pr.*

PRITCHARD, JAMES B. b. 1909 (ed.). *The Ancient Near East* (1973). An anthology of ancient Near East writing, newly translated by schol ars and representing the principal genres; includes the Gilgamesh epic. *P—Princeton U Pr.*

ST. JOHN, ROBERT b. 1902. *Ben-Gurion* (1959). A biography of Israel's first prime minister by a journalist who knows the Middle East. *H— Doubleday.*

SAVORY, R. M. b. 1925 (ed.). *Introduction to Islamic Civilisation* (1976). Contains 18 high-quality and lucid essays on various aspects of Islam: history, theology, law, literature, art, science, etc. *H & P— Cambridge U Pr.*

SAYEGH, FAYEZ ABDULLAH b. 1922. *Arab Unity* (1958). A nationalist Arab's commentary on the cultural and political aspects of Arab unity. *H—Devin.*

SYKES, PERCY MOLESWORTH 1867-1945. *A History of Persia* (3rd ed. 1930). Distinguished history covering from 3000 B.C. to the 20th century. *o.p.*

WATT, W. MONTGOMERY b. 1909. *Muhammad* (1974). Based on wide research, this volume, an abridgment of the author's *Muhammad at Mecca* and *Muhammad at Medina*, discusses the religious, political, social, and military activities of the Prophet. *P—Oxford U Pr.*

WILSON, EDMUND 1895-1972. *The Dead Sea Scrolls, 1947–1969* (1969). A thorough revision of the absorbing account of the discovery of the ancient scrolls, considering the results and implications of the scholarly work done since the discovery. *H—Oxford U Pr.*

8. East and South Asia

Oscar Shaftel

For over a century the two major determinants of change in Asian cultures have been the impact of the West and one of the effects of that impact, increasing literacy. The three leading nations, China, Japan, and India, as well as the lesser nations of Southeast Asia responded in varying ways. China, old and proud, tried to reject the invading and exploiting barbarians. India, infiltrated and colonized, tried to assimilate the language, legal system, and professed ideals of the British but remains divided through class structures and language groupings. Japan, perhaps too successful in adapting Western techniques in war and industry, today finds itself beset with social tensions that make for vigorous cultural achievement. The smaller nations, subjected to war and direct or indirect colonization, have been retarded in developing culturally beyond traditional folk modes.

The dominant Chinese classical form, beginning with the *Book of Odes* collected in Confucian times, was poetry, the pastime and solace of Confucian gentlemen. Folk and hero tales and ghost stories, at first the domain of the popular storyteller, were borrowed and published shamefacedly by literati down on their luck. And once the popular drama took hold in the 13th century, the old stories (especially the two great hero books, *The Three Kingdoms* and *The Water Margin*) found new expression, as they did yet again when the complex form called Peking opera developed its themes and formal traditions. Four great fictional classics, weighted with satire and social commentary, are *Journey to the West* (translated in part as *Monkey*), *Dream of the Red Chamber*, *Golden Lotus*, and *The Scholars*.

A sequel to the overthrow of the repressive Ch'ing dynasty in 1911 was the literary revolt that broke out in 1917, which condemned allusive, stilted, scholarly prose and called for colloquial language in essays and fiction. The literary rebels, led by Hu Shih

(1891-1962), turned to Western scientific and democratic ideas in order to free China from Western exploiters. Lu Hsun (1881-1936), critic and novelist, was a bridge between the imitative 1920s and the revolutionary 1930s. His *Madman's Diary* and *Ah Q*, almost surrealistic in depicting the horrors of urban existence, and his satires on Confucian ideals made him the laureate of the rising Communist movement after the split with the Kuomintang in 1927.

After victory and the founding of the People's Republic of China in 1949, universal literacy was established as a goal. Exhortation became the formal requirement of literature, stressing the released energies of workers and peasants, and especially of women, "who hold up half the sky." The Great Proletarian Cultural Revolution of 1966-1971 aimed to safeguard the masses from a recrudescence of "mandarinism" among ruling officials by combating elitism under the slogan "serve the people," but paradoxically it narrowed the scope of artistic forms such as fiction, film, ballet, and opera. The political upheaval after the death of Mao Tse-tung promised another period of "100 flowers blooming" and a less dogmatic control of the arts.

Japan emerged into history in the shadow of China. Despite its early borrowing of Chinese script (ill-adapted to polysyllabic Japanese) and literary, architectural, religious, and political forms, Japan soon fell into its own ways. Early legends, the source of Shinto belief, were written down in the *Kojiki* (712) and the *Nihon Shoki* (*Chronicles of Japan*, 720); and the fine collection of poetry, mostly by courtiers, the *Manyoshu*, was completed in 765. Japan responded creatively to Buddhism in sculpture, magnificent wooden temple complexes, and doctrinal innovations, often syncretized with native Shinto (Way of the Gods). Kana, a syllabary suited to Japanese sounds, came into use in the 9th century and encouraged literary practice, especially among court women. The inbred aristocratic Heian court gave the world the first great novel, the *Genji Monagatari*, by Lady Murasaki. Sei Shonagon, another attendant of the empress, wrote a fascinating gossip diary, the *Pillow Book*. Both works were typical of the Heian introspective esthetic sensibility, expressing melancholy awareness of evanescent joys.

The effete court was shoved aside in the power struggle between the Taira and Minamoto clans during the latter part of the 12th century, leading to the imposition of the shogun as the real power. The *Heike Monagatari* are romantic, chivalric tales of the brutal conflict. The events found new expression in the developing drama, both courtly and popular. The Noh play, a highly stylized, rarefied poetic form restricted to upper-rank audiences, expressed Zen Buddhist themes. Bunraku (with puppet characters) and Kabuki plays presented both traditional and topical incidents. Kabuki actors were favorite subjects, along with courtesans of the approved pleasure quarters, of the block-print artists. The finest poetic sensibility of the era was Basho (1644-1694), the supreme master of the haiku in seventeen syllables, a condensation of the older classical and more complex tanka.

Virtually cut off from the world after 1639 by the Tokugawa shoguns, Japanese culture was shaken after the opening to the West and the 1868 Meiji "restoration." Western technology, dress, food, and then literature and social ideas were emulated, but ambivalence grew as industrial and military success threatened old ways. Revised Shinto doctrine became ultranationalistic and justified Nipponese "elder-brother" imposition on the Western Pacific region during World War II.

Defeated in war and freed from military expenditure, Japan emerged as a leader in industry and in literary achievement with a highly literate populace. Such works as Akutagawa's *Rashomon*, Abe's *Woman in the Dunes*, and Takayama's *Harp of Burma* became significant films. Mishima was a paradoxical figure who combined modern techniques with a nostalgia for old military ideals. Kawabata, a 1970 Nobel laureate, expressed anew the indirect, intangible melancholy of the Heian age.

Indian expression is pervaded by religious vocabulary. The Vedic hymns, proclaimed as the basis of modern Hindu belief, were originally folk poetic expressions, prayers, and magic spells of a nomadic people who invaded the subcontinent from the northwest after 2000 B.C. Then the four collections of hymns became ritual formulae wielded by a specialized priesthood, the Brahmin caste. An offshoot of the Vedic tradition, the Upanishads, after 800 B.C., directly contravened the priesthood by exalting individual religious experience. What is called Hinduism developed out of the merging of cultures—the various native cultures and the Aryan invaders. Hindu religious and social doctrine was expressed in the sprawling *Mahabharata*, an oft-interrupted and embellished epic that tells of the struggle of the five sons of Pandu against their cousins, the Kauravas, for a kingdom. It combines exemplary tales, myths retold, and religious speculaton. The central document of Hinduism, the *Bhagavad-Gita* (Song of the Lord), seems to be a late insertion in the epic; in it a local low-caste folk deity, Krishna, is elevated to divine supremacy. Comfortingly, it legitimizes various ways to liberation from rebirth, especially *bhakti yoga*, the way of devotion, which opens the path even to outcastes and women.

The other great Indian epic, the more unified *Ramayana*, presents the just King Rama and the faithful wife Sita as paradigms of social virtue. In a deeper folk tradition, the great god Shiva presents greater psychic complexity in conflicting roles as ascetic, mystic, destroyer, and consort of various embodiments of the mother diety such as Durga and Kali. The various streams of myth reappear in the Puranas, religious wonder tales, and in the courtly refinements of Kalidasa, the foremost Sanskrit playwright, and Bhartrihari, an elegant erotic poetic. A supreme celebration of Krishna as god and lover is the *Gita Govinda* of Jayadeva, about

A.D. 1200. The non-Sanskritic languages of southern India had rich expression in their own legends and in their versions of the Aryan epics.

First the Muslim invasions, culminating in Mughal power in the 17th century, and then the British influence profoundly affected Indian life. English is still the most widely accepted language, and education and law still follow British forms. Today, Indian themes are expressed in Western forms—short stories and novels—such as Premchand's stories and his best-known novel, *Gift of a Cow*. Many Indian works, such as those of Tagore, are translated into English, and translation from one Indian language to others is encouraged by the government. Many writers use English, e.g., R. K. Narayan, Mulk Raj Anand, and Khushwant Singh.

General

ANDERSON, G. L. b. 1920 (ed.). *Masterpieces of the Orient* (rev. ed. 1977). Contains many examples from the standard classical literatures as well as modern material, including a revolutionary Chinese opera. *P—Norton.*

BURTT, EDWIN A. b. 1892. *The Teachings of the Compassionate Buddha* (1955). A sound introductory essay and a useful selection of scriptures and other sources of Theravada, Mahayana, Zen, and other doctrines. *P—NAL.*

CONZE, EDWARD b. 1904. *Buddhism: Its Essence and Development* (1951). An imaginative interpretation by a leading scholar and translator. *H—Peter Smith; P—Har-Row.*

DE BARY, WILLIAM T. b. 1919 (ed.). *Introduction to Oriental Civilizations: Sources of Indian Tradition* (1958), *Sources of Japanese Tradition* (1958), and *Sources of Chinese Tradition* (1960). An indispensable collection. Philosophical, religious, and historical materials are presented in depth; literary materials are less emphasized. *H—Columbia U Pr 3 vols; P—Columbia U Pr 6 vols.*

FAIRBANK, JOHN K. b. 1907, EDWIN O. REISCHAUER b. 1910, and ALBERT M. CRAIG b. 1927. *East Asia: Tradition and Transformation* (1973). A first-rate history, representing a reworking and condensation of several earlier books by the same authors; contains much necessary information, good illustrations, and useful maps. *H—HM.*

HISAMATSU, SHIN'ICHI. *Zen and the Fine Arts* (1971). Although it attempts to analyze the unanalyzable, this combination of historical, esthetic, and illustrative material in architecture, calligraphy, painting, tea, pottery, utensils, gardens, Noh, etc., saturates one in the essence of Zen. *H—Kodansha.*

LEE, SHERMAN E. b. 1918. *A History of Far Eastern Art* (rev. ed. 1974). A leading curator keeps abreast of a rapidly developing field. Well illustrated. *H—Abrams, P—H.*

YOHANNAN, JOHN D. b. 1911. *A Treasury of Asian Literature* (1959). A very useful yet inexpensive selection, including Gita Govinda, Tao Te Chingy, and an early Genji chapter. *P—NAL.*

China

BIRCH, CYRIL b. 1925 (ed.). *Anthology of Chinese Literature:* Vol. I—
From Early Times to the Fourteenth Century (1965); Vol. II—
From the Fourteenth Century to the Present (1972). An attrac-
tive selection of traditional materials. *H & P—Grove.*

———— (ed.). *Stories from a Ming Collection* (1968). Popular themes—
young scholars in love, faithful wives, scheming concubines, just and
unjust officials, witches, murderers—in realistic settings. *P—Grove.*

CONFUCIUS c. 551-479 B.C. *The Analects* (1938). Arthur Waley's translation and careful editing of the work that provided the basis for the
Confucian system. *P—Random.*

CREEL, H. G. b. 1905. *Confucius and the Chinese Way* (1949). A scholarly but readable account of how the original ideas of Confucius were
modified as they became "official" and of how they affected Western
thought and modern China. *P—Har-Row.*

————. *Chinese Thought from Confucius to Mao Tse-tung* (1953). A
basic popular study of the intertwining strands of developing ideas.
H & P—U of Chicago Pr.

DE BARY. *Sources of Chinese Tradition.* See page 57.

FUNG, YU-LAN b. 1895. *A Short History of Chinese Philosophy*
(1966). An abridged edition of a standard work by a universally respected scholar. *P—Free Pr.*

HINTON, WILLIAM. *Fanshen: A Documentary of Revolution in a
Chinese Village* (1966). A new classic, describing how peasants faced
their former landlords and themselves. *H—Monthly Rev; P—Random.*

HOOKHAM, HILDA 1915-1972. *A Short History of China* (1972). Up-
to-date survey, well-illustrated; ends with a sympathetic treatment of
the present regime. *P—NAL.*

KINGSTON, MAXINE HONG. *The Woman Warrior* (1976). A startling
revelation about two cultures: a Chinese village of the recent past and
present-day California. *H—Knopf.*

LIU, JUNG-EN (trans.). *Six Yuan Plays* (1972). Representing themes
and styles of the rapid-growth years of drama during the Mongol dynasty. *P—Penguin.*

LIU, WU-CHI b. 1907. *An Introduction to Chinese Literature* (1966).
A pleasant survey, including excerpts from major writers and works.
H & P—Ind U Pr.

————. and IRVING YUCHENG LO (eds.). *Sunflower Splendor: Three
Thousand Years of Chinese Poetry* (1975). The largest and most
impressive collection now available. *H—Ind U Pr; P—Doubleday.*

LO, KUAN-CHUNG c. 1330-1400. *Romance of the Three Kingdoms.*
Folk tradition leavening the formal history of the post-Han wars. *H—
C E Tuttle.*

LU HSUN (CHOU SHU-JEN) 1881-1936. *Selected Stories* (1972). Eighteen stories by "the chief commander of China's modern cultural revolution." *H & P—China Bks.*

MAO TSE-TUNG 1893-1976. *Mao Tse-tung: An Anthology of His Writings* (1971). Ed. by Anne Fremantle. A good introduction to Mao's philosophical ideas and polemical style. *P—NAL.*

_____. *Selected Readings* (1971). An official collection of representative writings and speeches. *H & P—China Bks.*

NEWMAN, RICHARD and LIN-TUNG TAN. *About Chinese* (1971). An effective and engaging analysis of how the Chinese language works. *P—Penguin.*

SCHURMANN, FRANZ b. 1926 and ORVILLE SCHELL. *The China Reader* (1967). The last two centuries are covered in three volumes of documents on Imperial, Republican, and Communist China. The introductions are enlightening. *P—Random.*

SHIH NAI-AN c. 1350. *Water Margin*. Social realism and lusty humor in the glorious band of outlaws of the Sung period. *P—Paragon.*

_____. *All Men Are Brothers*. The Shui-hu-Chuan rendered in archaic but pleasant prose by Pearl S. Buck. *H—John Day.*

SIREN, OSVALD 1879-1966. *The Chinese on the Art of Painting* (1963). Cites and explains clearly Chinese critical theory and practice. *P—Schocken.*

SZE, MAI-MAI. *The Way of Chinese Painting* (1959). A delightful explanation of how Taoist practice is applied; includes the Mustard-seed treatise on painting. *P—Random.*

TSAO HSUEH-CHIN 1717-1764. *The Dream of the Red Chamber (Hung Lou Meng)*. The first and still one of the greatest of the family-chronicle novels, rich in philosophical overtones. *H—Twayne; P—Doubleday, Penguin.*

WALEY, ARTHUR 1889-1966. *Three Ways of Thought in Ancient China* (1939). A conversational and anecdotal presentation of Taoism (Chuang Tzu), Confucianism (Mencius), and Legalism, with side references to other doctrines. *P—Doubleday.*

_____. *Monkey* (1942). A free version of one third of Wu Cheng-en's *Journey to the West* (Hsi-yu chi). Full of fun, on the Buddhist monk Hsuan Tsang's famous pilgrimage to India. *P—Grove.*

WELCH, HOLMES. *Taoism: The Parting of the Way* (1966). A sympathetic historical and philosophical treatment of the two ways of Tao: esoteric and popular. *P—Beacon Pr.*

WU CHING-TSU 1701-1754. *The Scholars*. A bitter satire on the intelligentsia, the mandarin administrators during the Ch'ing dynasty. *H—China Bks, Great Wall Pr.*

India

ANAND, MULK RAJ b. 1905. *Two Leaves and a Bud* (1942). A protest novel set in tea-producing country by the dean of editors and fiction writers in English. *P—InterCulture.*

_____. *The Untouchable* (1935). A fictional comment on India's abiding evil. *P—InterCulture.*

BASHAM, A. L. *The Wonder That Was India* (3rd ed. 1968). A rich and readable cultural history of pre-Muslim times; well illustrated. *H—Taplinger; P—Grove.*

Bhagavad-Gita (5th to 3rd cent. B.C.). The most popular book in Hindu religious literature. The modern version by P. Lal is graceful and literary (*P—InterCulture*). *Over 15 other eds.*

BROWN, D. MACKENZIE b. 1908. *The White Umbrella* (1953). Excerpts from classics in political thought from Manu to Mahatma Gandhi, with perceptive introductory essays. *P—U of Cal Pr.*

CHAUDHURI, NIRAD b. 1897. *Autobiography of an Unknown Indian*. A cantankerous anglophile looks at his compatriots.. *H—U of Cal Pr.*

DE BARY. *Sources of Indian Tradition*. See page 57.

FISCHER, LOUIS 1896-1970. *Gandhi* (1954). More admiring than some recent critical treatments of the leader's ideas and life but dependable in detail. *P—NAL.*

LAL, P. (trans.). *Great Sanskrit Plays in Modern Translation* (1964). Six pieces well rendered. *H & P—New Directions.*

LANNOY, RICHARD. *The Speaking Tree: A Study of Indian Culture and Society* (1971). Wide-ranging religious, sociological, and psychological study. *H & P—Oxford U Pr.*

MOORE, CLARK D. and DAVID ELDREDGE. *India Yesterday and Today* (1970). Packed with short excerpts, from the Vedas to newspaper articles of the 1960s, this book gives an idea of India's complex history and problems; explanatory material is skimpy. *P—Bantam.*

MORGAN, KENNETH W. b. 1908 (ed.). *Religion of the Hindus* (1953). A collection of helpful essays by noted scholars with good translations and interpretations of the religio-philosophical literature. *H—Ronald.*

NARAYAN, R. K. b. 1906. *The Bachelor of Arts* (1948). A leading novelist in English treats gently the indigent semiintellectual. *P—InterCulture.*

———. *The Financial Expert* (1952). A novel about the wiles of survival in a small town. *H—Mich St U Pr; P—FS&G.*

———. *The Ramayana* (1972). A shortened prose version of a great Sanskrit epic. *H—Viking Pr.*

O'FLAHERTY, WENDY D. b. 1940. *Hindu Myths* (1975). Brief but enlightening prefatory materials to translations from the Sanskrit introduce the complex and often brutal bases of popular religion as well as the "great tradition." *P—Penguin.*

PREMCHAND (pseud. of DHANPAT RAI SRIVASTAVA) 1881-1936. *The Gift of a Cow* (1968). A translation by G. Roadarmel of a classical Hindu-language novel about North Indian peasant life. *H & P—Ind U Pr.*

ROWLAND, BENJAMIN 1904-1972. *The Art and Architecture of India* (2nd ed. 1956). A traditional, judicious work, well illustrated. *H & P—Penguin.*

SINGH, KHUSHWANT. *Train to Pakistan* (1956). On the blood-spilling at the partition of British India in 1947. *P—Grove.*

_____ and JAYA THADANI (eds.). *Land of the Five Rivers* (1965). An interesting collection of stories from the Punjab. *P—InterCulture.*

TAGORE, SIR RABINDRANATH 1861-1941. *A Tagore Reader* (1966). Ed. by Amiya Chakravarty. Contains poetry and prose of India's best-known literary figure. *P—Beacon Pr.*

WISER, WILLIAM H. 1890-1961 and CHARLOTTE VIALL WISER. *Behind Mud Walls: 1930–1960* (1963). Two practical missionaries spent five years in a typical North India village, then returned for a follow-up study. *H & P—U of Cal Pr.*

Japan

BASHO, MATSUO 1644-1694. *The Narrow Road to the Deep North and Other Travel Sketches* (1974). The greatest haiku poet walked the byways, lived frugally, exchanged poems with admirers, and wrote memorable, simple prose. *H—Gannon; P—Penguin.*

BOWERS, FAUBION b. 1917. *Japanese Theatre* (1952). A good introduction to the various traditional forms, *Noh, Kabuki,* and *bunraku,* and helpful comments on modern drama. Contains three *Kabuki* plays. *H—Greenwood; P—C E Tuttle.*

CLAVELL, JAMES b. 1924. *Shogun* (1975). A long, fascinating historical novel about action and ethos in the time of the first Tokugawa shogun. *H—Atheneum; P—Dell.*

DE BARY. *Sources of Japanese Tradition.* See page 57.

HALL, JOHN W. b. 1916. *Japan* (1971). Formal in tone, sound in scholarship, ranging from prehistory to modern times. *P—Dell.*

HALLIDAY, JON. *A Political History of Japanese Capitalism* (1975). A Marxian analysis of the interplay of internal forces and foreign pressures that led to the Meiji upheaval and subsequent expansion. *H—Pantheon.*

HENDERSON, HAROLD G. b. 1889. *An Introduction to Haiku* (1958). Informative, with renderings of classic poets from Basho to Shiki that do not always benefit from rhyme. *H & P—Doubleday.*

HOUSTON, JEANNE WAKATSUKI and JAMES D. HOUSTON b. 1933. *Farewell to Manzanar* (1973). A gripping description of a Nisei family in the pressures of adjustment to a World War II relocation camp and afterward. *H—HM; P—Bantam.*

KAWABATA, YASUNARI 1899-1972. *Snow Country* (1969). A fair example of the teasing indirection of Japan's Nobel laureate. *H—Knopf; P—Berkley Pub.*

KEENE, DONALD b. 1922 (ed.). *Anthology of Japanese Literature* (1955-56). Not an exhaustive collection, but flavorful. *P—Grove 2 vols.*

_____ (trans.). *Four Major Plays of Chikamatsu* (1961). Representative pieces by the greatest classical playwright. *H & P—Columbia U Pr.*

KITAGAWA, JOSEPH M. b. 1915. *Religion in Japanese History* (1966). Helpful to an understanding of the undogmatic syncretism of Japanese belief. *H—Columbia U Pr.*

MISHIMA, YUKIO 1925-1970. *Death in Midsummer and Other Stories* (1966). A good sampling of the violent themes of the decadent who yearned for a pure absolute. *P—New Directions.*

——. *Five Modern Noh Plays* (1973). Retellings in modern settings of Noh classics. *P—Random.*

MORRIS, IVAN 1925-1977. *The World of the Shining Prince* (1964). A fascinating description of court life in ancient Japan during the era of Prince Genji. *H—Knopf.*

——. (trans.). *The Pillow Book of Sei Shonagon* (1971). The diary classic of Lady Murasaki's court rival. *P—Penquin.*

MURASAKI, LADY 978-1031? *The Tale of Genji*. The world's first novel and still one of the greatest. The 1976 translation by Edward G. Seidensticker is superb. *H—Knopf 2 vols.*

REISCHAUER, EDWIN O. b. 1910. *The Japanese* (1977). What the Japanese are like according to the former ambassador, and how they got that way. *H—Harvard U Pr.*

SANSOM, SIR GEORGE B. 1883-1965. *Japan* (rev. ed. 1962). Overall, the most balanced and penetrating study of the cultural history of Japan. *H—P-H.*

TANIZAKI, JUNICHIRO 1886-1965. *The Makioka Sisters* (1957). A directly told depiction of the persistence of old ways of thought in modern Osaka. *H—Knopf; P—Berkley Pub, G&D.*

WARNER, LANGDON 1881-1955. *The Enduring Art of Japan* (1952). A loving tribute to old Japanese craft artistry. *P—Grove.*

The Smaller Nations

BENDA, HARRY J. b. 1919 (ed.). *The World of Southeast Asia* (1967). A fact-filled background study through selected historical readings. *P—Har-Row.*

CASPER, LEONARD b. 1923. *New Writing from the Philippines* (1966). Contains a helpful introduction, interesting selections, and a comprehensive bibliography. *H—Syracuse U Pr.*

KANG, YOUNGHILL. *The Grass Roof* (new ed. 1975). An interesting autobiographical work. Bound with *The Yalu Flows*. *P—Norton.*

KARTINI, RADEN ADJENG 1879-1904. *Letters of a Javanese Princess* (1964). Insightful about life in Java. *P—Norton.*

RAFFEL, BURTON b. 1928 (ed.). *Anthology of Modern Indonesian Poetry* (2nd ed. 1968). A representative collection. *P—State UNY Pr.*

RAWSON, PHILIP b. 1898. *The Art of Southeast Asia* (1967). A compact but detailed treatment of the art of Cambodia, Vietnam, Thailand, Laos, Burma, Java, and Bali, with numerous illustrations well keyed to the text. *H & P—Praeger.*

RIZAL Y ALONSO, JOSÉ 1861-1896. *The Subversive* (1891). An anticolonial revolutionary political novel set in the Philippines. *H—Peter Smith; P—Norton.*

RUTT, RICHARD (ed. and trans.). *The Bamboo Grove* (1971). An introduction to *sijo*, the most popular Korean verse form. *H— U of Cal Pr.*

TOTH, MARIAN DAVIES. *Tales from Thailand* (1971). Gives insights into an exotic country. *H—C E Tuttle.*

9. Africa

Glenderlyn Johnson

Contrary to popular opinion, Africa is not one single homogeneous region. The second largest continent in the world, Africa is a complex kaleidoscope of peoples, cultures, traditions, and landscapes. Over one thousand ethnic groups inhabit the continent and speak a multitude of languages. The social organizations, directly related to the geographic locale, are generally classified in three categories: sedentary, pastoral, and nomadic.

The vast majority of Africans live in rural areas and sustain themselves by farming small plots of land and raising cattle. In recent years statisticians have noted a substantial increase in people migrating to urban areas in search of employment. As a result, many of Africa's cities have become overcrowded and troubled with serious social and economic problems. In direct contrast to the sedentary life of the urban dwellers is that of the nomads who inhabit vast desert areas. For centuries they have migrated over arid regions in search of grazing land for their cattle. Their survival is dependent on their adjustment to the harsh conditions of their environment. Even so, hundreds of thousands perished during the severe Sahelian droughts of 1973-1974. Several international organizations are working on projects designed to improve the living standards of the nomads and possibly integrate them into a more contemporary life-style. But integration into the modern world is not limited to the nomads; it is an issue throughout the continent.

To describe contemporary Africa as merely a changing continent is absurdly inadequate. Revolution—sometimes peaceful, sometimes violent—is sweeping the continent, effecting radical social and political changes. By far the most significant event of the last two decades has been the exodus of the colonial powers. Until the mid-1950s, there were only two independent Black African countries, Liberia and Ethiopia. In 1957 Ghana, formerly known as the Gold Coast, became the first of the new nations. Today there are nearly fifty independent countries.

After years of struggle and the loss of many lives, the goal of the African peoples to establish a continent of independent nations has almost been achieved. The racist apartheid system still continues to repress the lives of millions of Blacks in South Africa, but the escalation of the conflict demonstrates to the world that freedom is not negotiable; nor can it be parceled out piecemeal.

The long-drawn-out death of colonialism and the spread of nationalism have spawned many books about Africa, a great number by African authors. A distinctive yet diverse body of writing has accreted, an important contribution to world literature. It should not be forgotten, however, that written African literature has its origins in the oral tradition. For centuries African storytellers (commonly known as *griots* throughout West Africa) have told and retold indigenous legends, myths, and folktales. The griots have in fact been the custodians of African history, valued especially for their poetry and genealogical recitations. Even today it is not uncommon to find a group of villagers gathered around a storyteller, listening to tales that have been a part of their heritage for generations.

Although there is some writing in such indigenous languages as Swahili, Zulu, Yoruba, and Bemba, the bulk of contemporary published literature is written in either English or French, the languages of the former colonists. A popular theme of many novelists, especially since independence, is the clash of cultures and traditions. Chinua Achebe, Africa's foremost novelist, vividly portrays in his classic novel, *Things Fall Apart* (1958), the structural collapse and inner turmoil that take place in a typical Ibo village when Christianity and Western mores are introduced. This breakdown of traditional values is also depicted in novels that center around a protagonist who either leaves his village and moves to the city or returns to his village after being educated abroad. Time and again the clash of cultures and traditions becomes the thematic framework for African novels.

If one were to select a date that introduced contemporary Francophone African writing to an international audience, it would probably be 1922. In that year René Maran surprised the literary world by winning the prestigious Prix Goncourt for the best novel written in French, a first for a Black writer. Maran was born in Martinique but lived in Africa for over twenty years. His *Batouala* (1921) is based on his experiences as an employee in the French colonial service in the Central African Republic. Maran weaves an intriguing and explosive tale of an African village dominated by the chief Batouala. The reader experiences the sights and smells of daily life and, more important, the villagers' thoughts and feelings toward the French colonists. Viewed by the French establishment as a scathing attack on colonialism, *Batouala* was banned in all French African colonies. The ban heightened its political impact, and *Batouala* soon became a literary catalyst in Africa's preindependence movement.

Anglophone African writers gained an international audience some time later than their French counterparts. Most critics credit the Nigerian Amos Tutuola with being the forerunner of contemporary writing in English. Tutuola is indeed the doyen of African folklorists. His first novel, *The Palm-wine Drinkard*, caused a commotion when published in 1952. How, readers asked, could this semieducated Yoruba perform such wonders with myths and legends in pidgin English? The novel was simultaneously hailed and reviled, but it eventually found its place as one of the most popular African novels ever written. Now available in six languages, this novel is required reading in college courses in African literature.

In any introduction to African literature the writers belonging to the Négritude movement must be considered. This group of Black French-speaking African and West Indian writers emerged after World War II in response to what they perceived as the dissolution of their heritage. Simply put, Négritude is an affirmation of blackness or Africanness, an idea Léon Damas, Aimé Césaire, and Léopold Sédar Senghor dramatically enunciated in their works. A detailed analysis of this movement is given in Mphahlele's *African Image*.

Scholars and creative writers have begun to erase false or racist interpretations of Africa and to provide instead a more accurate portrait of its past and present history and culture. Many of these writers are Africans. Today's reader has available materials from which to gather informed insights into Africa's future.

African Literature

ABRAHAMS, PETER (South Africa) b. 1919. *Mine Boy* (1946). One of the first novels to portray vividly and passionately the dehumanizing system of apartheid. *P—Macmillan.*

ACHEBE, CHINUA (Nigeria) b. 1930. *Things Fall Apart* (1958). This first novel by Africa's most prominent novelist is already a classic. It dramatically depicts the tragic breakdown of African tradition upon contact with European culture. *H—Astor-Honor; P—Astor-Honor, Fawcett World.*

AIDOO, AMA ATA (Ghana) b. 1942. *The Dilemma of a Ghost* (1971). A brilliant play dramatizing the significance of motherhood in an African society, written by a leading woman writer. *P—Macmillan.*

ARMAH, AYI KWEI (Ghana) b. 1939. *The Beautyful Ones Are Not Yet* (1968). Gripping tale of violence and corruption in a modern-day, newly independent African nation. *P—Macmillan.*

BETI, MONGO (Cameroon) b. 1932. *The Poor Christ of Bomba* (1971). Witty, satirical novel centered around a Catholic mission school for girls run by French priests in French Colonial Africa. Its publication stirred the ire of the French church. *H & P—Humanities.*

EKWENSI, CYPRIAN (Nigeria) b. 1921. *Burning Grass* (1962). A leading African novelist weaves a simple but beautiful tale about the migration of Fulani herders and their cattle from northern Nigeria, after the burning of the grass, to the banks of the Niger. *P—Humanities.*

EMECHETA, BUCHI (Nigeria) b. 1944. *The Bride Price* (1976). Emecheta engages her readers in a stimulating cultural experience, showing the significance of a bride price, or dowry, in an African setting. *H— Braziller.*

_____. *Second-Class Citizen* (1975). In her desire to achieve personal goals, Adah, a young Nigerian woman living in England, struggles through myriad marital and racial problems. *H—Braziller.*

GORDIMER, NADINE (South Africa) b. 1923. *Selected Stories* (1976). A selection of previously published short stories by a writer internationally acclaimed for her works showing life in and around Johannesburg. *H—Viking Pr.*

HEAD, BESSIE (South Africa) b. 1937. *When the Rain Clouds Gather* (1969). Botswana is the setting for this first novel that questions the effects and consequences of independence on a traditional village. *H— S&S.*

KENNEDY, ELLEN CONROY (ed. and trans.). *The Négritude Poets* (1975). Well-researched, well-selected collection of the works of 27 French-speaking Black poets of the Négritude school. *H—Viking Pr.*

LAYE, CAMARA (Guinea) b. 1928. *Dark Child* (1954). Tender, sensitive autobiographical novel focusing on the author's adolescent years in Guinea. One of the most popular African novels. *H & P—FS&G.*

MARAN, RENÉ (Martinique) 1887-1960. *Batouala* (1921). A controversial, prizewinning first novel, depicting French colonialism. *H & P— Inscape Corp.*

NGUGI, JAMES (NGUGI WA THIONG O) (Kenya) b. 1938. *A Grain of Wheat* (1968). One of East Africa's foremost novelists portrays penetratingly Kenya's pre- and postindependence struggles. *P—Humanities.*

NIANE, DJIBRIL TAMSIR (Mali) b. c. 1920. *Sundiata* (1965). Beautiful tale about one of Africa's great ancient empires, Old Mali, told by the descendant of a long line of griots. *P—Humanities.*

NWAPA, FLORA (Nigeria) b. 1931. *Efuru* (1966). A provocative first novel, compassionately portraying the protagonist's rejection of many of the traditional roles of women in an African village. *P—Humanities.*

OYONO, FERDINAND (Cameroon) b. 1928. *Boy!* (1970). Humorous, biting satire on French colonialism taken from the "diary" of a houseboy. *P—Macmillan.*

PATON, ALAN (South Africa) b. 1903. *Cry, the Beloved Country* (1948). An acknowledged critic of apartheid dramatizes the race question in an intensely pulsating novel. *H & P—Scribner.*

SEMBÈNE, OUSMANE (Senegal) b. 1923. *God's Bits of Wood* (1962). Director, filmmaker, and novelist, Sembène focuses his pen on the 1947-1948 strike by African workers employed on the Dakar-Niger railroad. A moving novel based on actual events. *P—Doubleday.*

SENGHOR, LÉOPOLD SÉDAR (Senegal) b. 1906. *Nocturnes* (1971).
Senegal's president is recognized by literary critics as Africa's foremost
poet. Many of his most sensitive and poignant poems are in this collection. *H & P—Third Pr.*

SOYINKA, WOLE (Nigeria) b. 1934. (ed.). *Poems of Black Africa* (1975).
Ranges from traditional to contemporary poetry. Soyinka, himself an
internationally acclaimed poet, has assembled an excellent collection.
H & P—Hill & Wang.

TUTUOLA, AMOS (Nigeria) b. 1920. *The Palm-wine Drinkard* (1952). A
titillating folk tale written in a type of pidgin English; a classic. *P—
Grove.*

Books about Africa

ALLEN, PHILIP M. b. 1932 and AARON SEGAL b. 1938. *The Traveler's
Africa* (1973). A comprehensive guidebook full of valuable tips and
background information for anyone planning a trip to any part of
Africa. *H—Hopkinson, Scribner.*

AWOONOR, KOFI b. 1935. *The Breast of the Earth: A Survey of the
History, Culture, & Literature of Africa South of the Sahara*
(1976). Ambitious, scholarly, macrocosmic, thoroughly readable survey, emphasizing the literary tradition. *P—Doubleday.*

BEBEY, FRANCIS b. 1929. *African Music: A People's Art* (1975). Excellent introduction to traditional music and culture (the two are
inseparable). The many illustrations greatly enhance one's understanding of the tenacity of music in African societies. *H & P—Lawrence
Hill.*

CRANE, LOUISE b. 1917. *Ms. Africa: Profiles of Modern African
Women* (1973). Biographical sketches of 13 prominent women in fields
ranging from music to politics. *H—Lippincott.*

DAVIDSON, BASIL b. 1914. *Africa in History* (1974). Compact, readable,
thematic presentation of African history from ancient times to the
revolutionary movements of southern Africa. *H & P—Macmillan.*

D'AZEVEDO, WARREN L. (ed.). *The Traditional Artist in African
Societies* (1973). Noted Africanists examine the social functions of
the arts. *H & P—Ind U Pr.*

DIOP, CHEIKH ANTA b. 1923. *The African Origin of Civilization*
(1974). Absorbing and readable illustrated presentation of historical,
archaeological, and anthropological data supporting the thesis that
Egyptian civilization is of Negro origin. *H & P—Lawrence Hill.*

DU BOIS, WILLIAM E. 1868-1963. *World and Africa.* (rev. ed. 1965). First
published in 1946, a pioneer historical work that projects Africa in
clear, historical focus with the rest of the world. *H & P—Intl Pub Co.*

FANON, FRANTZ 1925-1961. *The Wretched of the Earth* (1965). This
book has become the "bible" for colonized people everywhere on earth.
It lays bare the dehumanizing aspects of colonialism and suggests
solutions for the oppressed of the Third World. *P—Grove.*

HAFKIN, NANCY J. and EDNA G. BAY (eds.). *Women in Africa* (1976).
Illuminating collection of essays by scholars from various disciplines

examining the social and economic changes in African women outside their traditional wife/mother role. *H—Stanford U Pr.*

HERDECK, DONALD E. b. 1924. *African Authors: A Companion to Black African Writing, 1300–1973* (1973). Excellent reference tool, alphabetically arranged by author, listing works and critiques in addition to hard-to-find biographical data. Many portraits. *H—Inscape Corp.*

JAHN, JANHEINZ 1918-1973. *Muntu* (1961). Broad survey of new African culture, embracing subjects such as art, religion, and philosophy. Jahn was a prime mover in introducing and popularizing African culture in Europe and America. *P—Grove.*

_____. *Neo-African Literature* (1969). Comprehensive, scholarly history of Black writing with extensive bibliographies. *P—Grove.*

JEFFERSON, LOUISE E. *The Decorative Arts of Africa* (1973). Through rich photographs and beautiful drawings the author takes us on an esthetic journey through the ritual and utilitarian uses of decorative arts. *H—Viking Pr.*

JEFFERSON, MARGO and ELLIOTT P. SKINNER b. 1924. *Roots of Time* (1974). Splendid, beautifully illustrated study of the mutual elements found throughout Africa in terms of family, tradition, religion, and politics. *H & P—Doubleday.*

JORDAN, ARCHIBALD CAMPBELL 1906-1968. *Towards an African Literature* (1973). Twelve lucid, scholarly essays analyzing literature written in Xhosa. *H—U of Cal Pr.*

JULY, ROBERT W. b. 1918. *A History of the African People* (rev. ed. 1974). Concise history in a political and social context with emphasis on the modern period. *H & P—Scribner.*

KENYATTA, JOMO b. c. 1893. *Facing Mount Kenya* (1938). A fascinating account of the social life and organizational structure of the Gikuyu (Kikuyu) tribe of Kenya, written by Kenya's president, grandson of a Gikuyu medicine man. *H—AMS Pr; P—Random.*

KILLAM, G. D. b. 1930 (ed.). *African Writers on African Writing* (1973). An introspective look into African literature by fourteen of Africa's most esteemed writers. *H & P—Northwestern U Pr.*

LA GUMA, ALEX b. 1925 (ed.). *Apartheid* (1972). Sixteen South African exiles describe life under apartheid. *P—Int Pub Co.*

MANDELA, NELSON b. 1918. *No Easy Walk to Freedom* (1974). A freedom fighter, Mandela received a life sentence in South Africa's infamous Robben Island prison. This is a piercing collection of his writings, speeches, and trial testimony. *P—Humanities.*

MBITI, JOHN S. b. 1931. *Introduction to African Religion* (1975). An African theologian analyzes the significance of religion in African societies in clear prose. *H—Praeger.*

MPHAHLELE, EZEKIEL b. 1919. *The African Image.* (rev. ed. 1974). A leading African literary critic takes us beyond the literary circle to a searching social and political discussion of the "African personality." *H—Faber & Faber, Praeger; P—Praeger.*

MURDOCK, GEORGE P. b. 1897. *Africa: Its People and Their Cultural History* (1959). Ethnographic survey of some of the social and political organizations of Africa. Not for the novice. Lengthy bibliographies conclude each chapter. *H—McGraw.*

NKETIA, JOSEPH H. b. 1921. *The Music of Africa* (1974). A survey of Africa's musical heritage in a historical, cultural, and social setting by a recognized musicologist. *H & P—Norton.*

NKRUMAH, KWAME 1909-1972. *Africa Must Unite* (rev. ed. 1970). A former president of Ghana describes the necessary steps African nations must take before full freedom and national development can be achieved. *H & P—Int Pub Co.*

———. *Ghana: The Autobiography of Kwane Nkrumah* (1971). An insightful account by one of Africa's most zealous liberation leaders about his struggles and triumphs that culminated in Ghana's independence. *H & P—Int Pub Co.*

PAULME, DENISE (ed.). *Women of Tropical Africa* (1963). An absorbing and enlightening study of African women in diverse geographical settings by six female anthropologists. *H & P—U of Cal Pr.*

RODNEY, WALTER. *How Europe Underdeveloped Africa* (1974). A provocative Marxian analysis of African history. *H—Howard U Pr. Panther Hse.*

SCHMIDT, NANCY J. b. 1936. *Children's Books on Africa and Their Authors* (1975). An exhaustive bibliography containing over 800 entries, each with descriptive and critical annotations and relevant biographical information. *H—Holmes & Meier.*

SNOWDEN, FRANK M., Jr. b. 1911. *Blacks in Antiquity* (1970). Engrossing historical account, with copious illustrations, of the role of Blacks (Ethiopians) in the Greco-Roman world. *P—Harvard U Pr.*

WILLIAMS, CHANCELLOR b. 1902. *The Destruction of Black Civilization* (1974). Clear, informative, scholarly analysis of the worldwide social, cultural, and political contributions of Africa. Contradicts many "Dark Continent" myths. *H & P—Third World.*

10. Latin America

Oswaldo Arana

Latin-American writing has gone through three distinct stages. During its colonial period, the writers—like the artists and architects—found their models in Spain and Portugal. During a revolutionary period that extended over two centuries, the literature of France—first the France of the Encyclopedists, then of the Symbolists—was the vital influence. Only very recently has Latin-American literature entered a renaissance. Compounded of North American techniques and developing from indigenous roots, it has the vitality of the plastic arts of the 1930s. This is especially true of the novel.

The Indians have always been a key (and problematic) figure in Latin-American letters. During the colonial period, these native Americans were either quaint Uncle Toms or even more fantastic and romantic Chingachgooks. During the various revolutionary cycles, they were first Rousseauesque "noble savages" and afterward faceless symbols of the oppressed. For the new generation of writers, however—especially in Mexico and to a lesser extent in Peru and Guatemala—they are complex protagonists of a deeply split but extraordinarily rich culture. Mexican writers such as Juan Rulfo, Rosario Castellanos, and Carlos Fuentes uncover in the Indian an ancient wisdom that the Toltecs and Maya possessed centuries before the conquistadores arrived on the scene. José Mariá Arguedas (Peru) and Miguel Angel Asturias (Guatemala) concentrate on probing the soul of the Indian in the struggle between the myths and symbols of a great past and the imperatives of a rather meager present.

In their creative preoccupation with who they are and what they mean, contemporary Latin-American writers have a fruitful literary tradition to explore and to which to return. The pre-Colombian legends—preserved by priest-ethnologists of the caliber of Sahagún and Ximénez and (today) Angel Garibay, or by European-educated natives such as the Incan Garcilaso—have a stylistic and symbol-packed richness resembling that of the Upanishads and the Old Testament. Works such as *Chilam Balam* and *Popol Vuh*, compiled long after the people whose legends and history they preserve had vanished, range in style and theme from a Grimm (and Freudian) fairy tale, through an Old Testament curse on the conquerors, to a Blakean myth of a New Jerusalem.

The colonial period produced some works of lasting importance. An Alarcón, a Sor Juana Inés de la Cruz—even a Lizardi, whose quasi-picaresque novel *The Itching Parrot* was the first written and published in this hemisphere—deserve more attention from students of international literature than they have been given.

During the revolutionary cycles, which can be divided into the 19th-century wars of independence and the continuing struggles against native dictators, much of the major writing was done by intellectuals turned soldiers—from Hidalgo to Martí. Their manifestos often took the form of poetry, novels, newspaper columns, and philosophic essays. To the latter phases of the revolutions we owe such vital works as those by Alegría (Peru), Arciniegas (Colombia), Azuela (Mexico), Da Cunha (Brazil), Gallegos (Venezuela), and Quiroga (Uruguay). Most such novels suffer, however, from being written too close to the scene—either as protest novels, or as combat diaries compiled by the light of the campfire on the eve of battle. In this genre the semi-fictionalized accounts of the Villa campaigns by Martín Luis Guzmán (Mexico) are notable. Though there is still no Latin-American *War and Peace*, some of the writers, sons of guerrillas, have composed battle scenes as convincing as Stephen Crane's.

The novelists and journalists fought and wrote. The poets tended to retreat to the ivory towers that Mallarmé and other Symbolists inhabited with great style. The early poetry of Rubén Darío (Nicaragua), the leader of the *modernistas*, is a prime example of this group. In Mexico the retreat took the form of the complex and opaque death-and-God-centered poetry of Villaurrutia and Gorostiza. The Spanish Civil War added a social focus to the anguished and esoteric poetry of César Vallejo (Peru) and Octavio Paz (Mexico). And the whole spectrum of human feelings and concerns runs through the poetry of Gabriela Mistral and Pablo Neruda, both Nobel Prize winners from Chile.

Meanwhile, a special genre of Latin-American writing—that echoes the bitter epigrams of *Chilam Balam* and borrows from such diverse sources as La Rochefoucauld and O. Henry—deserves attention. In the short story, prose poem, or short essay, such Latin Americans as Jorge Luis Borges and Julio Cortázar (Argentina), and Ramón López Velarde, Juan Rulfo, and Juan José Arreola (all of Mexico) have perfected forms as stylized as the Japanese haiku. Combining a European elegance of style with Indian impassivity, these pieces are a sharp commentary on human weakness and social conditions.

In very recent years American publishers have responded enthusiastically to new voices coming out of Latin America. Julio Cortázar, Mario Vargas Llosa (Peru), Alejo Carpentier, Gabriel Cabrera Infante, José Lezama Lima (all of Cuba), and Gabriel García Márquez (Colombia) provide remarkable examples of a neobaroque literary technique. The audacity of form and theme and the dazzling language of their novels or short stories—both in rural and urban settings—must be the joy and despair of the best translators. And the university presses in particular have been translating, or bringing back into print, Latin-American classics, old and new. Many are available in paperback.

Travel books on Latin America are often good reading as well as good guides. Not to be missed are John Dos Passos on Brazil (*Brazil on the Move*), Edmund Wilson on Haiti (*Red, Black, Blond, and Olive*), Graham Greene and Kate Simon on Mexico (*Another Mexico* and *Mexico: Places and Pleasures*), Sacheverell Sitwell on Peru (*Golden Wall*), and Selden Rodman on a number of countries.

We shall probably have to wait a generation, as we did after the Mexican Revolution, before writers of the stature of Rulfo and Fuentes can assess the Cuban happenings in terms of fictional art. Meanwhile, a book such as Azuela's *The Underdogs* etches a timeless picture of what revolution does to the revolutionaries.

Since Latin Americans blame North Americans for long neglect of their area and problems, we should do more to find out what they have to say about themselves. The quest for and the urge to assert national and cultural identity are a prime concern of Octavio Paz, Victor Alba, Samuel Ramos, Germán Arciniegos, Ezequiél Martínez Estrada, Gilberto Freyre, García Márquez, and others. Their works provide a keen insight into the multifaceted world of Mexicans, Cubans, Puerto Ricans, Chicanos, and other Latinos whose varied contributions are making a lasting mark on the culture of the United States.

Finally, scholarly research has produced a great number of studies on Latin American by experts in diverse fields in an effort to analyze the complex traditions inherited from the past and the socio-political and economic changes pointing to the future. Works by W. Rex Crawford, Edwin Lieuwen, Kalman H. Silvert, Carleton Beals, and Hubert Herring are worthy of our attention.

Latin-American Literature

ALEGRÍA, CIRO (Peru) b. 1909. *The Golden Serpent* (1935). One of the great novels. Reminiscent at times of Mark Twain, it deals profoundly and compassionately with boat people who live on the Amazon and the Indian villagers who live beside it. *o.p.*

AMADO, JORGE (Brazil) b. 1912. *Gabriela, Clove, and Cinnamon* (1962). Rabelaisian novel about a pretty country woman's effect on a seaport town. *H—Knopf; P—Avon.*

———. *Home Is the Sailor* (1964). Uproarious tale about a Brazilian Munchausen-Mitty. An imposter posing as a sea captain splits a town into factions and is unexpectedly unmasked. *o.p.*

ANDRADE, CARLOS DRUMOND DE (Brazil) b. 1902. *In the Middle of the Road* (1965). Poems in which irony, sadness, humor, and other traits of human life are vividly intertwined. *o.p.*

ARCINIEGAS, GERMÁN (Colombia) b. 1900. (ed.). *The Green Continent* (1944). Excellent anthology by more than 30 Latin-American historians, essayists, and novelists, revealing how our southward neighbors think and feel. *o.p.*

ASTURIAS, MIGUEL ANGEL (Guatemala) b. 1899. *El Señor Presidente* (1964). A forceful portrayal of the brutalization of life under the rule of a man who is the personification of the evils found in all dictators. *H & P—Atheneum.*

AZUELA, MARIANO (Mexico) 1873-1951. *The Flies* (1918) and *The Bosses* (1917). Two pungent novelettes about the Mexican Revolution. Published under the title *Two Novels of Mexico. P—U of Cal Pr.*

———. *The Underdogs* (1927). A starkly incisive novel about the Mexican Revolution. Probing the symptoms of revolution and the aftereffects, Azuela shows that in the end those who are betrayed are the people themselves. *P—NAL.*

BORGES, JORGE (Argentina) b. 1899. *Ficciones* (1962). A master of poetic *tour-de-force* and literary legerdemain pursues the unknowable in essays, detective stories, prose poems, and literary parodies. *P— Grove.*

———. *Labyrinths* (1962). Another anthology of literary fireworks based on Borges' favorite symbol, showing this great stylist at his best. *P— New Directions.*

———. *A Personal Anthology* (1967). In this collection, on which the author wants his reputation to rest, Borges mixes satire, myth, and parable, resembling Kafka, Mallarmé, and Swift. *P—Grove.*

CARPENTIER, ALEJO (Cuba) b. 1904. *The Lost Steps* (rev. ed. 1967). The search for the origins of Spanish-American culture set in a novel dominated by the magic realism of a lost but still longed-for world. *H—Knopf.*

CASTELLANOS, ROSARIO (Mexico) b. 1922. *The Nine Guardians* (1959). A rich novel about contemporary descendants of the Mayans. *o.p.*

COHEN, J. M. (England) b. 1903 (ed.). *Latin American Writing Today* (1967). A ranging, selective anthology. *H—Peter Smith.*

CORTÁZAR, JULIO (Argentina) b. 1914. *Hopscotch* (1966). Irony, humor, and a whimsical structure are skillfully combined in a cosmopolitan novel that questions through its characters the authenticity of various aspects of life. *H—Pantheon; P—Avon.*

CRANFILL, THOMAS M. (U.S.A.) b. 1913 (ed.). *Muse in Mexico* (1959). Elegantly produced anthology of contemporary Mexican art and literature. *H—U of Tex Pr.*

CUNHA, EUCLIDES DA (Brazil) 1866-1909. *Rebellion in the Backlands* (1902). An epic narrative of Brazil's struggle from tropic jungle to modernity. *P—U of Chicago Pr.*

DARÍO, RUBÉN (Nicaragua) 1867-1916. *Selected Poems* (1965). A varied sampler of rich poetry by a great innovator and a leading *modernista*. *H—U of Tex Pr.*

FUENTES, CARLOS (Mexico) b. 1929. *The Death of Artemio Cruz* (1964). Through the eyes of a dying robber baron we glimpse the tragedy of Mexico: the failure of the revolution. *P—FS&G.*

_____. *A Change of Skin* (1968). Fuentes' most ambitious novel, an existentialist epic involving four different kinds of travelers in a tragedy with Aztec overtones. *H—FS&G.*

_____. *Terra Nostra* (1976). A sprawling novel that spans from Genesis to New Year's Eve, 2000. A fantastic journey through reality as perceived by Fuentes' imagination, using key events in Western history as points of departure. *H—FS&G.*

GALLEGOS, RÓMULO (Venezuela) b. 1884. *Doña Bárbara* (1942). A symbolic novel about a *femme fatale*, developing the conflict between barbarism and civilization. *H—Peter Smith.*

GARCÍA MÁRQUEZ, GABRIEL (Colombia) b. 1928. *One Hundred Years of Solitude* (1970). A masterpiece in the neo-baroque style. A century-long history of a town and of a family, with subtle insights into the psychology of the people and the mores of Colombia. *H—Har-Row; P—Avon.*

_____. *The Autumn of the Patriarch* (1976). A novel about a dictator who spends his life in the ruthless exercise of power, told in brilliant language and with a deep awareness of the dictator's intimate tribulations and loneliness. *H—Har-Row; P—Avon.*

GARCILASO DE LA VEGA (Peru) c. 1540-1616? *Royal Commentaries of the Incas and General History of Peru* (1609). Son of an Inca princess and a Spanish conquistador, Garcilaso compiled an authentic chronicle of the origin, growth, and destruction of the Inca empire to correct the false picture given by the historians of his day. *H—U of Tex Pr 2 vols.*

GUZMÁN, MARTÍN LUIS (Mexico) 1890-1968. *The Eagle and the Serpent* (1930). A participant's fast-paced, dead-pan novel about campaigning with Pancho Villa. *H—Peter Smith.*

MACHADO DE ASSIS, JOAQUIM MARIA (Brazil) 1839-1908. *Epitaph of a Small Winner* (1880). Ironic psychological novel about a 19th-century Brazilian George Apley. *o.p.*

_____. *Esau and Jacob* (1965). Aristocratic twin brothers vie in turn for love of mother, a woman, political power. Witty, urbane political satire and "novel of the absurd." *H—U of Cal Pr.*

MAÑACH, JORGE (Cuba) b. 1898. *Martí, Apostle of Freedom* (1950). Fascinating biography of the martyr of Cuban independence and forerunner of modernism. *H—Devin.*

MISTRAL, GABRIELA (Chile) 1889-1957. *Selected Poems* (1957). Langston Hughes's translation of representative verse by a Nobel Prize winner. *P—Ind U Pr.*

Modern Brazilian Short Stories (1974). Ed. by William L. Grossman. A remarkable selection of contemporary writers exploring the complexities of the human condition in Brazil. *H & P—U of Cal Pr.*

ONIS, HARRIET DE (U.S.A.) b. 1899 (ed. and trans.). *The Golden Land* (rev. ed. 1961). A rich anthology of Latin-American writings from the Spanish conquest to 1961, chosen to show how native folklore has influenced literature. *H—Knopf.*

PAZ, OCTAVIO (Mexico) b. 1914 (ed.). *An Anthology of Mexican Poetry* (1958). This bilingual edition has a vital introduction by Paz and first-rate translations by Samuel Beckett. *H & P—Ind U Pr.*

————. *Early Poems 1935–1955* (rev. ed. 1973). Verse by Mexico's major poet beautifully translated by Muriel Rukeyser. *H—Ind U Pr; P—New Directions.*

Popul Vuh: The Sacred Book of the Ancient Quiché Maya (date unknown). A marvelous myth put into English by Delia Goetz and Sylvanus G. Morley. *o.p.*

QUIROGA, HORACIO (Uruguay) 1878-1937. *The Decapitated Chicken and Other Stories* (1976). Tales of love, madness, and death comparable to those by Poe, Kipling, and London. *H—U of Tex Pr.*

REYES, ALFONSO (Mexico) 1889-1959. *Mexico in a Nutshell and Other Essays* (1964). Scholar, humanist, classicist, revolutionary, Reyes, who had a wide range and the respect of the young, is especially brilliant on native themes. *o.p.*

ROMERO, JOSÉ RUBÉN (Mexico) 1890-1952. *The Futile Life of Pito Perez* (1967). A picaresque classic—scathing, poetic, touching. Pito, a typical Mexican hero, is an honest rogue who battles the establishment and generally lands in jail. *H—P-H.*

RULFO, JUAN (Mexico) b. 1918. *The Burning Plain and Other Stories* (1967). Wryly compassionate vignettes of Mexican peasant life, informed by a religion that is part Catholic, part Aztec. *H & P—U of Tex Pr.*

VARGAS LLOSA, MARIO (Peru) b. 1936. *The Time of the Hero* (1966). Action and suspense in a novel that inquires deeply into the nature of the Peruvian military caste as it perpetuates itself in a preparatory school for boys. *H—Grove.*

YAÑEZ, AGUSTÍN (Mexico) b. 1904. *Edge of the Storm* (1963). A probing study of the consciousness of a small Mexican town on the eve of the Revolution, told in poetic and evocative language. *H & P—U of Tex Pr.*

Books about Latin America

ALBA, VICTOR b. 1916. *The Mexicans: The Making of a Nation* (1970). An incisive analysis of the culture, problems, and possibilities by a keen observer. *P—Pegasus.*

ARCINIEGAS, GERMÁN b. 1900. *Caribbean: Sea of the New World* (1946). Weaves a rich tapestry of clashing empires, merging cultures, struggles, and achievements. *o.p.*

CALDERÓN DE LA BARCA, FRANCES E. 1804-1882. *Life in Mexico* (1931). Classic account by a 19th-century diplomat's wife; still largely accurate. *H—AMS Pr, Dutton.*

CASO, ALFONSO b. 1896. *The Aztecs* (1959). A superb history with style and learning. *H—U of Okla Pr.*

COVARRUBIAS, MIGUEL 1904-1957. *Indian Art of Mexico and Central America* (1957). A brilliant, handsome work, both revolutionary and definitive. *o.p.*

CRAWFORD, WILLIAM REX b. 1898. *A Century of Latin-American Thought* (rev. ed. 1961). A classical study providing the background for the understanding of Latin-American ideas today. *o.p.*

DÍAZ DEL CASTILLO, BERNAL c. 1492-1581. *Discovery and Conquest of Mexico* (1632). Blunt, engaging chronicle by one of Cortes' conquistadores. *H—Octagon; P—FS&G.*

DOS PASSOS, JOHN 1896-1976 *Brazil on the Move* (1963). A major novelist with Portuguese roots approaches modern Brazil with the feeling for landscapes and political figures that distinguishes his novels. *H—Greenwood.*

FLORNOY, BERTRAND b. 1910. *The World of the Inca* (1956). Authoritative, literate account of a colorful, vanished empire. *o.p.*

FREYRE, GILBERTO b. 1900. *Masters and the Slaves* (1964). Using buildings to symbolize Brazil's history from colonial times to the present, from country to city life, Freyre pontificates with verve. *H—Knopf; P—Phila Bk Co.*

HERRING, HUBERT C. b. 1889. *History of Latin America* (3rd ed. 1968). The standard work, tracing a kaleidoscopic interplay of varied cultures and forces upon an immense, rich continent. *H—Knopf.*

HITCHCOCK, HENRY RUSSELL b. 1903. *Latin American Architecture Since 1945* (1955). Daring triumphs of modern design reflecting the new civilization that has taken shape. *H—Arno.*

LEWIS, OSCAR 1914-1970. *The Children of Sánchez* (1961). Tape recorded interviews with a typical Mexico City slum family edited to produce an anthropological documentary on the culture of poverty that reads like a novel. *H & P—Random.*

LIEUWEN, EDWIN b. 1923. *Venezuela* (2nd ed. 1965). Compact history of this unstable country from conquistador days to 1965. *o.p.*

MADARIAGA, SALVADOR DE b. 1886. *Latin America Between the Eagle and the Bear* (1962). A scholar's viewpoint of the two major forces pulling at the continent south of us. *H—Praeger.*

MORLEY, SYLVANUS G. 1883-1948. *The Ancient Maya* (3rd rev. ed. 1956). Classic account of the "Greeks" of Central America. *H & P—Stanford U Pr.*

PAZ, OCTAVIO b. 1914. *The Labyrinth of Solitude* (1962). A major modern poet analyzes the ambivalence of Mexicans—their sudden pendulum swings from sensuality to asceticism, from rhetoric to taciturnity, from social explosion to solitariness—in a sociological and literary classic of our time. *P—Grove.*

PRESCOTT, WILLIAM HICKLING 1796-1859. *Conquest of Mexico* (1843) and *Conquest of Peru* (1847). Colorful classics of historical writing. *Over 10 eds., mostly abr.*

RAMOS, SAMUEL b. 1897. *Profile of Man and Culture in Mexico* (1963). This acute analysis of the Mexican character by an Adlerian psychologist has had an immense influence on Mexican writers from

Paz to Fuentes. Ramos underlines the split between past and present to explain the inferiority complex in the *mestizo*. *H & P—U of Tex Pr.*

RODMAN, SELDEN b. 1909. *Haiti, the Black Republic* (rev. ed. 1963). Rounded poetic view of a strange, complex island country. *o.p.*

SILVERT, KALMAN H. b. 1921. *Essays in Understanding Latin America* (1976). An incisive analysis of this region's perennial problems and the possibilities for a better future. *H—Inst Study Human.*

TORRES-RÍOSECO, ARTURO b. 1897. *The Epic of Latin American Literature* (1959). A crowded panorama, filled with insight; an excellent guide to reading in the field. *H—Peter Smith; P—U of Cal Pr.*

VAILLANT, GEORGE 1901-1945. *The Aztecs of Mexico* (rev. ed. 1962). A classic revised. *H—Gannon; P—Penguin.*

WAGLEY, CHARLES b. 1913. *An Introduction to Brazil* (rev. ed. 1971). Illustrated and updated, this book provides a first-rate interpretation of the culture and civilization of contemporary Brazil. *H & P—Columbia U Pr.*

Literary Types

11. The Novel

19th-Century Continental Novels

Arthur Waldhorn

More good novels were written in Continental Europe during the 19th century than in any other place or period. It seems doubtful that this was mere happenstance. The arts flourish in peace, and there were no great wars after Napoleon's defeat in 1815. A novelist feeds on his or her time, and Continental Europe in the 19th century served varied and nourishing fare. Ferment in art, science, and politics leavened the age and infused the novel with new ideas and new points of view. For those with intellectual appetite, it was a zestful time to live and to write.

France and Russia showed the greatest activity. Out of the turmoil of French politics a new middle class was arising. Increasingly, careers were open to talent instead of to aristocratic privilege. The greatest French novelists—Balzac, Zola, Stendhal, Flaubert—were bourgeois, and it was the rise of their class that they portrayed with varying degrees of disapproval. Where the French Romantics saw men and women as passionate individuals, nobler or baser than they consistently were, Balzac placed the individual in society, and in his novels the Romantic goals of an abstract liberty or an exalted love change to money and social ambition. His *Comédie Humaine* had the most comprehensive plan any novelist ever made, nothing less than to depict in a series of novels a whole nation, the France of his time, as it actually was. For Zola, actuality was scientific: "Study men like simple elements and note their reactions," he advised. His novels about the Rougon-Macquart families shocked France to the core although they never quite achieved the scientific objectivity he aimed for: a strong moral disapproval shows through. In his three chief novels Stendhal wrote the same story three times, that of a young man making his way in the world: in *The Red and the Black*, a poor young man in a real France; in *Lucien Leuwen*, a rich young man; but in *The Charterhouse of Parma* (sometimes called the greatest French novel), a young aristocrat fails to gain happiness in an imaginary Italian principality. The actions, operatic and extravagant, are moved by a hard-boiled modern psychology.

With Flaubert's *Madame Bovary*, the novel changed. Although Flaubert was called a realist in his time, it can now be seen that he not only fused the Realistic and the Romantic ideas but he moved the novelist out of the book. The characters seem to think and act by themselves. His intense care for structure and the fall of the individual sentence gave novelists everywhere a new sense of the seriousness of their art; thus he is the bridge to Joyce and through him to the 20th century.

In Russia the situation was different. The Czars, frightened by the democratic ideas that had spread from revolutionary France, tried to shut them out by suppressing freedom of assembly and imposing a strict censorship. It is possible that most Russian novels, although politically "correct," were a defiant response to these pressures. Tolstoi was a rich nobleman, an army officer, and had none but the artist's obligation to be a novelist at all. Yet in *War and Peace, Anna Karenina,* and *Resurrection,* he tries to portray the permanent, essential Russia, regardless of the accidents of politics, and his vision is so profound that he gives us not merely Russians but very human beings. After a term in Siberia as a political offender, Dostoevski was tormented by the problems of Christian belief and the existence of evil. His lifelong aim was to write a huge work called *Life of a Great Sinner,* but he never did. However, his great novels, *The Brothers Karamazov, Crime and Punishment,* and *The Possessed,* may be fragments of this work. He owed much to Dickens, but he treats his characters with a psychological penetration that often foreshadows Freud and makes Dickens seem at times naive. Turgenev, like Tolstoi, was a rich nobleman; he was sent to jail for depicting serfs as human beings in his *Sportsman's Sketches.* In *Fathers and Sons* he examines with great clarity the impact of liberal ideas on two generations of Russians. Isolated though they were, these Russian novelists have a power and intensity that abolish national boundaries.

Other European countries had fewer great novelists, but fine novels were published nevertheless. Manzoni's *The Betrothed* and Verga's *The House by the Medlar Tree* were the best to come out of Italy. The charm of Alarcón's *The Three-Cornered Hat* and Pérez Galdós' *Doña Perfecta* makes one wish that Spain had been more prolific. Among German novels, *Wilhelm Meister,* although not Goethe's greatest work, is still a product of one of the most fertile minds of the age. Novels by Scandinavian, Polish, Hungarian, Belgian, Dutch, and Portuguese authors had merit but made little stir internationally.

In 1800 the novel had been a new thing, scarcely to be ranked with poetry or drama as serious literature. By 1900 the novel was clearly the most popular and most influential of all literary forms.

ALARCÓN, PEDRO ANTONIO DE (Spain) 1833-1891. *The Three-Cornered Hat* (1874). After *Don Quixote*, the most famous of Spanish tales. A clever, witty, and charming account of how a miller's wife fooled an amorous mayor. *P—Barron, Dufour, Penguin.*

BALZAC, HONORÉ DE (France) 1799-1850. *Eugénie Grandet* (1833). One of the greatest of *La Comédie Humaine*, Balzac's series of novels that record French life from the fall of Napoleon to 1848. Grandet, a provincial bourgeois miser, sacrifices his daughter's happiness upon the altar of greed. Powerful realism and sweeping imagination color the portrayal of emotional sterility. *Over 6 eds.*

_____. *Old Goriot* (1834). Balzac's version of the King Lear theme, an agonizing, searing, and relentlessly objective tale of an old father's humiliation at the hands of his monstrous daughters. *Over 10 eds.*

_____. *Cousin Bette* (1846). "A serious and terrible study of Parisian manners," Balzac called it. Many consider this brutal study of vice, jealousy, and vanity his finest work. Certainly the characterizations—the vindictive Bette, the debauched Hulot, and the dazzling "beast of prey" Valerie—number among his most unforgettable. *P—Har-Row, Penguin.*

CONSTANT, BENJAMIN (France) 1767-1830. *Adolphe* (1815). One of the earliest psychological novels, it draws upon Constant's long and dramatic relationship with Mme. de Staël. *H—St Martin; P—Larousse.*

DOSTOEVSKI, FEDOR (Russia) 1821-1881. *Notes from the Underground* (1864). A terrifying analysis of psychic alienation and impotence. In many ways the protagonist is the archetypal anti-hero of 20th-century existential fiction. *P—Bantam, T Y Crowell, Dell, Dutton, NAL.*

_____. *Crime and Punishment* (1866). A half-starved student with superman aspirations murders two women, then seeks a motive for his crime. On one level a superb detective story; on a deeper level a trenchant analysis of human impulses. *Over 10 eds.*

_____. *The Idiot* (1868-69). An eccentric epileptic emerges as a Christ figure in this complex study of unworldly saintliness in a harshly realistic world. *Over 6 eds.*

_____. *The Brothers Karamazov* (1880). Dmitri Karamazov and his debauched father vie for the affections of the loose and lusty Grushenka. Smerdyakov, an illegitimate son and an epileptic, murders the father, but Dmitri is tried and convicted on circumstantial evidence. Beyond the intricate plot and compelling characterizations, the novel gains force from its profound investigation of good, evil, and faith. The climactic novel of Dostoevski's career. The Magarshack translation is recommended: *P—Penguin. Over 6 other eds.*

DUMAS, ALEXANDRE (France) 1802-1870. *The Count of Monte Cristo* (1844). An exciting story that dramatizes French history with melodramatic romance and adventure. *Over 6 eds.*

FLAUBERT, GUSTAVE (France) 1821-1880. *Madame Bovary* (1857). Often called the first modern realistic novel, *Madame Bovary* reveals consummate precision in language, structure, and irony. Emma Bovary seeks vainly in a dull marriage the romance she has read and dreamed of. Disillusioned, she searches for adventure in illicit amours, but again encounters disappointment and monotony. At last, she

destroys herself, a victim of her own failure to distinguish appearance
from reality. The Steegmuller translation is recommended: *H & P—
Modern Lib. Over 10 other eds.*

FRANCE, ANATOLE (France) 1844-1924. *The Crime of Sylvestre Bonnard* (1881). Presented against a background of gentle humor, pathos,
urbanity, Bonnard is one of the most lovable characters of French
literature. *H—Dodd.*

_____. See also "20th-Century Continental Novels," page 89.

GAUTIER, THÉOPHILE (France) 1811-1872. *Mademoiselle de Maupin*
(1835). A romantic, sensual love story by the fine poet who first preached
the gospel of "art for art's sake." *H & P—French & Eur.*

GOETHE (Germany). See "The 18th Century," page 45.

GOGOL, NIKOLAI (Russia) 1809-1852. *Dead Souls* (1842). Chichikov, the
rascally hero, journeys across Russia purchasing the names of dead
serfs for their tax value. Beneath the genial, comic surface run twin
streams of satire against fraud and compassion for the underprivileged. *Over 6 eds.*

_____. *The Overcoat* (1842). "We have all come out of Gogol's overcoat,"
Dostoevski observed, conscious in his jest of Gogol's sure-handed style,
pungent social satire, and heartfelt warmth. All appear in this curi-
ously realistic tale that steps over into the realm of fantasy. The
Magarshack translation in *Tales of Good and Evil* (which also contains *The Nose*) is recommended: *P—Norton.*

GONCHAROV, IVAN (Russia) 1812-1891. *Oblomov* (1859). Oblomov,
a rich landowner, is the laziest man in the world. The account of his
getting up in the morning is one of the funniest, most touching passages
in fiction. *P—Dutton.*

HUGO, VICTOR (France) 1802-1885. *The Hunchback of Notre Dame.*
See "The Middle Ages," page 20.

_____. *Les Misérables* (1862). Jean Valjean, Javert, and Fantine, three
of the most memorable characterizations of the great French roman-
ticist, act out their drama of pathos and poverty in post-Napoleonic
France. *Over 6 eds.*

HUYSMANS, JORIS KARL (France) 1848-1907. *Against Nature* (1884).
A lavish portrait of a decadent searching relief from the banality of
bourgeois life. The exotic proclivities of the aristocratic Des Esseintes
whetted many tastes, not least among them Oscar Wilde's; *The Picture
of Dorian Gray* avowedly imitates portions of Huysmans' fascinating
tale. *P—Penguin.*

LOUŸS (France). *Aphrodite.* See "Greece," page 9.

MANZONI, ALESSANDRO (Italy) 1785-1873. *The Betrothed* (1826). A
splendid historical novel of 17th-century Italy, replete with robber
barons, the plague, and eternal love. *H & P—Dutton.*

MAUPASSANT, GUY DE (France) 1850-1893. *Bel-Ami* (1885). A scoun-
drel makes his way by his good looks. *P—Penguin.*

MÉRIMÉE, PROSPER (France) 1803-1870. *Carmen* (1845). Famous in
story, opera, and film, this gypsy girl enslaves and destroys her lover
but makes the experience seem worthwhile. *P—Barron, Larousse,
Odyssey.*

NERVAL, GÉRARD DE (France) 1808-1855. *Sylvie* (1853). An affecting, semiautobiographical narrative of adolescent love recollected in maturity. *o.p.*

PÉREZ GALDÓS, BENITO (Spain) 1843-1920. *Doña Perfecta* (1876). The finest of Galdós' several portraits of Spanish life. The scene is provincial, the time before the Carlist war, the treatment at once romantic and realistic. *P—Barron.*

STENDHAL (HENRI BEYLE) (France) 1783-1842. *The Red and the Black* (1830). Julien Sorel, one of the supreme opportunists and hypocrites of literature, turns profitably from "red" (the military life) to "black" (the clerical life) in this sharply drawn study of post-Napoleonic France. Brilliant characterizations, memorable episodes, and an overwhelming irony combine to make this one of the great novels of the century. *Over 6 eds.*

_____. *The Charterhouse of Parma* (1839). An intricately wrought but colorful and forceful novel of love and politics. *H—Liveright; P—NAL, Penguin.*

_____. *Lucien Leuwen* (1894). One of the sharpest political novels ever written. Published in America as two novels: *The Green Huntsman* and *The Telegraph. H & P—New Directions.*

TOLSTOI, LEO (Russia) 1828-1910. *War and Peace* (1866). One of the supreme novels of all time. Historically, it chronicles on an epic scale Napoleon's invasion of Russia. But its grandeur and sweep derive chiefly from the pulsating force of characterization, the dynamic interplay of ideologies in conflict. Noble and base, wise and foolish, heroic and cowardly—every type finds a place in Tolstoi's all-embracing scheme. *Over 10 unabr. eds.*

_____. *Anna Karenina* (1877). An engrossing story of adultery among the Russian nobility. Thomas Mann called it the greatest novel of society in the history of the world. *Over 6 eds.*

_____. *The Kreutzer Sonata* (1889). An absorbing problem novel about an unconventional attitude toward marriage. *H—Oxford U Pr.*

TURGENEV, IVAN (Russian) 1818-1883. *Sketches from a Hunter's Album* (1852). A vigorous attack on Russian serfdom, defending the peasant as a man possessed of "a soul of his own." A subtle book despite its propagandistic intent. *P—Penguin.*

_____. *Fathers and Sons* (1862). Although Bazarov, the hero, embodies the principles of political nihilism that led to the October Revolution, he is also a spokesman for youthful rebellion against the authority of the older generation. *Over 12 eds.*

VERGA, GIOVANNI (Italy) 1840-1922. *The House by the Medlar Tree* (1890). A graphic and tragic account of the lives of Sicilian fishermen. *P—NAL.*

ZOLA, ÉMILE (France) 1840-1902. *L'Assommoir* (1877). The terrors of poverty, alcoholism, and debauchery hound Zola's tortured souls into animalized nonexistence. Some rate this novel second only to *Germinal* in its enormous force. *H—Peter Smith; P—French & Eur., Penguin.*

_____. *Nana* (1880). With stunning if sometimes excessive detail—a characteristic of his naturalistic method—Zola describes the bizarre life of a harlot during the Second Empire. *Over 6 eds.*

_____. *Germinal* (1885). Relatively free of the confining limitations of the "scientific method" of naturalism, the novel rages through the agonies of an unsuccessful strike by impoverished French coal miners. Scenes of brutality and bestiality, courage and compassion follow hard upon one another in this relentless but overwhelmingly moving story. The translation by L. W. Tancock is recommended: *P—Penguin.*

20th-Century Continental Novels

Arthur Waldhorn and Arthur Zeiger

Works of literature form a continuum, and the centuries mark off convenient but artificial fragments. By the middle of the 19th century realism had been firmly established with Stendhal and Flaubert, and soon Zola developed naturalism, a deterministic and characteristically pessimistic variation (or aberration, as some critics insist). Symbolism, inevitable in any fictional construct, became linked to a new theory and attained a new density in Huysmans and the decadents. Dostoevski's novels, integrated by a searing psychological vision, anticipated the findings of psychoanalysts by a half century and sometimes (as in *Notes from the Underground*) of the existentialists as well. Hardly a genre, mode, or technique (hallucinatory images, stream of consciousness, expressionistic distortion, surrealistic fantasy, subverted narrative) that courses through the 20th-century novel has not its spring in the century—really, centuries—preceding.

And yet the shape of the modern novel, its total configuration, must impress us as very different. The multiple shocks our time has suffered—monstrous wars, genocide, cataclysmic redistribution of lands and peoples—have shattered traditional values and overthrown venerated authorities. The writer, deeply responding to these dislocations, has been driven to an intensified and heightened isolation. Without a compelling perception of wholeness, or even worth, of the sort that Balzac or Tolstoi had inherited, he or she cannot project images of wholeness and symmetry. Characteristically, then, writers see their world as a landscape of despair, fragmented, torn by force.

The consequences for the modern novel are momentous. The novelistic perspectives of the 19th century have been violently wrenched. The writers of our time introduce nightmare variations upon familiar themes, anathematize traditional certainties, like Céline. Or they escape the burden of reality through a mystic descent, like Hesse. Or they precisely and dispassionately annotate the phenomena of consciousness, like Robbe-Grillet. Or they devise a humanistic but contingent morality as a surrogate for a once-confident faith, like Camus. Or they arrange a counterpoint of pain and fantasy in evoking the past to evade its impact, like Grass.

These are schematic comments, however; novels may not be subsumed by catalogs of characteristics. For each of the writers cited, it would not be impossible to adduce, with much qualification, a 19th-century analogue. Despite a variety of differences, for example, Grass surely has affinities to Gogol. And Silone and Malraux, no less than Mauriac and Undset, are actuated by traditional principles of morality—though the traditions are of course diverse. Moreover, the novelists generally acknowledged to be the most significant of our century elude generalization. Proust, whose complex interweaving of themes is essentially modern, nevertheless presents a fictional world as solid as that created by any of his 19th-century forebears—distorted certainly, but compelling belief. And Mann, whose vast mythic journeys to discover the sources of our pervasive spiritual illness are still *avant garde*, is yet allied to Goethe and Schiller among other great ancestors. In every novelistic development in the 20th century, the "new" has been conditioned by the "old," the beginning is implicit in every progression.

BEAUVOIR, SIMONE DE (France) b. 1908. *The Mandarins* (1955). A lively, prize-winning *roman à clef* about the personalities, politics, and philosophy of existentialism by one of its most famous adherents. *H—French & Eur.*

BECKETT, SAMUEL (Ireland, now France) b. 1906. *Three Novels: Molloy; Malone Dies;* and *The Unnamable* (1951-1953). A trilogy (1959) of sorts: its element, despair; its matter, the absurdity of human existence; its manner, wit and farce. *P—Grove.*

————. *Murphy* (1938). A comedy of failure: no individual escape into the recesses of self is possible for Murphy because the big booming confusion of the macrocosm (his friends, disciples, and beloved) keeps breaking through. *H & P—Grove.*

BELY, ANDREY (Russia) 1880-1934. *St. Petersburg* (1911). Nabokov ranks this with the works of Joyce, Kafka, and Proust. Simple in plot— a revolutionist son in conflict with a conservative father during the ferment of 1905—but complex and virtuoso structurally, stylistically, and symbolically. *H—M McCosh Bkslr; P—Grove.*

BÖLL, HEINRICH (Germany) b. 1917. *Billiards at Half Past Nine* (1959). How three generations of a family of architects lived before, during, and after two world wars—between 1880 and 1958. Böll characterizes better than he plots, affords a many-faceted experience. *P— Avon, McGraw.*

BROCH, HERMANN (Austria) 1886-1951. *The Sleepwalkers* (1932). A trilogy of modern dissolution; set in Germany, 1888 to 1918, this masterly novel surveys the disparate lives of three men (Romantic, Anarchist, and Realist) to achieve a kind of synthesis. *o.p.*

CALVINO, ITALO (Italy) b. 1923. *Invisible Cities* (1974). A subtle fantasy that resolves the eternal conflict between multiplicity and unity as Kubla Khan discerns a pattern in Marco Polo's travel memories. *H—HarBarceJ.*

CAMUS, ALBERT (France) 1913-1960. *The Stranger* (1946). A compelling story of the absurdity of life when man's aspirations and values have no cosmic status. *H—Knopf; P—Random.*

_____. *The Plague* (1948). Bubonic plague in Oran forces choices of action: bewildered faith, passivity, flight, suicide, helping others. Symbolically, the story of the Nazi Occupation and of people's responses to any sort of human plague. *H—Knopf, Modern Lib; P—Modern Lib.*

ČAPEK, KAREL (Czechoslovakia) 1890-1938. *War with the Newts* (1937). The Newts take over: science fiction, excellent as humor, social commentary, and story. *H—AMS Pr, Gregg; P—Berkley Pub.*

CÉLINE, LOUIS FERDINAND (DESTOUCHES) (France) 1894-1961. *Journey to the End of the Night* (1932). The colloquially and semiautobiographically reported adventures and misadventures of Bardamu, first in World War I, then in America and Africa, and at last as an embittered doctor. Though gusty and vigorous, the novel is heavy with loathing for humanity and a pervasive sense of life's emptiness. *P—New Directions.*

_____. *Death on the Installment Plan* (1936). Boyhood and adolescence in all their agony, comedy, and tenderness, but with a large measure of paranoia added for bad measure. *P—New Directions.*

COLETTE, SIDONIE GABRIELLE (France) 1873-1954. *Six Novels* (1960). Six novellas, perhaps the best introduction to a writer whose stylistic elegance no less than her subtle, precise, often malicious perception of life (even when it is oppressive) is an unfailing delight. *o.p.*

DUERRENMATT, FRIEDRICH (Switzerland) b. 1921. *The Pledge* (1959). Thought-arousing *recit*, sparsely written, of a police-force captain whose logic is defeated by reality. *o.p.*

_____. *The Quarry* (1961). Police commissioner Barlach—an old, brave, dying Christian—must find and arrest Dr. Emmenberger, surgeon-torturer and archetype of renascent Nazism. A chilling, inspiring, different detective-story myth for our times. *o.p.*

FRANCE, ANATOLE (France) 1844-1924. *Penguin Island* (1908). Deceits, tricks, pathetic follies of the rich, poor, haters, lovers, predators, idealists when, as penguins become humans, they repeatedly make and break "civilizations." *P—NAL.*

GENET, JEAN (France) b. 1910. *Our Lady of the Flowers* (1942). The first novel by the notorious thief and literary man, a flamboyant but powerful narrative—idyllic, brutal, comic, and absurd—of love and death among Parisian pimps and male whores. *P—Grove.*

GIDÉ, ANDRE (France) 1869-1951. *The Counterfeiters* (1927). Technically, a virtuoso performance: a novel within a novel; multiple points of view and diverse accents. Thematically, a study of how we "counterfeit" our actual identity, deceiving ourselves as well as others. *H—Modern Lib; P—Random.*

_____.*The Immoralist* (1902). A masterfully patterned short novel tracing the career of the Immoralist from conformity to hedonism, leaving him poignantly aware of the nature and implications of his sexuality. *H—Knopf; P—Bantam, Random.*

GRASS, GÜNTER (Germany) b. 1927. *The Tin Drum* (1959), *Cat and Mouse* (1961), and *Dog Years* (1963) are Rabelaisian diagnoses and prescriptions for the sick conscience of modern Germany—and by extension of the modern world. Difficult black humor as full of dirt and drollery as *Gulliver's Travels*. The author is Germany's most acclaimed writer since Thomas Mann. *Over 6 eds.*

HAMSUN, KNUT (Norway) 1859-1952. *Growth of the Soil* (1920). An unsophisticated farmer, Isak resists the temptations and corruptions of society to achieve a kind of serenity on his Norwegian farm. *H— Knopf; P—Random.*

HANDKE, PETER (Germany) b. 1942. *The Goalie's Anxiety at the Penalty Kick* (1972) and *Short Letter, Long Farewell* (1974). Two short novels by the most important new talent to emerge in Germany in the past dozen years. Distinct in subject—the one a thriller that is also a psychological and philosophical study, the other a *bildungsroman* that is also a fantasy and a "scale model of America." Both are complex, intense, intriguing. *H—FS&G.*

HASEK, JAROSLAV (Czechoslovakia) 1883-1923. *The Good Soldier Schweik* (1923). With peasant guile, Schweik outwits and outlives both ally and enemy. Devoid of honor or morality, he epitomizes—with grim good humor—the brutal emptiness of war. *H—TY Crowell; P— NAL, TY Crowell, Ungar.*

HESSE, HERMANN (Germany) 1877-1962. *Steppenwolf* (1929). An introspective, psychoanalytically oriented novel that probes the dilemma of the intellectual divorced from society and terrified of isolation. Harry Haller, the autobiographical hero, confronts the "steppenwolf" (animal) of his inward self in one of the most remarkable scenes in modern fiction. *H—HR&W; P—Bantam, HR&W.*

――――. *Siddhartha* (1951). A poignantly lyrical tale about a young Indian who learns to fuse the worlds of flesh and spirit. Though steeped in mysticism, the brief story speaks eloquently to Western minds struggling toward unity in a schizophrenic world. *H—New Directions; P— Bantam, New Directions.*

KAFKA, FRANZ (Czechoslovakia) 1883-1924. *The Trial* (1937). In this our life, Joseph K. is up for trial. But for what? He is never really tried by the High Court. Yet, finally, he is taken to a quarry and stabbed in the heart. Is this a neurotic Jew's anxiety dream—or a revelation for Everyman? *H—Knopf, Modern Lib; P—Random, Schocken.*

――――. *The Castle* (1926). At the same time a parable and a nightmare, the novel records the futile attempt of a surveyor to communicate with the Castle (to attain grace?), suggesting the essential nature of the metaphysical problem but not of its solution. *H—Knopf; P—Modern Lib, Random, Schocken.*

KAPEK. See Čapek, page 89.

KAZANTZAKIS, NIKOS (Greece) 1885-1957. *Zorba the Greek* (1952). Zorba is fuller of the joy of life than continents of today's "hollow men." He obeys the law of his own being which, like that of his prototype Ulysses, is compounded of cunning, fellowship, and picaresque heroism. *H & P—S&S.*

KOESTLER, ARTHUR (Hungary; England) b. 1905. *Darkness at Noon* (1941). Penetrating, memorable dramatization of the ideological and psychological forces in a Communist purge trial. *H—Macmillan; P—Bantam.*

LAGERKVIST, PÄR (Sweden) b. 1891. *Barabbas* (1951). The 1954 Nobel Prize winner writes a powerful character study of the man released to the mob instead of Jesus. *P—Bantam, Random.*

LEVI, CARLO (Italy) 1902-1975. *Christ Stopped at Eboli* (1945). A moving autobiographical novel about a genteel, sophisticated northern Italian discovering the agony and humanity of southern villagers under Fascist dominion. *P—FS&G.*

MALRAUX, ANDRÉ (France) 1901-1976. *Man's Fate* (1933). Individuals— Communists and non-Communists—together yet solitary, brave yet absurd, commit themselves to danger and death in the attempt to control Shanghai during the Chinese civil war (1927). Not history but existentialist vision; not man's fate but Malraux's fate for man. Malraux's heroes set the pattern for "picaresque saints." *P—Modern Lib, Random.*

MANN, THOMAS (Germany) 1875-1955. *Buddenbrooks* (1901). The ineluctable decline from wealth and honor to mean-spirited poverty and extinction of a too-complacent mercantile family. Interesting for its delineation of social changes; of temperaments, motives, marriages, and measures among the Buddenbrooks and their connections. *H— Knopf; P—Random.*

_____. *The Magic Mountain* (1924). One of the most profound and provocative novels of our time, picturing a mountaintop sanitarium as a symbol of humanity in a pathological universe. *H—Knopf; P—Modern Lib, Random.*

_____. *The Joseph Tetralogy* (1924-44). A vivid, highly suggestive recreation of ancient Egypt and the biblical saga of Joseph. *H—Knopf.*

MAURIAC, FRANÇOIS (France) 1885-1970. *Thérèse* (1927). A guilt-ridden woman remains inwardly tormented despite acquittal of trying to poison her husband. As in most of Mauriac's taut, absorbing fiction, characters try vainly to comprehend what can be known only to God. *P—FS&G.*

MORAVIA, ALBERTO (Italy) b. 1907. *The Time of Indifference* (1953). That "indifference" itself is a kind of action is realized as the shocked reader watches the Marengos—mother, daughter, and son—maneuvered into sexual and moral ruin by an amoral businessman. Neorealistic satire without a smile. *H—Greenwood; P—Manor Bks.*

_____. *Two Adolescents* (1950). Agostino and Luca suffer the torments of social, familial, and sexual pressure in these two sensitively perceived novellas of youth. *H—Greenwood, M McCosh Bkslr.*

MUSIL, ROBERT (Austria) 1880-1942. *The Man Without Qualities* (3 vols 1931-1943). Unfinished but heroic novel; set in pre-World War I Austria, it investigates the collapse of an empire and the disintegration of an individual consciousness. Witty, learned, passionate, ironic, it is a great, complex, and difficult work. *P—Putnam.*

PASTERNAK, BORIS (Russia) 1890-1960. *Dr. Zhivago* (1958). Yuri Zhivago, orphaned at ten, later an upper-class doctor, poet, husband, lover, philosopher, struggles successfully, despite upheavals and regimentation in his beloved Russia, to preserve his humanity and spiritual independence. *H—Pantheon; P—NAL.*

PAVESE, CESARE (Italy) 1908-1950. *The Moon and the Bonfire* (1950). His last, most autobiographical, and most mature novel. About the narrator's tragic quest in a Piedmontese village for the truth about his past and possibilities for the future. *H—Greenwood.*

PROUST, MARCEL (France) 1871-1922. *Remembrance of Things Past* (1913-28). In recovering his past through the dedicated exercise of memory, Proust lays bare in a series of seven novels—from *Swann's Way* (the best known) to *Time Regained*—a growing self, a changing age, a many-stranded philosophy. To read Proust, slowly, is to experience, in entertaining and enlightening fashion, his special world. *H—Random 2 vols.*

REMARQUE, ERICH MARIA (Germany) 1897-1970. *All Quiet on the Western Front* (1929). Perhaps the best-known World War I novel; blends images of war's bestiality with scenes of the battle-born brotherhood of men. *H—Little; P—Fawcett World.*

ROBBE-GRILLET, ALAIN (France) b. 1922. *The Voyeur* (1958). An exceptionally readable example of the French "New Novel." Enveloped by ambiguity and charged with suspense, it records, with sometimes painful detail and unvarying objectivity, the surface consciousness of a man who may be a traveling salesman of watches or a monstrous criminal. *P—Grove.*

ROMAINS, JULES (France) 1885-1972. *The Death of a Nobody* (1911). A poignant, haunting account of the impact an unimportant man's death has upon the lodgers in his boardinghouse. *H—Fertig.*

————. *Men of Good Will* (1932-47) A 27-volume *roman fleuve* embracing the feverish years 1908 to 1933, commingling real characters (Lenin, Poincaré, the Kaiser) and imaginary ones; admirable for its epic scope and memorable tableaux (e.g., the battle of Verdun). Often talky and naïve but a valuable document of misguided optimism. *H—AMS Pr 14 vols.*

SARRAUTE, NATHALIE (France) b. 1902. *The Golden Fruits* (1964). A sparkling brief satire on the vanities of literary critics and on how solid-seeming fictions dissolve into "process" when examined by many or when reexamined by one. *o.p.*

SARTRE, JEAN PAUL (France) b. 1905. *Nausea* (1938). Antoine Roquentin, the antihero protagonist, records in his diary the dizzying elements of his existential vertigo: time, things, bourgeois bad faith, others, and himself. A disturbing but bracing portrait of Sartre's wasteland. *P—New Directions.*

SHOLOKHOV, MIKHAIL (Russia) b. 1905. *The Silent Don* (1934-41). Includes two novels of epic scope—*And Quiet Flows the Don* and *The Don Flows Home to the Sea*—about Russian life from late Czarist days through World War I and the revolution. *H—Knopf; P—Random.*

SILONE, IGNAZIO (Italy) b. 1900. *Bread and Wine* (1936). The hero, Pietro Spina, an independent Communist, is primarily a humanitarian who risks all to rally the exploited away from Mussolini. A novel that has everything: great story; memorable characterizations; humor and pathos; major implications for church, society, and the individual. *P—NAL.*

SOLZHENITSYN, ALEKSANDR (Russia) b. 1918. *The First Circle* (1964; 1968). Stalin's Russia as it terrorizes a broad range of free-minded scientists, writers, and other intelligentsia. More journalistic than literary but undeniably powerful. *H—Har-Row; P—Bantam.*

———. *The Cancer Ward* (1968). Based partially upon the author's own bout with cancer, a dramatic and emotional detailing of life in a prison hospital toward the end of Stalin's regime. *H—Dial, FS&G; P—Bantam, Dell, FS&G.*

UNDSET, SIGRID (Norway) 1882-1949. *Kristin Lavransdatter* (1920-22). A fictional trilogy about medieval Scandinavia: the passion of Kristin's bridal wreath, the tragedy of her married life at Husaby, and the cross she bore to the end. *H—Knopf; P—Bantam.*

WERFEL, FRANZ (Austria) 1890-1945. *The Forty Days of Musa Dagh* (1934). Saga of seven Armenian villages resisting the Turks in 1915. *o.p.*

ZAMYATIN, YEVGENY (Russia) 1884-1937. *We* (1924). Orwell acknowledged his debt to this satiric fantasy of a metronomic metropolis where dreaming is a disease and an individual is always "we," never "I." *H—Gregg; P—Bantam, Dutton.*

19th-Century British Novels

Joan Schulz

With thousands of new novels published each year in the United States alone, with many of them addressed to concerns central to our lives today, and with hundreds of them available in the corner drugstore, why should anyone read a 19th-century novel?

Why indeed? To begin with, the great novels of Victoria's England not only portray the social texture of the period but also convey the sense of self that prevailed at the time. Second, the best of the Victorian novelists, like the best of contemporary novelists, are grappling with the questions of how people do and how they should live their lives. Moreover, since the world they describe is not our own, we can more dispassionately examine there the answers to psychological and moral problems that are no less relevant today.

For students of literature, the Victorian novels offer models of the traditional novel form from which they can gain perspective on and understanding of the changes that have occurred in our century. For all readers, the Victorians—at least many of them—tell good stories. This is important because a novel ought to satisfy that primitive urge to hear an engrossing tale.

Start reading anywhere. Start with Sir Walter Scott and what he called his "Big bow-wow stuff"—those marvelously broad and spacious canvases that nevertheless seem crowded with vivid characters and intriguing events with all the stir and bustle of life, or with his Scottish novels, which seem to achieve an added dimension from his strong historical sense. Scott's novels are exciting also because he had the storyteller's awareness of the great scene and how to use it. So did Meredith, and so did Jane Austen working on what she called her "little pieces of ivory . . . two inches wide," on which she created witty, perceptive satires out of the material of everyday life in a world where a clumsily handled teacup and the response it brought might reveal more about the persons involved than would a major crisis in their lives.

Or dip into Trollope, who, like Miss Austen, possessed of a gift for sharp observation of human behavior, could turn the unremarkable into delightful stories, stories characteristically colored with either pathos or good-natured irony and not infrequently directed at the Establishment.

While Trollope is the great armchair raconteur, Hardy is a storyteller out of the primitive oral tradition, able to create suspense and mystery and at the same time to make the action significant on a cosmic scale. Hardy has the power to draw elemental figures who retain human dignity in spite of the relentlessness and inevitability of their suffering.

Or try one of the most inventive and exciting storytellers of them all, Charles Dickens. He creates a world so lively and peoples it with characters so eccentric, exaggerated, or extravagant that we don't care how clumsy and inept his plots are. With the exception of Jane Austen, whose novels are technically sophisticated, 19th-century novelists, great storytellers though they were, had creaky plots. For a well-plotted novel, turn to Wilkie Collins, whose *The Moonstone* and *The Woman in White* are still among the best mystery and detective fiction ever written.

For stories in which the sensational and melodramatic have real significance, one must go either to Hardy or to the Brontë sisters, who brought poetry and passion to their brilliant novels. *Jane Eyre* convinces us that the sensational can exist within the commonplace and reveals an ability to move through realism to the highest romance; *Wuthering Heights*, which G. K. Chesterton said "might have been written by an eagle," recounts a story of fierce and transcendent human passions in conflict with the ordinary social world.

The Brontës were among the few 19th-century English novelists who explored in depth the private self and private emotions. Mainly the Victorian novel concerned itself with the problems of the human being in society; many novels are topical in their comment on and criticism of the Victorian scene but also have universal relevance and meaning. Among them are some of the novels of Dickens, whose pictures of social evil and inequity are as moving as his solution is puerile. Never merely a social reformer, Dickens was as much dedicated to symbolic attacks on oppressive institutions as to real attacks on existing ones. Or there is Thackeray, who, though no social reformer, levels a satiric gaze on his society and uncovers in a vast panorama the snobbishness and hypocrisy of bourgeois society. Thackeray's achievement lies in the enormous variety of circumstances, in the succession of brilliant scenes, in the sharply drawn and contrasted characters, and in the incisiveness of his picture of human beings as social creatures.

If we then turn to George Eliot, who, herself a rebel against conventions, changed the course of the English novel chiefly by deepening it morally and making it a more serious work of art, we are in a different but no less exciting world. Eliot's world is dominated by intense moral concerns and inhabited by a large, diverse collection of characters given perceptive psychological analysis by their creator.

What, in sum, keeps the 19th-century novel alive? Certainly the enormous inventiveness of the Victorians as spinners of intriguing stories and as creators of memorable characters is partly responsible, as are the great liveliness and diversity of them. These novels are often fast-moving, seldom plodding; they are Gladstone bags stuffed with interesting things for our inspection. There is sharp satire and keen criticism, pure comedy and pathos and tragedy. Some are distinguished by high intensity in a narrow scope, others by a leisurely pace and panoramic views of man and society. All in all, the range is broad; the mood various.

AUSTEN, JANE 1775-1817. *Sense and Sensibility* (1811). In deft strokes of brilliant and sometimes brutal irony, this antisentimental domestic comedy traces the fortunes of two very dissimilar sisters—one a figure of subtle intelligence and good sense, the other a victim of romantic sentimentality. *Over 10 eds.*

_____. *Pride and Prejudice* (1813). One of the world's greatest novels, a sparkling comedy of manners of intense vision and perfection of form, in which the hero's haughty pride of class is opposed by the heroine's natural prejudice with nearly disastrous results. *Over 15 eds.*

_____. *Mansfield Park* (1814). To some readers, the protagonist, Fanny Price, is priggish and insipid; to others, she is touching and right. For both, there is great delight in the marvelously contrasting portraits of the pompous, the vapid, and the selfish as seen through Fanny's perceptive gaze. *Over 10 eds.*

_____. *Emma* (1816). An almost faultlessly structured novel in which a subtle irony is directed at the egotistical but engaging heroine for her misguided meddling in the love affairs of others and for her failures in self-knowledge. *Over 10 eds.*

BRONTË, CHARLOTTE 1816-1855. *Jane Eyre* (1847). Romance is joined with realism to produce a fantastic love story and a piercing and radical social analysis of what it means to be female, poor, intelligent, and sexually passionate in mid-Victorian England. *Over 15 eds.*

_____. *Villette* (1853). Less popular than *Jane Eyre*, but more relentless in its account of a young woman who, appearing colorless and uncommunicative to others, without beauty or family, and therefore without "prospects," nevertheless powerfully engages reader interest. Unwilling to be either "influence" or nurturer and strengthened by determination and clarity of vision, Lucy Snowe achieves her two most precious objectives—freedom and renewal. *H—Dutton, Oxford U Pr; P—Dutton, HM.*

BRONTË, EMILY 1818-1848. *Wuthering Heights* (1847). The action of this extraordinarily intense novel, conceived at the highest imaginative level, centers around the fiercely passionate relationship between Catherine and Heathcliff, figures of elemental force and towering strength. *Over 20 eds.*

BUTLER, SAMUEL 1835-1902. *Erewhon* (1872). A satire upon sham in education, religion, social custom, and ethics. As sharply pointed as Aristophanes, and as clearly relevant. *Over 6 eds.*

_____. *The Way of All Flesh* (1903). At once modern and Victorian, this semiautobiographical novel is one of the earliest studies of a young male protagonist's alienation and search for identity. At the same time it savagely attacks the hypocrisy and horror of the Victorian family and of Victorian Christianity. *Over 6 eds.*

CARROLL, LEWIS (CHARLES L. DODGSON) 1832-1898. *Alice in Wonderland* (1865). Ostensibly a children's story, this wildly fantastic and uproarious tale of Alice's adventures may be read as a terrifying journey into the subconscious mind. *Over 20 eds.*

COLLINS, WILKIE 1824-1889. *The Moonstone* (1868). The first full-scale detective story—an involved, action-filled mystery concerning the theft of a precious jewel. *Over 10 eds.*

CONRAD. See "20th-Century British Novels," page 103.

DICKENS, CHARLES 1812-1870. *Oliver Twist* (1838). The violence and terror of the 19th-century London underworld among the outcasts of society is powerfully depicted in a story of crime and punishment. *Over 6 eds.*

_____. *David Copperfield* (1850). Dickens' favorite, perhaps because it reflects his own youth, this novel is essentially a long retrospective look into David's memory, in which reside some of the most fascinating characters Dickens ever invented. *Over 10 eds.*

_____. *Bleak House* (1853). On one level, an artfully contrived detective story employing melodramatic effects; on another level, Dickens' most mature criticism of the whole social fabric of Victorian society, in which the failure of caring and responsibility takes its enormous toll in human lives and well-being. *Over 6 eds.*

_____. *Hard Times* (1854). Dickens' most straightforwardly serious response to contemporary civilization, this short novel shows the world of rational hard-headedness and calculated self-interest in all its absurdity and in all its potential for destroying what is best in life. *Over 6 eds.*

_____. *A Tale of Two Cities.* See "The 18th-Century," page 47.

_____. *Great Expectations* (1861). Employing all the appurtenances of melodrama, Dickens manages to create a profoundly moving novel of symbolic import based on the rise, fall, and rise again of a humbly-born young orphan. *Over 15 eds.*

EDGEWORTH, MARIA 1767-1849. *Castle Rackrent* (1800). Told with verve and vivacity, this short novel shows the decline and fall of an aristocratic Irish family through three generations of riotous and un-reformed living habits. *Over 6 eds.*

ELIOT, GEORGE (MARY ANN EVANS) 1819-1880. *Adam Bede* (1859). The charm of the English countryside pervades this simple story of four young people: the uncorruptible workman, Adam Bede; the rich, pleasure-seeking squire; the romantic young woman desired by both; and the Methodist preacher, Dinah Morris, whose healing influence is felt by all. *Over 6 eds.*

_____. *The Mill on the Floss* (1860). An ugly duckling with a tragic end, Maggie Tulliver suffers for her difference both as duckling and as swan, expiates her "sin" through massive renunciation—of lover, friends, family, home—and finally dies to save the brother for whose love she thwarted and denied herself. *Over 6 eds.*

_____. *Middlemarch* (1872). A comprehensive and penetrating analysis of early Victorian provincial life, employing a multiple plot integrated by the character of Dorothea Brooke, whose splendid aspirations are initially defeated by her failure in self-knowledge and by her ignorance of the limits set by her society on female behavior and ideal achieve-ment. *Over 6 eds.*

GASKELL, ELIZABETH 1810-1865. *Mary Barton* (1848). One of the best of the 19th century's "protest novels," which extensively and realistically explore social problems, this novel examines in compelling detail the miserable living conditions of the poor and the hostile relations between masters and workers and recounts the life of a poor young woman caught in the dilemmas of being female in 19th-century England. *H—Dutton; P—Dutton, Norton, Penguin.*

GISSING, GEORGE 1857-1903. *The Odd Women* (1893). The "odd women" are those who, by choice or necessity, do not conform in their lives or temperaments to the ordinary Victorian conception of the role of women. In a moving and probing story of trouble and hardship, some run risks, and a few remain true to their perceptions of themselves and of their claim to equality. *H—AMS Pr.; P—Norton.*

HARDY, THOMAS 1840-1928. *Far from the Madding Crowd* (1874). Hardy depicts a society of rural people who must compromise their ideals and consume much of their vital energy before attaining some degree of contentment. *Over 6 eds.*

———. *The Return of the Native* (1878). A story of joy, sorrow, and defeat set against the somber background of Egdon Heath, which has a great influence on the lives of the characters. *Over 6 eds.*

———. *The Mayor of Casterbridge* (1886). A drunken man sells his wife and child to a stranger: such is the extraordinary opening scene in this nearly classical tragedy, which tells the story of a man of heroic ambition who achieves great success and then is thwarted and finally destroyed by the excess of his own character. *Over 6 eds.*

———. *Tess of the d'Urbervilles* (1891). The poignant tragedy of a young girl who grows into womanhood dogged by unhappiness and misfortune—beginning with seduction and ending with murder—for which she is only remotely responsible. *Over 10 eds.*

———. *Jude the Obscure* (1896). A shocking and powerful drama of a man and woman whose quests for intellectual fulfillment and emotional freedom are frustrated at every turn by past values, contemporary society, and their own limitations. *Over 6 eds.*

JAMES. See "19-Century American Novels," page 112.

KINGSLEY, CHARLES 1819-1875. *Westward Ho!* (1855). Bitterly anti-Jesuit, but an exciting historical romance of the time when Queen Elizabeth knighted sea captains for piracy against the Spaniards. *Over 6 eds.*

MEREDITH, GEORGE 1829-1909. *The Ordeal of Richard Feverel* (1859). The moving story of a young man "scientifically" educated by his misogynistic and dogmatic father and the disastrous effects of that education, on both young love and wholeness of being. *Over 6 eds.*

———. *The Egoist* (1879). High comedy in the prolix and convoluted Meredith manner. The story of a man whose solipsistic sense of self-importance is finally shattered by the women whom his aggressive selfishness has exploited, with consequences that arouse our delight and then, unexpectedly, our pity. *H—Oxford U Pr.*

MOORE, GEORGE 1852-1933. *Esther Waters* (1894). This novel, which introduced French Naturalism into England, is a sympathetic portrayal of lower-class life in the story of a servant whose brief enjoyment of life is overshadowed by overwhelming misfortune. *H—Liveright, Oxford U Pr; P—Dutton.*

READE. *The Cloister and the Hearth*. See "The Middle Ages," page 21.

SCOTT, SIR WALTER 1771-1832. For his ever-popular historical novels dealing with the Middle Ages, the Renaissance, and the 17th century, see pages 21, 33, 40.

SHELLEY, MARY WOLLSTONECRAFT 1797-1851. *Frankenstein* (1818). The most famous and one of the best of the gothic romances—a tale of terror, at times surprisingly poignant, in which a scientist stumbles onto the dangerous secret of breathing life into an eight-foot human figure he has constructed. *Over 10 eds.*

STEVENSON, ROBERT LOUIS 1850-1894. *Dr. Jekyll and Mr. Hyde* (1886). Pre-Freudian prototypical novel of the divided self. An absorbing story in which fantasy and romantic adventure are used to explore the irrational forces of evil to be found in the depths of even the most rational and humane scientist. *Over 6 eds.*

_____. *The Master of Ballantrae* (1889). Stevenson's best—a novel of character with a fast-moving and complicated plot of the success and failures of two aristocratic Scottish brothers whose bitter hatred for each other reaches a ghastly climax in the wilderness of America. *Over 6 eds.*

THACKERAY, WILLIAM MAKEPEACE 1811-1863. *Vanity Fair* (1847-48). A sometimes merry, nearly always biting satire, complete with large and lively comic scenes, and two nonheroines—one an extremely clever, engaging, but hardheaded (to some readers, hardhearted) plotter, the other a virtuous, sweet, but conventional and pallid young woman. Their alternating, interrelated fortunes are the basis for a searching judgment on society. *Over 6 eds.*

TROLLOPE, ANTHONY 1815-1882. *The Warden* (1855). A delightfully muddleheaded and generous old clergyman and those under his care are made miserable by a well-intentioned young reformer who raises a delicate ethical question. *Over 6 eds.*

_____. *Barchester Towers* (1857). A leisurely paced and gently satiric story about the petty gossip and sometimes involved intrigues of a small mid-19th-century English cathedral town is made especially attractive by the memorable characters created by Trollope. *Over 6 eds.*

WILDE, OSCAR 1854-1900. *The Picture of Dorian Gray* (1891). A modern-day Narcissus falls in love with his own beauty in a portrait. His demonic wish to remain young while the portrait ages is granted and he pursues a hedonistic and evil life that ends in horror. *Over 6 eds.*

20th-Century British Novels

Arthur Zeiger

In the decade preceding World War I some very impressive British novels were written: John Galsworthy's *The Man of Property* (1906), first volume of *The Forsyte Saga;* Arnold Bennett's *The Old Wives' Tale* (1908); H. G. Wells's *Tono-Bungay* (1909). Produced by perceptive novelists who respected truth and their craft, these are serious and substantial works.

Yet the younger novelists found them unsatisfying. Galsworthy had conceived his Philistine saga ironically, but in execution the iron melted. The author became the novelist member of the Forsyte family, esteeming them—and their solid possessions—almost as much as they did. Sentiment blurred his vision, and the Forsytes seem never wholly in focus.

Bennett built compacter, perhaps more durable, structures. In his best, most deeply felt novel, he placed two sisters against a drab industrial background—Bursley, one of the "five towns" of Staffordshire. He pictured their unlovely, joyless lives in immense and accurate detail, so that one knows all *about* them—but never quite *knows* them, never feels their life as they felt it. Like other naturalistic novels, *The Old Wives' Tale* impresses by its massed data, not by the immediacy with which it enables us to know the characters it describes.

H. G. Wells had formidable novelistic equipment: curiosity, intelligence, social conscience, fertility of invention, and an incapacity for dullness. Yet, proudly regarding himself as a journalist and deprecating the artist's role, he willfully sacrificed form to social reform. His people seem frequently to illustrate a thesis rather than to live even a fictitious life.

Admitting the virtues of Wells, Bennett, Galsworthy, and their industrious school, Virginia Woolf, the most articulate advocate of the opposition, denounced their resolute externality, their documentary materialistic bias, their refusal to immerse in the stream of consciousness. *To the Lighthouse* (1927) illuminates her structures. The author enters the consciousness of her characters, reproduces sensitively the quality and content of their feeling, and herself intrudes only obliquely. From the subtle, lambent prose, one deduces not only the characters and their relationships but also the environment itself. An admirable stylistic achievement, *To the Lighthouse* becomes at times impalpable and rarefied as the shadow of a flame. One admires, but longs for plot and incident, for more solidity, more substance.

Virginia Woolf did not, of course, inaugurate the subjective novel: she acknowledges two great ancestors, Henry James and James Joyce. James's involute sentences, which at first block the reader's progress and obscure the dramatic structure of his fiction by their dislocated clauses, fragmented phrases, displaced adverbs, piled-up punctuation, and wrenched rhythms, seem ultimately right; for they capture the delicate, fleeting, apparently ineluctable nuance of feeling. Joyce's mythic ordering of the flux of contemporary experience, his dedication to the word, his comic vision, and above all his power of rendering the inward life of his characters, make *Ulysses* a triumph of the introvertive method.

Because of the compelling examples of Joyce, James, and (to a lesser extent) Virginia Woolf, many novelists since have progressively shunned external reality, preferring instead to record—intensively, almost raptly—the feelings and thoughts it induces. The unhappy fact, however, is that the reality itself often attenuates or disintegrates. As practiced by most contemporary English writers, the novel has lost force and breadth (and readability) and gained technique. Writers in our time generally have turned their backs on the elements that vitalize technique.

But charting the development of the 20th century thus broadly, one inevitably distorts. A number of writers refuse to submit to facile classification. Two with whom Virginia Woolf associated herself in the revolt against the realistic and naturalistic novel, E. M. Forster and D. H. Lawrence, escape the perils incident to both the extrovertive and introvertive novel. Each novelist has a central, governing theme. Forster, beautifully, lucidly, penetrates the moral situation of our time, the difficulties we have "connecting" with one another, establishing truly human attitudes. Lawrence, in passionate, thrusting prose, probes the vital relationship between men and women, their failures to achieve fulfillment, the deepest longings of their subterranean beings.

Other names arise to undermine generalization concerning the progressive inwardness of the novel during this century. Aldous Huxley, Evelyn Waugh, and George Orwell attained notable success in satire, a genre that, requiring a definite credo, finds the climate of our divided age inhospitable. Nevertheless, Huxley, Waugh, and Orwell, men firmly grounded in belief (the first in Vedanta, the second in Roman Catholicism, the last in socialism), withstood the forces impelling to unbelief.

Finally, traditional novelists—novelists who have never abjured plot, chronology, climax, never renounced the world outside us from which presumably our impressions derive—have flourished. Somerset Maugham, an astute craftsman, has produced clever and extremely readable novels, though hardly anyone would claim that they were searching or powerful creations, enlarging our apprehension or increasing our sensibility. Christopher Isherwood has not realized the promise of his Berlin novels—penetrating, moving, prophetic evocations of pre-Hitler Germany; but *The Last of Mr. Norris* and *Goodbye to Berlin* stand, perhaps, as the best "social" fiction in this century. Graham Greene freights his well-made novels of suspense with theological insight—unlikely matter, but far from capsizing, it imparts gravity and dimension to them. Joyce Cary, nearly alone among the contemporaries, has dedicated his splendid novelistic abilities—a marvelous creative vigor, a warm and sympathetic insight into human imperfections, a flexible and resilient style—to celebrating the enduring, vaulting spirit.

Though C. P. Snow and Lawrence Durrell received most attention, the 1950s were dominated by the Angry Young Men—writers like Kingsley Amis, John Wain, J. P. Donleavy, Alan Sillitoe, and John Braine. "Angry" certainly seems an inappropriate designation for most of them: far more they were disaffected, disassociated, or "disaffiliated." No member of the group (whether he voluntarily enlisted or was dragooned by the critics) has yet published a great novel. And, in spite of their various excellences, the novels they have so far produced bear too marked a resemblance to one another.

While a literary critic with even minor qualifications as a prophet might have a decade earlier foreseen the remarkable increase of such phenomena as the long novel and the novel sequence, only one gifted with extraordinary clairvoyance could have divined the main course of English literature since 1960. The Angry Young Men have made their peace with things as they are; Amis and Braine, indeed, have migrated far to the right and now assault the currently estranged generation as vigorously (if not perhaps as cogently) as once they assaulted the old Establishment. Iris Murdoch, who seemed to have tenuous affinities with them, has seceded wholly: her novels in the "crystalline" mode, informed by myth and structured by symbol, strain to reveal the pattern of our existence—but without much anger. Doris Lessing, after her sustained and dedicated concentration on the social, political, and sexual realities of our discordant age, has digressed to Sufism, a variety of mysticism that hardly seems to gear with her essential talent. Neither the 1960s nor the 1970s have been notable for new directions nor brave achievements in the British novel. The years they embrace have been, rather, a period of novelistic stasis, of consolidation. The stillness may be deceptive; it may signalize, as recurrently in the novel's history, the gathering of force, the onset of a stirring age, a time when novels will once again show forth the shape and meaning of our lives through characters who inhabit the real world and are bound to it.

AMIS, KINGSLEY b. 1922. *Lucky Jim* (1954). A funny, at times cruel, story of a young, inept instructor on probation at an English college, his difficulties and fortunes in love. *P—Viking Pr.*

———. *One Fat Englishman* (1964). A destructive, immensely clever portrait of a "U-type" Englishman, whom some will loathe and others relish; it is also a sly critique of America and American ways. *H—HarBraceJ; P—Penguin.*

BECKETT. *Molloy*. See "20th-Century Continental Novels," page 88.

BEERBOHM, MAX 1872-1956. *Zuleika Dobson* (1911). Undergraduate Oxford is disrupted by the maddening beauty of Zuleika in this deft comic fantasy. *o.p.*

BENNETT, ARNOLD 1867-1931. *The Old Wives' Tale* (1908). Slowly, almost imperceptibly, the grimy Midlands town presses life from Sophia and Constance Baines. *o.p.*

BOWEN, ELIZABETH 1899-1973. *The Death of the Heart* (1938). A deeply moving tragedy of adolescence, brought about by adult cruelty and insensitivity. *H—Knopf; P—Random.*

BRAINE, JOHN b. 1922. *Room at the Top* (1957). A brilliant chronicle of the fortunes—and ultimate misfortune—of a young man who knows all prices but no values. *P—NAL.*

BURGESS, ANTHONY b. 1917. *A Clockwork Orange* (1962). Remarkable for its linguistic virtuosity, this antiutopian novel relentlessly presses its alternatives: a world in which men and women possess free will and are cruel, inhuman, bad; or one in which they have been deprived of free will and are powerless to do evil, inhuman, "good." *H—Knopf; P—Bantam, Norton.*

CARY, JOYCE 1888-1957. *The Horse's Mouth* (1944). Last and best of a trilogy including *Herself Surprised* (1941) and *To Be a Pilgrim* (1942). Exuberant history of Gulley Jimson, visionary painter and outrageous person, told by himself. (In the other volumes, Sarah, his beloved, and Wilcher, his lawyer rival, tell their complementary stories.) *H—Har-Row.*

COMPTON-BURNETT, IVY b. 1892. *Bullivant and the Lambs* (1948). A comedy of manners, couched in antinaturalistic epigrammatic dialogue, involving a stingy father, his sinister children, and Bullivant, the butler, who never loses control. *o.p.*

CONRAD, JOSEPH 1857-1924. *The Nigger of the Narcissus* (1897). Extraordinary delineation of a common man of the sea. *H—Doubleday; P—Penguin.*

———. *Lord Jim* (1900). The hero suffers dishonor through cowardice; he atones, endures heroic defeat, and gains redemption. *Over 10 eds.*

———. *Heart of Darkness* (1902). A short novel revealing the heart's darkness, deeper than Africa's. *Over 6 eds.*

———. *Nostromo* (1904). An intricately structured political novel, recounting in full detail the genesis and course of a South America revolution and pointing up the corrupting power of silver. *P—HR&W, NAL, Penguin.*

DONLEAVY. *The Ginger Man*. See "20th-Century American Novels," page 121.

DOUGLAS, NORMAN 1868-1952. *South Wind* (1917). Amusing, cynical symposium on conventional morality. The setting is a Mediterranean island whose shifting winds effect shifts in moral values among its visitors. *H—Int Pubns Serv, Scholarly; P—Penguin.*

DURRELL, LAWRENCE b. 1912. *Justine* (1957), *Balthazar* (1958), *Mountolive* (1959), and *Clea* (1960). A stunning baroque "Quartet" of novels about Alexandria—the shimmering, monstrous, beautiful, unreal city—and the "truth" about some exotic people who live there told from shifting perspectives. *H—Dutton; P—Dutton, PB.*

FORD, FORD MADOX (FORD MADOX HUEFFER) 1873-1939. *The Good Soldier* (1915). A subtle, beautifully duplicitous account, told by an "obtuse narrator" (or are the readers obtuse?) of four people who moved together with an intimacy that seemed "like a minuet"—until the music shattered. *P—Random.*

_____. *Parade's End* (1924-28). A tetralogy comprising The Tietjens Saga, in which "the last Tory" emerges from manifold tribulations (World War I merely one of them) into the modern world—where he has no place. *H—Knopf.*

FORSTER, E. M. 1879-1970. *The Longest Journey* (1907). A sensitive young man regularly accepts illusion for reality, an error that leads to a destroying marriage and ultimate destruction. *P—Random.*

_____. *A Passage to India* (1924). Focusing on a dramatic situation, this philosophical novel explores the tensions between the English and the Indians—and, symbolically, other, more basic tensions as well. *H & P—HarBraceJ.*

FOWLES, JOHN b. 1926. *The Magus* (1966) and *The French Lieutenant's Woman* (1969). Completely captivating narratives with strong story lines and deliberately ambiguous shadings. *H—Little; P—Dell, NAL.*

GALSWORTHY, JOHN 1867-1933. *The Forsyte Saga* (1906-21). A series of 12 novels affectionately centering on a large, wealthy, middle-class family from 1886 to 1920, and tracing the effect on them of property and the possessive instinct. *H—Scribner.*

GOLDING, WILLIAM b. 1911. *Lord of the Flies* (1954). "Boys will be boys"—which, Golding implies in this brilliant, merciless allegory, means they will be, quite literally, savage. *H—Coward; P—Putnam.*

GREEN, HENRY (HENRY VINCENT YORKE) 1905-1973. *Loving* (1945). A comic-pathetic realistic novel, set against a romantic Irish background; the story concerns the love of Edith, a housemaid, for Raunce, a butler. *H—Dufour.*

GREENE, GRAHAM b. 1904. *Brighton Rock* (1938). One of Greene's "entertainments," involving pursuit, gang warfare, and murder—encompassed by terror and informed with theological doctrine. *H—Viking Pr; P—Bantam, Viking Pr.*

_____. *The Heart of the Matter* (1948). A "theological thriller," but equally a tale of frustrated goodness and thwarted love. *P—Viking Pr.*

HUDSON, W. H. 1841-1922. *Green Mansions* (1904). Romantic tale, set in the tropical forests of South America, recounting the ill-starred love of Rima, the "bird-girl," and the narrator, Mr. Abel. *Over 6 eds.*

HUGHES, RICHARD 1900-1976. *A High Wind in Jamaica* (also titled *The Innocent Voyage*) (1929). A revealing study of the separate world of childhood; a group of children, captured by pirates, undergo a violent voyage into experience. *H—Watts; P—Har-Row.*

HUXLEY, ALDOUS 1894-1963. *Point Counter Point* (1928). Through "parallel contrapuntal plots," Huxley atomizes the upper-class world in pursuit of "pleasure"—sensuality, debauchery, parasitism, and purposelessness. *H & P—Har-Row.*

_____. ***Brave New World*** (1932). Satire on the mechanized, dehumanized world of the future; the time is 632 A.F. (After Ford). *H—Har-Row; P—Bantam, Har-Row.*

ISHERWOOD, CHRISTOPHER b. 1904. ***The Berlin Stories*** (1946). Two short novels that hauntingly evoke Berlin in the five years before Hitler—its degeneration, futility, ominous brutality. Source of the musical *Cabaret. P—New Directions.*

JOYCE, JAMES 1882-1941. ***Portrait of the Artist as a Young Man*** (1916). A semiautobiographical "novel of initiation": the young artist strives to gain his freedom—from religion, country, family—to practice his art untrammeled. *H & P—Viking Pr.*

_____. ***Ulysses*** (1922). Ostensibly the record of a single day filtered through the consciousness of Leopold Bloom and Stephen Dedalus; but more than that, a great comic-epic poem, a paradigm of modern man's search for values. *H—Modern Lib, Random; P—Random.*

KIPLING, RUDYARD 1865-1936. ***Kim*** (1901). A vivid picture of India and its people is given in this exciting tale of secret-service activity. *Over 6 eds.*

LAWRENCE, D. H. 1885-1930. ***Sons and Lovers*** (1913). A semiauto-biographical novel, powerfully dramatizing the sexually inhibiting force of excessive mother-love. *Over 6 eds.*

_____. ***The Rainbow*** (1915). An analysis (sometimes concrete, sometimes mystical) of the nature of sexuality, divisive and unifying—and ultimately insufficient. *P—Penguin, Viking Pr.*

_____. ***Lady Chatterley's Lover*** (1928). Long censored because of the author's unreticent description of the processes of passionate love, the novel seems old-fashioned today in spite of the plain language but is still valid as a study in contrasts—industrialism versus "nature," the decadent upper class versus the vigorous lower. *H—Modern Lib; P—Bantam, Grove, NAL.*

LESSING, DORIS b. 1919. ***Children of Violence*** (1965-69). Five novels tracing the movement through several hells—social, political, and emotional—of Martha Quest, beginning in "Zambesia" before World War II and ending in an apocalyptic fate. Occasionally tedious, ultimately rewarding. *H—Knopf; P—Bantam, NAL.*

LOWRY, MALCOLM 1909-1957. ***Under the Volcano*** (1947). A powerful phantasmagoric novel, "a vision of hell," centering on the last day in the life of a British consul in Mexico, whose compulsive drinking has led to his total alienation. *H—Lippincott; P—NAL.*

MAUGHAM, W. SOMERSET 1874-1965. ***Of Human Bondage*** (1915). An engrossing "educational novel," based on the author's life: the hero comes to the realization of his individual identity through suffering, defeat, and tragic love. *Over 6 eds.*

_____. ***The Moon and Sixpence*** (1919). This *roman à clef* (the prototype of the hero is Paul Gauguin, the French impressionist painter) tells of an artist whose only morality is in his art. *P—PB.*

MURDOCH, IRIS b. 1919. ***The Flight from the Enchanter*** (1956). Fascinating simply as story, this symbolic "fantasia" centers on a

group of Londoners drawn into the orbit of the powerful, shadowy enchanter, Mischa Fox, and on how each suffers change or extinction.
P—Warner Bks.

———. *A Severed Head* (1961). A "metaphysical examination of love,"
in its several varieties, through shock narrative. *P—Viking Pr.*

NAIPAUL, V. S. b. 1932. *A House for Mr. Biswas* (1961). A long, densely
populated, richly comic novel about Mohun Biswas' determination to
give shape (by owning his own home) to an apparently shapeless existence in colonial India. *P—Penguin.*

———. *Guerrillas* (1975). Loosely based on the actual murder of an
Englishwoman in Trinidad, Naipaul's novel is set vaguely in the
Caribbean. The internal landscape is—though never slavishly—
Conradian: dark, turbulent, profoundly revealing of psychic torment
and despair. *H—Knopf; P—Ballantine.*

O'FLAHERTY, LIAM b. 1897. *The Informer* (1926). Dublin during "the
Trouble" is the scene; what passed through the mind of a man who
betrayed his best friend to the English enemy. *P—NAL.*

ORWELL, GEORGE 1903-1950. *Animal Farm* (1945). Brilliant satirical
allegory on dictatorship, especially on its penchant for devouring its
own. *H—HarBraceJ; P—NAL.*

———. *1984* (1949). A nightmare projection of a future police-state
ruled by "Big Brother," where "War Is Peace" and all values are trans-
valued. *H—HarBraceJ; P—NAL.*

PATON. *Cry, the Beloved Country*. See "Africa," page 67.

POWELL, ANTHONY b. 1905. *A Dance to the Music of Time* (1951-73).
An 11-volume sequence (which Powell regards as a single novel)
chronicling urbanely and wittily the adventures of Nicholas Jenkins
and his odd friends, most very upper-class, from before the wars to
the recent past. The first installment, *A Question of Upbringing* (1951),
is perhaps the best place to begin. *H—Little; P—Popular Lib.*

PRIESTLEY, J. B. b. 1894. *The Good Companions* (1929). Long, divert-
ing, picaresque tale involving a troupe of wandering English players.
H—Har-Row.

RHYS, JEAN b. 1894? *Quartet* (1928). *Good Morning, Midnight* (1939),
and *Wide Sargasso Sea* (1966). Lately emerged, extraordinarily popular novels—but one may be enough for most readers. Each novel
chronicles the downward spiral (always downward) of a woman
deceived, humiliated, rejected. *H—Har-Row.*

SILLITOE, ALAN b. 1928. *Saturday Night and Sunday Morning* (1958).
The career of a young worker, trapped by the system and angry with it,
described authentically from a proletarian (even a lumpenproletarian)
point of view. *H—Knopf; P—NAL.*

———. *The Loneliness of the Long-Distance Runner* (1959). A short
novel, the quintessence of "disaffiliation," about a Borstal reform
school boy who deliberately refuses to win a race—rejecting any
triumph, no matter how gratifying, which gratifies the authorities as
well. *H—Knopf; P—NAL.*

SNOW, C. P. b. 1905. *Strangers and Brothers* (1940-70). An 11-volume
sequence that forms the fictional biography of Lewis Eliot, an English

lawyer, in his wanderings in the "corridors of power." An absorbing entry into the sequence is *The Masters* (1951), a realistic and poignant account of the election of a new master to a Cambridge college. *P— Scribner.*

SPARK, MURIEL b. 1918. *Memento Mori* (1959). A group of oldsters, their prepossessions and prejudices merely ossified by time, take brief positions in this funny and sad dance of death. *P—Avon.*

TOLKIEN, J. R. R. 1892-1973. *The Lord of the Rings* (1954-56). This trilogy, enormously popular with undergraduates (and others), consists of *The Fellowship of the Ring, The Two Towers*, and *The Return of the King*. The three novels describe the perilous exploits of two extraordinary hobbits, Frodo and Sam, their valiant efforts to destroy a ring and with it the power of the Dark Lord: at once an allegory, a heroic romance, a moral mythology, a fairy story, a repository of elf-lore, a fascinating language game, and, above all, an engrossing adventure story. *H—HM; P—Ballantine.*

WAUGH, EVELYN 1903-1966. *A Handful of Dust* (1934). A satire of the contemporary wasteland: the career of Tony Last, the man of goodwill, ends in tragic-absurd fashion, as captive reader to a Dickens-loving lunatic. *P—Dell.*

_____. *Brideshead Revisited* (1945). A muted satirist in this novel written from a Catholic stance, Waugh presents dissipation, boredom, and insurmountable hopelessness as the only alternative to faith and works. *o.p.*

WELLS, H. G. 1866-1946. *Tono Bungay* (1908). Vigorous history of the rise and fall of the promoters of a patent-medicine fraud, with perceptive sidelights on the evils commercialism breeds. *P—HM.*

WHITE, PATRICK b. 1912. *Voss* (1957). A dramatic multidimensional novel, set in 19th-century Australia but shedding a wide radiance. The most memorable work of an Australian Nobel Prize winner. *H—Viking Pr; P—Avon.*

WILSON, ANGUS b. 1913. *Anglo-Saxon Attitudes* (1956). A witty and corrosive satire, centering on the ranging reactions of a scholar who discovers a fraud—a heathen idol buried in the tomb of a Saxon bishop. *P—Popular Lib.*

WOOLF, VIRGINIA 1882-1941. *To the Lighthouse* (1927). From shifting centers of consciousness, this beautifully textured symbolic novel shows rather than describes Mrs. Ramsey and her widening effect (even after she has died) on the lives that touch hers. *H & P—HarBraceJ.*

_____. *Orlando* (1928). The hero turns heroine in this pseudobiography, which is also a survey of England's history and literature since Elizabethan times. *P—HarBraceJ.*

19th-Century American Novels

Daniel Gerzog

Cultural independence is harder to win than political independence. It took the American novel almost three-quarters of a century after 1776 to finish its own struggle for liberty. Not until the middle of the 19th century can it be said to have completely freed itself of English apronstrings. In the meantime, scores of fictional early-American heroines relived the moral anguish of Richardson's Pamela, and as many Yankee Robinson Crusoes survived the hazards of primitive existence. Charles Brockden Brown transported Godwin's gothic settings to the outskirts of Philadelphia, and H. H. Brackenridge fashioned a Pennsylvania Don Quixote and an Irish Sancho Panza, set them on the western frontier, and acknowledged the debt his satire owed to Fielding and Swift. Some of these early attempts have their excellent moments, but none is an enduring work of art.

The first important American novelist, James Fenimore Cooper, consciously imitated Sir Walter Scott. Because America lacked knights in full panoply and the romance of the Highlands, he exploited the closest parallels—the frontier, with its "noble savages" and dauntless pioneers; and the Revolution, with its larger-than-life heroes on both land and sea. Like Scott, Cooper created some unforgettable scenes and characters, but his adventure stories are best read in adolescence. Mature readers have found, however, that the Cooper novels concerned with American social problems—*The Pioneers* and *The Prairie* (the best of the Leatherstocking series); and the "Rent-War" trilogy, especially *Satanstoe*—yield rewarding if highly opinionated insights into the growing pains of our turbulent formative years.

Whereas the American novel can be said to have started slowly and imitatively, it came of age in that creative flowering of the early 1850s that has come to be known as the first American renaissance. In successive years two of the greatest novels in any nation's literature were published—Hawthorne's *The Scarlet Letter* and Melville's *Moby Dick*.

Not only had America discovered a subject matter in its own past and present, but it had found a form in which to present it. Although both novels are, in the broadest sense, romances (neither Hawthorne's Salem nor Melville's *Pequod* is a world that ever was), both men create out of the materials of romance rich fabrics of highly complex symbolism, woven through with dark threads of enigmatic moral and metaphysical inquiry. In Melville's words, they "dove deep" and surfaced with treasures that lie unseen by those who swim in the shallows of human awareness. Because Hawthorne and Melville raised troublesome questions in an essentially optimistic age, neither was fully appreciated in his day. But in our darker times they are rightly considered two of the giants of American—and world—letters. The depth of psychological insight and the profundity of theme in these novels will sustain the reader through several rereadings and many hours of reflection.

Hawthorne went on to write other provocative romances, but he never again achieved the economy of expression and tightness of form that elevate *The Scarlet Letter* and the best of his short stories to the highest level of literary accomplishment.

Moby Dick marks the high point of Melville's output. Of the five novels he produced in the five years before its publication, four are fictionalized accounts of his adventures at sea. One, *Mardi*, does attempt the philosophic scope of his masterpiece, but fails to achieve its dramatic and poetic power. After *Moby Dick*, Melville's somber vision produced two more novels, but neither strikes the happy balance between exciting realism and significant speculation that we experience following Ahab in search of the white whale. Late in life, in the short novel *Billy Budd*, Melville again used shipboard life as a microcosm to illuminate humanity's metaphysical dilemma. Read with sensitivity to its author's sharp satiric bent and powerful irony, it reaffirms the dark genius of the mind that spawned America's greatest novel.

The strength that the romance had achieved with Hawthorne and Melville was dissipated over the next two or three decades. The serious literary figures from 1830 to 1870—perhaps still intimidated by the Puritan skepticism of "storytelling"—wrote poetry or essays. The novelists ground out precursors of today's sentimental soap operas. *Little Women* illustrates the type, although it far surpasses in quality the trivial productions it foreshadowed. From this genre, too, came *Uncle Tom's Cabin*, important for its immense effect on the antislavery movement. We might pause to consider *Elsie Venner* by Dr. Oliver Wendell Holmes, whose medical interest in the nature of the mind and in the moral and social problems raised by psychological determinism has new significance in our post-Freudian times. But not until the novel received vital transfusions from two regenerative springs did it regain its lost power.

The United States emerged as a nation from the Civil War, and with the awareness of wider vistas came the desire to create real pictures of the sprawling country. The best of the "local color" writing appeared in short stories, but at least one of the novels arising from the movement, G. W. Cable's *The Grandissimes*, etches sharp portraits not only of individuals but of the impact of slavery and miscegenation on the culture of antebellum New Orleans. The movement helped encourage Mark Twain to write the novels whose wit, humor, and sharp social and political satire dominate the last quarter of the century. In his greatest novel, *Huckleberry Finn*, we travel down the mainstream of the nation on a raft—seeing not only the Mississippi but the world with the eyes and mind of a wise-innocent boy through whose vision Mark Twain forces us to question our basic assumptions about society. Twain chose satire as his weapon to attack the far-from-idyllic America of the 1870s and 1880s. Although he can hardly be called gentle or subtle, until late in his life he always made his readers laugh at what angered him.

The second powerful influence brought with it the seeds of a much harsher form of social criticism. William Dean Howells, who had spent the war years in Italy, brought home the gospel of literary realism. Howells was primarily concerned that the novel reflect a true image of the situations it portrayed. He wrote in conformity with his doctrine, observing carefully, but rarely penetrating the surface of what he saw. Perhaps more important than his novels was his pervasive influence as editor and literary critic. He praised, justly, De Forest's *Miss Ravenel's Conversion* for its realistic scenes; encouraged writers as different as Henry James and Mark Twain; and fought to gain public acceptance for younger writers like Garland, Crane, Norris, and the first important Black American novelist, Charles W. Chesnutt.

This new realism took vastly divergent paths. Henry James used it as a magnifying glass for in-depth explorations of human consciousness in novels that are subtle, carefully wrought studies of the motivations and interactions of real people. But for the younger group, the new realism was a harsh white spotlight to be cast, in the manner of Zola, into the dark corners of the contemporary scene. Stephen Crane wrote *Maggie* in 1893 and *The Red Badge of Courage* in 1895. Norris was soon to follow with *McTeague* and Dreiser with *Sister Carrie* in 1900.

The troublesome social and economic conditions that had prompted Twain's satire and Bellamy's utopian prescription in *Looking Backward* gave rise to a full-fledged literature of protest, which carried the American novel into its position of dominance as a literary form in the 20th century.

ALCOTT, LOUISA MAY 1832-1888. *Little Women* (1868). A sentimental story of domestic life in New England. The characters exude a certain charm but live life as we'd like it to be rather than as it is. *Over 12 eds.*

BELLAMY, EDWARD 1850-1898. *Looking Backward* (1888). One of the most popular utopian romances in English: a vision of our nation in the year 2000, showing how economic planning and nationalization of industry can create prosperity of both body and spirit. *Over 6 eds.*

CABLE, GEORGE WASHINGTON 1844-1925. *The Grandissimes* (1880). Episodic but rich, sensitive treatment of the New Orleans of the year of the Louisiana Purchase, by a man who loved the South while repudiating its values. *H—Peter Smith; P—Hill & Wang.*

COOPER, JAMES FENIMORE 1789-1851. *The Pioneers* (1823). The earliest and least idealized of the Leatherstocking tales. Cooper's pioneer hero, Natty Bumppo, past middle age, struggles against the encroachments of civilization on the New York State frontier in 1793. *H—Dutton; P—Airmont, HR&W, NAL, WSP.*

_____. *The Prairie* (1827). The most lasting of the Leatherstocking series—tied together by the force of the Great Plains themselves. Natty Bumppo lives out his last days reflecting on and waiting for death among a cast of characters that ranges the social gamut from naked Indian to born-to-the-blood aristocrat. *P—Airmont, NAL.*

_____. *Satanstoe* (1845). The first novel in a trilogy that presents the author's brief for the necessity of a landed aristocracy. In this story of the youthful adventures of Cornelius Littlepage, colonial life on three social levels is vividly portrayed. *P—U of Nebr Pr.*

CRANE, STEPHEN 1871-1900. *Maggie: A Girl of the Streets* (1893). A short, impressionistic novel about a young New York streetwalker. Social protest etched in the acid of bitter irony. *P—Airmont, Fawcett World, WSP.*

_____. *The Red Badge of Courage* (1895). This Civil War story divests that over-romanticized war—or any war—of much of its false glory. So vivid that its readers cannot believe that Crane had never known war first hand, yet subtly symbolic and far-reaching in its implications. *Over 25 eds.*

DE FOREST, JOHN WILLIAM 1826-1906. *Miss Ravenel's Conversion from Secession to Loyalty* (1867). A surprisingly realistic novel of manners, delineating characters neither good nor bad, and projecting a well-balanced view of the Civil War. *H—Brown Bk., Peter Smith; P— Brown Bk.*

FREDERIC, HAROLD 1856-1898. *The Damnation of Theron Ware* (1896). The story of a Methodist minister whose superficial faith, based on self-satisfaction, crumbles as he begins to see more deeply. By implication, the story symbolizes America's loss of innocence. *H— Peter Smith; P—Harvard U Pr, HR&W.*

HAWTHORNE, NATHANIEL 1804-1864. *The Scarlet Letter*. See "The 17th Century," page 40.

_____. *The House of the Seven Gables* (1851). A novel about sinister hereditary influences within an old New England family, sunnier than Hawthorne's other works despite its grim subject. *Over 12 eds.*

_____. *The Marble Faun* (1860). The Fall of Adam reset amidst the ruins and art treasures of Rome. *H—Ohio St U Pr; P—Airmont, NAL.*

HOLMES, OLIVER WENDELL 1809-1894. *Elsie Venner* (1861). A young woman's struggle with a hereditary moral flaw raises important questions of moral and social responsibility in a novel that would be greater if it had a less creaky structure. *o.p.*

HOWELLS, WILLIAM DEAN 1837-1920. *A Modern Instance* (1882). A realistic study of average people, a young newspaperman and his wife, and of their marital difficulties. *P—HM.*

_____. *The Rise of Silas Lapham* (1885). A self-made man chooses not to recoup his losses at the expense of others and thus "rises" morally if not socially and financially. Made less trite than the plot line would suggest by Howells' careful attention to realistic detail and characterization. *Over 6 eds.*

_____. *A Hazard of New Fortunes* (1890). Howells' best novel, written when his moral outrage at the injustices of industrial conflict had driven him toward a Tolstoian socialism. A personal experience with socio-economic injustice awakens the novel's protagonist to his total involvement with his fellow men. *H—Ind U Pr; P—NAL.*

JAMES, HENRY 1843-1916. *The American* (1877). Wealthy, capable, candid Christopher Newman goes to Paris to "live" and to get a wife who would be "the best article on the market." An early novel, direct in style, and a good introduction to James. *Over 6 eds.*

_____. *The Portrait of a Lady* (1881). Isabel Archer, the counterpart of Christopher Newman, hopes to find in Europe the best of life and men. Another incisive contrast of American and European types and codes. *Over 10 eds.*

_____. *The Turn of the Screw* (1898). A fascinating psychological ghost story. *Over 6 eds.*

_____. *The Wings of the Dove* (1902). Kate Croy and Merton Densher weave a subtle scheme to enmesh the American heiress Milly Theale, who surprisingly reveals them to themselves in a complicated psychological novel with a background of stately London residences, shabby lodging houses, and twisting Venetian canals. *Over 6 eds.*

_____. *The Ambassadors* (1903). James's richest novel, contrasting the European and American traditions. Slowly, slowly, in a novel of great psychological suspense, the American Lambert Strether falls under the spell of the liberal European way of life and sheds his new-world provincialism. *Over 10 eds.*

_____. *The Golden Bowl* (1905). In this story set in Victorian London, a beautiful but flawed golden bowl symbolizes the marriage of the Italian prince Amerigo and the wealthy American girl Maggie Verver, who eventually surmounts all difficulties in another working out of James's "international theme." *Over 6 eds.*

MELVILLE, HERMAN 1819-1891. *Typee* (1846). A fictionalized account of Melville's stay in the Marquesas Islands. Chiefly descriptive of the islanders' simple and lovely way of life and critical of Western ways. *Over 6 eds.*

_____. *Omoo* (1847). Well-developed episodes and 20 characters sharply realized as Melville recounts in fictional form his Tahiti adventures. *H—Hendricks House; P—Northwestern U Pr.*

_____. *Moby Dick* (1851). A rich, complex, highly symbolic narrative which explores the deepest reaches of our moral and metaphysical dilemma at the same time that it tells a gripping, realistic sea story. A paean to the human spirit which nevertheless faces up to its darker, less comforting side. Perhaps Melville raises more questions than he answers, but this is as it should be in the highest order of literary art. Soaring poetic prose, dramatic conflict, unforgettable character-izations—in a book to be read and reread. *Over 20 unabr. eds.*

_____. *Billy Budd* (c. 1891, pub. 1924). Goaded beyond endurance, Adam-like Billy strikes down his satanic persecutor and is executed in a scene suggesting the Crucifixion in this ironic quasi-allegory of human and divine justice. *Over 10 eds.*

NORRIS, FRANK 1870-1902. *McTeague* (1899). A realistic study of the disintegration of character, ending in murder. *Over 6 eds.*

_____. *The Octopus* (1901). The story of battles between California wheat growers and the intruding railroad "octopus" is the beginning volume of a naturalistic trilogy Norris never completed. *Over 6 eds.*

STOWE, HARRIET BEECHER 1811-1896. *Uncle Tom's Cabin* (1852). Powerful antislavery propaganda. The prose is dated but the characters are surprisingly vivid, especially when contrasted with stereotypes from later stage versions. *Over 10 eds.*

TWAIN, MARK (SAMUEL LANGHORNE CLEMENS) 1835-1910. *The Adventures of Tom Sawyer* (1876). This book for young and old pictures the life of boys in little, lazy Hannibal, Missouri, contrasting their superficial cussedness with their inner decency. *Over 15 eds.*

_____. *Adventures of Huckleberry Finn* (1885). Mark Twain's imagination elevates this tale of a boy seeking freedom on a raft he shares with a runaway slave into a true comic epic of American life. Huck—who sees the world with a marvelous combination of wisdom and innocence—tells his own story in a direct, colloquial idiom that is a perfect vehicle for Mark Twain's social satire. *Over 20 eds.*

_____. *A Connecticut Yankee in King Arthur's Court* (1889). A modern American finds himself among the Knights of the Round Table and discovers that Yankee ingenuity is more than a match for medieval magic and superstition. *Over 6 eds.*

_____. *Pudd'nhead Wilson* (1894). A nonconformist too wise for his backwoods community, Wilson solves several mysteries. Partly a triumph of bitter humor, partly a daring treatment of miscegenation. *Over 6 eds.*

20th-Century American Novels

Arthur Waldhorn

1900–1945

During the first five years of the new century, Henry James published a trio of novels (*The Wings of the Dove, The Ambassadors*, and *The Golden Bowl*) exquisite in psychological and moral perception (see "19th-Century American Novels"). James's refined achievement left sparse opportunity for immediate literary descendants. American fiction had urgent need for new voices, harsher and coarser perhaps, but more consonant with the rough energy of American life.

Theodore Dreiser was the first of these voices to be heard. For more than twenty years after he published *Sister Carrie* in 1900, Dreiser sounded his gloomy message that natural and social forces shape and direct human affairs—or, characteristically, misshape and misdirect them. What he lacked in stylistic grace and precision he made up in epic abundance of detail and a craggy sincerity. However plodding and awkward his lengthy accounts of the sordid, his acute reportorial vision and his profound compassion for humanity affected generations of realistic and naturalistic American writers—from Jack London to Erskine Caldwell and Richard Wright.

A more able craftsman than Dreiser, Sherwood Anderson recorded the impact of inward as well as environmental forces, zeroing in on his characters' bewildered groping as they grappled with the vast emptiness of life in the corn belt.

Others focused their critical vision on regional centers. Upton Sinclair explored the slums of Chicago's South Side; Sinclair Lewis fixed narrowly on tribal manners among midwestern small-town and small-city ritualists; and Thomas Wolfe rhapsodized about his childhood in Asheville, North Carolina. Edith Wharton perceived the excesses of elegant urbanites, and Ellen Glasgow scanned and satirized the foibles of her fellow Virginians.

Some novelists stumbled beyond the geographical limits of their material into cosmic regions. Thus, Willa Cather achieved a profound sense of human experience in her portrait of the Nebraskan prairies and of those who live and work on them. And no American novelist of this century has more wholly captured a region at once particular and universal than has William Faulkner. His mythic

Yoknapatawpha County, Mississippi, site of most of his novels and stories, is populated by Indians, Black servants, laborers, and farm-workers, decadent Southern aristocrats, and shrewd, amoral carpet-baggers. But Faulkner's people and themes are not merely Southern; instead, they are universal and timeless—all humanity and its sense of unexpiated guilt; its struggle with nature; and its agonized effort to reconcile values past and present.

During the great years of the 1920s, when much of America's best fiction of the century was written, two of the most famous pub-lic literary figures—Ernest Hemingway and F. Scott Fitzgerald—wrote their finest work too, each memorializing the impact of the "lost generation," that Jazz Age outcropping of shattered idealism and morality that exploded lives into myriad paths, most of them dead ends.

By the end of the 1930s—whose sordid record of economic de-pression and social unrest were most effectively recorded by John Dos Passos, John Steinbeck, and James Farrell—America was again ready for new voices. But they would not be heard until the din of war had receded.

ANDERSON, SHERWOOD 1876-1941. *Winesburg, Ohio* (1919). In the vein of Edwin Arlington Robinson's Tilbury Town of New England and of Edgar Lee Master's Midwestern Spoon Rover, this unified medley of tales—Anderson's finest work—is the prose equivalent of those poems, a gallery portrait of the frustrated men and women of a small town at the end of the last century. *H & P—Viking Pr.*

_____. *Poor White* (1920). A novel emblematic of the arrival of the indus-trial revolution in the Middle West, this is the story of Hugh McVey, the Lincolnian and Huck Finn-like folk-hero inventor, and of his attempt to launch a successful marriage. *o.p.*

CALDWELL, ERSKINE b. 1903. *God's Little Acre* (1933). The Georgia mountaineer, Ty Ty Walden, and his daughters Rosamund and Darling Jill are the hilariously grotesque central characters of this notable American folk comedy. *H—Norton; P—NAL.*

CATHER, WILLA 1873-1947. *My Antonia* (1918). The red grass and white snows of the Nebraska prairies provide the scenery of this compelling story of a 19th-century immigrant and her American friends. *H & P—HM.*

_____. *The Professor's House* (1925). There are two houses in Pro-fessor St. Peter's life, and two worlds representing different values, in this impressive scrutiny of American civilization in terms of a family's experiences. *H—Knopf; P—Random.*

DOS PASSOS, JOHN 1896-1970. *U.S.A.* (1937). A powerful trilogy, includ-ing *The 42nd Parallel* (1930); *1919* (1932); and *The Big Money* (1936), of disillusion with the American dream. Dos Passos' "four-eyed vision"—an amalgam of diverse narrative techniques—adds dramatic force to his tale of ordinary and famous Americans during the first three decades of the 20th century. *H—HM.*

DREISER, THEODORE 1871-1945. *Sister Carrie* (1900). Carrie Meeber drifts upward—from poverty in Chicago to fame on the New York stage in the 1890s. The decline of her lover, Hurstwood, establishes a moving counterpoint. *Over 6 eds.*

_____. *The Financier* (1912). The best of his "Trilogy of Desire" based on the career of the Chicago robber-baron Charles Yerkes. The famous scene of a lobster devouring a squid sets the tone for Frank Cowperwood's rise to power in finance and sex. The succeeding volumes, *The Titan* (1914) and *The Stoic* (published posthumously, 1947) suffer from excessive documenting and flaccid philosophizing. *P—NAL.*

_____. *An American Tragedy* (1925). Drawn from an actual murder case, the story of Clyde Griffith's hollow dreams and nightmare reality is overly long but still gripping. Is Clyde's fall a tragedy of his failure of will or of the American way of success? *P—Apollo Eds, NAL.*

FARRELL, JAMES T. b. 1904. *Studs Lonigan* (1935). The overwrought but forceful Lonigan trilogy, including *Young Lonigan* (1932), *The Young Manhood of Studs Lonigan* (1934), and *Judgment Day* (1935), tells the story of the middle-class Irish on Chicago's South Side, particularly of the degenerating effects of school, church, and family upon the weak, bragging Studs in the years between World War I and the depression. *P—Avon.*

FAULKNER, WILLIAM 1897-1962. *The Sound and the Fury* (1929). A superb evocation of the decay and degeneration of a Southern family. Technically complex, its devices—stream-of-consciousness, multiple points of view, dislocated time sequence, and symbolism—nevertheless reward an attentive reader with a memorable image of human fate. *H & P—Modern Lib, Random.*

_____. *As I Lay Dying* (1930). The Bundren family takes the ripening corpse of Addie, wife and mother, on a gruesomely comic journey that is interrupted by such elemental matters as fire and flood. *H—Modern Lib, Random; P—Random.*

_____. *Light in August* (1932). A profound and violent tale of isolation and endurance. Of the people Faulkner studies here, Joe Christmas is the most affecting in his complex and fatal quest for a reason for living. *H & P—Modern Lib, Random.*

_____. *Absalom, Absalom!* (1936). The Civil War, miscegenation, and murder run through this macabre and complex story of a decadent Southern family. *H & P—Modern Lib, Random.*

FITZGERALD, F. SCOTT 1896-1940. *The Great Gatsby* (1925). A major scrutiny of American values through the experiences of a near-mythic hero and his grand, though ill-fated masquerade during the Jazz Age. *H & P—Scribner.*

_____. *Tender Is the Night* (1934). The slow, poignant dissolution of a gifted psychiatrist who gives too easily and too much to those who need him—and, ironically, whom he needs almost as much. *H & P— Scribner.*

_____. *The Last Tycoon* (1941). Unfinished at Fitzgerald's death, this engrossing legend of Hollywood affords a compelling portrait of Monroe Stahr, a driving, artistic producer—the "last tycoon." *H—Scribner; P—Bantam, Scribner.*

GLASGOW, ELLEN 1874-1945. *Barren Ground* (1925). A poor young Virginian with aristocratic connections, Dorinda Oakley is betrayed by a weak-natured young doctor in this tale of madness and murder written elegantly but powerfully. *H—Peter Smith; P—Hill & Wang.*

———. *Vein of Iron* (1935). Ada Fincastle, daughter of a scholarly former Presbyterian minister in Virginia, loses the man she loves but finally regains him and, despite losses from the depression, faces life with her vein of iron. *P—HarBraceJ.*

HEMINGWAY, ERNEST 1899-1961. *The Sun Also Rises* (1926). In this 20th-century masterwork, Hemingway's hero, Jake, blasted in the war, lives in Paris among Left Bank expatriates who make sidetrips to Spain for the bullfighting and search for values through the alcoholic fog of the "lost generation." *H & P—Scribner.*

———. *A Farewell to Arms* (1929). Told in terse and rhythmic understatement, with nicely calculated repetitions, this star-crossed romance of an American ambulance driver and an English nurse in the Italy of 1917 is one of the finest war novels of our time. *H & P—Scribner.*

———. *For Whom the Bell Tolls* (1940). Hemingway's most ambitious but not his most successful novel. Sprawling and occasionally sentimental, this panoramic story of the Spanish Civil War boasts, nevertheless, tremendous emotive power gained through magnificent scenes and unforgettable portraits of Spanish guerrillas. *H & P—Scribner.*

LEWIS, SINCLAIR 1885-1951. *Main Street* (1920). A doctor's wife and minor-league Madame Bovary, Carol Kennicott is severely defeated in her ill-considered attempts to bring culture to the Midwestern town of Gopher Prairie. *H—HarBraceJ; P—NAL.*

———. *Babbitt* (1922). A clownish businessman in the mythical city of Zenith, George F. Babbitt (the prototype of the hustler and conformist) tries to break the grip of tribal customs—and fails grotesquely. *H—HarBraceJ; P—NAL.*

———. *Arrowsmith* (1925). A young doctor who becomes a bacteriologist has to battle both germs and the Establishment. *H—HarBraceJ; P—NAL.*

LONDON, JACK 1876-1916. *The Call of the Wild* (1903). London's most popular story, about Buck, a dog who regresses to wolf after his master dies during the Klondike Gold Rush. *Over 10 eds.*

MARQUAND, J. P. 1893-1960. *The Late George Apley* (1937). Ostensibly a biographical tribute by a friend, this neat satire of a proper Bostonian shows the dignified and not unlovable Apley and his tribal rituals in a dry comic light. *H—Little; P—NAL.*

MILLER, HENRY b. 1891. *Tropic of Cancer* (1931). Miller's exuberant, influential, and controversial masterpiece records, in simple but ecstatic prose, the adventures of an American vagabond merrily sponging on his Left Bank friends. *P—Grove.*

O'HARA, JOHN 1905-1970. *Appointment in Samarra* (1934). In his first novel, a compact one unlike his loose-jointed later efforts, the prolific O'Hara tells a striking story strikingly well, unreeling a little saga of the country-club set in a Pennsylvania town during the bootleg era. *P—Popular Lib.*

SINCLAIR, UPTON 1878-1968. *The Jungle* (1906). An impressive piece of dramatized journalism that paints a grim picture of the Chicago stockyards of the period. *H—Bentley; P—Airmont, NAL.*

STEIN, GERTRUDE 1874-1946. *Three Lives* (1909). A trio of novellas about three women—two, German immigrants, the third, a Black—who

suffer painful and, at last, futile lives. Each tale experiments stylistically, but "Melanctha" (about a Black woman's affair with a doctor)
dares most. *P—Random.*

STEINBECK, JOHN 1902-1968. *In Dubious Battle* (1936). This forcefully
dramatized story of a fruit pickers' strike in California has remained
Steinbeck's most impressive novel. *H—Viking Pr; P—Bantam, Viking
Pr.*

_____. *The Grapes of Wrath* (1939). The 1962 Nobel Prize winner's most
famous novel. Describes the plight of dispossessed Oklahoma Dust
Bowl tenant farmers during the depression vividly and compassionately but, too often, melodramatically. *H—Viking Pr; P—Penguin,
Viking Pr.*

WESCOTT, GLENWAY b. 1901. *The Grandmothers* (1927). From the
stories told by his grandmother and other relatives, and from the
evidence in family albums, a Wisconsin boy pieces together the vivid
story of his pioneer heritage. *P—Atheneum.*

WEST, NATHANAEL 1906-1940. *Miss Lonelyhearts* (1933). An unhappy
newspaperman assigned to write the lovelorn column at first scorns the
stricken people who write in but gradually becomes tangled in their
destinies. *P—New Directions.*

_____. *The Day of the Locust* (1939). A surrealistically grotesque
comedy about Hollywood. Distorted, hopeless, but powerful dreams of
beauty and romance translate into bizarre reality; enacted by an extraordinary array of psychically bankrupt characters. *P—Bantam.*

WHARTON, EDITH 1862-1937. *The House of Mirth* (1905). Wharton's
masterpiece is a compelling novel of manners in which the glamorous,
well-connected, but poverty-ridden Lily Bart desperately goes toward
her doom. *H—Scribner; P—NAL.*

_____. *Ethan Frome* (1911). Grim and icy New England dominates this
tragedy of a farmer who falls in love with the cousin of his wife,
who, after a catastrophe to the lovers, triumphs bitterly over them. *H—
Watts; P—Scribner.*

WILDER, THORNTON 1897-1975. *The Bridge of San Luis Rey* (1927).
The earliest of Wilder's three Pulitzer Prize novels and his most enduringly popular. Five travelers plunge to death when a bridge col-
lapses in 18th-century Peru. A witness reconstructs their life histories to
probe the justice of their fate. *H—Har-Row; P—WSP.*

_____. *Heaven's My Destination* (1934). A modern comic novel about
a traveling textbook salesman, a priggish amateur evangelist whose
quixotic attempts to meddle in the lives of others usually end in hilarious but pathetic disasters. *o.p.*

WOLFE, THOMAS 1900-1938. *Look Homeward, Angel* (1929). Wolfe's
best novel tells in occasionally forceful but too often rhetorical
prose, the story of the turbulent Eugene Gant's first 19 years in his
native Southern town and at his state university. *H & P—Scribner.*

WRIGHT, RICHARD 1908-1960. *Native Son* (1940). Crude but magnetic,
the story of Bigger Thomas, a Black man overthrown by his own
impulses and society's bias. The novel remains an unusually effective
and timely novel of social protest. *H & P—Har-Row.*

1945–Present

At no time in our literary history has American fiction seemed more profoundly anxious than since World War II. The horrors of corporate echnologized war—in Europe and the Pacific, Korea, and Vietnam—diminished radically the potential of the individual, the "imperial self," by reducing human dignity to near insect level. Hero gave way to antihero; lyricism to parody; reason to madness. Norman Mailer, James Jones, and Joseph Heller, the best of our war novelists, mirror the cancellations and negations of aspiration and decency. With grim humor they prophesy the manner and message of a new age: a malignant survival of cruelty and injustice, an absurd, irrational persistence of destructive impulse.

Starting in the 1950s, many novelists stepped outside the mindless mainstream of history to contemplate their own images in a kind of desperate commitment to salvaging self. Bernard Malamud, Saul Bellow, Philip Roth, Herbert Gold, and many others puzzled over the complexities of being an American Jew. Ralph Ellison, James Baldwin, Ishmael Reed were among many who examined sensitively and, often, angrily the exasperating alienation of the Black in northern as well as southern America. The troubled consciousness of the Southerner found powerful expression among the literary descendants of William Faulkner: Robert Penn Warren, William Styron, Carson McCullers, Flannery O'Connor, and Walker Percy. And some writers, particularly J. D. Salinger, quested in adolescence and childhood some shred of innocence to shore against the ruins. Vladimir Nabokov's *Lolita* effectively ended that scant hope.

By the 1960s paranoia passed, for many, as normal. The asylum, hallucination, junk artifacts, V-2 rockets, fire bombings, cannibalism—these are salient images in the fiction of Ken Kesey, William Burroughs, Donald Barthelme, Thomas Pynchon, Kurt Vonnegut, and John Hawkes, leaders of the vanguard of new fiction. Their vision coincides with that of John Barth, who reminds us, ironically and despairingly, in the title of one of his novels that we are *Lost in the Funhouse*. It is too late to *do* anything, the philosopher-novelist William Gass insists; the artist can only show us what reality is and write so compellingly that we must at least confront that reality, perhaps for the first and only time in our lives.

Despite their fantasies of violence and doom, the novelists have stayed at their craft—and crafted with extraordinary virtuosity. Indeed, the technical skills of American novelists have never been more substantial or more original. As Mailer and Bellow paid homage to Hemingway, Dos Passos, and Faulkner, then forged their own way, so a new generation of novelists is stretching beyond the masters of the 1950s. Writers like Thomas Berger, Robert Coover, Joan Didion, John Gardner, Jerzy Kosinksi, Joyce Carol Oates, John Updike, and Larry Woiwode are others among the novelists of the 1960s and 1970s who will determine whether the novel will prove restorative or degenerative. The samples on hand suggest that it will not at any rate prove comforting or genteel.

AUCHINCLOSS, LOUIS b. 1917. *The Rector of Justin* (1964). The famous head of a famous preparatory school, having reached his eighties, is viewed at various times in his career by different people who knew him and who make a composite picture of his many-faceted personality. *H—HM; P—Avon.*

BALDWIN, JAMES b. 1924. *Go Tell It on the Mountain* (1953). At once ironic and intense, this novel (largely autobiographical) traces the lines of force that meet in the conversion of the Black child and youth who is the central character. *H—Dial; P—Dell, Noble.*

BARTH, JOHN b. 1930. *End of the Road* (1958). A classic case of contemporary psychic paralysis, Jacob Horner fails to escape his corner, despite innovative, often funny, but at last destructive efforts. *P— Bantam, GAD.*

_____. *The Sot-Weed Factor* (1960). A freewheeling picaresque novel, a Rabelaisian satire of human pretensions, a bawdy prose-extension of Ebenezer Cooke's 18th-century lampoon, *The Sot-Weed Factor*, or a "moral allegory cloaked in the material of colonial history" (as the author affirms)—Barth's narrative is certainly an astonishing fusion of witty *tour de force* and comic epic. *H—Doubleday; P—Bantam.*

BARTHELME, DONALD b. 1931. *Snow White* (1967). An unsweetened parody in which Snow White finds no prince but settles grumpily for her dwarfs, with whom she shares occasionally bed and bath. *H & P— Atheneum.*

_____. *The Dead Father* (1975). To his familiar techniques of collage, irony, and parody, Barthelme adds an Oedipal plot as a son accompanies his father's mammoth corpse ("dead only in a sense") to a burial site. Often comic, sometimes outrageous, the novel is also a painful gloss on modern culture and familial patterns. *H—FS&G; P—PB.*

BELLOW, SAUL b. 1915. *The Adventures of Augie March* (1953). A plump novel about the wanderings of a passive *picaro* from Chicago. War, sex, and shipwreck play roles in his maturation. *P—Fawcett World.*

_____. *Seize the Day* (1956). A powerful short novel whose antihero, Tommy Wilhelm, struggles to survive and to understand despite his pitiable ineffectuality. *P—Viking Pr.*

_____. *Herzog* (1964). Both highly individualized and deeply representative, Moses Herzog is an extravagantly and sadly comic portrait of the modern intellectual caught in a series of emotional traps. *H & P—Viking Pr.*

_____. *Mr. Sammler's Planet* (1969). Though a septuagenarian, Mr. Sammler resembles most of Bellow's heroes in his compassion for his fellows and his commitment to the fullness of life. *H & P—Viking Pr.*

BERGER, THOMAS b. 1924. *Little Big Man* (1964). A chunky Western about Jack Crabb, the 120-year-old sole survivor of Custer's Little Bighorn disaster. Fact and fiction intermingle to create a vigorous, often hilarious, mock-heroic parody of American myth. *P—Fawcett World, S&S.*

BURROUGHS, WILLIAM b. 1914. *Naked Lunch* (1959). A panoramic excursion through the moral underground, this surrealistic and hallucinatory novel is a ferocious (and linguistically scatological) depiction of the horrors of unbridled appetite. *P—Ballantine, Grove.*

CAPOTE, TRUMAN b. 1924. *Other Voices, Other Rooms* (1948). Capote's first and best novel about the grim rite of passage of a sensitive Southern boy trapped in a decadent gothic household. *H—Random; P—NAL.*

CHEEVER, JOHN b. 1913. *The Wapshot Chronicle* (1958) and *The Wapshot Scandal* (1964). An episodic, subtly farcical but haunted account of the failure of the solidly middle-class Wapshot family of St. Botolphs, Mass.—and particularly the brothers Moses and Coverly—to cope with the intricacies of contemporary mores and morality. *P—Har-Row.*

COOVER, ROBERT C. b. 1932. *The Universal Baseball Association, Inc., J. Henry Waugh, Prop.* (1968). A compelling allegorical fantasy about Waugh, a middle-aged accountant who peoples an entire baseball league with imaginary teams and players, complete with biographies and statistics—all dependent upon the dice Waugh throws to determine fate. *H—NAL.*

DIDION, JOAN b. 1934. *Play It as It Lays* (1970). Stylistically taut and understated, this novel explores the burned-out emotional shell of an actress whose possibilities as a woman—wife, mother, and artist—have atrophied. *H—FS&G; P—Bantam.*

DONLEAVY, J. P. b. 1926. *The Ginger Man* (1955). Although for some years a resident of Ireland, Donleavy may still be counted as an American writer, notably for this vigorously funny picaresque story of a young American's adventures and misadventures in Dublin and London. *P—Berkley Pub, Dell.*

ELLISON, RALPH b. 1914. *Invisible Man* (1952). In this compelling story, symbolic of modern alienation, an anonymous Black man undergoes a series of baffling adventures, first in the South and later in New York, during a fervent quest for personal identity and social visibility. *H—Modern Lib, Random; P—Random.*

GADDIS, WILLIAM b. 1922. *Recognitions* (1955). Twenty years after its publication, this first novel of more than 900 pages has at last won deserved acclaim (just as Gaddis' second novel, the equally long *JR*, made its appearance). At surface, a story about forging paintings; beneath is "recognition" that inauthenticity clutters and infects every facet of our lives and ourselves. *P—Avon.*

GARDNER, JOHN 1934. *The Sunlight Dialogues* (1972). An existential criminal—the Sunlight Man—in melodramatic conflict with a small-town "law and order" police chief. On this simple narrative base, Gardner constructs an ingenious and sometimes interminable series of dialogues about the ethical, social, and cultural paraphernalia of modern American society. *H—Knopf; P—Ballantine.*

GASS, WILLIAM b. 1924. *Omensetter's Luck* (1966). Novelist and philosopher Gass exercises a virtuoso control of language as he mounts a strange and imaginative conflict between good and evil in a rural Midwestern setting. *P—NAL.*

GOLD, HERBERT b. 1924. *Fathers* (1967). Sweeping across years and countries, Gold employs the memoir technique to tell the story of his father and himself as father in a crowded, tense, vital narrative. *o.p.*

HAWKES, JOHN b. 1925. *The Lime Twig* (1961). A novel of gothic atmosphere and force about the English underworld, the theft of a racehorse, and the violent death of a man under the hooves of horses during a race. *P—New Directions.*

_____. *Second Skin* (1964). Hawke's finest work, a densely textured complex of images and episodes that records the central character's passage from nightmare and death to dream and life. *P—New Directions.*

HELLER, JOSEPH b. 1923. *Catch-22* (1961). The total madness and horror of war captured through a farrago of comic absurdities at an American bomber base in World War II. *H—Delacorte, S&S; P—Dell, Modern Lib.*

JONES, JAMES 1921-1977. *From Here to Eternity* (1951). Barracks life in Hawaii just before Pearl Harbor; notable for its portraits of Pfc. Prewitt, sensitive, rebellious, doomed, and of Sgt. Warden, the professional soldier who controls the entire army post—enlisted men, officers, and officers' wives. *H—Scribner.*

_____. *The Thin Red Line* (1962). Less melodramatic and sentimental than *From Here to Eternity* but truer to the dully ferocious reality of combat; here the mission is to recapture a group of hills on Guadalcanal. *P—Avon.*

KESEY, KEN b. 1935. *One Flew over the Cuckoo's Nest* (1962). Set in a mental hospital, this story dramatizes the conflict between a stubborn patient and the bullying figure known as Big Nurse, a conflict full of dramatic tension and sometimes painful comedy. *H—Viking Pr; P—NAL, Viking Pr.*

KOSINSKI, JERZY b. 1933. *The Painted Bird* (1965). An accidentally abandoned child, terrified into loss of speech, drifts silently from place to place during World War II, spectator and victim alike to vicious abuses, each a kind of metaphor for what humanity has become. Not a line of dialogue appears in this shocking first novel. *H—HM, Modern Lib; P—Bantam.*

McCULLERS, CARSON 1917-1967. *The Heart Is a Lonely Hunter* (1940). A bizarre group in a southern town—a man who owns a lunch counter, a woman with musical ambitions, an alcoholic radical, and a Black doctor—confide their troubles to a deaf mute in this beautifully fashioned story. *H—HM: P—Bantam.*

MAILER, NORMAN b. 1923. *The Naked and the Dead* (1948). A collective picture of a reconnaissance squad in action against the Japanese on an island in the Pacific; this is one of the finest and grimmest of American war novels. *H—HR&W; P—NAL.*

_____. *An American Dream* (1964). A novelistic projection of themes from Mailer's famous essay "The White Negro"—sex and death, good and evil, magic and madness. A flawed book, but dazzlingly energetic, original, and passionate. *H—Dial; P—Dell.*

_____. *Why Are We in Vietnam?* (1967). A psychopathic young narrator details the grotesqueries of an Arctic hunting expedition with his father and assorted Texans. Idylls give way to mayhem and madness as the barbarism of modern technology degrades and destroys what is good in nature. *P—Berkley Pub.*

MALAMUD, BERNARD b. 1914. *The Assistant* (1957). An affecting novel in which a wayward young Italian "assistant" learns some special meanings of suffering from a profoundly human Jewish grocer. *H—FS&G; P—Dell, FS&G.*

MORRIS, WRIGHT b. 1910. *The Works of Love* (1952). A touching, sympathetic portrait of Will Brady, a decent but weak Midwesterner who offers love too freely and suffers inevitable frustration. *P—U of Nebr Pr.*

_____. *The Field of Vision* (1956). A series of interior monologues by some eccentric Midwesterners who attend a bullfight in Mexico which becomes their rite of passage. *P—U of Nebr Pr.*

NABOKOV, VLADIMIR 1899-1977. *Lolita* (1955). Not Nabokov's best book but his most popular, a hilarious but also rather chilling account of a nubile, predatory "nymphet" and her hapless middle-aged lover. *H—Ardis Pubs, McGraw; P—Berkley Pub, Putnam.*

_____. *Pale Fire* (1962). An extraordinary comic *tour de force* about appearance and reality. Nabokov teases, traps, and enchants readers in his labyrinth of passages and deadfalls leading to understanding the fatal implications of a seemingly harmless task—editing and translating a modern epic poem called "Pale Fire." *P—Berkley Pub.*

OATES, JOYCE CAROL b. 1938. *Them* (1969). A big and rather old-fashioned naturalistic family chronicle about three decades in the lives of the Wendells of Detroit, a shabby, not-too-bright clan struggling to rise above their stifling emptiness. *H—Vanguard; P—Fawcett World.*

O'CONNOR, FLANNERY 1925-1964. *The Violent Bear It Away* (1960). Set in the backwoods of Tennessee, this comically macabre and complex novel, her finest, tells of a young man's terrifying initiation as a religious prophet. *P—FS&G.*

PERCY, WALKER b. 1916. *The Moviegoer* (1961). Percy's first and best novel, a National Book Award winner about a New Orleans broker who rejects the banalities of traditional society but can substitute only movies as functional reality. *H—Knopf; P—FS&G.*

PURDY, JAMES b. 1923. *Malcolm* (1959). The gothic adventures of a complicatedly simple young man who, before he dies unexpectedly, meets a bizarre group of people, including a midget, a Black undertaker, a wealthy woman who calls her home "The Chateau," and a torch singer whom he marries. *H—FS&G.*

PYNCHON, THOMAS b. 1937. *V.* (1963). A landmark of Black humor, *V.* is a lively picaresque novel set in America, Africa, Italy, and elsewhere, and tells an absurd story about two men, one of them on a classical "quest." A mysterious female, whose initial gives the book its title, overshadows the narrative. *H—Lippincott; P—Bantam.*

_____. *Gravity's Rainbow* (1973). This time the quarry is V-2, a rocket rather than a spy. Physics (especially principles of entropy and indeterminacy), cybernetics, and a dollop of paranoia are metaphors of modern chaos in this long, funny, and often exasperating novel. *H—Viking Pr; P—Bantam, Viking Pr.*

ROTH, PHILIP b. 1933. *Portnoy's Complaint* (1969). The ultimate fictional case history of the suffering Jewish mothers inflict upon their sons. Pitiless comedy and inspired mimicry with a broad base of sadness and bitterness. *H—Random; P—Bantam.*

————. *My Life as a Man* (1974). An ingenious triple play in which a writer offers two of his short stories, then appends a lengthy autobiographical account of the miseries (not unlike Portnoy's, only substitute wife for mother) that inspired the fiction. *P—Bantam.*

SALINGER, J. D. b. 1919. *The Catcher in the Rye* (1951). In his own brand of flavorful but sometimes monotonous slang, a prep-school adolescent named Holden Caulfield relates his attempts to evade adulthood in this mischievous and slyly comic novel. *H—Little; P—Bantam.*

STYRON, WILLIAM b. 1925. *Lie Down in Darkness* (1951). A powerful story of the decay of a Virginia family; drunkenness, incest, and suicide are all evoked with force in a haunting, nightmarish style. *P—NAL, Viking Pr.*

UPDIKE, JOHN b. 1932. *Rabbit Run* (1960) and *Rabbit Redux* (1971). As the earlier novel scanned the inward, private problems of the 1950s, its successor confronts the explosive public issues of the 1960s. In his twenties, Rabbit Angstrom, a former star athlete who could not grow up, abandoned his wife and kept on running. Ten years older in the companion volume, Rabbit has settled into responsibility—but now the world runs beyond him. Updike's finest work, a powerful attempt to comprehend the violently disparate forces of our time. *H—Knopf; P—Fawcett World.*

VONNEGUT, KURT b. 1922. *Slaughterhouse Five* (1969). The firebombing of Dresden warps Billy Pilgrim's consciousness of time, space, and reality, compelling him to seek refuge and perspective elsewhere—on Vonnegut's now familiar planet, Tralfamadore. Possibly the best of his imaginative if occasionally sentimental satires. *H—Delacorte; P—Dell.*

WARREN, ROBERT PENN b. 1905. *All the King's Men* (1946). The best novel of a first-rate American poet, critic, and scholar tells the story of a corn-pone dictator, markedly like Huey Long. *H—HarBraceJ, Random; P—Bantam.*

WIESEL, ELIE b. 1928. *Night* (1960). A Rumanian Jew by birth, survivor of Auschwitz and Buchenwald, Wiesel is now an American citizen. His first novel is one of the most searing accounts of the Holocaust—as experienced by a 15-year-old boy. *H—Hill & Wang; P—Avon.*

————. *A Beggar in Jerusalem* (1970). Although set during the Six-Day War, the agonies and aspirations of the characters are timeless. *H—Random; P—Avon.*

WOIWODE, LARRY b. 1941. *Beyond the Bedroom Wall* (1975). Four generations of the Neumiller family of North Dakota lovingly and lengthily recollected in a full-bodied projection of the land and the people. *H—FS&G; P—Avon.*

12. The Short Story

Arthur Zeiger

From the first nameless storytellers, masters of oral narrative, who enlarged on occurrences, interpreted rituals, and transmitted traditions; through the earliest papyri, centuries later, upon which tales were inscribed in hieroglyphics; through the great ages of literature, the short story had a long and not inglorious history before the 19th century distinguished it as a specific genre.

Though Washington Irving, Edgar Allan Poe, and Nathaniel Hawthorne have variously been called "Father of the Short Story," they are at best its stepfathers. Poe, however, did define most explicitly, and stringently, the requirements for the form: it must aim at a single effect and every line must conduce to that end. Consequently, to insure its totality of effect, its "unity," it must require "from a half-hour to one or two hours for its perusal"— neither more nor less.

Poe succeeded admirably by following his prescription. But other writers refused to be confined. Romantic fantasy (Tieck and Hoffmann in Germany), realistic analysis (Mérimée and Balzac in France), local color verism (Bret Harte and Mark Twain in America), psychological "depth-diving" (Gogol and Dostoevski in Russia) demanded forms and techniques different from Poe's.

Yet a kind of design became increasingly apparent in the 19th-century story. Length became standardized within generous limits—from 500 to 15,000 words (shorter, it became a "short-short story"; longer, a "short novel"). Plot, a causal chain of episodes, dominated: the story had a beginning, a middle, and an end; a knot was tied, more or less complexly, and gradually untied— with enough doubt about the possibility of untying to generate suspense. Character tended to be subordinated to plot (though occasionally, as in Melville's tales, plot evolved from character). And a kind of unity, at least of feeling, was generally sought and in the best stories attained.

But as the century progressed, the "well-made story" suffered a series of assaults. Even Maupassant, exemplar of the taut story with a surprise ending, sometimes broke the restraints to write poignant, evocative, nearly plotless stories (e.g., "Little Soldier"). Henry James, while tracing the formal pattern of the story, transcended it—because of his dedication to the "organic principle," his belief that a work of fiction is "a living thing, all one and continuous" (e.g., "The Beast in the Jungle"). Turgenev, especially, centered on quite ordinary characters, and as they revealed themselves, quite casually, almost incidentally, they compose the story (e.g., "The Country Doctor"). The most important practitioner of the modern short story, however, is surely Chekhov. He perceived the essential falsity of the story grounded in plot, wedded to unitary effect, proceeding to climax, all precisely calculated like the shelves of a cabinet. He insisted on a "middle action," with little or nothing before or after: a coachman, oppressed by troubles, tries to tell them to his passengers and fellows; rebuffed by both, he goes to the stable and confides to his horse ("A Coachman"). The readers are forced into active collaboration: they flesh out the story through memory, sympathy, insight, and they feel its truth as immediately as a toothache. The story makes Poe's effects seem trumpery.

With significant exceptions (Faulkner, for example), the great forgers of modern short fiction have continued in the direction toward which Chekhov pointed: Joyce, Mansfield, Anderson, Lawrence, Hemingway are each unique, yet in some sense descended from Chekhov. Nevertheless, the well-made story still prevails, of course; and it ought to. It delights, or thrills, or sends shivers through us. The world of story would be much poorer without Saki, or Conan Doyle, or Jackson. Literature is large; it can include multitudes.

And it needs to. For in the last two decades other forms of story have proliferated. Some attempt to show the disconnection of things (Barthelme); others their occult connection (Borges). Some point to the hollowness at the center of our lives (Gass); others—fewer, certainly—to at least a fragile hope (Bellow). Some are grounded in hallucination (Cortázar); others in the enduring folk past (Singer). Some reject all religious sanction (Camus); others accept it as a first principle (Flannery O'Connor). But if the multitudes seem uncountable, it is a matter for rejoicing. The multitudinousness, the plenitude, of the story implies its continuing force and vigor. The more ways for fiction the better, if not the merrier.

Books listed in earlier chapters that contain short narratives not generally considered to be short stories include Aesop's *Fables* ("Greece"), Ovid's *Metamorphoses* ("Rome"), Chaucer's *The Canterbury Tales* ("The Middle Ages"), Boccaccio's *Decameron* and Cervantes' *Don Quixote* ("The Renaissance and Reformation"), Addison and Steele's *The Spectator* ("The 18th Century"), and *Arabian Nights* and the *Bible* ("The Middle East"). Collections of short stories by writers of the regions are listed in "The Middle East," "East and South Asia," "Africa," and "Latin America."

Anthologies

There are countless good paperbound and hardcover anthologies of short stories old and new. Listed below are a few representative titles.

44 Irish Short Stories (1955). An excellent anthology edited by Devin Garrity: from Yeats and Joyce to O'Connor, O'Faolain, and Mc-Laverty. *H—Devin.*

French Stories and Tales (1954). Representative collection from Balzac and Flaubert to Gide. *P—WSP.*

Great American Short Stories (1959). From Poe to the 1950s. *P—Dell.*

Great English Short Stories (1959). A representative collection. *P—Dell.*

Great German Short Novels and Stories (1952). Fifteen stories and short novels, including Goethe's *Sorrows of Young Werther* and Mann's *Death in Venice. H—Modern Lib.*

Great Russian Short Stories (1959). A stimulating and representative collection. *P—Dell.*

Great Spanish Short Stories (1959). Another good assortment. *P—Dell.*

Individual Authors

ALEICHEM, SHOLOM (SHALOM RABINOWITZ) 1859-1916. **Stories and Satires.** The "Jewish Mark Twain," Aleichem writes with understanding, compassion, and love about the Yiddish-speaking Jews of Eastern Europe. *Over 6 colls.*

ANDERSON. **Winesburg, Ohio.** See "20th-Century American Novels," page 115.

BABEL, ISAAC 1894-1938. **Collected Stories** (1955). Stories of civil war and of Russian life before and after the Revolution by a Russian master believed to have died in a concentration camp. *P—NAL.*

BARTH, JOHN b. 1930. **Lost in the Funhouse** (1968). Witty, technically adroit, occasionally overingenious but immensely enjoyable nevertheless. *H—Doubleday; P—Bantam, G&D.*

BARTHELME, DONALD b. 1933. **Unspeakable Practices, Unnatural Acts** (1968). Brilliant, often surreal fragments by a satirist who is also an extraordinary stylist: perfect sentences, words that "twitter, bong, flash and glow signals of exquisite distress." *H—FS&G; P—PB.*

BENÉT, STEPHEN VINCENT 1898-1943. **Selected Works** (1960). Colorful, romantic stories dealing mostly with America's past. *H—HR&W.*

BIERCE, AMBROSE 1842-1914. **In the Midst of Life** (1898). Sardonic sketches of soldiers and civilians in the terrifying world of our Civil War and after. *P—NAL.*

BORGES. **Ficciones** and **Labyrinths.** See "Latin America," page 74.

BRADBURY, RAY b. 1920. **The Golden Apples of the Sun** (1953). One of several first-rate collections of tales of fantasy and science fiction by a master of the genre. *H—Greenwood; P—Bantam.*

CALDWELL, ERSKINE b. 1903. *Complete Stories* (1953). Tales of ribald humor, social protest, and tragedy. *H—Little.*

CAPOTE, TRUMAN b. 1924. *The Grass Harp and A Tree of Night and Other Stories* (1950). Nebulous, haunting stories. *P—NAL.*

CHEEVER, JOHN b. 1912. *The Enormous Room* (1953), *The Housebreaker of Shady Hill* (1958), and *The Brigadier and the Golf Widow* (1964). Wry commentaries on individual and societal manners in contemporary American metropolis, suburbia, and exurbia. *o.p.*

CHEKHOV, ANTON 1860-1904. *Short Stories.* Carefully wrought, skeptical commentaries on Russian life and character. Chekhov's indirect, implicational narrative technique has profoundly influenced 20th-century fiction. *Over 12 colls.*

COLETTE (SIDONIE GABRIELLE COLETTE) 1873-1954. *My Mother's House* (1953). Reminiscences of childhood by one of the most celebrated French writers of this century. *P—FS&G.*

CONRAD, JOSEPH 1857-1924. *Stories.* The master of the sea story is equally the master of the psychological tale. Incisive probings into the dark places of the human psyche. *Over 6 colls.*

COOVER, ROBERT b. 1932. *Pricksongs and Descants* (1969). Biblical episodes, myths, and fairy tales transmuted by psychological realism into startling and intriguing modern stories. *P—NAL.*

COPPARD, A. E. 1878-1957. *Collected Tales* (1948). The major work of a British master, ranging from naturalism to fantasy to symbolism. *H—Bks for Libs.*

CRANE, STEPHEN 1871-1900. *Stories.* Narratives by a pioneer of realism in America. *Over 6 colls.*

DE LA MARE, WALTER 1873-1956. *Stories.* Fascinated by the "twilight side of life," de la Mare created stories and tales of an unforgettable world of fantasy, dreams, and the supernatural. *Over 6 colls.*

DINESEN, ISAK (BARONESSE KAREN BLIXEN) 1885-1962. *Seven Gothic Tales* (1934). Jewel-like, richly embroidered tales of a romantic past peopled by cavaliers, maidens, and ghosts. *P—Random.*

FARRELL, JAMES T. b. 1904. *Stories.* Stories of 20th-century urban America by the author of *Studs Lonigan. H—Vanguard.*

FAULKNER, WILLIAM 1897-1962. *Stories.* Richly varied short fiction ranging in time from the early settling of Mississippi to post-World War II days, by a master of form, subtlety, symbolism, and psychological insight. *H—Modern Lib, Random.*

FITZGERALD, F. SCOTT 1896-1940. *Stories* (1951). Gay and tragic stories by the spokesman for the Jazz Age. *H & P—Scribner.*

FORSTER, E. M. 1879-1970. *The Celestial Omnibus* (1911). Graceful, witty, delightful exercises in fantasy. *P—Random.*

GASS, WILLIAM b. 1924. *In the Heart of the Heart of the Country* (1968). Diverse and remarkable "experimental" stories—ranging from a dispassionate recording of correlatives of pain to the earthy interior monologue of a "latter-day Molly Bloom." *H—Har-Row; P—PB*

GOGOL, NICOLAI V. 1809-1952. *The Overcoat and Other Tales of Good and Evil* (1957). Seven stories, all enormously important in the development of modern fiction: grotesques, moralities, acute psychological revelations, biting satires. *H—Norton.*

GORDIMER. *Selected Stories.* See "Africa," page 67.

HAWTHORNE, NATHANIEL 1804-1864. *Stories and Tales.* Deeply symbolic and carefully wrought studies of sin and retribution and romantic tales of colonial New England, by a master who helped establish the form as a serious literary type. *Over 12 colls.*

HEMINGWAY, ERNEST 1899-1961. *Short Stories.* Various collections of the short fiction by one of the most significant, influential, and controversial writers of our time. *H & P—Scribner.*

HENRY, O. (WILLIAM SYDNEY PORTER) 1862-1910. *Short Stories.* Ingenious, swiftly paced, skillfully plotted trick- or surprise-ending stories by a most widely read and imitated practitioner. *Over 6 colls.*

IRVING, WASHINGTON 1783-1859. *Sketch Book* (1820). Warmly colored, romanticized sketches, tales, and essays, such as "Rip Van Winkle" and "Legend of Sleepy Hollow." *H—Dodd, Dutton; P—NAL.*

JACKSON, SHIRLEY 1919-1965. *The Lottery* (1949). Terrifying and macabre vignettes of the tensions underlying contemporary life. *P— Popular Lib.*

JAMES, HENRY 1843-1916. *Short Stories.* Intricate analyses of conflicting personalities and their psychological and emotional reactions by a consummate craftsman. *Over 12 colls.*

JOYCE, JAMES 1882-1941. *Dubliners* (1914). Joyce sought his material in the lives of insignificant people in "dear, dirty Dublin." Rich in insight, subtly symbolic, essentially simple in structure, *Dubliners* is a towering landmark in the evolution of the short story. *H—Modern Lib, Viking Pr; P—Viking Pr.*

KAFKA, FRANZ 1883-1924. *Selected Short Stories.* Strikingly existentialist commentaries on the meaninglessness of modern life presented in terms of grotesque imagery and surrealistic symbols. *P— Modern Lib.*

KIPLING, RUDYARD 1865-1936. *Stories.* One of the last of the great romantics ranges from the hill towns of India to the jungles of Mowgli, Kaa, and Rikki-Tikki-Tavi. *Over 6 colls.*

LARDNER, RING 1885-1933. *Best Short Stories.* Satirical tales—sometimes humorous, often bitter—debunking hypocrisy in American life. *P—Scribner.*

LAWRENCE, D. H. 1885-1930. *Complete Short Stories* (1961). Lawrence's "religion of the blood" animates these vigorous and provocative stories of confrontations between man and woman, child and adult. *P—Viking Pr 3 vols.*

LONDON, JACK 1876-1919. *Stories.* Narratives of violence, action, and atmosphere, set from the Far North to the South Seas. *Over 10 colls.*

MALAMUD, BERNARD b. 1914. *The Magic Barrel* (1958) and *Idiots First* (1963). Ironic, highly individualistic stories of American Jews at home and abroad, tempered by nostalgia for the Jewish past. *H—FS&G: P—FS&G, PB.*

MANN, THOMAS 1875-1955. *Stories of Three Decades*. Masterly, lengthy short stories on themes ranging from the adolescent to the artist. *H—Knopf.*

MANSFIELD, KATHERINE 1888-1923. *Stories*. Penetrating character studies in the Chekhov manner, and impressionistic portraits of situations. *H—Collins-World, Knopf; P—Random.*

MAUGHAM, W. SOMERSET 1874-1965. *Complete Short Stories*. Dramatic accounts by a popular raconteur, mostly dealing with strange people in faraway places. *P—WSP 4 vols.*

MAUPASSANT, GUY DE 1850-1893. *Stories*. Realistic impressions of French life, deftly constructed and brilliantly ironic. *Over 6 colls.*

MELVILLE, HERMAN 1819-1891. *Stories*. Impressive, usually provocative tales. *Over 6 colls.*

MISHIMA, YUKIO 1925-1970. *Death in Midsummer and Other Stories* (1966). Frequently sensational but riveting tales by the Japanese writer who has made the deepest impress on the West. *P—New Directions.*

O'CONNOR, FLANNERY 1925-1964. *A Good Man Is Hard to Find* (1955) and *Everything That Rises Must Converge* (1965). Artistry, social awareness, the grotesque, and the need for faith characterize these stories of the contemporary South. First title: *H—HarBraceJ; P—Doubleday.* Second title: *H & P—FS&G.*

O'CONNOR, FRANK 1903-1966. *Stories* (1952). Humor, insight, and satire mark these representative stories by a leading Irish writer. *H—Knopf.*

O'FAOLAIN, SEAN b. 1900. *Short Stories* (1961). Effective narratives about contemporary Ireland. *P—Little.*

O'HARA, JOHN 1905-1970. *Short Stories*. Social satire of individual and societal absurdities. *P—Popular Lib.*

POE, EDGAR ALLAN 1809-1849. *Tales*. Memorable stories of atmosphere, horror, and ratiocination by a founder and master of short fiction. *Over 20 colls.*

PORTER, KATHERINE ANNE b. 1894. *Stories*. Beautifully wrought and subtle narratives of varied moods, themes, and settings. *H—HarBraceJ; P—NAL.*

PRITCHETT, V. S. b. 1900. *The Sailor, Sense of Humor, and Other Stories* (1956). Mostly about the double lives of middle-class Britishers tormented by changing social forces. *o.p.*

PURDY, JAMES b. 1923. *Color of Darkness* (1957) and *Children Is All* (1962). Misfits trapped in a purgatory of the unloved, the unwanted, and the alienated, by an outstanding "Black humorist." *P—New Directions.*

ROTH, PHILIP b. 1933. *Goodbye, Columbus, and Five Short Stories* (1959). Roth writes with irony and understanding about the American Jew in a variety of settings ranging from army training camp to big city. *H—Modern Lib.*

SAKI (H. H. MUNRO) 1870-1916. *The Best of Saki* (1961). Sophisticated treatment of affectations of English society; short-short stories of fantasy and surprise with an undercurrent of serious commentary. *P—Viking Pr.*

SALINGER, J. D. b. 1919. *Nine Stories* (1953). Perceptive depiction of problems of children and child-like adults, narrated with warmth, understanding, and sympathy. *H—Little; P—Bantam.*

SAROYAN, WILLIAM b. 1908. *My Name Is Aram* (1940). Fresh and exuberant stories of a young Armenian in Fresno, California. *H—HarBraceJ; P—Dell.*

SINGER, ISAAC BASHEVIS b. 1904. *Gimpel the Fool & Other Stories* (1957) and *The Spinoza of Market Street* (1961). Marvelous stories, rooted deep in folk memory, intensely real even when the theme is supernatural. First title: *H—FS&G.* Second title: *H—FS&G; P—Avon.*

STAFFORD, JEAN b. 1915. *Collected Stories* (1966). Disturbing depictions of neuroses in contemporary American life enlivened by occasional humorous stories of "bad" characters in Colorado. *H & P—FS&G.*

STEINBECK, JOHN b. 1902-1968. *The Long Valley* (1938). Powerful short fiction about the American West. *P—Bantam, Viking Pr.*

THOMAS, DYLAN 1914-1953. *Adventures in the Skin Trade* (1955). Includes individualistic short stories and sketches, employing melodrama, fantasy, humor, and surrealism. *P—NAL, New Directions.*

THURBER, JAMES 1894-1961. *The Thurber Carnival* (1945). Selections from an American humorist, one of the best of our time, whose warmth and insight are tempered by a gratifying malice. *H—Har-Row, Modern Lib; P—Dell, Har-Row.*

TURGENEV, IVAN 1818-1883. *Sketches from a Hunter's Album* (1852). Enormously influential and absorbing stories in which plot evolves from character, naturally and convincingly. *P—Penguin.*

TWAIN, MARK (SAMUEL L. CLEMENS) 1835-1910. *Stories.* Collections of the shorter works of America's greatest humorist. *Over 6 eds.*

UPDIKE, JOHN b. 1932. *Pigeon Feathers and Other Stories* (1962), *The Music School* (1966), and *Museums and Women* (1972). The often engaging stories of a talented and prolific writer, sometimes a bit slick but always crafted, intelligent, and genuinely perceptive. *H—Knopf; P—Fawcett World.*

VERGA, GIOVANNI 1840-1922. *She Wolf and Other Stories.* Highly skillful reconstructions of Sicilian life in the 1860s. *P—U of Cal Pr.*

WELTY, EUDORA b. 1909. *Stories.* Sensitive, masterly worked tales about contemporary Mississippi. *H—HarBraceJ, Modern Lib; P—HarBraceJ.*

WODEHOUSE, P. G. 1881-1976. *Most of P. G. Wodehouse* (1969). A generous sampling of the hilarious effects achieved by intricate plotting and soufflé dialogue. Psmith, Jeeves, Bertie Wooster, and Mr. Mulliner are maybe stock characters but surely enduring ones. *H & P—S&S.*

WOLFE, THOMAS 1900-1938. *The Hills Beyond* (1941). Semiautobiographical stories reminiscent of his loose novels but more carefully and economically written. *H—Har-Row; P—NAL.*

WRIGHT, RICHARD 1908-1960. *Uncle Tom's Children* (1938) and *Eight Men* (1961). Relentlessly honest, moving accounts of the Black experience in a hostile white world. First title: *H & P—Har-Row.* Second title: *P—Pyramid Pubns.*

13. Poetry

Paul Oppenheimer

Poetry is really the birthright art. We are all born to it and with it, and our need of it persists throughout our lives at the heart of our humanity. For poetry is simultaneously the natural speech of the soul and the language of our brains and feelings as they gather the universe and its values into our shapes and acts of being. Poetry is thus the sort of language that we speak and sing and read, and talk to ourselves, first—before we are aware of language as language—and last too: whenever we crave clarity of life instead of mere information. We turn to it whenever we know that we must hear some, any, truth lest we die or freeze up because, in Wordsworth's phrase, "the world is too much with us." We seek it whenever the pain, horror, beauty of our lives simply require the musical fine prayers and diagnoses of words rightly used, intensely felt and thought—the fantasy and power of ordinary language suddenly firecracking with extraordinary flashes and meanings and insights.

So the first fact to accept about poetry may be its amazing proximity—that every one of us makes the art, is a poet naturally, even easily, in conversations when these touch the soul, at the lightning-rod points of them, when they unabashedly groom us with holy and sweet loveliness, and in everybody's occasional swift phrases of passionate exactness. The only difference, perhaps, between most of us and the professional poets of genius lies in the loyalty to the flashes. The professional poets devote themselves to perfecting language with truths—realizing that when poems work and are good or better than good, they (to paraphrase Milton) justify the ways of the universe to our hearts and brains in their panics and joys.

That is why the complexity, when it is there, is worth it. (Most poetry, of course, is amazingly simple, clear: it is often the reader who is superfluously complex, who resists original ideas.) The broad epic poems of Homer, Vergil, Dante, Milton open our imaginations, increase our very intelligence and range of feelings—and this with invitations to love, to think, to refashion into meaningful orders the whole of human experience on all of its physical, mental, and spiritual levels. With lyric poetry, that briefer, more personal sort of shot in the dark, the invitations challenge our personal anarchies: to arrange for comprehension our fears and pains and pleasures—to hospitalize them within the generous complete forms of right words. Creating such forms, such shapes for experience, is the hard, happy task and art of the true poet, who enters, as William Faulkner has put it, the "workshop" of the human heart, to make, from what the Irish poet Yeats has called our "quarrels with ourselves," a language for our solitude.

The greatest poems, in fact, become unforgettable because they are secretaries of the human spirit, expressing not merely private wounds and healings but universal sufferings and hopes. Their techniques—of rhythm, rhyme, meter, metaphor, surrealistic leaps and unpredictable similes—are merely extensions of the mind's natural methods, are echoes of truth beyond the just plain personal. Such techniques objectify and make more honest the lines, make possible in poetry what Socrates meant by the examined life— and what Shelley meant when he said that the poet "reveals the hidden analogies of things." To thrill to real poetry is therefore to thrill to oneself—and this with all the complex and natural methods by which, perhaps, even the universe may be said to be thrilling to, and examining, its own beauty.

Guides and Anthologies

AUDEN, W. H. 1907-1973 and NORMAN HOLMES PEARSON b. 1909. (eds.). *Poets of the English Language* (1950). Five volumes, ranging from Middle English to the present century. Indispensable collection, with superb essays by Auden. *P—Viking Pr.*

BROOKS, CLEANTH b. 1906 and ROBERT PENN WARREN b. 1905 (eds.). *Understanding Poetry* (4th ed. 1976). Anthology of American and English poetry, with a sound introduction. *P—HR&W.*

DEUTSCH, BABETTE b. 1895. *Poetry Handbook* (4th ed. 1974). A useful guide to technical terms and techniques. *H—Funk&W.*

ELLMANN, RICHARD b. 1918 and CHARLES FEIDELSON b. 1918 (eds.). *The Modern Tradition* (1965). Sources of modern poetry. *H— Oxford U Pr.*

ENGLE, PAUL b. 1908 and WARREN CARRIER b. 1918 (eds.). *Reading Modern Poetry* (1955). Good anthology, with helpful critical discussions. *P—Scott F.*

FRIAR, KIMON b. 1911 and JOHN MALCOLM BRINNIN b. 1916 (eds.). *Modern Poetry* (1st ed. 1950). Valuable discussions of the poems. *o.p.*

HIEATT, A. KENT b. 1921 and WILLIAM PARK b. 1930 (eds.). *The College Anthology of British and American Poetry* (2nd ed. 1972). Excellent, balanced selection from Chaucer to the present, with a good chapter on versification. *H—Allyn.*

HOFFMAN, DANIEL G. b. 1923 (ed.). *American Poetry and Poetics* (1962). Poets from the Puritans to Robert Frost discussing how they write, their methods. *o.p.*

KINSLEY, JAMES b. 1922 (ed.). *The Oxford Book of Ballads* (1969). The standard, excellent collection. *H—Oxford U Pr.*

LARKIN, PHILIP b. 1922 (ed.). *The Oxford Book of Twentieth-Century English Verse* (1973). A comprehensive but highly personalized anthology. *H—Oxford U Pr.*

MATTHIESSEN, F. O. 1902-1950 (ed.). *The Oxford Book of American Verse* (1950). Still the best summary-anthology of American poetry. *H—Oxford U Pr.*

NIMS, JOHN FREDERICK b. 1913 (ed.). *Western Wind: An Introduction to Poetry* (1974). Splendid thematic anthology, treating poems from points of view such as "senses," "mind," "emotions." *P—Random.*

PALGRAVE, FRANCIS T. 1824-1897 (ed.). *The Golden Treasury* (1861). The "classic, first" modern anthology, still a superb guide to taste. *Over 6 eds.*

PERKINS, DAVID. *A History of Modern Poetry* (1976). The most far-reaching study to date. *H—Harvard U Pr.*

POULIN, A. Jr. b. 1938 (ed.). *Contemporary American Poetry* (2nd ed. 1975). A good collection of poets prominent since 1945. *P—HM.*

PREMINGER, ALEX b. 1915 (ed.). *Encyclopedia of Poetry and Poetics* (1965). Reference text for techniques, terms, history. *H & P—Princeton U Pr.*

ROSENTHAL, M. L. b. 1917. *The New Poets: American and British Poetry Since World War II* (1967). Excellent discussions of the sources and meanings of modern poetry. *H—Oxford U Pr.*

SIMPSON, LOUIS b. 1923 (ed.). *An Introduction to Poetry* (1972). Fine, wide-ranging anthology, with valuable commentaries. *P—St Martin.*

SPEARE, M. E. b. 1884 (ed.). *Pocket Book of Verse.* An excellent inexpensive collection. *P—WSP.*

STAUFFER, DONALD BARLOW b. 1930. *A Short History of American Poetry* (1974). A good study, from the beginnings. *P—Dutton.*

WAGGONER, HYATT H. b. 1913. *American Poetry from the Puritans to the Present* (1968). Thoroughgoing studies of trends. *H—HM.*

WAGNER, JEAN b. 1919 (ed.). *Black Poets of the United States: From Paul Laurence Dunbar to Langston Hughes* (1973). The best anthology, to date, of Black poetry. *H—U of Ill Pr.*

WALLENSTEIN, BARRY b. 1941. *Visions and Revisions: An Approach to Poetry* (1971). Studies through compared texts of how great poems have evolved. Enormously valuable. *P—T Y Crowell.*

WHICHER, GEORGE F. 1889-1954 (ed.). *Poetry of the New England Renaissance, 1790–1890* (1950). An indispensable collection. *o.p.*

Poets to 1800

The ten chapters on "Historical and Regional Cultures" contain listings for the major world poets from Homer through Blake and Goethe. None of these is relisted or cross-referenced in this chapter.

Poets from 1800 to the Early 20th Century

The entries listed below are limited to the best poets writing in English in the 19th and early 20th centuries—except for a few major poets who wrote in languages other than English and whose influence on the development of English and American poetry has been profound.

ARNOLD, MATTHEW 1822-1888. *Poems*. Poetry conceived thoughtfully, often brilliantly, as a "criticism of life." *Over 6 eds.*

BAUDELAIRE, CHARLES 1821-1867. *Les Fleurs du mal* (1857). His use of symbolism, evocative power, and careful artistry in developing the theme of the antagonism between good and evil have influenced profoundly the development of modern poetry. *Over 6 eds.*

BROWNING, ELIZABETH BARRETT 1806-1861. *Sonnets from the Portuguese* (1850). Among the best of English sonnets. *Over 6 eds.*

BROWNING, ROBERT 1812-1889. *Poems*. Masterful monologues, having an enormous influence on modern poets. *Over 10 eds.*

BYRON, GEORGE GORDON 1788-1824. *Poems*. Satiric, romantic, and cynically witty long and short poems. *Over 6 eds.*

COLERIDGE, SAMUEL TAYLOR 1772-1824. *Poems*. Haunting poetry of beauty and terror by "the heaven-ey'd creature" (Wordsworth's phrase) of fantasy. *Over 6 eds.*

DICKINSON, EMILY 1830-1886. *Poems*. Brilliant short lyrics by a genius who probed deeply into the human spirit. *Over 6 eds.*

EMERSON, RALPH WALDO 1803-1882. *Poems*. Verses with a stern but kindly moral tone by America's first major poet and philosopher. *Over 6 eds.*

HARDY, THOMAS 1840-1928. *Poems*. First modern poetry with themes of antiwar and disillusionment. *H & P—Macmillan, St Martin.*

HEINE, HEINRICH 1797-1856. *Selected Poems*. Powerful lyrics and satirical ballads that successfully survive translation. *H—Oxford U Pr; P—Citadel Pr, Random.*

HOLMES, OLIVER WENDELL 1809-1894. *Poetical Works*. Serene, intelligent, civilized poetry. *H—HM.*

HOPKINS, GERARD MANLEY 1844-1889. *Poems*. Lovely and powerful "sprung-rhythm" verses; strongly influential. *H & P—Oxford U Pr.*

HOUSMAN, ALFRED EDWARD 1859-1936. *A Shropshire Lad* (1896). Deeply moving poetry with Horatian tones about the passions and disillusionment of youth. *H—Peter Pauper; P—Avon, Branden.*

KEATS, JOHN 1795-1821. *Poems*. The greatest odes in English, written by a genius who died young. *Over 15 eds.*

LONGFELLOW, HENRY WADSWORTH 1807-1882. *Poems*. Poetry still loved and esteemed despite changes in fashion. *Over 6 eds.*

POE, EDGAR ALLAN 1809-1849. *Poems*. Fantastical, often decadent poems; new appreciation of their excellence is increasing. *Over 6 eds.*

RIMBAUD, ARTHUR 1854-1891. *Complete Works*. Poetry by an amazingly precocious genius whose career as poet of the soul's disorder was over by the time he was 19. *H—Har-Row.*

SHELLEY, PERCY BYSSHE 1792-1822. *Poems*. Profound and light lyrics, often highly intellectual, often very lovely. *Over 15 eds.*

SWINBURNE, ALGERNON CHARLES 1837-1909. *Poems*. Romantic decadence in sensuous melodic lines. *o.p.*

TENNYSON, ALFRED 1809-1892. *Poems*. Familiar poetry by a late romantic, typical Victorian, and superb technician. *Over 10 eds.*

WHITMAN, WALT 1819-1892. *Leaves of Grass* (1855). His songs praising democracy and celebrating the individual profoundly charted the direction of modern American poetry. *Over 15 eds.*

WILDE, OSCAR 1854-1900. *Poems*. A lyric poet of high gifts, best known for "The Ballad of Reading Gaol." *P—Dutton, Penguin, Viking Pr.*

WORDSWORTH, WILLIAM 1770-1850. *Poems*. Poetry revealing the extraordinary beauty and significance of simple people and things by one of England's greatest romantic poets and philosophers. *Over 10 eds.*

Modern Poets

AIKEN, CONRAD 1889-1973. *Selected Poems*. A tough-minded verse, psychoanalytically directed. *H & P—Oxford U Pr.*

AUDEN, W. H. 1907-1973. *Collected Longer Poems* (1975) and *Selected Poetry* (1971). Among the modern masters of poetry as art; widely influential. *P—Random.*

BENÉT, STEPHEN VINCENT 1898-1943. *John Brown's Body* (1928). One of America's best long narrative poems. *H—HR&W.*

BERRYMAN, JOHN 1914-1971. *The Dream Songs* (1969). Striking, tormented, highly regarded poems and sonnets. *H & P—FS&G.*

CULLEN, COUNTEE 1903-1946. *On These I Stand* (1947). One of the most important Black poets. *H—Har-Row.*

CUMMINGS, E. E. 1894-1962. *Poems*. Deep poetic insight powerfully expressed in unorthodox forms and manners. *H—HarBraceJ; P—Grove, HarBraceJ.*

ELIOT, T. S. 1888-1965. *Complete Poems and Plays, 1909–1950* (1952). One of the most important modern poets in English to date. *H—HarBraceJ. Numerous other colls. in paper.*

FROST, ROBERT 1874-1963. *Poems*. Master of pentameter, with a passionate interest in evil. *H—HR&W; P—HR&W, WSP.*

HUGHES, LANGSTON 1902-1967. *Poems*. Strong, beautiful lyrics by one of America's foremost Black poets. *H—Knopf; P—Random.*

MACLEISH, ARCHIBALD b. 1892. *Collected Poems* (1952). A forceful "public" poet—rare in these times. *P—HM.*

MACNEICE, LOUIS 1907-1963. *Collected Poems*. Spare, satiric, solid lyrics often in traditional forms by one of the "Oxford Poets." *H—Oxford U Pr.*

MILLAY, EDNA ST. VINCENT 1892-1950. *Sonnets*. Laconic, witty poems showing great technical mastery. *H & P—Har-Row.*

MOORE, MARIANNE 1887-1972. *Poems*. Conversational, steely style; influential in early 20th century. *H—Macmillan; P—Viking Pr.*

PARKER, DOROTHY 1893-1967. *Poems*. A poet of dashing, casual, often bitter wit. *H & P—Viking Pr.*

PATTERSON, RAYMOND b. 1929. *26 Ways of Looking at a Black Man* (1969). Strong, intelligent lyrics. *P—Univ Pub & Dist.*

PLATH, SYLVIA 1932-1963. *Ariel* (1965). Well-wrought, moving, influential lyrics. *H & P—Har-Row.*

POUND, EZRA 1885-1972. *Selected Poems* (1957). Difficult poetry by an expatriate American whose influence on younger poets was great. *P— New Directions.*

RANSOM, JOHN CROWE 1888-1974. *Selected Poems* (3rd ed. 1969). Intellectual, hard, compassionate lines. *H—Knopf.*

ROBINSON, EDWIN ARLINGTON 1869-1935. *Poems*. Powerful lyrics and narratives in blank verse and other forms. *H & P—Macmillan.*

ROETHKE, THEODORE 1908-1963. *Collected Poems* (1958). "Madness" intensifying humanity in often superb lyrics. *H & P—Doubleday.*

SANDBURG, CARL 1878-1967. *Poems*. Sophisticated minstrelsy, in Whitmanesque style. *H & P—HarBraceJ.*

STEVENS, WALLACE 1879-1955. *Collected Poems* (1954). Intricate, contrapuntal lines of great beauty and wit; an important poet in the Romantic tradition. *H—Knopf.*

TATE, ALLEN b. 1899. *Poems* (1960). Passionate, muted lyrics, less influential than simply loved. *P—Swallow.*

THOMAS, DYLAN 1914-1953. *Poems*. A word-magician, with powerful imagination, whose poetry is not only influential but popular. *H—New Directions.*

THOMAS, EDWARD 1878-1917. *Collected Poems* (1964). Poet of nature, experiment, and deep intellectual passions. *H & P—Norton.*

WILLIAMS, WILLIAM CARLOS 1883-1963. *Pictures from Brueghel* (1962). Certainly one of the most important 20th-century American poets. *H & P—New Directions.*

WYLIE, ELINOR 1887-1928. *Collected Poems* (1932). Witty, powerful poems by an influential conservative in verse. *H—Knopf.*

YEATS, WILLIAM BUTLER 1865-1939. *Collected Poems* (2nd ed. 1956). The most important poet since Donne, winner of the Nobel Prize, leading poet of the Irish Renaissance. *H—Macmillan.*

Poetry on Records, Tapes, in Performance

This century has witnessed—is witnessing—an extraordinary explosion of talent and fine poems, by gifted young poets, in the United States: a period that some have wished to call America's Elizabethan Age of poetry. Together with the equally extraordinary advances in technology, familiar to everyone, this means that poets and their poems in performance (whether on tapes or records or live) are available straight across the country, and especially at colleges and universities, where a good many of the more prominent practicing poets currently teach. The greatest poets of previous ages have also been recorded, often by accomplished actors and actresses, and these are easily available to those eager to learn, to excite their imaginations, and to open their minds to the art. Catalogs such as those of Schwann and Caedmon (and frequently radio-recorded tapes of poets) may be had for the asking—and the rewards are rich. For above all else, poetry like music is meant to be heard; and not only heard, but allowed to happen to the ears and heart, as well as the head, of the listener.

14. Drama

J. Sherwood Weber

Reading a play is only an expedient substitute for seeing it on the stage. Because a play is properly a story acted on a stage before an audience, its printed version is at best only a partial art form. Story, dialogue, some few stage directions are supplied, but missing are scenery, costumes, stage movement, voice inflection and timing, facial expression, sometimes music—all of which are part of the dramatist's original conception or the director's version of that conception, none of which translates clearly to the printed page. Yet plays can be read—and with considerable understanding and satisfaction, for a first-rate play retains much of its dramatic power even when merely read.

When only read, however, a good play is a highly condensed, closely packed, carefully structured literary form; it lacks the novel's expanse, full detail, and orientation to the reader. The reader must therefore supply through a cultivated dramatic imagination what theatrical production normally adds to enhance the playwright's dialogue. During a second reading (or a third) analogies, symbols, overtones will become clear—elements that would cause only a few puzzled brows if the same play were well produced in the theatre.

Because a play must immediately excite an audience or fail in production, the drama is a thoroughly social art. It must speak movingly and persuasively to large groups of people, or quickly perish. Thus almost all great playwrights have been publicly recognized and generally acclaimed during their lifetimes. To win such recognition the dramatist has to employ action, conflict, characters, and theme emanating from the bedrock of all lasting art, our common humanity.

On this bedrock many different structures for theatre have been built, ranging from the huge, formal open-air amphitheatre of the Greeks through the intimate, flexible apron stage of the Elizabethans to the detached picture frame (or proscenium-arch) or versatile epic (open or arena) stages of today. The theatre has nurtured many forms, from slapstick farce to austere poetic tragedy—all of which involve an orderly distortion of reality through dramatic art and artifice. It has employed the allied arts of music, dance, architecture, sculpture, painting, to express itself vividly, and it has combined these elements with endless variation. Through continual adaptation to contemporary needs, the theatre has remained vital. The play reader can learn about theatre history and development through Macgowan and Melnitz's handsomely illustrated *The Living Stage* or Brockett's excellent *History of the Theatre*.

One unchanging factor in the theatre is the audience's desire to be entertained—though ideas about what constitutes entertainment have shifted greatly in various cultures through the ages. Playwrights, always mindful of popular acclaim, have often exhibited a fondness for the spectacular, the melodramatic, the sentimental. In almost every age the plea of the critical minority—from Aristotle to Walter Kerr and John Simon—has been for less show and more art.

Perhaps the most effective way to learn to read plays perceptively is by using a critical, skillfully edited anthology such as Goodman's *Drama on Stage*, Bentley's *The Play*, or Kernan's *Character and Conflict*. All of these contain a variety of theatre classics, from Sophocles to Pinter, as well as apparatus for developing a capacity to visualize imaginatively. Paperbound anthologies provide the most good plays for the least money, and the book list that follows favors them. By browsing in them the reader can discover periods of the drama and specific playwrights to explore further—in books, on records or tapes, and in the theatre.

Earlier chapters of this book contain selective material on the classic dramatic localities: Greece, with its unrivaled quartet of Aeschylus, Sophocles, Euripides, and Aristophanes; Renaissance England, with Marlowe, Shakespeare, and Jonson; 17th-century France, with Corneille, Molière, and Racine; Restoration and 18th-century England, with Congreve and Sheridan. All of these, and many others, helped build the solid foundations of modern and contemporary drama.

Since the late 19th century the world has taken such a lively interest in the social art of drama that it has vied with the novel for popularity. Fifteen Nobel Prizes for literature have been awarded to playwrights, and the familiarity of names such as Ibsen, Chekhov, Pirandello, Shaw, O'Neill, Brecht, Williams, Genet makes one realize how large the dramatist bulks in the total literary scene.

Today in the United States and elsewhere the drama has flourished—quantitatively if not always qualitatively—in the cinema and on television as well as in the amateur, college, regional, and commercial theatres. Though some form of realism has been the prevailing mode, experimentation abounds. In recent decades the theatre has become at its best a forum for provocative social thought:

O'Casey, Sartre, Odets, Miller, Hellman, Albee, Pinter, Bullins, Stoppard have written plays that are both eminently theatrical and socially alert. To read representative American, British, Continental, Asian, and African plays is to become aware of the most challenging and disturbing developments of our confused and confusing times.

Anthologies

BENTLEY, ERIC b. 1916 (ed.). *The Play: A Critical Anthology* (1951). One play each by Sophocles, Molière, Ibsen, Strindberg, Rostand, Wilde, and Miller, and two by Shakespeare, plus unusually illuminating critical analyses, constitute an excellent introduction to the study of drama. *H—P-H.*

———. (ed.). *The Modern Theatre* (1955-60). Stimulating collections containing 30 otherwise hard-to-find modern European and American plays. *H—Peter Smith; P—Doubleday 6 vols.*

———. (ed.). *The Classic Theatre* (1958-63). Good collections from major national theatres—Italian, German, Spanish, and French. *H—Peter Smith 3 vols; P—Doubleday 4 vols.*

BLOCK, HASKELL M. b. 1923 and ROBERT G. SHEDD b. 1921 (eds.). *Masters of Modern Drama* (1962). An impressively edited, monumentally proportioned anthology, containing 45 plays by 35 modern world dramatists from Ibsen and Strindberg through Beckett and Duerrenmatt. *H—Random.*

CARTMELL, VAN H. 1896-1966 and BENNETT A. CERF 1898-1971 (eds.). *24 Favorite One-Act Plays* (1958). A collection showing the variety of form and subject used by modern masters of the short play until the 1960s. *H & P—Doubleday.*

DOWNER, ALAN S. b. 1912 (ed.). *American Drama* (1960). Traces the history of play writing in the United States through specimen plays. *o.p.*

Eight Great Comedies (1957). From Aristophanes to Shaw. *P—NAL.*

Eight Great Tragedies (1957). From Aeschylus to O'Neill. *P—NAL.*

Genius of the Theatre Series. Includes eight carefully edited and compact volumes—one each on the Early English, Late English, French, German, Irish, Italian, Oriental, and Scandinavian theatres—containing a half dozen or more representative plays each. *P—NAL.*

GOODMAN, RANDOLPH b. 1908 (ed.). *Drama on Stage* (1961). A first-rate introduction to the serious study of plays, containing sample dramas from major periods as well as many essays about theatres, dramatic production, and acting. *P—HR&W.*

Jacobean Drama Anthology (1968). Ed. by Richard C. Harrier. A representative collection of early 17th-century plays. *P—Norton 2 vols.*

KERNAN, ALVIN B. b. 1923 (ed.). *Character and Conflict* (2nd ed. 1969). An excellent introduction to drama, containing 11 plays from various periods with elaborate commentaries. *P—HarBraceJ.*

LAHR, JOHN b. 1941 (ed.). *Grove Press Modern Drama* (1975). Six

plays by Baraka, Brecht, Feiffer, Genet, Ionesco, and Mrozek epitomize the most nontraditional trends in world theatre today. *P—Grove.*

New American Plays (1965-71). Vol. I ed. by Robert W. Corrigan, Vols.
II-IV by William M. Hoffman. Representative samplings of the kinds
of plays being written in the 1960s and produced off-Broadway, off-
off-Broadway, and in college theatres. Like many plays, these often
act better than they read. *H & P—Hill & Wang 4 vols.*

Nineteenth-Century Russian Plays (1973). A good collection, ed. and
trans. by F. D. Reeve. *P—Norton.*

REINERT, OTTO b. 1923 (ed.). ***Classic Through Modern Drama*** (1970).
An introductory anthology surveying the history of drama through 15
plays from Greek to contemporary with extremely cogent critical essays. *P—Little.*

Ten Greek Plays in Contemporary Translations. See "Greece," page
6.

Twentieth-Century Russian Plays (1963). Ed. and trans. by F. D.
Reeve. An excellent collection. *P—Norton.*

Classics of the Drama

For plays by, and books about, the classical Greek dramatists
(Aeschylus, Sophocles, Euripides, Aristophanes), see "Greece,"
pages 6 to 8. Elizabethan and Jacobean drama, including Shakespeare, is covered in "The Renaissance and Reformation," pages
28 to 34. For classical French drama (Corneille, Molière, Racine), see
"The 17th Century," pages 37 to 40. Distinctive plays from all the
greater and lesser dramatic periods are contained in many of the
critical and standard anthologies cited above.

Modern Drama

Many plays by modern and contemporary playwrights are in-
expensively available in anthologies such as those listed above.
Only collections of a single dramatist's work are included below.
An up-to-date listing of single plays in paperbound editions can be
found in the latest *Paperbound Books in Print*, either in the author
section under the author's name or in the subject section under
"Drama."

ALBEE, EDWARD b. 1928. ***The American Dream and The Zoo Story***
(1962) and ***Who's Afraid of Virginia Woolf*** (1962). Short and long
plays by a leading contemporary dramatist whose plays delight,
anger, and sometimes merely irritate. First title: *P—NAL.* Second title: *P—Antheneum, PB.*

ANDERSON, MAXWELL 1888-1959. ***Four Verse Plays*** (1959). Contains the best tragedies (including *Winterset*) of a modern playwright
who tried with varying success to blend poetry and social commentary with his own tragic vision. *P—HarBraceJ.*

ANOUILH, JEAN b. 1910. *Five Plays* (1959). Distinctive and diverse plays by a French master of theatricalism. *P—Hill & Wang.*

BECKETT, SAMUEL b. 1906. *Waiting for Godot* (1954), *Endgame* (1958), and *Krapp's Last Tape and Other Dramatic Pieces* (1960). Ambiguous, sensitive, controversial "theatre of the absurd" pieces by a man much in tune with his times. *H & P—Grove.*

BRECHT, BERTOLT 1898-1956. *Parables for the Theatre* (1957). The best-known "epic theatre" dramas—including *The Good Woman of Setzuan* and *The Caucasian Chalk Circle*—by a skillful Communist playwright who employed the stage for social protest. *H—U of Minn Pr.*

CHEKHOV, ANTON 1860-1904. *Plays*. Superb, realistic, subtle analyses of timeless human nature, with Russian variations. *Over 6 colls.*

ELIOT. *Complete Poems and Plays, 1909–1950*. See "Poetry," page 136.

GIRAUDOUX, JEAN 1882-1944. *Four Plays* (1958). Four theatricalist dramas, including *The Madwoman of Chaillot*, in Maurice Valency's excellent translations and adaptations from the French. *P—Hill & Wang.*

HELLMAN, LILLIAN b. 1905. *Collected Plays* (1972). A realist, moralist, and deft dramatic artist analyzes contemporary society in modern classics such as *The Children's Hour. H—Little.*

IBSEN, HENRIK 1828-1906. *Plays*. Naturalistic, symbolic, poetic plays that have shaped significantly both the form and content of drama ever since his time. *Over 12 colls.*

IONESCO, EUGÈNE b. 1912. *Four Plays* (1958). Antirealistic, symbolic plays by a leading exponent of the experimental European theatre since World War II. *P—Grove.*

LORCA, FEDERICO GARCÍA 1899-1936. *Three Tragedies* (1956). Powerful poetic tragedies by the leading author of 20th-century Spain. *P—New Directions.*

MILLER, ARTHUR b. 1915. *Collected Plays* (1957). Tragedies and social parables that prompt some critics to rank Miller as a major contemporary dramatist. *P—Viking Pr.*

O'CASEY, SEAN 1884-1964. *Three Plays* (1957). The three best plays, including *The Plough and the Stars*, by the most powerful modern Irish playwright. *P—St Martin.*

O'NEILL, EUGENE 1888-1953. *Three Plays* (1959). Three of the best-known tragedies of a prolix but deeply probing major 20th-century dramatic genius. *P—Random.*

PIRANDELLO, LUIGI 1867-1936. *Naked Masks* (1952). In five enigmatic, provocative plays, an experimental Italian playwright probes into the confusing nature of reality. *P—Dutton.*

SARTRE, JEAN-PAUL b. 1905. *No Exit and The Flies* (1947). Incisive dramatizations of French existentialist thought by its leading literary spokesman. *H—Knopf.*

SHAW, GEORGE BERNARD 1856-1950. *Plays*. Witty, talky dramas dedicated to the proposition that reason should rule over 20th-century men and women. *Over 6 colls.*

STRINDBERG, AUGUST 1849-1912. *Plays.* Misogynistic, moving dramas by a mordant Scandinavian playwright, important for his psychological probing and symbolist technique. *Over 10 colls.*

WILDER, THORNTON 1897-1975. *Three Plays* (1957). Includes *The Skin of Our Teeth* and *Our Town;* experimental, lucid, much-revived plays by a modern who retained his faith in humanity and God. *H—Har-Row.*

WILLIAMS, TENNESSEE b. 1914. *Theatre of Tennessee Williams* (1972). Strange poetic tragedies about warped, frustrated lives by a leading American dramatist. *H—New Directions 4 vols.*

History and Criticism

BENTLEY, ERIC b. 1916. *The Playwright as Thinker* (1955). Perceptive, informed analyses of the thought in drama of Cocteau, Ibsen, Pirandello, Sartre, Shaw, Strindberg—most useful after the reader knows the plays well. *P—HarBraceJ.*

——. (ed.). *The Theory of the Modern Stage* (1968). A ranging introduction to theatre today through essays by representative directors, critics, and scholars. *P—Penguin.*

BROCKETT, OSCAR G. b. 1923. *History of the Theatre* (2nd ed. 1974). For both readability and scholarship, the best one-volume history of the theatre from ancient Egypt down to "happenings." Rich in material, objective on controversial matters, with well-chosen but poorly reproduced illustrations. *H—Allyn.*

—— and ROBERT R. FINDLAY b. 1932. *Century of Innovation* (1973). Comprehensive, generously illustrated survey of the past 100 years of European and American theatre, stressing how and why we reached the current state. *H—P-H.*

BROOK, PETER b. 1925. *The Empty Space* (1968). One of the most brilliant and controversial directors in the theatre today explains his views on theatrical production. *P—Avon.*

ESSLIN, MARTIN b. 1918. *Reflections* (1969). A series of essays in casual language offering sensible, perceptive, and thorough analyses of the whole theatre situation today, viewing the newer trends (e.g., epic, absurdist) as fusing into the traditional mainstream. *H—Doubleday.*

FERGUSSON, FRANCIS b. 1904. *The Idea of a Theatre* (1968). An often profound, often brilliant, sometimes difficult study of ten great plays, from *Oedipus Rex* to *Murder in the Cathedral*, with focus on the changing art of drama. *H & P—Princeton U Pr.*

KERR, WALTER b. 1913. *Tragedy and Comedy* (1967). A sensible, persuasive, readable effort to write a modern poetics by a foremost contemporary drama critic. *P—S&S.*

LAHR, JOHN b. 1941. *Up Against the Fourth Wall* (1970). Stimulating essays on the radical theatre of the 1960s (playwrights such as Pinter and Kopit, groups such as Living Theatre and La Mama), viewing drama as a reflection of our social and cultural upheavals. *P—Grove.*

MACGOWAN, KENNETH 1888-1963 and WILLIAM MELNITZ b. 1900. *The Living Stage* (1955). Fascinating, lively, handsomely illustrated history of world theatre from the beginnings to recent times. *H—P-H.*

SIMON, JOHN b. 1925. *Singularities* (1975). A provocative and probing critic of our cultural scene writes short, acerbic essays on dramatic productions, playwrights, and directors. *H & P—Random.*

TYNAN, KENNETH b. 1927. *Curtains* (1961). A stimulating collection of essays by a critic with taste and convictions. *o.p.*

Drama on Records

Listening to recorded plays is a compromise measure—sometimes more satisfying than reading them but less rewarding than seeing them. The library of plays on records and tapes is extensive. Standard classics, from Aeschylus through Shakespeare to Ibsen, can be heard; and many new plays are recorded shortly after they are produced. Play recordings are particularly useful for an understanding of plays difficult to read. Schwann's catalog contains up-to-date listings of recorded dramas available. And most college and public libraries today have growing record and tape collections—of plays as well as of poetry and music.

15. Biography

Philip Roddman

Is it possible to learn the truth about any individual, living or dead? And would the discovery of the truth explain the intricate, the accidental, the elusive life led from day to day by the subject of this truth? When reconstructing a life, all biographers must assume an affirmative answer to these two great questions. Whereas novelists and playwrights aim to *create* life in order to intensify the mystery of personality, biographers aim to *re-create* life in order to clarify the mystery. For the purpose of biography is to introduce, as history does, a sense of continuity into human affairs, as well as to excite our wonder and satisfy our doubts by making life a function of truth, as religion does. Biography is therefore a branch of history and frequently an ally of religious philosophy. In fact, for a culture such as ours, bred in the Judeo-Christian tradition, it has been the universal art form, as exemplified by the lives of the patriarchs and heroes of the Old Testament and by that of Jesus in the New. So it may well be that the enormous popularity of biography in our time—over 2,000 are published annually in English alone—expresses the wish for a general, perhaps a religious, thaw in the icy reaches of Technopolis—biography being a reassuring documentary art form that infuses the meshes of history with the magic of personality.

There are, of course, many kinds of biography to fit the many kinds of truth. The thoughtful reader, seeking both pleasure and instruction, should examine the half-dozen masterpieces in the two mainstreams of biographical writing: the stream of being— what a person is; and the stream of action—what a person does. The first stream flows from Plutarch's *Lives of the Noble Grecians and Romans*, the second from Suetonius' *Lives of the Twelve Caesars*. Plutarch, influenced by the idea of destiny in Greek tragedy, portrays human nature as changeless and the conflict between will and fate in terms of a morality play. Suetonius, influenced by

Lucretius and the Atomists, conceives of the individual as a bundle of sensations, as an ever-changing I, a "coral-reef of diverse personalities," as a vehicle for a fund of restless energies that add up to a "happening" rather than a play.

Plutarch's concept of "the ruling passion" and the unitary sense of things has been reinforced in modern history by Calvin's dogma of predestination, by Freud's theory of the ineluctable unconscious, and by Lenin's insistence on the inexorability of class determinism. Suetonius' emphasis on our mixed nature and the pervasiveness of chance has received support from the British empirical thinkers, from John Locke, David Hume, John Stuart Mill, and Charles Darwin, as well as from the libertarian ideas in the Declaration of Independence and from Einstein's Theory of Relativity.

The Plutarchian tradition of "the ruling passion" conferring symmetrical order upon the ages of man—youth, middle age, old age—appears in Dr. Johnson's *Lives of the Poets*, though not in his theories regarding experience. In Boswell's *The Life of Samuel Johnson*, the supreme biography in English, "the ruling passion" motif does not appear at all. Consider an example from each. After observing of Dean Swift that "he was always careful of his money," Johnson continues: "At last his avarice grew too powerful for his kindness; he would refuse a bottle to a guest, and in Ireland no man visits where he cannot drink." He then concludes that Swift's loneliness and desolation brought on his madness. The root cause, seemingly, of Swift's great misfortunes was in large part his "love of a shilling." Johnson's point of view is clear-cut and imposed with much force and wit. His biographer, James Boswell, on the other hand, follows the realistic tradition of Suetonius, where the character steadily characterizes himself—in and by his very voice, his style, and his habits. Here is Boswell's rendering of a dinner table conversation: "Mr. Arthur Lee mentioned some Scotch who had taken possession of a barren part of America, and wondered why they should choose it. Johnson: Why, Sir, all barrenness is comparative. The Scotch would never know it to be barren." Boswell tells us that Johnson kept dried orange peel in his pockets and that he had a dread of solitude. All manner of detail shapes and reshapes the Johnsonian presence. Boswell vividly re-creates the man who converted his outrageous prejudices into counters for fun and games and transmuted the ugly matter of physical pain and early sorrow into the bright essences of reason.

Of 20th-century biographies, perhaps the most important in the first category are Ernest Jones's *The Life and Work of Sigmund Freud* and Edgar Johnson's *Charles Dickens: His Tragedy and Triumph*, while Lytton Strachey's *Queen Victoria* and Amy Kelly's *Eleanor of Aquitaine and the Four Kings* are examples of the second.

Ever since St. Augustine's *Confessions*, men and women have yearned to tell their own side of the story in the unequal struggle with existence, impelled as much by the need to obtain absolution as by the desire for self-justification in a cold and hostile universe.

Autobiography, therefore, is as much a branch of psychology as of history. Its interest for us resides in the personal answer, both conscious and unconscious, which it gives to those four simple and all-encompassing questions that psychology is forever asking: Why do we laugh? Why do we cry? Why do we forget? Why do we lie? The responses to these questions in autobiographies of men and women of genius have universal value because they carry a charge of consciousness surpassed only by the greatest novelists. In projecting the self as hero, an autobiographer sets out to serve the secret fantasies of the heart, but ends by serving knowledge and truth. In the process of vindicating the massive illusions and ambitions of the inner life, he or she uncovers the way they are put together. Cellini's *Autobiography*, Rousseau's *Confessions*, Boswell's *London Journal*, Gibbon's *Autobiography*, De Quincey's *Confessions of an English Opium-Eater*, Mill's *Autobiography*, Gide's *Journals*, Planck's *Scientific Autobiography*, Einstein's *Out of My Later Years*, Van Gogh's *Dear Theo*, Stravinsky's *Themes and Episodes*, Frank Lloyd Wright's *Autobiography*, Stein's *The Autobiography of Alice B. Toklas*, Churchill's *Memoirs of the Second World War*, Sartre's *The Words*, and, most recently, Russell's *Autobiography*—all attest to the variety, the wisdom, the psychological reality of this form of revelation.

The first ten chapters of this book, dealing with "Historical and Regional Cultures," list a few autobiographies and many biographies—both those written during the historical period or in the cultural area and those written mainly in recent decades about important political leaders and monarchs, writers, scientists, social reformers, and artists. These numerous biographies are not relisted or cross-referenced in this "Biography" chapter. The reader is advised to consult the "Books About" sections of Chapters 1 through 10 for additional recommendations and data about other biographies rewarding to read.

ACKERMAN, JAMES S. b. 1919. *Palladio* (1966). Perhaps the most imitated architect in history is presented in his social and cultural environment. *P—Penguin.*

ADAMS, HENRY 1838-1918. *The Education of Henry Adams* (1906). The scion of one of the "first families" of New England in quest of the meaning of life. *H—Berg, Modern Lib; P—HM.*

ALI, MUHAMMAD b. 1942. *The Greatest: My Own Story* (1975). A world's champion boxer emerges as a great-hearted, imaginative, arrogant, yet irresistible American. *H—Random; P—Ballantine.*

ALLEN, GAY WILSON b. 1903. *The Solitary Singer* (1955). America's master poet, Walt Whitman, in a well-documented work that lays bare his life in his art. *H—NYU Pr.*

ARMITAGE, ANGUS b. 1902. *The World of Copernicus* (1947). The life of the Renaissance cleric-astronomer who changed our view about the structure of the universe. *P—Beekman Pubs.*

AUCLAIR, MARCELLE. *Teresa of Avila* (1953). An extraordinarily vivid book about an extraordinary woman, founder of the Carmelite order. *P—Doubleday.*

AUDUBON, JOHN JAMES 1785-1851. *Eighteen Twenty Six Journal* (1967). The personal record of the artist-ornithologist whose contribution to American culture is of unparalleled splendor. *H & P—U of Okla Pr.*

BEAUVOIR, SIMONE DE b. 1909. *All Said and Done* (1974). Views on feminism, religious belief, change, chance as they form in the life experiences of the existentialist novelist and critic. *H—Putnam; P—Warner Bks.*

BELL, QUENTIN b. 1910. *Virginia Woolf* (1972). A major English novelist caught to the life in a frank biography by her nephew. *H & P—HarBraceJ.*

BERGER, JOHN b. 1926. *Success and Failure of Picasso* (1966). The matchless artist of the 20th century considered in relation to the setting of his time and the evolution of his genius. *H—Peter Smith.*

BERLIN, ISAIAH b. 1909. *Karl Marx* (3rd ed. 1963). The mover and shaker of the modern world depicted by a celebrated English scholar. *P—Oxford U Pr.*

BERLIOZ, HECTOR 1803-1869. *Memoirs of Hector Berlioz* (1969). The great composer self-revealed as a passionate intellect. *H—Knopf, Peter Smith; P—Dover, Norton.*

BLAKE, ROBERT b. 1916. *Disraeli* (1966). The gifted and mysterious man—Queen Victoria's favorite prime minister—comes to life. *H—St Martin.*

BLOTNER, JOSEPH LEO b. 1916. *Faulkner* (1974). A detailed life of the Nobel Prize novelist whose vision of Southern anguish since the Civil War has enriched world literature. *H—Random 2 vols.*

BOWEN, CATHERINE DRINKER 1897-1973. *Yankee from Olympus* (1944). The fascinating life of a magnificent man, Justice Oliver Wendell Holmes. *H—Little.*

———. *John Adams and the American Revolution* (1950). A recreation of an entire era in the image of a leading historical figure. *H—Little; P—G&D.*

CHESTERTON, GILBERT KEITH 1874-1936. *Saint Thomas Aquinas* (1933). The authoritative theologian of Roman Catholicism refreshingly presented by a "prince of paradox" among biographers. *P—Doubleday.*

CURIE, EVE b. 1904. *Madame Curie* (1937). A daughter's tribute to the genius of her mother, a great scientist. *H—Doubleday; P—PB.*

DAICHES, DAVID b. 1912. *Moses* (1975). The Hebrew lawgiver and prophet delineated by a many-sided Scottish scholar. *H—Praeger.*

DANA, RICHARD HENRY 1815-1882. *Two Years Before the Mast* (1840). A young Harvard dropout adventuring aboard a windjammer over a century ago. *Over 6 eds.*

DARWIN, CHARLES 1809-1882. *The Voyage of the Beagle* (1840). Perhaps the most significant voyage since Columbus, leading to the formulation of the theory of evolution and to a new concept of history. *H—Har-Row (abr.); P—Dutton, Natural Hist.*

DELACROIX, EUGENE 1798-1863. *Journals* (repr. 1969). A towering artist of immense energy, interested in politics and literature and sex, setting himself down in a daily journal from the age of 23 to the year of his death. *P—G&D.*

DE QUINCEY, THOMAS 1785-1859. *Confessions of an English Opium-Eater* (1822). An account of drug addiction in brilliant prose. *H & P—Dutton.*

DU BOIS, WILLIAM EDWARD BURGHADT 1868-1963. *Autobiography* (1968). The champion of complete civil and political equality for Black Americans in a self-portrayal that reveals great nobility of character and mind. *H & P—Intl Pub Co.*

EDEL, LEON b. 1907. *Henry James* (1953-72). A five-volume definitive biography of the subtlest master of the American novel. *H—Lippincott.*

ELLMANN, RICHARD b. 1918. *James Joyce* (1959). An engrossing and immensely learned biography of a literary genius. *H & P—Oxford U Pr.*

ESSLIN, MARTIN b. 1918. *Antonin Artaud* (1977). A study of the lucid madman whose theories have revolutionized the modern theatre. *P—Penguin.*

FRANK, ANNE 1929-1945. *Diary of Anne Frank* (1952). The unforgettable journal of an adolescent girl who with her family hid in an Amsterdam house before capture and death in a Nazi extermination camp. *H—Modern Lib.*

FRANK, PHILIPP 1884-1966. *Einstein* (1947). Einstein's successor in the professorship of theoretical physics at the University of Prague writes a magisterial account of a scientific genius. *H—Knopf.*

FREEMAN, DOUGLAS SOUTHALL 1886-1953. *R. E. Lee* (1935). The hero of the Confederacy and his lieutenants delineated in a monumental work of historical scholarship. *H—Scribner 4 vols.*

GOLDSTONE, RICHARD HENRY b. 1917. *Thornton Wilder* (1975). A synthesis of the life and achievements of a widely read playwright, novelist, scholar, and critic. *H—Sat Rev Pr.*

GRAHAM, SHIRLEY 1907-1977 and GEORGE D. LIPSCOMB. *Dr. George Washington Carver* (1944). An engaging account of a Black American scientist of international renown, whose work as an agricultural chemist has so extensively improved the culture of crops as to affect the culture of civilization. *H—Messner; P—Archway.*

GUTMAN, ROBERT W. b. 1930. *Richard Wagner* (1968). The genius of the music-drama and "endless melody" brilliantly portrayed. *P—HarBraceJ.*

HAMMARSKJÖLD, DAG 1905-1961. *Markings* (1964). The spiritual struggle of a man who headed the United Nations like a modern Pericles. *H—Knopf.*

HIGHAM, CHARLES b. 1931. *The Adventures of Conan Doyle* (1976). The life of a great and just man, who in the Holmes-Watson team created one of the absolute successes in world literature. *H—Norton.*

HINGLEY, RONALD. *A New Life of Anton Chekhov* (1976). A scrupulous rendition of the known facts about the life of a writer whose plays and short stories are among the world's masterpieces. *H—Knopf.*

HOMER, WILLIAM INNES b. 1929. *Alfred Stieglitz* (1977). About the photographer and painter who counseled and sustained native genius in the arts long before America's awakening to the existence of the School of Paris. *H—NYGS.*

ISHERWOOD, CHRISTOPHER b. 1904. *Christopher and His Kind* (1976). Remarkably objective autobiography of the novelist who caught a vision of suicidal inhumanity in the Berlin of the 1930s. *H—FS&G.*

JOHN XXIII, POPE 1881-1963. *Journal of a Soul* (1963). The record of a noble spirit in a troubled world, reminiscent of Thomas à Kempis' *The Imitation of Christ. H—Chr Classics.*

JOHNSON, EDGAR b. 1901. *Charles Dickens* (1952). An outstanding work about the tragedy and triumph of one of the best and most beloved of English novelists. *H—Greenwood.*

JONES, ERNEST 1879-1958. *The Life and Work of Sigmund Freud* (1953-57). A classic biography of the man who reshaped the consciousness of the modern world. *H—Basic 3 vols; P—Basic abr.*

JOSEPHSON, MATTHEW 1899-1978. *Edison* (1963). An accurate account of the inventor forever associated with light, power, and the organization of the research laboratory as the center of modern civilization. *P— McGraw.*

KAPLAN, JUSTIN b. 1925. *Mr. Clemens and Mark Twain* (1966). The man, the writer, and the performer acutely studied, his comic genius perceptively analyzed. *H & P—S&S.*

KELLER, HELEN 1880-1968. *The Story of My Life* (1903). A document of first importance about the miraculous achievements of a human being who in early childhood had lost the power to hear and see. *Over 6 eds.*

KING, CORETTA SCOTT b. 1927. *My Life with Martin Luther King, Jr.* (1970). The poignant story of the assassinated human-rights activist by his wife, a remarkable leader in her own right. *P—Avon.*

KLEE, PAUL 1879-1940. *The Diaries of Paul Klee* (1964). The painter who believed that art is *process* illuminates his own work and that of abstract impressionism. *H & P—U of Cal Pr.*

LÉLY, GILBERT. *Marquis de Sade* (1962). Novelist, diabolist, sadist, the Marquis, the ultimate monster in modern psychology, portrayed as neighbor and "our bedfellow." *P—Grove.*

LEVY, JULIEN. *Memoir of an Art Gallery* (1977). A rich record of the years 1931-1948 that recalls the struggle of the *avante-garde* to reach the American public at a time when the business aspect of art meant not money but lightness of heart, unorthodoxy of mind, and "plenty of pleasure." *H—Putnam.*

LUDWIG, EMIL 1881-1948. *Napoleon* (1927). The tempestuous life of the general and emperor who won and lost kingdoms by sacrificing millions of lives to his massive ambition. *H—Liveright; P—PB.*

LUKE, MARY M. b. 1919. *Gloriana: The Years of Elizabeth I* (1973). A sumptuous biography of England's most admired ruler, covering her entire reign. *H—Coward.*

LYONS, F. S. L. b. 1923. *Charles Stewart Parnell* (1977). The fascination of a career, both political and romantic, that captured the imagination of geniuses like Yeats and Joyce as well as the average person. *H—Oxford U Pr.*

MADARIAGA, SALVADOR DE b. 1886. *Christopher Columbus* (1967). A well-conceived life of the explorer. *H—Ungar.*

MALCOLM X 1925-1965. *The Autobiography of Malcolm X* (1964). A devastating depiction of life in the jungle of cities by a man of fine intelligence who rose, against heavy odds, above the bondage of his surroundings. *P—Ballantine.*

MARCHAND, LESLIE b. 1900. *Byron* (1957). A definitive biography of a great 19th-century poet, individualist, and activist. *H—Knopf 3 vols.*

MAUROIS, ANDRÉ 1885-1967. *Lélia: The Life of George Sand* (1953). The most famous woman in French letters, celebrated for 80 novels, a dozen liaisons, and numerous social reforms, drawn with a steel pen. *P—Penguin.*

———. *Prometheus: The Life of Balzac* (1966). The definitive biography of a titan of the novel and rated by French critics as Maurois' masterpiece. *H—Har-Row.*

MEHTA, VED b. 1934. *Mahatma Gandhi and His Apostles* (1976). A vivid rendering of Gandhi's habits and daily conduct against the background of his beliefs, precepts, and enormous influence. *H—Viking Pr.*

MERTON, THOMAS 1915-1968. *The Seven Storey Mountain* (1948). Challenging account of a poet's conversion to Roman Catholicism and of his discovery of a vocation in a Trappist monastery in Kentucky. *P—Doubleday, NAL.*

MILL, JOHN STUART 1806-1873. *Autobiography* (1873). The education of a prodigy by a father whose psychological theories stressed environmental factors rather than heredity. *Over 6 eds.*

MILLER, EDWIN H. b. 1918. *Melville* (1975). A psychobiography whose primary evidence is Melville's fiction and poetry. *H—Braziller; P—Persea Bks.*

MIZENER, ARTHUR b. 1907. *The Far Side of Paradise* (1951). Fascinating account of F. Scott Fitzgerald, who in his novels caught the sense of life prevailing between the two world wars. *P—Avon, HM.*

MOORE, RUTH E. b. 1908. *Niels Bohr* (1966). A dramatic and thoughtful portrayal of the physicist and the milieu that helped place America first in the Atomic Age. *H—Knopf.*

MORGAN, CHARLES H. b. 1902. *The Life of Michelangelo* (1960). The pithiest one-volume account of the greatest sculptor between Phidias and Rodin and the most sumptuous of muralists. *H—Reynal.*

MURRAY, K. M. ELIZABETH. *Caught in the Web of Words* (1977). The founding editor of the great *Oxford English Dictionary*, to whom we all owe "an unpayable debt," memorialized in a biography of drama and power. *H—Yale U Pr.*

NABOKOV, VLADIMIR 1899-1977. *Speak, Memory* (1966). A masterly evocation of the aristocratic life in pre-Communist Russia by the author of *Lolita. H—Putnam; P—Putnam, Pyramid Pubns.*

NEWMAN, JOHN HENRY 1801-1890. *Apologia pro Vita Sua* (1864).

One of the stellar stylists in English examines his life and his conversion to Roman Catholicism. *Over 6 eds.*

PAINTER, GEORGE D. b. 1914. ***Proust*** (1959-65). One of the great novelists of the 20th century delineated so vividly and precisely as to emerge as a Proustian creation. *o.p.*

PARKMAN, FRANCIS 1823-1893. ***The Oregon Trail*** (1849). The classic account by a historian of life on the westward trek, including experiences shared with a band of Sioux. *Over 6 eds.*

PERNOUD, RÉGINE b. 1909. ***Joan of Arc*** (1969). A remarkable document illuminating an incredible life. *P—Stein & Day.*

PÉTREMENT, SIMONE. ***Simone Weil*** (1976). A passionate thinker of the 20th century; mystic, rationalist, martyr, in a sympathetic biography. *H—Pantheon.*

QUENNELL, PETER C. b. 1905. ***John Ruskin*** (1949). The absorbing story of an outstanding art critic and social reformer, the man who defended the innovative painter Turner and inspired the esthetic concepts of Proust. *H—R West.*

RIIS, JACOB 1849-1914. ***The Making of an American*** (1901). A classic in the literature of immigration to the United States by a Dane who became a successful journalist and social reformer. *H—Macmillan.*

RODINSON, MAXIME b. 1915. ***Mohammed*** (1971). The prophet and lawgiver of Islam in a biography that emphasizes his religious genius and political acumen. *H—Pantheon; P—Random.*

SANDBURG, CARL 1878-1967. ***Abraham Lincoln*** (1926). Lincoln depicted against his native background, the prairie, in a biography rich in detail, poetic in conception. *H—HarBraceJ; P—Dell, HarBraceJ.*

SANTAYANA, GEORGE 1863-1952. ***Persons and Places*** (1944-53). The memories, reflections, and assessments of one of the wisest and most frequently quoted philosophers of our time. *o.p.*

SARTRE, JEAN-PAUL b. 1905. ***The Words*** (1964). The existentialist philosopher describing his life up to the age of ten in terms of the language of human experience. *P—Fawcett World.*

SCHOENBAUM, SAMUEL b. 1927. ***William Shakespeare: A Documentary Life*** (1975). The best essential life to date. *H—Oxford U Pr.*

SCHWEITZER, ALBERT 1875-1965. ***Out of My Life and Thought*** (1933). The story of an amazing man—teacher, theologian, musician, humanitarian, doctor-missionary in Africa. *P—HR&W, NAL.*

SHEAFFER, LOUIS b. 1912. ***O'Neill: Son and Playwright*** (1968) and ***O'Neill: Son and Artist*** (1973). A double biography of America's Nobel playwright, perhaps the most autobiographical of all our artists. *H & P—Little.*

STEEGMULLER, FRANCIS b. 1906. ***Cocteau*** (1970). An account of the man, his work, and the banquet years that does justice to the kaleidoscopic artist: poet, novelist, playwright, filmmaker. *H—Little.*

STEFFENS, LINCOLN 1866-1936. ***Autobiography*** (1931). One of the trail-blazing books about graft and corruption in American city politics during the early 1900s. *H & P—HarBraceJ.*

STEIN, GERTRUDE 1874-1946. *The Autobiography of Alice B. Toklas* (1933). The classic re-creation of the life of geniuses living and working in the great epoch of early 20th-century Paris. *H—Peter Smith; P—Random.*

STRACHEY, LYTTON 1880-1932. *Queen Victoria* (1921). A master biographer draws a vivid picture of the Queen-Empress in the enthusiasm of youth, the loneliness of middle age, and the eccentricities of old age. *H & P—HarBraceJ.*

SULLIVAN, J. W. N. 1886-1937. *Beethoven* (1927). A fine introduction to the life and work of a master composer. *H—Knopf; P—Random.*

SWANBERG, W. A. b. 1907. *Norman Thomas: The Last Idealist* (1976). The American voice for socialism and six times his party's candidate for president clearly portrayed as the product of the Protestant tradition of service and the Emersonian philosophy of optimism. *H—Scribner.*

THOMPSON, LAWRANCE 1906-1973. *Robert Frost* (1966-77). America's "poet laureate" shown objectively, with all his strengths and weaknesses. *P—U of Minn Pr 3 vols.*

THOREAU, HENRY DAVID 1817-1862. *Walden* (1854). The essential American loner seeking communion with nature, self-revealed in classic prose. *Over 20 eds.*

TROTSKY, LEON 1879-1940. *Lenin: Notes for a Biography* (1925). A firsthand report of the international revolutionary figure by a messianic visionary who was his closest partner in the overturning of the Czarist regime. *H & P—Putnam.*

TURNER, W. J. 1889-1946. *Mozart* (rev. ed. 1966). A sound analysis and appreciation of a pure genius. *o.p.*

VAN GOGH, VINCENT 1853-1890. *Dear Theo* (1937). Perceptive letters to his brother by one of the tenderest and most anguished of artists. *P—NAL.*

WARD, AILEEN b. 1919. *John Keats* (1963). An award-winning biography of the immortal poet whose life has become an allegory of the suffering and transfiguration of early and ill-fated genius. *o.p.*

WASHINGTON, BOOKER T. 1856-1915. *Up from Slavery* (1901). The epic story of a resurrection, from bondage to freedom, by the influential Black educator. *Over 6 eds.*

WECHSBERG, JOSEPH b. 1907. *Verdi* (1974). A life of the endearing composer whose music and whose humanism project what is most beautiful in Mediterranean civilization. *H—Putnam.*

WILLIAMS, TENNESSEE (THOMAS LANIER WILLIAMS) b. 1914. *Memoirs* (1975). The frank and open-handed life of a major living American dramatist. *H—Doubleday; P—Bantam.*

WILSON, EDMUND 1895-1972. *The Twenties* (1976). Fascinating journal by the dean of American literary critics about the high decade of love and poetry and aspiration in Greenwich Village and seacoasts of Bohemia. *H—FS&G; P—Bantam.*

WRIGHT, FRANK LLOYD 1869-1959. *Autobiography* (1943). A wise, impressive, and provocative book covering the long career of a creative mind in architecture. *H—Horizon.*

WRIGHT, RICHARD 1908-1960. **Black Boy** (1945). Grim autobiography of an American who yearned for the intellectual and physical freedom denied him in a country ruled by whites. *H & P—Har-Row.*

YEATS, WILLIAM BUTLER 1865-1939. *Autobiography* (1936). The beautifully composed memoirs of the celebrated poet, Nobel Prize winner, founder of the Abbey Theatre, and Irish patriot. *H & P—Macmillan.*

16. Essays, Letters, Criticism, Magazines

J. Sherwood Weber

Much of the nonfiction we read, whether in books, magazines, or newspapers, is in essay form. Long, rather formal, and intellectually stimulating essays fill the pages of the *Atlantic Monthly*, the *New York Review of Books*, and *Scientific American*. Short essays abound in weeklies and newspapers—on the editorial pages, in columns such as those by Russell Baker, and in book, drama, music, art, and dance reviews.

Because essays vary so greatly in length, purpose, and style, the essay, like most art forms, is difficult to describe. It is generally defined as a short prose piece exploring one subject and reflecting the perceptions and feelings of the writer. There is no restriction on the subject matter or its treatment. The writer chooses a subject freely, whether trivial or earthshaking, and develops it in any style that seems appropriate. This vague definition suggests the wide range of essays to be found: Bacon may pinpoint the essence of friendship, Lamb may jest about the origin of roast pig, Richard Rovere may analyze a meeting of foreign ministers, Russell Baker may aim barbs at the Internal Revenue Service, T. S. Eliot may tell us that Shakespeare failed to write a great play in *Hamlet*, Susan Sontag may defend pop art, and several hundred thousand college freshmen each year explain to teachers and classmates how they spent the summer or why marijuana should be legalized.

The important matter for the reader of an essay is generally the personality of the writer. We demand that the essayist have something new, something interesting to say on a subject that appeals to us. Even more, we want the writer to attract us as a person, for we react to the essayist as to the people we meet: with some we come to an immediate understanding, others we must know for some time before admitting them to our friendship, and still others we never want to meet again. We must make the same effort to relate to the essayist as to a close friend; and as in all good relationships, we will often find ourselves putting in words of opposition. In sum, the appreciation of an essay is often an individual matter; we return to those writers we would like to know. Fortunately, the range is wide, and anyone can respond intimately, intensely, fondly, or with hostility to the writers of essays, from Montaigne to Irving Howe.

The letter is the most confidential of essays because the writer normally addresses intimates rather than a large, distant audience. Through the letters of famous and not-so-famous men and women we often come to know them and their times better than we might through a biography or history. Those interested in the genesis of a work of art can follow the agonizing steps that led to the finished work. One may follow the daily progress of Flaubert's *Madame Bovary* or encounter the changing notions about life and art of D. H. Lawrence and come away with a greater appreciation of the author's work. Any confirmed reader of the "Letters to the Editor" section of a newspaper or magazine will recognize how the letter reveals the mind and temperament of its writer. With the letters of great people the revelations are simply more rewarding.

Criticism is a specialized, often formal, form of the essay, an interpretation and/or evaluation of a work of art that should aim to foster better understanding of it. Like the essay, criticism appeared late in the history of civilization. Only after the Greeks developed drama and other forms of literature did Plato and Aristotle begin to analyze the results; ever since, the critic has generally followed the creator.

As with the essay, criticism occurs on many levels, from the hurried newspaper review of last night's opening play or opera to the carefully formulated reflections of one who has spent a lifetime reading poetry or fiction, viewing paintings, or listening to music. Again, the approach is personal, and the reader will turn repeatedly only to those critics who prove most compatible, reliable, and helpful. It must be noted, however, that one can find fresh insights in any fine critic, even though one may not share the biases or agree with the judgments; irritation often stimulates learning. Since there are many critical systems (almost as many, one sometimes thinks, as there are critics), the reader should have no difficulty finding useful ones. The acute reader will probably not accept completely any of the printed interpretations of any work but will find in each new insights that will promote greater understanding and appreciation of the work of art itself.

Essay Anthologies. Essay collections are legion, as any college freshman knows. The following inexpensive anthologies represent the scope and variety of the essay and include examples from many essayists of diverse interests and styles: *American Essays*, ed. by Charles B. Shaw (P—NAL); *The Art of the Essay*, ed. by Leslie Fiedler (P—Crowell); *Great English and American Essays*, ed. by Edmund Fuller (P—Avon);

Great Essays, ed. by Houston Peterson (*P—WSP*); and *A Liberal Arts Reader*, ed. by Robert B. Partlow, Jr. (*H—P-H*).

ADDISON and STEELE. *The Spectator*. See "The 18th Century," page 44.

AGEE, JAMES 1909-1955. *Letters of James Agee to Father Flye* (1962). One of our potentially great authors and a fine film critic writes about his frustrations and conflicts over his writing to his substitute father. *o.p.*

AUDEN, W. H. 1907-1973. *The Dyer's Hand* (1962). An important poet-critic has collected and edited his favorites among his own critical works, dealing with matters as diverse as the detective story and Shakespeare. *P—Random*.

AUERBACH, ERICH 1892-1957. *Mimesis* (1946). A remarkably perceptive and illuminating study of the ways Western writers from Homer to Virginia Woolf have used language and rhetoric to project their unique versions of reality. *H & P—Princeton U Pr.*

BACON. *Essays*. See "The Renaissance and Reformation," page 28.

BAKER, RUSSELL b. 1925. *No Cause for Panic* (1964) and *All Things Considered* (1965). The keen "Observer" of the *New York Times* editorial page views the contemporary scene with devastating humor and sharp satire that are often more penetrating than the learned analyses of the social scientists. *H—Lippincott*.

BENCHLEY, ROBERT C. 1889-1945. *The Benchley Roundup* (1954). Nathaniel Benchley has chosen some 90 pieces, representing the best of his father's reactions to the petty irritations of daily life. *H & P— Har-Row.*

CAMUS, ALBERT 1913-1960. *The Myth of Sisyphus and Other Essays* (1955). The French novelist's searching personal essays on the absurdity of human life and on the necessity of carrying it on. *H— Knopf; P—Random.*

CHESTERFIELD. *Letters to His Son*. See "The 18th Century," page 44.

Columbia Essays on Modern Writers. Ed. by William York Tindall. Over 75 50-page critical studies of varying quality on individual contemporary American, British, and Continental novelists, poets, and dramatists of artistic and intellectual significance—each written by an authority and each bearing the title of its subject. *P—Columbia U Pr.*

COWLEY, MALCOLM b. 1898. *Exile's Return* (rev. ed. 1951). Recollections of the "lost generation" of the 1920s and of its writers by one who shared their lives and ideals. *P—Viking Pr.*

CRÈVECOEUR. *Letters from an American Farmer*. See "The 18th Century," page 44.

DREW, ELIZABETH 1887-1965. *Discovering Poetry* (1933). A splendid introduction to the understanding and appreciation of poetry. *H & P— Norton.*

ELIOT, T. S. 1888-1965. *Selected Essays* (1950). A great poet and influential critic surveys literature and religion in one of the classics of modern criticism. *H—HarBraceJ.*

EMERSON, RALPH WALDO 1803-1882. *Essays*. The views of an important transcendentalist on many subjects. *Over 10 eds.*

FLAUBERT, GUSTAVE 1821-1880. *The Selected Letters of Gustave Flaubert* (1954). An excellent selection edited by Francis Steegmuller, showing the life and labor that went into the writing of *Madame Bovary. H—Bks for Libs.*

FORSTER, E. M. 1879-1970. *Aspects of the Novel* (1927). A conversational and penetrating treatment of the novel as an art form by one of England's most civilized novelists and essayists. *H & P—HarBraceJ.*

_____. *Two Cheers for Democracy* (1951). Urbane, familiar essays, some on political matters, others on literary, all written with wit and tolerance. *P—HarBraceJ.*

GOLDEN, HARRY b. 1902. *Only in America* (1958), and *For 2¢ Plain* (1959). Amiable, witty essays about New York's Lower East Side, segregation, and America in general. *H—Greenwood.*

GOODMAN, PAUL 1911-1972. *The Structure of Literature* (1954). A personal and enjoyable discussion of the values of formal literary analysis. *P—U of Chicago Pr.*

_____. *Growing Up Absurd* (1960). An attempt to explain the various aspects of contemporary Establishments and why the prevailing moral climate engendered alienation and revolt in the youth of the 1960s. *H & P—Random.*

HAZLITT, WILLIAM 1778-1830. *Table Talk* (1821). A wholly honest man writes about his personal reactions to people and the passing show. *H—Dutton.*

HIGHET, GILBERT 1906-1977. *The Anatomy of Satire* (1962). A classicist defines satire with ably told examples and much wit. *H & P—Princeton U Pr.*

HOLLAND, NORMAN. *Poems in Persons: An Introduction to the Psychoanalysis of Literature* (1975). A trenchant analysis of the insight psychology can bring to literature. *P—Norton.*

HOWE, IRVING b. 1920. *The Critical Point* (1974). A "democratic socialist" with political commitments and keen literary perception covers a range of literary topics. *H—Horizon; P—Dell.*

ISAACS, JACOB 1896-1973. *The Background of Modern Poetry* (1952). A lucid and informative introduction to modern poetry addressed to the often puzzled general reader. *P—Dutton.*

JARRELL, RANDALL 1914-1965. *Poetry and the Age* (1953). A good poet and better critic writes about modern poetry and the conditions under which it is written. *H—Octagon; P—FS&G.*

KEATS, JOHN 1795-1821. *Letters 1814–1821* (1958). Hyder Rollins has assembled the definitive edition of a young genius's letters, which read almost as well as his poetry. *H—Harvard U Pr 2 vols.*

KRUTCH, JOSEPH WOOD 1893-1970. *The Measure of Man* (1954). Provocative thinking and effective writing on freedom, human values, survival, and the modern temper. *H—Peter Smith.*

LAMB, CHARLES 1775-1834. *Essays of Elia* (1823, 1833). Sometimes gentle, always incisive, these essays helped to establish the definition of an art form; the picture of a loving, kind man shines through. *Over 6 eds.*

LIEBLING, A. J. 1904-1963. *The Most of A. J. Liebling* (1963). A fine reporter and expert literary caricaturist writes delightfully on a broad range of subjects from food to the foibles of the press. *P—S&S.*

LINCOLN, ABRAHAM 1809-1965. *Speeches and Letters.* Lincoln's depth of character is easily seen in the dignity and directness of his personal communications. *Over 6 eds.*

LIPKING, LAURENCE I. b. 1934 and A. WALTON LITZ b. 1929 (eds.). *Modern Literary Criticism, 1900–1970* (1972). An interesting introduction to the problems, methods, and major figures in contemporary literary criticism. *P—Atheneum.*

MACHIAVELLI, NICCOLÒ 1469-1527. *The Letters of Machiavelli* (1961). Trans. and ed. by Allan H. Gilbert. These letters by the man whose name has wrongly become a synonym for political evil help us to understand the Renaissance mind and to explain *The Prince. P—Putnam.*

MANN, THOMAS 1875-1955. *Essays of Three Decades* (1947). The noted novelist and critic discusses some of the great artists: Goethe, Tolstoi, Wagner, Freud, Cervantes. *o.p.*

MAUGHAM, W. SOMERSET 1874-1965. *Points of View* (1959). Essays, mostly on writers and writing, by an extremely civilized author. *H—Arno, Greenwood.*

MENCKEN, H. L. 1880-1956. *Prejudices: A Selection* (1958). A good collection of the most trenchant essays from the shocker and debunker of the 1920s. *P—Random.*

MONTAIGNE. *Essays.* See "The Renaissance and Reformation," page 27.

MOZART, WOLFGANG AMADEUS 1756-1791. *Letters of Wolfgang Amadeus Mozart* (1972). At times the most delightful, at times the most unhappy of composers reveals his problems and his great moments. *P—Dover.*

ORWELL, GEORGE 1903-1950. *A Collection of Essays* (1954). The author of *1984* discusses books, humor, language, politics, and provides, unintentionally, a good introduction to his novels. *H & P—HarBraceJ.*

Pamphlets on American Writers. A continuing series of 48-page biographical and critical essays about individual American authors, major and minor, done with conciseness and insight—each by a different authority. *P—U of Minn Pr.*

READ, HERBERT 1893-1968. *The Tenth Muse* (1958). Genius in the arts gets attention here, with essays on painters, writers, and philosophers. *H—Bks for Libs.*

RICHARDS, I. A. b. 1893. *Practical Criticism* (1929). A pioneer and now classic work in modern criticism, placing emphasis on close reading of the poem. *P—HarBraceJ.*

RUSKIN, JOHN 1819-1900. *Sesame and Lilies* (1865). His most popular work, detailing his views on the importance of education and the arts. *H—Dutton.*

SARTRE, JEAN-PAUL b. 1905. *What Is Literature?* (1962). France's leading existentialist writer defines the art of writing, its purpose, and its audience. A fascinating treatment of the role of the writer in society. *H—Peter Smith.*

SCOTT, WILBUR S. b. 1914 (ed.). *Five Approaches to Modern Literary Criticism* (1962). Moral, psychological, sociological, formalistic, and archetypal approaches are analyzed and each illustrated by three essays by well-known critics. Most helpful in giving an overall view of modern criticism. *H & P—Macmillan.*

SEWALL, RICHARD B. b. 1908. *The Vision of Tragedy* (1959). Brilliant inquiry into the nature of tragedy through examination of eight works from *Job* to Faulkner. *H—Yale U Pr.*

SHAW, GEORGE BERNARD 1856-1950. *Advice to a Young Critic* (1955). Letters to Reginald G. Bright, edited by F. J. West, illustrating both Shaw's insight into the problems of the theatre and his business ability. *P—Putnam.*

SONTAG, SUSAN b. 1933. *Against Interpretation and Other Essays* (1966). A coruscating, sometimes mannered, spokeswoman for new trends in the arts writes about modern novels, theatre, and films. *H— FS&G; P—Dell.*

STEVENSON, ROBERT LOUIS 1850-1894. *Virginibus Puerisque* (1881). Gracefully written informal essays in the Lamb tradition. *H— Bks for Libs.*

STRACHEY, LYTTON 1880-1932. *Portraits in Miniature and Other Essays* (1931). Witty essays on minor, but quite interesting, English eccentrics, by the man who did much to make history and biography readable. *o.p.*

THOREAU. *Walden.* See "Biography," page 154.

THURBER, JAMES 1894-1961. *The Owl in the Attic* (1931). One of the greatest humorists discusses the English language and other difficulties of modern life. *P—Har-Row.*

_____. *Thurber Country* (1953). Thurber's mad and threatening world is brilliantly captured here. *H & P—S&S.*

Treasury of the World's Great Letters (1940). Ed. by M. L. Schuster. Interesting letters from ancient times to recent. *P—S&S.*

TYNAN. *Curtains.* See "Drama," page 145.

WALPOLE. *Letters.* See "The 18th Century," page 47.

WELLEK, RENÉ b. 1903 and AUSTIN WARREN b. 1899. *Theory of Literature* (rev. ed. 1956). An excellent introduction to the "New Criticism" (concentration on the structure and detail of a literary work rather than on its historical and social background). *P—HarBraceJ.*

WHITE, E. B. b. 1899. *The Points of My Compass* (1962). The old *New Yorker*'s superb writer of personal essays looks back at the past with nostalgia and at much of the present with horror. *H—Har-Row.*

_____ and KATHARINE S. WHITE 1892-1977 (eds.). *Subtreasury of American Humor* (1941). The classic collection. *P—Putnam.*

WILDE, OSCAR 1854-1900. *The Letters of Oscar Wilde* (1962). Ed. by Rupert Hart-Davis. These letters bring to life the wit and tragedy of the leader of the esthetic movement in the late 19th century. *H—HarBraceJ.*

WILSON, EDMUND 1895-1972 (ed.). *The Shock of Recognition* (1943, 1955). A great critic collects literary documents from James Russell Lowell to Sherwood Anderson, writers dealing mostly with their contemporaries. *H—Octagon.*

WOOLF, VIRGINIA 1882-1941. *The Common Reader* (1925). Comments on literary themes and people by one of England's most perceptive novelists and critics. *P—HarBraceJ.*

Magazines

Magazines generally publish weekly, monthly, or quarterly; they may be highly specialized or they may address a large number of timely topics. As a rule, the less frequently a magazine is issued, the more specialized its content and the more intellectual its tone. But in the better quarterlies, despite subject specialization, the writing is lucid and the arguments cogent; rarely are they academic or pompous.

Many of the best-known quarterlies deal with literature. Larger than their predecessors, the little magazines of the 1920s, literary quarterlies today abet the critical and social rather than the creative. Although fiction and poetry do appear, the chief function of the literary quarterlies is to illuminate the work of art; and most of the best critics of today serve the function effectively.

But literature by no means holds the field. Nonliterary quarterlies abound, some broad in scope, some rather confined, many offering informed and provocative discussion in readable and frequently lively prose. These journals may range widely and probe deeply into politics and contemporary affairs (regional and global), economics, history, philosophy, science, ecosophy, psychology, and the arts.

Good writing and good reading appear frequently in monthly and weekly magazines too, and no person who wants to keep informed should neglect reading several with regularity. Factual and interpretive surveys of current events are presented weekly in *Time*, *Newsweek*, and the "Week in Review" of the *New York Times* Sunday edition. Monthly, the *Atlantic* appraises social and political developments and trends, often with the high seriousness and acute perceptivity that have characterized this magazine for a century; and *Commentary* has won respect for its outstanding essays on social and cultural problems. The *New York Review of Books* twice a month gives long reviews and topical essays, most of liberal persuasion, on a high intellectual level. And weekly, the *New Yorker*, no longer the great magazine it once was, relies on urbane wit to point its gently satiric thrusts at the doings and inhabitants of an absorbing, confused, and elitist world.

The 25 magazines described below are all worth knowing. Together they constitute the best available in the extensive world of magazines today.

The American Scholar (Quarterly—Washington, D.C.) An excellent review, published by the Phi Beta Kappa Society, directed to the intelligent reader and covering a wide range, from social issues to the arts.

The Atlantic Monthly (Monthly—Boston, Mass.) Perhaps the best of the general-interest review magazines, containing quality fiction and poetry as well as influential essays on a consistently high level.

Bulletin of the Atomic Scientists (10/yr—Chicago, Ill.) Directed to the educated lay reader and aimed at bridging the worlds of the scientist and humanist, offering informed, well-written articles by experts on science and world affairs, with special emphasis on the social responsibilities of scientists.

Commentary (Monthly—New York, N.Y.) This Jewish-sponsored, but not parochial, magazine, no longer a bastion of liberalism, contains literate discussions on current social, political, and artistic issues.

Daedalus (Quarterly—Amer. Acad. of Arts and Sciences, Cambridge, Mass.) A scholarly journal of readable, intelligent essays on a large variety of contemporary subjects, with each issue covering one subject in breadth and depth.

Ebony (Monthly—Chicago, Ill.) Long on photographs and short on text, this Black-oriented magazine affords, on a popular level, the best insight into an ethnic culture.

Economist (Weekly—London, England) Well-written, authoritative, cosmopolitan articles on politics, economics, and world affairs.

Fortune (14/yr—New York, N.Y.) Slick, polished magazine of special appeal to arrived and arriving management types, discussing vividly and in documented detail world affairs, finance, politics, and new industries and products.

Hudson Review (Quarterly—New York, N.Y.) An outstanding literary magazine, publishing fiction, poetry, drama, criticism, and essays on American cultural life by some of the most sensitive and astute writers of our day.

Human Behavior (Monthly—Los Angeles, Calif.) Well-written, thoroughly grounded articles covering the whole range of the social sciences and directed at the average educated reader.

Ms. (Monthly—New York, N.Y.) Slick and often strident in tone, but nevertheless the single best general magazine for women in the movement and for all women and men interested in social change.

The Nation (Weekly—New York, N.Y.) One of the oldest and best liberal weeklies, running clear, well-documented essays on world affairs and politics as well as literary and dramatic criticism.

National Review (Biweekly—New York, N.Y.) The well-modulated intellectual voice of conservatism in America.

Natural History (10/yr—American Museum of Natural History, New York, N.Y.) Semipopular, authoritative, outstandingly illustrated essays for the nature lover, covering conservation, anthropology, geography, astronomy.

The New Republic (Weekly—Washington, D.C.) A liberal, lucid, often hard-hitting weekly concerned with all aspects of current American and international events.

New York Review of Books (Biweekly—New York, N.Y.) The major reviewing source in this country, publishing long review essays and timely articles by distinguished writers, characteristically those with liberal leanings and thoroughly defined opinions.

New York Times Sunday Edition (Weekly—New York, N.Y.) "The Week in Review" is the best short news summary available; the *New York Times Book Review* is uneven but necessary; and the *New York Times Magazine* contains a half dozen high-quality articles on timely subjects.

The New Yorker (Weekly—New York, N.Y.) Urbane fiction, witty commentary, trenchant criticism, well-wrought but stereotyped cartoons, and special features addressed to a liberal but affluent audience.

Newsweek (Weekly—New York, N.Y.) A sound, often detailed, generally objective summary of the week's news.

Scientific American (Monthly—New York, N.Y.) A handsomely illustrated journal containing articles that interpret scientific and technological advances and theories to the educated lay reader.

Sewanee Review (Quarterly—Univ. of the South, Tenn.) The oldest and often most up-to-date journal of criticism in the United States, printing literature and review articles that are in no way limited by regional interests.

Time (Weekly—New York, N.Y.) One of the better general news review periodicals, written in lively, sometimes strained, prose.

Unesco Courier (Monthly—New York, N.Y.) A superior publication, handsomely illustrated, that opens a window on the cultures of the world with emphasis on all the arts.

Virginia Quarterly Review (Quarterly—Univ. of Virginia, Va.) Perceptive, well-written articles on literary subjects, on national and international affairs, and on problems of the South.

Yale Review (Quarterly—Yale Univ., Conn.) A major periodical whose timely articles by specialists range from philosophy to international politics, from poetry to economics.

Humanities, Social Sciences, and Sciences

17. Fine Arts and Design

Kenneth G. Wallace

Art begins in necessity and culminates in satisfaction. When Stone Age folk fashioned their primitive tools, it is doubtful that they considered themselves artists. While they attempted generation after generation to make their hammers, scrapers, and stabbers ever better and neater, more efficient and more shapely, it is doubtful that they conceptualized the relationship between form and function. But as form and function somehow fused and merged, control over human existence increased.

It is, of course, a truism—or should be—that humanity's needs are esthetic and spiritual as well as practical and material. If Stone Age people painted scenes from their daily lives on the walls of caves, they did so because they felt compelled to leave some evidence of having been on earth. If the result of this need was something we choose to call "beautiful" (an extremely dangerous, if not meaningless, word), then an esthetic need had been satisfied. As civilization moved through time, the needs remained pretty much the same; only the expressions changed.

These changes in the modes and methods of artistic expression are responsible for the false notion, unfortunately widespread, that art is something special, fancy, precious, existing for the very few, and remote from life. While art is not life, in its finest form it is an honest expression of the condition of all humanity. The fact that any expression in words, paint, stone, or sound generally reflects a historical period or style should not lessen one's understanding about the nature of art, nor does it cause art to be remote and removed from life. On the contrary, art can change existence at its very basis and involve all in that change.

Another false notion about the nature of art, resulting largely from Western civilization's espousal of platonic idealism, is that it must possess utilitarian value, must offer some profit in the form of beauty, truth, goodness. A work of art offers none of these vague qualities inherently; at best—and surely this should be enough—it projects a vision of the joy, the fear, the despair, and the mystery of the human condition. The "truth" that art offers is its very existence. When we avert our eyes or close our ears, the finest work of art has no meaning.

People with a sensitive awareness of the human condition have not chosen to turn away from a painting, a building, a symphony, for experiencing art is similar to experiencing people. We reveal this when we speak of going "to hear Beethoven" or "to see a Picasso." As a rule, before one can care deeply for a person, one must know that person very well. So with art. Before one can really grasp what attracts in particular art forms, one must take the time to acquire an informed understanding. For one takes from a work of art—as from life in general—only in proportion to what one brings to it. Any person can take delight in or respond to Bach or Mozart, Renoir or Moore, without knowing a thing about them or their lives or their times. But if one knows something about the personalities involved, something about classicism or romanticism or impressionism, something about the various periods of expression in the work of Picasso, something about tone, volume, space, dynamics, rhythm—then one is prepared to hear in the music or see in the paintings or buildings significances and subtleties that the uninformed never recognize. By cultivating sensitive, sympathetic, and imaginative understanding of what any artist is attempting, one develops the capacity to come to terms more fully with the work of art, to probe more deeply, to enjoy more fully—in short, to become a part of the artist's vision.

The books listed below are a means—but only one of many—whereby the eyes and ears may be more widely and wisely opened, so that any person may be among those who relish fully the finest achievements of the greatest painters, sculptors, architects, composers, photographers, and dancers of all time. Through books about art and artists one can develop a capacity to understand and share some aspects of the human condition that any great artist offers.

Many specialized histories of art, architecture, and music dealing with the arts of early historical periods or major cultural areas, and some biographies of leading artists from these periods or areas, are listed in the "Books About" sections of Chapters 1 through 10. Additionally, the "Biography" chapter lists numerous biographies or autobiographies of painters, sculptors, architects, composers, and other artists. None of these many books about art and artists is relisted or cross-referred in this chapter.

The reader is advised to explore the eleven chapters cited above as well as the Index for additional good reading.

Basic Principles and General Histories

ARNASON, H. H. b. 1909. *History of Modern Art* (rev. ed. 1976). Exhaustive study of modern art from the late 19th century to the provocative movements of the 1970s. *H—Abrams.*

BATTCOCK, GREGORY b. 1937 (ed.). *Minimal Art* (1968). An impartial collection of valuable essays concerning the minimal art movement by critics and artists. *P—Dutton.*

———. (ed.). *The New Art* (rev. ed. 1973). A first-rate anthology of criticism by contemporary art critics, covering painting, sculpture, design, dance, and film. *P—Dutton.*

EICHENBERG, FRITZ b. 1901. *The Art of the Print* (1976). A master printmaker himself, Eichenberg writes for the lay reader and artist alike a brilliant history of printmaking and explains lucidly its various techniques. *H—Abrams.*

FRY, ROGER E. 1866-1934. *Vision and Design* (1920). A famous art critic and former curator of the Metropolitan Museum of New York discusses the relation between perception and esthetic form. *P—NAL.*

GHISELIN, BREWSTER b. 1903 (ed.). *The Creative Process* (1952). Symposium by writers, painters, sculptors, musicians about the process of creation. *P—NAL.*

GOMBRICH, E. H. b. 1909. *The Story of Art* (12th ed. 1974). A sound and detailed history of Western art from its primitive beginnings through modern movements. *H & P—Phaidon.*

JANSON, HORST W. b. 1913. *History of Art* (rev. ed. 1977). A splendid survey of the major visual arts from the beginning of history to the present day. Magnificent illustrations include 80 color plates, many with gold. *H—P-H.*

KRAMER, HILTON. *The Age of the Avant-Garde* (1973). Stimulating, perceptive essays on artists and movements of the last few decades, tracing the rise of the avant-garde as a historical phenomenon. *H—FS&G.*

MALRAUX, ANDRÉ 1901-1976. *The Voices of Silence* (1953). A monumental and unique history of art, profusely illustrated and based on the concept that "the museum without walls is by definition a place of the mind." *o.p.*

TAYLOR, JOSHUA C. b. 1917. *Learning to Look: A Handbook of the Visual Arts* (1966). Clear, concrete explanations of what to look for in viewing art, particularly useful for the relatively uninitiated. *H & P— U of Chicago Pr.*

Painting and Sculpture

To enjoy fully great works of art, reading about them is less valuable than looking at them, studying them, getting to know them—as originals in museums, as good prints on the walls, as reproductions in the rich variety of excellent art books, hardcover and paperbound. Three series are outstanding:

Landmarks of the World's Art. Abbreviated but useful introductions to various periods in the history of world art. The series ranges from the ancient to the modern world and includes both Eastern and Western cultures. *H—McGraw.*

Pelican History of Art. An unusually well-written and handsomely illustrated series of books on art and architecture of various countries, areas, and periods. *H—Penguin.*

Skira Art Books. Volumes with illuminating but dullish texts and magnificent color plates. Of special interest is the Art-History-Ideas series: 14 volumes giving the art-history-total cultural backgrounds of both the Eastern and Western worlds. *H—Skira.*

Also extremely valuable are four series of smaller, less ambitious, less expensive, but amazingly well-printed books.

Barnes and Noble Art Series. *P—B&N.*

Compass History of Art Series. *P—Viking Pr.*

Praeger World of Art Paperbacks. *P—Praeger.*

UNESCO Art Series. *P—NAL.*

Art Since 1945. A series of modest critical essays on the world art scene since 1945. Internationally known scholars write on the major European countries and the United States, often showing, for a change, how America influences Europe. *P—WSP.*

BARR, ALFRED H., Jr. b. 1902. *What Is Modern Painting?* (rev. ed. 1958). A clear introductory analysis of the methods and techniques of modern painting as well as an excellent explanation of how to look at modern art. *P—NYGS.*

BERENSON, BERNARD 1865-1959. *Aesthetics and History in the Visual Arts* (1948). A master critic analyzes the reasons for changing styles in the arts. *H—Somerset Pub.*

BOAS, FRANZ 1858-1942. *Primitive Art* (1927). The classic study of the subject by a great anthropologist. *H—Peter Smith; P—Dover.*

BOUSQUET, JACQUES b. 1923. *Mannerism: The Painting and Style of the Late Renaissance* (1964). Close to the definitive study of one of the most controversial periods in art history, arguing convincingly for mannerism as a valid style. *o.p.*

BOWIE, HENRY. *On the Laws of Japanese Painting* (1952). Clear, fascinating explanation. *H—Peter Smith; P—Dover.*

BRION, MARCEL b. 1895. *Art of the Romantic Era* (1960). Illuminating, stimulating, excellently illustrated study of the 19th-century Romantic period. *P—Praeger.*

CHASTEL, ANDRÉ b. 1912. *The Age of Humanism* (1963). Exhaustive study of one of the most productive periods in the arts—Europe from 1480 to 1530: profusely illustrated. *o.p.*

CLARK, KENNETH M. b. 1903. *The Nude* (1956, 1959). Witty, learned, graceful analysis of the nude in art through the ages as an expression of imaginative, idealized experience. *H—Princeton U Pr; P—Doubleday, Princeton U Pr.*

_____. *The Romantic Rebellion* (1974). Clearly, but with considerable caution, discusses the Romantic quality of the work of 13 important artists from the middle of the 18th century to the middle of the 19th century. *H—Har-Row.*

_____. *Landscape into Art* (rev. ed. 1976). Authoritative analysis of four possible ways artists have tried to clarify the complexities of natural appearances. *H—Har-Row.*

EVANS, DAME JOAN b. 1893 (ed.). *The Flowering of the Middle Ages* (1960). Magnificently illustrated study of the art and culture of the Middle Ages, containing readable essays by scholars of such calibre as Christopher Brooke, George Zarnecki, John Harvey. *o.p.*

FALLICO, ARTURO B. b. 1909. *Art and Existentialism* (1962). A significant attempt to reconcile art with the philosophy that interprets life as an encounter with nothingness. *o.p.*

LARKIN, OLIVER W. b. 1896. *Art and Life in America* (rev. ed. 1960). Solid, readable study of the relationship of the visual-plastic arts to the growth of American civilization. *H—HR&W.*

LIPPARD, LUCY R. b. 1937. *Pop Art* (1966). Lucid, informative survey and appraisal of a controversial contemporary art style. *P—Praeger.*

LULLIES, REINHARD b. 1907 and MAX HIRMER. *Greek Sculpture* (rev. ed. 1957). Superior photographs are illuminated by Lullies' authoritative criticism of the successive trends. *H & P—Abrams.*

MASTAI, M. L. *History of Pictorial Illusionism* (1975). Fascinating and comprehensive study of *trompe l'oeil* as practiced by nearly all famous artists in almost every generation since antiquity. *H—Abaris Bks.*

NADEAU, MAURICE b. 1911. *The History of Surrealism* (1965). The definitive study of this 20th-century art movement by a distinguished French critic. *o.p.*

NEWTON, ERIC b. 1893. *European Painting and Sculpture* (rev. ed. 1961). Excellent summary introduction. *o.p.*

———. *The Romantic Rebellion* (1965). Valid, convincing, yet intensely personal view of Romanticism and the Romantic temperament which Newton sees as epitomized in "mystery, abnormality, conflict." *o.p.*

OZENFANT, AMEDÉE 1886-1966. *The Foundations of Modern Art* (1952). A scholarly investigation of backgrounds. *H—Peter Smith; P—Dover.*

RHEIMS, MAURICE b. 1910. *19th Century Sculpture* (1976). A fresh appraisal of the 19th-century works by sculptors from 28 countries. *H—Abrams.*

RICHTER, HANS 1888-1976. *Dada: Art and Anti-Art* (1966). Excellent history of a highly controversial movement in 20th-century art by a man who was part of it. Contains many primary sources: documents, manifestos, etc. *o.p.*

ROBB, DAVID M. b. 1903. *The Harper History of Painting* (1951). A first-rate survey of Western painting since the Old Stone Age, with over 500 illustrations. *o.p.*

SCHAPIRO, MEYER b. 1904. *Romanesque Art* (1976). A great art historian's collected innovative essays on Romanesque sculpture and medieval esthetic ideas. *H—Braziller.*

SCHÖNBERGER, ARNO b. 1915 and HALLDOR SOEHNER. *The Rococo Age* (1960). Brilliantly conceived, superbly illustrated survey of the art and civilization of the 18th century. *o.p.*

STRUPPECK, JULES b. 1915. *The Creation of Sculpture* (1952). Analysis of the nature and techniques of sculpture for those who wish to appreciate or produce it. *H—HR&W.*

SYPHER, WYLIE b. 1905. *Rococo to Cubism in Art and Literature* (1950). Stimulating, provocative survey of the arts from the 18th century to today, arguing for Rococo as an authentic style, and developing interrelationships among the arts in terms of style and cultural values. *o.p.*

WILENSKI, REGINALD HOWARD 1887-1975. *Modern French Painters* (rev. ed. 1963). Correlates the principal artists and movements with social and cultural trends from 1863 to 1938. *H—HarBraceJ.*

Architecture and Design

GIEDION, SIGFRIED 1893-1968. *Space, Time and Architecture* (4th ed. 1962). A fundamental text illuminating our times and the interrelation of materials, techniques, and human needs in terms of architectural design and city planning. *H—Harvard U Pr.*

GREENOUGH, HORATIO 1805-1852. *Form and Function* (1947). Remarks on art, design, and architecture by a prophet of modern architecture. *P—U of Cal Pr.*

GROPIUS, WALTER 1883-1969. *Apollo in the Democracy* (1968). Collection of profound essays and addresses by the founder of the famous Bauhaus School examining the cultural obligation of the architect. *o.p.*

HAMLIN, TALBOT FAULKNER 1889-1956. *Architecture Through the Ages* (rev. ed. 1953). Excellent illustrated survey. *H—Putnam.*

HOLLAND, LAURENCE B. b. 1920 (ed.). *Who Designs America?* (1966). Stimulating collection of critical essays by leading design critics showing the effects of both good and bad design in America. *H—Peter Smith.*

LE CORBUSIER (CHARLES ÉDOUARD JEANNERET) 1887-1965. *The Modular* (1954, 1958). Two volumes of provocative, intensely personal argument for an ideal system of proportions based on the human body and the golden mean. *H—Harvard U Pr; P—MIT Pr.*

Makers of Contemporary Architecture. A series of well-illustrated studies of influential modern architects, including Fuller, Johnson, Kahn, Saarinen, Tange. *H—Braziller.*

Masters of World Architecture. A series of compact analyses of the works of outstanding modern architects and designers, with illustrations and biographies. Included are such as Aalto, Gaudí, Gropius, Le Corbusier, van der Rohe, Nervi, Neutra, Sullivan, and Wright. *H & P—Braziller.*

MUMFORD, LEWIS b. 1895. *The Culture of Cities* (1938). The past, present, and hoped-for future of urban civilization—a panorama survey rich with factual data and provocative positions. *P—HarBraceJ.*

———. *Sticks and Stones* (rev. ed. 1955). Critical analysis of American architecture from the 18th century to the 20th, stressing integration of structure with site. *H—Peter Smith; P—Dover.*

PEHNT, WOLFGANG (ed.). *Encyclopedia of Modern Architecture* (1964). An invaluable aid to students, architects, critics, civil engineers, lay readers for browsing or reference, involving the contributions of 31 authorities from 16 countries. *o.p.*

PEVSNER, NIKOLAUS b. 1902. *An Outline of European Architecture* (rev. ed. 1960). A first-rate introduction, sound and readable, with pointed, incisive comments. *P—Penguin.*

————. *Pioneers of Modern Design* (rev. ed. 1964). A standard work on designers from William Morris to Walter Gropius showing how these men moved from Victorianism to modernism. *P—Penguin.*

SCOTT, ROBERT GILLAM b. 1907. *Design Fundamentals* (1951). Analysis of problems of visual relationship illustrated through step-by-step designing of this book. *H—McGraw.*

TUNNARD, CHRISTOPHER b. 1910. *The City of Man* (1955). Stimulating and richly illustrated commentary on the development of American city design. *o.p.*

WRIGHT, FRANK LLOYD 1869-1959. *The Future of Architecture* (1953). A collection of prophetic lectures concerning the author's own works as well as the future of architecture. *H—Horizon; P—NAL.*

————. *Writings and Buildings* (1960). Chronological summary of the master architect's major periods, with photographs, drawings, floor plans, illustrative writings. *H—Horizon.*

Music

AUSTIN, WILLIAM W. b. 1920. *Music in the 20th Century* (1966). A panorama of musical composition designed not only as a history but also as a means of arousing the reader's interest in contemporary musical forms from Debussy to Stravinsky. *H—Norton.*

BARZUN, JACQUES b. 1907 (ed.). *The Pleasures of Music* (1977). Fascinating anthology of "words on music" culled from a large variety of sources. *P—U of Chicago Pr.*

————. *Berlioz and His Century* (1956). Splendid evocation of a man, his time, and his work. *H—Peter Smith.*

BERNSTEIN, LEONARD b. 1918. *The Unanswered Question* (1977). Brilliant lectures by America's leading conductor-composer concerning the future of music, discussing music from primal sources to the most complex compositions. Boxed with three recordings. *H—Harvard U Pr.*

BLUME, FRIEDRICH b. 1893. *Renaissance and Baroque Music* (1967). A comprehensive survey by a distinguished musicologist, filled with fresh insights. *H—Peter Smith.*

BROCKWAY, WALLACE b. 1905 and HERBERT WEINSTOCK 1905-1975. *Men of Music* (rev. ed. 1950). Good critical biographies. *H & P—S&S.*

CHASE, GILBERT b. 1906. *America's Music* (rev. 2nd ed. 1966). Exhaustive study of American music from the Pilgrims to the age of electronics. *H—McGraw.*

COPLAND, AARON b. 1900. *What to Listen for in Music* (rev. ed 1957). A distinguished composer explains lucidly the interrelation of rhythm, melody, harmony, and tone color in musical patterns. *H—McGraw; P—NAL.*

EWEN, DAVID b. 1907. *Encyclopedia of Opera* (1963). A very valuable, comprehensive reference that answers almost any question about opera the reader may pose. *H—Hill & Wang.*

GROUT, DONALD JAY b. 1902. *A History of Western Music* (rev. ed. 1973). A shortened version of the author's very lengthy history of music from the ancients to the modern masters of atonalism and dodecaphony. *H & P—Norton.*

HODIER, ANDRE. *The Worlds of Jazz* (1972). An analysis of the various kinds of jazz, intended primarily for the lay person, emphasizing in depth the sociology of jazz. *P—Grove.*

LANG, PAUL HENRY b. 1901. *Music in Western Civilization* (1941). The definitive one-volume history—scholarly, detailed, yet very readable. *H—Norton.*

LOESSER, ARTHUR 1894-1969. *Men, Women, and Pianos* (rev. 1964). A fascinating history of keyboard instruments and of piano virtuosos. *P—S&S.*

McKINNEY, HOWARD D. b. 1889 and W. R. ANDERSON b. 1891. *Music in History* (1940). Relates music to the other fine arts and to the cultural climate in which it was written. *o.p.*

SACHS, CURT 1881-1959. *The History of Musical Instruments* (1940). Traces the evolution of rhythmic sound instruments from prehistory to the modern symphony, jazz band, and electronic devices. *H—Norton.*

SANDBURG, CARL 1878-1967. *The American Songbag* (1927). Gives unexcelled background for 280 songs, ballads, ditties as well as the music for them. *H—HarBraceJ.*

SCHONBERG, HAROLD C. b. 1916. *The Great Pianists* (1963). The music critic for the *New York Times* writes engagingly and knowledgeably about pianism and pianists from Mozart to the present for the music lover as well as for the specialist. *H & P—S&S.*

STEVENS, DENIS W. b. 1922 (ed.). *History of Song* (1961). Covers all the noteworthy song composers in 15 Western countries from the Middle Ages to the present. *P—Norton.*

ULRICH, HOMER b. 1906. *Chamber Music* (2nd ed. 1966). Summarizes the evolution of music from the early canzones and sonatas through Haydn, Mozart, and Beethoven to the present. *H & P—Columbia U Pr.*

WINTERNITZ, EMANUEL b. 1898. *Musical Instruments of the Western World* (1963). Excellent, informative discussion of the history of musical instruments, their creators, and aspects of the interconnection between the instruments and music of any given age. Exceedingly beautiful photographs by Lilly Stunzi. *H—McGraw.*

The Dance

BALANCHINE, GEORGE b. 1904. *Complete Stories of the Great Ballets* (rev. ed. 1968). The celebrated choreographer's stories of more than 100 ballets still performed, guide to watching ballet, history of ballet, and discussion of the study of ballet—all directed to the ballet-goer. *H—Doubleday.*

DE MILLE, AGNES b. 1908. *Dance to the Piper* (1952). Entertaining autobiography of a significant contributor to the popularity of ballet today. *o.p.*

FONTEYN, DAME MARGOT b. 1919. *Autobiography* (1976). The life of one of the world's great dancers told with honesty and humility. *H— Knopf.*

HASKELL, ARNOLD b. 1903. *The Wonderful World of Dance* (1960). Intended for children, this is also a good introduction to the dance for adults. It shows how people in various cultures reveal in their dances their way of living and thinking. *o.p.*

HUMPHREY, DORIS 1895-1958. *The Art of Making Dances* (rev. ed. 1962). Illustrated guide to an appreciation of American modern dance as an art form, by a great dancer and choreographer. *P—Grove.*

LEATHERMAN, LEROY b. 1922. *Martha Graham* (1966). Beautifully illustrated and fascinating biography of one of America's greatest dance innovators. *o.p.*

REYNOLDS, NANCY. *Repertory in Review: 40 Years of the New York City Ballet* (1977). A unique comprehensive history of a great ballet company, combining photographs, performance programs, interviews, and the author's commentary. *H—Dial.*

SACHS, CURT 1881-1959. *World History of the Dance* (1937). A scholarly history of the dance (defined as rhythmical motion not related to work itself) in different cultures. *P—Norton.*

Photography and Film

BUNNELL, WALTER. *The New Photography* (1967). An illustrated description of modern developments in photographic techniques. *o.p.*

CARTIER-BRESSON, HENRI b. 1908. *The World of Henri Cartier-Bresson* (1968). An excellent collection of the work of a brilliant humanist photographer who strives for precise reporting of fact. *o.p.*

DORR, NELL. *Of Night and Day* (1968). A handsome photographic essay on the quest for the meaning of life. *H—Scrimshaw Calif.*

EISENSTAEDT, ALFRED b. 1898. *Witness to Our Time* (1968). An exciting photographic history of people and events since World War I. *o.p.*

EISENSTEIN, SERGEI 1898-1948. *Film Form* (1969). Famous Soviet director's brilliant explanation of the esthetics of filmmaking. *P— HarBraceJ.*

———. *The Film Sense.* (1968). Twelve essays demonstrating key points of the author's film theory, including diagrams and halftones. *P— HarBraceJ.*

Focal Encyclopedia of Photography (rev. ed. 1972). An informative reference work, presenting 2,400 articles by many experts. *H—McGraw.*

GOSLING, NIGEL b. 1901. *Nadar* (1977). Contains 359 unusually fine photographs of leading artistic figures of the 19th century by the pioneer photographer Nadar, whose real name was Félix Tournachon (1820-1910). *H—Knopf.*

HUSS, ROY G. b. 1927 and NORMAN SILVERSTEIN b. 1922. *The Film Experience* (1968). An enlightening analysis of the principles and techniques of filmmaking from all periods and all countries. *H—Har-Row; P—Dell.*

KAEL, PAULINE b. 1919. *Reeling* (1976). A well-known film critic writes 74 perceptive and often provocative essays on major films from 1926 to 1976. *H—Little.*

POLLACK, PETER b. 1911. *The Picture History of Photography* (rev. ed. 1970). From the earliest experiments to the recent accomplishments of contemporary photographers. *H—Abrams.*

SARRIS, ANDREW b. 1928. *The Films of Josef von Sternberg* (1966). A comprehensive survey of a great director's work. *P—Mus of Mod Art.*

SCHARF, AARON b. 1922. *Pioneers of Photography* (1976). Compelling story of the early years of photography, using excerpts from the diaries and letters of the photographers as well as 175 of their photographs. *H—Abrams.*

STEICHEN, EDWARD 1879-1973. *Family of Man* (1956). Reproduces the famous exhibition (503 photographs from 68 countries) created by Steichen for the New York Museum of Modern Art. *H—S&S; P—NAL.*

18. Philosophy

Philip Roddman

Philosophy is essentially a skill like medicine and an invention like music. The philosopher by means of language investigates the known, explores the unknown, and infers the unknowable. This art, as in doctoring and composing, entails many methods or procedures. The methods of philosophy are as various as the imaginations that entertain it. Of those imaginations, the mathematical, the common-sensible, the literary, and the religious are the most prominent in the philosophical thought of our time.

Contemporary thinkers tend to speak of philosophy as an activity rather than as a repository of wisdom. Accomplishments, in the sense of therapies for "mental cramp" and hints for penetrating existence, now count for more than doctrines about humanity's place in nature or supernature. Of the two most influential philosophies of the 20th century, one confines itself to the critique or analysis of language, while the other inquires into the predicament of the individual in the chaos of being. The analytic philosophers, whose appeal is either to mathematics or to common sense as manifested in ordinary speech, disclose the meaning and unmeaning of verbal constructions expressing beliefs and ideas. Examining articulations among and within codes of communication, they are much like physicians or surgeons diagnosing and prescribing for states of illness and delusion. The moral philosophers, whose appeal is to conditions of suffering and privation, to forces in a state of crisis, produce a poetry of feeling meant to educate the heart or suggest a new horizon to the mind. These philosophers are akin to musicians who inflect the pang of a painful emotion into its ideal import.

The linguistic philosophers use symbolic logic and everyday discourse, as far as these resources can go, to ascertain the meaning of facts, propositions, material objects, and the meaning of meaning. They call upon the authority of the senses and of the general rules of language to draw the line between sense and nonsense. The grammar of language, its structure and arrangement, in the opinion of the "logisticians," is a basic world view. Hence their metaphysics or system of first principles is the form and syntax of language itself, words used as signs or tools and as images or parables. They insist, quite literally, that in the beginning was the word.

The existentialists or moral philosophers dramatize a state of affairs in which acts, decisions, resolutions create worlds of value. Their gospel reads that in the beginning was the deed. Although theirs is a cosmology that presupposes a totality devoid of purpose and design, they present a highly flattering, if overstrenuous, vision of the individual as his or her own invention: own keeper, own judge, and own priest.

For the logisticians, philosophy is "a battle against the bewitchment of our intelligence." For the existentialists, philosophy is a training in courage "for an attack on one's convictions."

It is precisely for leading the youth of Athens to lose faith in their convictions by exposing the inconsistencies and nonsense in their beliefs that Socrates, the patron saint of philosophy, was put to death. Socrates was both an analytic and a moral philosopher, a physician of the mind and a composer of new visions. His ontology (analytic metaphysics) and his cosmology (speculative metaphysics) are of a piece. Love for him is the cosmological process, the dynamo, that drives us to the ontological reality of truth, goodness, and beauty. Philosophy, a dialogue between sense and reason, culminates in a feast of intelligence and love. Compounded of the words *philos* (love) and *sophia* (wisdom), philosophy, in the Socratic definition, is the passion for self-knowledge. To make our ideas and beliefs clear to ourselves and to others is to bring the truth out of hiding, to distinguish what we are and what we do from what we think we are and what we think we do. The key sentence in Socrates' life, still the most powerful declaration of moral principle in Western culture, occurs in Plato's *Apology:* "The unexamined life is not worth living."

But is self-knowledge possible? In fact, is reliable knowledge of any kind attainable? Doctrines of knowledge and truth, classified as epistemology, have mustered much ingenuity in order to answer these still unanswered questions. Is true knowledge, as Plato says, a recollection, from prenatal existence, of an eternal Idea or Principle? Or is it, as Lenin says, a transition from non-knowledge to knowledge? In sum, is it a gift or a conquest?

If a gift, then it is the gift of self-recovery. Here the fundamental unit in morals is the individual giving birth to an authentic self. True knowledge harmonizes in us impulses and passions the way music organizes random sounds into intelligible forms. In the Socratic-Platonic theory, virtue and knowledge, morality and waking consciousness, are one. It is not our experience of the world but our commitment to what is permanently best that can define the meaning of justice, courage, loyalty. The moral individual is like a fugitive dancer intuiting the timeless pattern of a dance.

Knowledge as conquest is knowledge for service, not for self-possession. The collectivity, of which the individual is a module, is the unit in morals. Marxism-Leninism holds that the class struggle in history shifts the accent of moral judgments according to the needs of the working class. Moral beliefs need constant revision, since moral values depend on modes of production and the alterable body of social life. The individual is a pawn aspiring to a command of the game, never to command the game.

Job in the Old Testament and Prometheus in Greek religion personify, in large measure, the two ethical systems under discussion. Job is in quest of himself; Prometheus, in quest of social justice. Job, in an access of cosmic piety, acknowledges the Power that made him and must unmake him in the end as living proof of the moral government of the world. For Job the right is the good. Prometheus accuses the king of the gods of a vile conspiracy against humanity, of disloyalty to what makes for the good. For Prometheus, only the good can be right. Job bows before the divine secret that has brought about the kinship of all creation. Prometheus steals the secret of fire from the tyrant god in order to liberate humanity from the darkness of bondage. Job's recognition of the limits of his understanding frees him from illusion and inspires in him a boundless sympathy for all that lives and breathes. Prometheus' rebellion redeems humankind from alienation and endows it with consciousness of its own destiny. In both moral systems reason or understanding is the key to happiness. But in the Socratic-Biblical system, understanding brings about a change of heart, while in the Promethean-Marxist system, understanding brings about a change of situation. The life of reason may lead, as in Spinoza, to "the intellectual love of God"; or it may, in the reforming zeal of modern revolutionaries, govern passion by passion.

When the existentialists declare that "man creates his own values," they are close to the Marxist principle of value. So to a degree are those linguistic philosophers who reduce moral principles to the commitments we choose to make in life—games whose policy-rules change with circumstances. Neither school subscribes to the historical determinism of Marxist ideology. The linguistic philosophers, however, who are also structuralists, imply that language is command, and its complex rules introduce a large element of determinism.

If we grant that language is command, we may well ask whose language is more likely to be obeyed: the classic language of the oppressor or the street language of the oppressed? Is it possible that languages collide, fight, and destroy one another as men and women and nations do? Moreover, experience and science everywhere remind us that there is a force in things which no set of invented forms can ever contain. Is there between the will-to-live and the will-to-dominate a web of indeterminate circumstance that neither a philosophy of freedom nor a philosophy of determinism can ever hope to encompass or circumvent?

The ancient questions of Whence? Why? Whither?—in metaphysics, in epistemology, in ethics—are like the Flying Dutchman, doomed to sail the seas of thought forever, without hope of putting into some miraculously permanent haven. Yet the youngest branch of philosophy, esthetics, embracing families of felt quality (the Beautiful, the Ugly, the Tragic, the Comic, the Heroic, the Vulgar, the Noble, the Sublime, the Useful, the Useless, the Boring), has gained an independent haven in the fine arts.

The immense need for the assimilation of experience that has developed in industrial societies is creating a host of metaphysical, epistemological, and ethical issues that find their most attractive formulation in esthetic terms. Very likely, too, the mutations of religious categories have multiplied the perspectives of esthetics, for the same fundamental question resides in esthetics as in religion: What, without any ulterior reason, is objectively most admirable and infinitely cherishable?

Because works of art and of criticism materialize esthetic feelings and perceptions more successfully, certainly more visibly, than other forms of human activity, the philosophy of art and the philosophy of criticism have proved as various and as polemical as the study of theology in the heyday of scholasticism. Definitions of art are as multifarious as the ideologies and the imaginations of the definers. But about the function of the work of art there seems to be general agreement. It is this: a painting, a poem, a sculpture, a piece of music, when successful, serves as an organ of life. For a philosopher like Aristotle a work of art completes nature and thereby offers us a second life. For an artist like Tolstoy art expresses the morality of the brotherhood of man and hence is the essential condition of human life. For a critic like Walter Pater art lights the flame of perception and thus recovers the powers of life.

In the esthetics of the 20th century, the major concern is the relation of function to form. In existentialist esthetics, form follows function, as essence follows existence, or as actuality precedes meaning or purpose. In structuralist esthetics function follows form, the way operations of a language follow its grammar, or as the movements of the body depend on the articulation of bone and muscle. To an existentialist the air of anxiety and dread informing a work by the sculptor Alberto Giacometti or by the painter Francis Bacon is the expression of a being choosing freedom, an existence choosing its essence, even, or especially, in a trap or cage. To a structuralist the same work is a transformation of several motifs in the history and in the medium of painting. Its meaning is its esthetic organization of, say, the composition of the age and the sensibility or technique of the artist—external and internal codes or forms deeply interfused. Here the meaning of a symbol is its power to translate into other symbols, as if we said that Socrates the philosopher is in one aspect the foe of tradition, in another the prototype of the Christian martyr. In existentialism, on the other hand, the symbol is a light beam that locates causes and consequences, as if we said that Socrates leading the life of the barefoot idler of Athens concretized philosophy. It is, however, possible to assert that the echo of Socrates' thought has grown so much more resonant than the actuality of the man in ancient Athens that essence has not only overtaken but completely swallowed existence. What, then, shall be our position in respect to knowledge that is given in nature and in social intercourse and knowledge formed by art and imagination?

At the outset we compared the discipline of philosophy to that of medicine and music—to a science and an art. We now may add that philosophy, in a systematic manner, carries on the task suggested by those two world symbols earlier described: Job and Prometheus. Like Job, philosophy inquires into the nature and limits of knowledge. Like Prometheus, it indicates the possibilities of experience. Activities such as these, at least according to Aristotle, create the one permanent field of happiness.

Classics in Philosophy

The following descriptions, read in chronological order, from Plato through Russell, will give the reader a thumbnail history of philosophy.

ARISTOTLE 384-322 B.C. *Basic Works*. "The master of those who know" (Dante's phrase), Aristotle emphasizes "rationalism": the reliance on human capacities for intelligent behavior. The major works are *Nicomachean Ethics* ("the middle way" of common sense not as compromise but as hitting the bull's-eye in thought and action); *Physics and Metaphysics* (nature as the dynamic realm of matter and form set in eternal motion by the eternal unmoved first mover); and *Poetics* (art considered, like nature, a dynamic principle of creativity). *Over 6 eds. of each title.*

AUGUSTINE, SAINT 354-430. *The City of God*. Biblical fervor and Platonic ontology combine to create the philosophy of "illuminism." God (effluence of bright essence) enters history, preparing that mystical city where the individuality of the soul can efface the slave stamp of the body, as light obliterates darkness. The heavenly city is constituted of the union of souls in the love of the Divine Being. *H—Cath U Pr 3 vols, Dutton 2 vols, Harvard U Pr 7 vols; P—Penguin (abr.).*

BERKELEY, GEORGE 1685-1753. *Three Dialogues Between Hylas and Philonous* (1713). Berkeley repudiates the existence of a material world. His "empirical" or "subjective idealism," which identifies sense perception wholly with a mental reality, puts the source of all our knowledge in the divine language of our sensations. What Spirit, the eternal perceiver, creates has its passing moment of existence in the human mind and its eternal moment in the mind of God. *P—Bobbs, Open Court.*

DESCARTES, RENÉ 1596-1650. *Discourse on Method* (1637). Assuming a mind-body dualism, Descartes makes thinking the essence of the individual, and mathematical dynamism the essence of matter. *Cartesianism* (philosophical dualism, or even tri-alism, with God as the connective) divorces science from theology and frees the individual consciousness from forms fixed by tradition, custom, and community. *Over 6 eds.*

DEWEY, JOHN 1859-1952. *Experience and Nature* (1925) and *Art as Experience* (1935). Effecting the union of theory and practice, as in Greek thought, but breaking with the dogma of a changeless super-static truth, Dewey's "pragmatism" defines experience as a web of collective transactions. His "instrumentalism" looks to the scientific method and the democratic process as instruments for converting desire into intelligence. Since for Dewey meanings dwell neither in things nor in individual minds but in shared experience, he points the way toward activities whose fulfillment is esthetic and open-ended. First title: *H—Open Court, Peter Smith; P—Dover, Open Court.* Second title: *P—Putnam.*

HEGEL, GEORG W. F. 1770-1831. *The Philosophy of History* (1837). What Hegel calls "objective idealism" is really Kant's spirituality, the feeling of the ethical as an intimation of God, freedom, and immortality, transformed into an active, cunning, and self-realizing Spirit. The method used by Spirit is a dialectic of tensions and assimilations, packed with the whole realm of nature, humanity, and history, leading to ever higher successes. Esthetically, Hegel's Spirit is a composer and his dialectic a development of themes and counterthemes in ever richer complexities. Morally, his Spirit is a fighter and his dialectic a machinery of conflict for realizing giant organizations for the sake of greater giants, never for the individual. *H—Peter Smith.*

HOBBES, THOMAS 1588-1679. *Leviathan* (1651). Breaking with all past philosophies of perfectionism and rationalism, and following the new science of Galileo and Bacon, Hobbes posits "materialism" (matter and motion as the basis of all perceptions) as the sole form of philosophy. His materialism views everything, including human beings, in terms of physical force, or matter in motion. It is the ferocious wolfishness of humanity in a state of nature that drives people to worship power and to accept, for reasons of survival, sovereign power in the state and in religion. *Over 6 eds.*

HUME, DAVID 1711-1776. *Enquiry Concerning Human Understanding* (1748). With a thoroughgoing "skepticism," the doctrine that the truth of all knowledge is in doubt, Hume undermines the entire traditional structure of philosophical and commonsensible thought and belief: the self, substance, identity, the existence of the external world, causal necessity. He uses as his means an empirical criterion, holding that every impression is a distinct, isolated, independent, particular unit of experience. *Over 6 eds.*

JAMES, WILLIAM 1842-1910. *Pragmatism* (1907) and *The Meaning of Truth* (1909). For James "the stuff" out of which everything is composed, including all connections and connectives, is experience, a cosmic continuum. In his particular kind of pragmatism, "radical empiricism," consciousness and truth are functions and instruments of experience. James opts for personal experience as knowledge itself. He thus restores a living warmth to the varieties of imagination and belief. *Over 4 eds. of each title.*

KANT, IMMANUEL 1724-1804. *The Critique of Pure Reason* (1781), *The Critique of Practical Reason* (1788), and *The Critique of Judgment* (1790). "Transcendentalism" in Kant means the critique or analysis of all knowledge as arising from the structure of the human mind organizing experience. Kant discovers two selves in every human being: the phenomenal or empirical self that conforms to ordered sense-impressions, and the noumenal self that hints at eternal values. The phenomenal self, in tune with mechanical or causal necessity, makes scientific knowledge possible. The noumenal self, in tune with intimations of God, freedom, and immortality, leads to ethical and esthetic judgments of universal import. First title: *P—Doubleday, Dutton, St Martin.* Second title: *P—Bobbs.* Third title: *H—Oxford U Pr; P—Hafner.*

LOCKE, JOHN 1632-1704. *An Essay Concerning Human Understanding* (1690). In revolt against Descartes's concept of innate ideas and their self-evident character of clarity and distinctiveness, Locke considers sensory experience the sole source of knowledge. This philosophy of "empiricism" induces Locke to describe the human mind as one long autobiography of unnumbered experiences and to conceive nature, under the influence of Newton, as a free mechanism subject to indefinite change. *Over 6 eds.*

LUCRETIUS c. 94-55 B.C. *On the Nature of Things.* This classic work, based on the Epicurean philosophy of "atomism" (primary reality as a fertile dust—material and mechanical) and "naturalism" (nature as its own standard), announces that all creation arises from destruction. Everything tends toward death, and "death is the mother of beauty." *Over 6 eds.*

MARCUS AURELIUS ANTONINUS 121-180. *Meditations.* In the most famous work of "stoicism," a philosophy that weds "pantheism" (the order of nature identified as divinity) to "fatalism" (acceptance of the inevitable as recognition of the divinity that shapes our ends), the author balances a scientific logic (the stoic world-reason) against his personal life and vocation as emperor and general. *Over 10 eds.*

MARX, KARL 1818-1883. *Economic and Philosophical Manuscripts* (1844). From Hegel, Marx derives the belief that reason is central to history, but in terms of class conflict, not in Hegelian terms of nations and epochs playing subsidiary parts in the ultimate mission of Absolute Spirit. For Marx the idea of progress is not divine but human, going deeper than any code of ethics. He sees morals and religions as political passions, passions reflecting the way society makes its living and distributes its wealth. Divining the dénouement of future history as a prophet of old divined the Day of Judgment, Marx's "dialectical and historical materialism" holds that truth is the reality of power demonstrated in practice. *H & P—Int Pub Co.*

NIETZSCHE, FRIEDRICH 1844-1900. *The Will to Power* (1906). Anarchist in morals, absolutist in politics, foe of social reform or progress, poet of the "eternal return" (the periodic reembodiment of certain patterns in world history), Nietzsche resurrects the Greek tragic hero, who, having outgrown his gods and rejected all limits, is to be the superman of the future. Converting Darwin's theory of natural selection and the struggle for life into the will-to-power, power to reverse all values at will, Nietzsche proclaims the terrible beauty of the imperial self, the philosophy of "romantic egotism." *H—Gordon Pr 2 vols; P—Random.*

PLATO c. 427-347 B.C. *Dialogues.* All philosophy is a footnote to Plato (Whitehead). Maintaining that all reality is mental, as do all idealists, Plato posits two principles: (1) the Eternal Mind is changeless; (2) all motion arises from the love inspired by the Eternal Mind. Among the major dialogues are *The Phaedo* (the ontology or nature of Ideas), *The Timaeus* (the cosmogony), *The Meno* and *The Theaetetus* (the epistemology), *The Republic* (the structure of justice, of science, and of the soul), and *The Symposium* (love as the ladder to truth). *H—Liveright, Oxford U Pr 4 vols, Random 2 vols; P—HM, WSP.*

PLOTINUS 204-275. *The Enneads.* Defining God as the Beloved whose emanations we are and whose center we forever seek, Plotinus creates a logic of feeling known as "neo-Platonism" that, for later centuries, becomes the ruling principle of such various institutions as Byzantine art, monastic discipline, feudalism, and the system of courtly love. *Over 6 eds.*

RUSSELL, BERTRAND 1872-1970. *An Inquiry into Meaning and Truth* (1940). A master logician (*Principia Mathematica*, 1913, with Alfred North Whitehead) and epistemologist (*Our Knowledge of the External World*, 1914), Russell wishes to assimilate philosophy to science. A leader in the movement known as Logical Analysis, Russell writes that its chief merits are "the introduction of scientific truthfulness into philosophy" and the invention of "a powerful method by which [philosophy] can be rendered fruitful." He is a mighty moralist in the tradition of Spinoza and John Stuart Mill. *H—Humanities.*

SCHOPENHAUER, ARTHUR 1788-1860. *The World as Will and Representation* (1819). Into the philosophy of "voluntarism" (the priority of desire over intellect), Schopenhauer introduces an evolutionary tendency that deepens the possibilities for pain and suffering engendered by that irrational and insane force, the will to live. To reach the extremes of cruelty, the will pursues its manifestations from the mineral to the vegetable to the animal to the human kingdom. In the human kingdom desire triumphs over all forms of knowledge, save in the case of the Buddhist saint who kills the will to live, save also in those moments of freedom that we achieve in passive contemplation of the wildness of the will revealed in works of art. It is spirit, the intuitive intellect in us, that on such occasions eclipses the will, spirit that is an offshoot of the will in the human kingdom as is a medicinal herb in the vegetable kingdom. But spirit is ultimately impotent. *H—Peter Smith 2 vols; P—Dover 2 vols.*

SPINOZA, BARUCH 1634-1677. *The Ethics* (1677). Spinoza asumes the eternal rightness, and therefore goodness, of God or Universal Nature. Of this Universal Nature, infinite in attributes, we know but thought and matter and their infinitude of instances. Descartes says: When I think, I am. Spinoza says: When I think, Nature thinks in me. Spinoza transforms pantheism, the belief that God is everything and everything is God, into "pan-in-theism," the belief that God or Nature embraces everything. Spinoza's scientific attitude requires identifying necessity with freedom. For him, the understanding of scientific laws, what he calls "the intellectual love of God," offers the power and wisdom to elude the pitfalls of wishful thinking, illusion, and delusion. *P—Citadel Pr.*

THOMAS AQUINAS, SAINT 1225-1274. *Summa Theologica.* To close the gap between Creature and Creator and to fashion an undivided universe in a continuous hierarchy of intelligences, "Thomism" reconciles Aristotelian rationalism with divine revelation, reason with faith, in the synthesis of Christian humanism. Dante's *Divine Comedy* is a Thomist poem of the levels of reality, from the innermost recesses of the heart to the farthest reaches of the stream of destiny. *Over 6 eds.*

Modern and Contemporary Thought

AUSTIN, J. L. 1911-1960. *Philosophical Papers* (1961). The significance of nuances in ordinary language by an Oxford professor noted for his theory of "speech acts." *H—Oxford U Pr.*

AYER, A. J. b. 1910. *Language, Truth, and Logic* (1936). Important work in the exposition of logical empiricism. *H—Peter Smith; P—Dover.*

BERGSON, HENRI 1859-1941. *The Two Sources of Morality and Religion* (1935). The interplay of instinct and intelligence brilliantly presented in a seminal work. *H—Greenwood.*

BUBER, MARTIN 1878-1965. *Between Man and Man* (1947). A religious existentialist relating the "I—Thou" principle to communication, society, education, and modern philosophies. *P—Macmillan.*

CASSIRER, ERNST 1874-1945. *The Philosophy of Symbolic Forms* (1923). Detailed analyses of the significance of symbolic forms in the intellectual activities of our culture. *H & P—Yale U Pr 3 vols.*

FRANK, PHILIPP 1884-1966. *Modern Science and Its Philosophy* (1941). Einstein's successor at the University of Prague relating 20th-century physics to the logic of science, metaphysics, and education. *H—Arno.*

HEIDEGGER, MARTIN 1889-1977. *Existence and Being* (1949). Four essays by the existentialist philosopher, two dealing with the essence of metaphysics, two with the essence of poetry in relation to Hölderlin. *P—Regnery.*

HUSSERL, EDMUND 1859-1938. *Ideas* (1913). A philosopher who greatly influenced the 20th-century existentialists here contrasts pure phenomenology with psychology. *H—Humanities; P—Macmillan.*

KIERKEGAARD, SØREN 1813-1855. *Either/Or* (1843) and *The Sickness unto Death* (1849). Musical-erotic problems, "original sin," the importance of pure choice, the existing self as against Hegel's objective thinker dramatically examined by an exponent of Christian existentialism. *H—Peter Smith; P—Doubleday.*

MILL, JOHN STUART 1806-1873. *On Liberty* (1859) and *Utilitarianism* (1863). The great inductive logician and philosopher of science in a brilliant defense of individual freedom and the ethics of the greatest good for the greatest number. *Over 6 eds.*

MOORE, G. E. 1873-1958. *Some Main Problems of Philosophy* (1953). One of the fathers of analytical philosophy in essays relating problems in logic and metaphysics to common sense. *H—Humanities.*

OGDEN, C. K. 1889-1957 and I. A. RICHARDS b. 1893. *The Meaning of Meaning* (1938). The famous study of the influence of language upon thought and of the science of symbolism. *P—HarBraceJ.*

PEIRCE, CHARLES S. 1839-1914. *Philosophical Writings* (1940, 1955). Popular and technical essays on logic, evolution, and the cosmos presenting key ideas in American thought. *P—Dover.*

QUINE, W. V. O. b. 1908. *Word and Object* (1960). The definitive examination of the notion of meaning and the linguistic mechanisms of object reference in the philosophy of a noted logician. *P—MIT Pr.*

SANTAYANA, GEORGE 1863-1952. *The Life of Reason* (1906). Next to James's *Principles of Psychology*, Santayana's work is the most distinguished masterpiece in American philosophy. *o.p.*

SARTRE, JEAN-PAUL b. 1905. *Being and Nothingness* (1943). Atheistic existentialism presented by a philosopher who is also a novelist and playwright. *P—Citadel Pr, WSP.*

SUZUKI, D. T. 1870-1966. *Zen Buddhism* (1956). The search for the entirely and vividly concrete. *P—Doubleday.*

WHITEHEAD, ALFRED NORTH 1861-1947. *Modes of Thought* (1938). The relations of value to language and physics to life explained by a philosopher whose work in mathematics and logic is of first importance. *P—Free Pr.*

WITTGENSTEIN, LUDWIG 1889-1951. *Tractatus Logico-Philosophicus* (1921). A key contribution to the philosophy of logical atomism. *H & P—Humanities.*

———. *Philosophical Investigations* (1953). An important contribution to linguistic philosophy. *H—Basil Blackwell; P—Macmillan.*

Histories and Anthologies

Age of Analysis (1955). Ed. by Morton White. Well-selected pages from key works of the 20th century with lucid commentaries. *P—NAL.*

Contemporary Philosophic Problems (1959). Ed. by Y. H. Krikorian and A. Edel. Selections from influential thinkers dealing with meaning, knowledge, being, value, and action. *o.p.*

DURANT, WILL b. 1885. *The Story of Philosophy* (rev. ed. 1933). Popular, readable, and selective account of Western thinkers. *H—S&S: P—PB, S&S.*

Existentialism from Dostoevsky to Sartre (1956). Ed. by Walter Kaufmann. An anthology for the lay person of selections from literary and religious imaginations in philosophy. *H—Peter Smith; P—NAL.*

FLOWER, ELIZABETH and MURRAY G. MURPHY. *A History of Philosophy in America* (1977). A comprehensive study of the origins and interrelations of American philosophical thought from Puritanism to Conceptualistic Pragmatism. *H—Putnam 2 vols.*

JONES, W. T. b. 1910. *A History of Western Philosophy* (1952). The classical, the medieval, and the modern minds simply and forcefully presented. *o.p.*

Logical Positivism (1959). Ed. by A. J. Ayer. Authoritative expositions of doctrines associated with logical positivism. *P—Free Pr.*

MARÍAS AGUILERA, JULIÁN b. 1914. *History of Philosophy* (22nd ed. 1966). A Spanish scholar's philosophical treatment of the history of philosophy from the pre-Socratics to Heidegger and Ortega. *P—Dover.*

Ordinary Language (1964). Ed. by V. C. Chappell. Essays on the uses of language with an introduction relating linguistic philosophy to Wittgenstein and Oxford professors. *o.p.*

Readings in Philosophy (3rd ed. 1972). Ed. by J. H. Randall, Jr. Excerpts from Plato through Descartes and Mill to Whitehead, grouped to emphasize philosophic perspectives. *P—B&N.*

RUSSELL, BERTRAND 1872-1970. *History of Western Philosophy* (1945). Lucid, candid, wise analysis of philosophical systems and of their connections with political and social circumstances. *H & P—S&S.*

Source Book in Indian Philosophy (1957). Ed. by S. Radhakrishnan and C. A. Moore. Selections from the Vedic and Epic periods as well as from the heterodox and orthodox and contemporary systems with enlightening introductions. *H & P—Princeton U Pr.*

STUMPF, SAMUEL E. b. 1918. *Socrates to Sartre* (1966). For beginners in philosophy an up-to-date introduction to the great issues of thought. *H—McGraw.*

WINDELBAND, WILHELM 1848-1915. *A History of Philosophy* (1901). A classic in its field by an idealist philosopher of some distinction. *P—Har-Row.*

19. Religion

Susan E. Crockford

Among the earliest traces of human life, the archaeologist finds relics, works of art, and symbolic objects, the functions of which are not merely functional and most often must logically be ascribed to religious purposes. The effort that humanity has expended through the millenia to define itself in relation to the natural, animate, and spiritual worlds is one of the most basic and consistent examples of intellectual struggle. Although there are many examples of the individual's traditional quest for personal meaning outside the communal religious expression, by far the greater body of work relates to the varieties of spiritual and religious belief within large cultural or ethnic groups. Individuality is often defined in reaction to and interaction with what has evolved as an organized or shared religious expression.

The major world religions are expressed chiefly in three forms: the sacred texts, which, in poetry or prose, reveal the fundamental traditions, principles, and perceptions; the theology, which reveals the dogma and interpretive perceptions that guide the faithful community; and the church, or religious establishment, which embodies the theology and provides current commentary as society and the world changes. Additionally, a wealth of interpretive, historical, and analytical material is written on all forms of religious expression and experience.

None of the sacred texts of the world's major religions was originally written in English. Fortunately, the translations available today, many of them excellent, represent the scholarship and dedication of centuries of endeavor to bring the vitality of the original texts to the English language. The reader need not be a member of the community for which the texts have special meaning to find the combined challenge of great literature, boundless imagination, and intellectual stimulation.

The crises and strains of world events have necessarily affected religions in a profound way. The need of human beings to reassess the definitions of previous generations has influenced the churches and their critics and has produced major new interpretive works. The vast literature of religion is continuously enriched as men and women apply current historical, philosophical, and sociological insights to the ageless questions about the reasons for the existence of humanity, for the origins of the physical world, and for the role of the individual and the community in the cosmos.

Sacred Texts

Bhagavad-Gita (5th to 3rd cent. B.C.). See "East and South Asia," page 60.

Bible (800 B.C. to A.D. 300). The scriptures of Judaism and Christianity in the Old Testament, the New Testament, and the Apochrypha. Over 50 English translations of the Bible have appeared since Wycliffe's in 1382; the King James (Authorized) Version, first published in 1611, is widely considered the most beautiful. The King James Version is available in countless editions, including *The Dartmouth Bible* (1950) (*H—HM*), an abridgment with superb notes.

Modern translations of the Bible include *The New English Bible* (1961), *H & P—Oxford U Pr;* a new Catholic translation, *The Jerusalem Bible* (1966), *H—Doubleday; The Anchor Bible*, still under revision by its Catholic, Protestant, and Jewish collaborators (*H & P—Doubleday*); and the *American Revised Standard Version or RSV* (*H—Nelson; P—World Pub*).

Numerous biblical guides and commentaries are available to aid the reader. Two important concordances are *Cruden's Concordance* (*over 6 eds.*) and *Harper's Topical Concordance* (*P—Har-Row*). A notable commentary, which includes the texts of the King James Version and the *RSV*, is *The Interpreter's Bible* (12 vols. 1951-57; *H—Abingdon*) and its companion, *The Interpreter's Dictionary of the Bible* (5 vols. 1962; *H—Abingdon*), which provides references to the personalities, places, and topics of the scriptures. *A New Catholic Commentary on Holy Scripture* (1969; *H—Nelson*) is designed as a companion to the *RSV* and includes much post-Vatican II thought.

BUDDHA 563-483 B.C. *Teachings of the Compassionate Buddha* (1955). An anthology of the basic texts of Buddhism, with introduction and notes by E. A. Burtt. *P—NAL.*

CONFUCIUS. *The Analects*. See "East and South Asia," page 58.

Hindu Scriptures (1966). Ed. and trans. by R. C. Zaehner. Includes the Bhagavad-Gita, and selections from the Upanishads, Rigveda, and Atharvaveda. *P—Dutton.*

Koran. See "The Middle East," page 51.

LAO-TZU c. 604-531 B.C. *The Way and Its Power* (1956). Arthur Waley's excellent translation and editing of the basic Taoist document, the Tao Te Ching. *H—Allen Unwin; P—Grove.*

Reader on Islam (1962). Ed. by A. Jeffrey. Selections from the standard Arabic writings, including the Koran, the *Traditions*, and other major Muslim texts. *o.p.*

Sacred Texts of China (1891). Trans. by J. Legge. This remains a classic English translation of Taoist texts. *H—Krishna Pr.*

World's Great Scriptures (1962). Ed. by L. Browne. Selections from the sacred texts of Babylonian and Egyptian religions, Hinduism, Buddhism, Confucianism, Taoism, Zoroastrianism, Judaism, Christianity, and Islam. *P—Macmillan.*

Writings of the Great Theologians

FOSDICK, HARRY EMERSON b. 1898 (ed.). *Great Voices of the Reformation* (1952). Major writings of Protestant reformers, from Wycliffe to Wesley, with biographies and commentary. *o.p.*

GOLDIN, JUDAH b. 1914. (ed. and trans.). *The Living Talmud* (1957). A selection from one of the treatises of the Talmud, with an introduction to the world of the Talmud; the archives of 700 years (300 B.C.-A.D. 400) of oral biblical interpretation, commentary, and debate that constitute rabbinic law. *P—NAL.*

HUNT, GEORGE L. b. 1918 (ed.). *Twelve Makers of Modern Protestant Thought* (rev. 1971). Barth, Buber, Niebuhr, and Tillich are among those represented. *P—Assn Pr.*

NOVECK, SIMON b. 1914 (ed.). *Great Jewish Thinkers of the Twentieth Century* (1963). Ten authorities discuss Jewish religious, intellectual, and social attainments since Moses. *P—B'nai B'rith.*

PEGIS, ANTON C. b. 1905 (ed.). *The Wisdom of Catholicism* (1949). Important writings of Catholics through the centuries: church fathers, ecclesiastics, mystics, philosophers, and lay authors. *o.p.*

Books on Religion and the Churches

AHLSTROM, SYDNEY E. b. 1919. *The Religious History of the American People* (1972). A major new study of the role religion has played in American life and history. *H & P—Yale U Pr.*

ALTIZER, THOMAS, J. J. b. 1927 (ed.). *Toward a New Christianity* (1967). Anthology of major writings necessary to an understanding of the "Death of God" movement in the United States and Europe. *H—HarBraceJ.*

BENZ, ERNST b. 1907. *The Eastern Orthodox Church* (1963). Good treatment of Eastern Orthodoxy—its church, traditions, thought, and dogma. *o.p.*

BLACK, ALGERNON D. b. 1900. *Without Burnt Offerings: Ceremonies of Humanism* (1974). A leader in the Ethical Culture movement presents nonritualistic ways of marking such occasions as birth, marriage, and death—invoking not God but "those elements of the human spirit that dignify and enoble human life." *H—Viking Pr.*

BLAU, JOSEPH L. b. 1909. *Modern Varieties of Judaism* (1965). Well-documented study of the chief movements within Judaism today, including Zionism. *H & P—Columbia U Pr.*

BURROWS. *The Dead Sea Scrolls.* See "The Middle East," page 50.

BURTT, EDWIN A. b. 1892. *Types of Religious Philosophy* (1951). Objective treatments, designed to enable the reader to make independent critical judgments, of the essential assumptions and outlooks of Catholicism, Protestant orthodoxy, the religion of science, agnosticism, ethical idealism, modernism, and humanism. *H—Har-Row.*

CHASE, MARY ELLEN 1897-1973. *The Bible and the Common Reader* (rev. 1952). The scriptures as literature and history, emphasizing the Old Testament, King James Version, and written with charm and scholarly grasp. *P—Macmillan.*

CONE, JAMES H. b. 1938. *A Black Theology of Liberation* (1970). Analyzes the role of Christianity and the theology of liberation in modern Black American society. *P—Lippincott.*

ELLIS, JOHN T. b. 1905. *American Catholicism* (2nd ed. 1969). Objective, documented review of the growth of the Catholic Church in the United States since Colonial times, coordinating ecclesiastical and secular history. *H & P—U of Chicago Pr.*

FRANKFORT, HENRI b. 1897. *Kinship and the Gods* (1948). Using the concept of kinship as a basis, Frankfort presents an analysis of the theology and traditions of Egypt, Mesopotamia, and the ancient Near East, emphasizing their integration of society and nature. *H—U of Chicago Pr.*

FRAZER. *The Golden Bough.* See "Greece," page 8.

GLAZER, NATHAN b. 1923. *American Judaism* (rev. 1972). Study of the Jewish faith in America since 1953, with sociological considerations and religious insight. *H & P—U of Chicago Pr.*

GRAVES. *The Greek Myths.* See "Greece," page 8.

GREELEY, ANDREW M. b. 1928. *The American Catholic: A Social Portrait* (1977). A sociological study of the American Catholic today aimed at dispelling myths and stereotypes held by non-Catholics. *H—Basic.*

GUILLAUME, ALFRED b. 1888. *Islam* (2nd rev. ed. 1956). Muhammad, the Koran, the evolution of Islam, the various schools of thought, and the place of Islam in the world today. *P—Penguin.*

HOPKINS, THOMAS J. b. 1930. *Hindu Religious Tradition* (1971). The values and traditions of Hindu life clearly presented chronologically and historically. *P—Dickinson.*

HUDSON, WINTHROP b. 1911. *American Protestantism* (1961). Evaluation of the development of Protestant churches since the Puritans through religious and cultural history. *H & P—U of Chicago Pr.*

HUMPHREYS, CHRISTMAS b. 1901. *Buddhism* (rev. 1958). Exposition of the various schools of Buddhism, including Zen, by the leader of the Buddhist Society in England. *P—Penguin.*

JAMES, WILLIAM 1842-1910. *Varieties of Religious Experience* (1902). The classic study of spiritual experiences as psychological phenomena. *H—Modern Lib; P—Collins-World, Macmillan, NAL.*

LATOURETTE, KENNETH S. b. 1884. *A History of Christianity* (rev. 1975). A definitive, comprehensive work. *P—Har-Row.*

MBITI, JOHN S. b. 1931. *African Religions and Philosophy* (1969). Presents aspects of pre-colonial Africa's traditional beliefs and practices, concentrating on those uninfluenced by either Christianity or Islam. *P—Doubleday.*

NEILL, STEPHEN CHARLES b. 1900. *Christian Faith and Other Faiths* (2nd ed. 1970). Intended for the Christian's understanding of and dialogue with Judaism, Islam, Hinduism, Buddhism, and Existentialism. *H & P—Oxford U Pr.*

NICHOLS, JAMES H. b. 1915. *Primer for Protestants* (1947). Concise, clear historical and doctrinal exposition of Protestant principles. *H—Greenwood.*

OBERHOLTZER, W. D. (ed.). *Is Gay Good? Ethics, Theology, and Homosexuality* (1971). Thirteen essays ranging over the subject of homosexuality and its theological and ethical implications. *P—Westminster.*

PARRINDER, EDWARD G. b. 1910. *African Traditional Religion* (1962). Sketches the broad concepts of African traditional religions with comparative material from the entire African continent. *H—Negro U Pr, Greenwood; P—Har-Row.*

ROSE, HERBERT J. 1883-1961. *Handbook of Greek Mythology, Including Its Extension to Rome* (6th ed. 1958). A good guide to the Greek myths, organized for both general and specific use, with scholarly notes and index. *P—Dutton.*

SUZUKI. *Zen Buddhism*. See "Philosophy," page 186.

UNDERHILL, EVELYN 1875-1941. *Mysticism* (1911). The classic study of the subject, with material drawn from mystics such as St. Teresa of Avila, Meister Eckhart, St. John of the Cross, and William Blake. *H—Rowman; P—Dutton, NAL.*

Women's Liberation and the Church (1970). Ed. by S. B. Doely. Essays by eight women, themselves active in both the lay and ordained communities, emphasizing the need for a new definition of the role of women in the Christian churches. *o.p.*

20. History

Austin L. Venable and Bernerd C. Weber

Carl Becker defined history as "a knowledge of things said and done." But history at its best does more than present a miscellaneous collection of the varied experiences of the human race. It may show, although sometimes imperfectly, the whole spectrum of behavior and belief and illustrate the range and depth of human experience.

A knowledge of history can serve as a valuable corrective to the common habits of vague generalization or of too narrow particularism. Historical knowledge explains how things have come to be what they are and hence helps to make the world more intelligible. The more one delves into the past, the deeper and broader will be one's comprehension of the present and insight into the future. The value of a knowledge of the past to the understanding of society today has been recognized by all the major historians from Thucydides on. Sir Charles Firth clearly expressed this idea: "History is not easy to define; but to me it seems the record of the life of societies of man, of the changes which those societies have gone through, of the ideas which have determined the actions of those societies, and of the material conditions which have helped or hindered their development."

By its very nature history is vibrant with life and inevitably concerns each of us. The 19th-century British historian Edward A. Freeman defined history as "past politics," but this definition is no longer considered adequate. Modern historians in writing about the past have increasingly turned attention to what James Harvey Robinson termed "the new history"—in other words, to economic, social, and cultural behavior of all people as well as to political, military, and constitutional events. Geographically, too, the whole base of history has broadened. No longer are Western historians concerned just with Europe or the Americas: Africa, Asia, and the island world of the Pacific are a vital part of the total drama of human experience and endeavor. Thus, all that has been thought and done on this earth falls within the province of history.

One of the pleasures of history grows out of its relationship with literature. Since the time of Herodotus of Halicarnassus, written history has been a major form of literary expression, and many major historians of the past have been distinguished writers. Not only have historians created literature by writing history, but, in varying degrees, a knowledge of the history they write is necessary for an understanding and appreciation of the poetry, drama, fiction, architecture, art, and music of any country or period.

History thus represents the sum of the total past of the world. If it is read and studied to any purpose, it is not "a confused heap of facts" (Lord Chesterfield) or "always tedious" (Anatole France) but makes an intelligent and often fascinating relationship between cause and effect that contains wisdom for all ages.

Many important historical books are listed in over a dozen other chapters of *Good Reading*. For dates and other reference data, extremely useful volumes include *Annals of European Civilization, 1501-1900* (1949) by Alfred Mayer; *Encyclopaedia of American History* (5th ed. 1976) edited by Richard B. and Jeffrey B. Morris; *An Encyclopaedia of World History* (5th ed. 1972) edited by William L. Langer; *Historical Atlas* (9th ed. 1964) by William R. Shepherd; and *The Timetables of History: A Horizontal Linkage of People and Events* (1975) by Bernard Grun. Available in paperback is *Historical Atlas of the World* (1961) edited by R. R. Palmer (*P—Rand*). See also the subdivision History in the "Reference Books" chapter.

General

Several hundred specialized histories—that is, histories limited to various historical periods and geographical areas—are contained in the book lists of Chapters 1 through 10. Histories that span the ages and often continents but examine only an aspect of culture (e.g., art, music, philosophy) are listed in the chapters on "Fine Arts and Design," "Philosophy," "Religion," "Economics," and "Anthropology." Additionally, many biographies of men and women important in history are listed in "Biography." Because of the profusion of history titles listed elsewhere, none is cross-referred in this chapter.

BRIDENTHAL, RENATE b. 1935 and CLAUDIA KOONZ (eds.). *Becoming Visible: Women in European History* (1977). An excellent collection of essays by various scholars stressing the role of women throughout European history. *P—HM*.

BRINTON, CRANE 1898-1968. *Ideas and Men* (2nd ed. 1963). A well-written and sound analysis of the major concepts in Western thought that have helped shape the course of Western civilization. *H—P-H*.

———— et al. *History of Civilization* (5th ed. 1976). A readable, thorough, well-illustrated survey. *H—P-H 3 vols.*

CHURCHILL, SIR WINSTON 1874-1965. *History of the English-Speaking Peoples* (1956-58). The great English statesman presents in his inimitable style the history of England, the United States, and the British Commonwealth as a unified story. *H—Dodd 4 vols.*

CLYDE, PAUL H. b. 1896 and BURTON F. BEERS b. 1927. *The Far East* (6th ed. 1975). A well-organized and clearly written account that stresses the impact of the West upon eastern Asia. *H—P-H.*

DEAN, VERA MICHELES b. 1903. *The Nature of the Non-Western World* (1957). A useful introduction emphasizing the West's influence upon older, traditional cultures. *P—NAL.*

FAIRBANK, JOHN K. b. 1907. *The United States and China* (3rd ed. 1971). An excellent general introductory account of the history of American-Chinese relationships. *H & P—Harvard U Pr.*

HALECKI, OSKAR 1891-1973. *A History of Poland* (1976). A readable survey by a Polish-born scholar. *H—McKay.*

KNAPTON, ERNEST JOHN b. 1902. *France: An Interpretive History* (1971). A well-written and clearly organized survey. *P—Scribner.*

McNEILL, WILLIAM H. b. 1917. *The Rise of the West: A History of the Human Community* (1963). A fascinating and provocative work, monumental in scope, that attempts to integrate the entire history of human societies into one continuous and cohesive story. *H & P—U of Chicago Pr.*

———. *Plagues and Peoples* (1975). A lively analysis of the role of disease in history. *H—Doubleday.*

MAHAN, ALFRED T. 1840-1914. *The Influence of Sea Power upon History, 1660–1783* (1890). A work that has become a classic. *H—Little, Peter Smith; P—Hill & Wang.*

PINSON, KOPPEL S. 1901-1961. *Modern Germany* (2nd ed. 1966). A clear and readable survey. *H—Macmillan.*

RANDALL, JOHN HERMAN, Jr. b. 1899. *The Making of the Modern Mind* (rev. ed. 1976). A learned and stimulating explanation of the forces from the Middle Ages onward that have contributed to modern ways of thinking and acting. *H & P—Columbia U Pr.*

TOYNBEE, ARNOLD J. 1889-1975. *A Study of History* (1934-61). A masterly monumental inquiry into the causes of the rise and decline of civilizations. *H & P—Oxford U Pr 12 vols.*

TREVELYAN, GEORGE M. 1876-1962. *History of England* (3rd ed. 1945). A classic account written by an outstanding English historian. Presupposes some previous knowledge of English history. *P—Doubleday 3 vols.*

Ancient and Medieval

For many additional titles see Chapters 1 through 3.

CHILDE, V. GORDON 1892-1957. *The Prehistory of European Society* (1958). A useful survey by a distinguished archaeologist. *o.p.*

HAY, DENYS b. 1915. *Europe in the Fourteenth and Fifteenth Cen-*

turies (1966). A well-organized survey of the last two centuries of the medieval period. *H & P—Longman.*

PARKES, HENRY B. b. 1904. *Gods and Men* (1959). A good narrative account of the origins of Western culture, with a critical analysis of the important shaping ideas and ideals. *H—Knopf.*

PETERS, EDWARD MURRAY b. 1936. *Europe: The World of the Middle Ages* (1977). An excellent recent survey provided with extensive bibliographies for further reading. *H—P-H.*

PLUMB, JOHN HAROLD b. 1911. *The Italian Renaissance* (1965). A concise survey. *P—Har-Row.*

SCHEVILL, FERDINAND 1868-1954. *The Medici* (1960). Traces with vivid detail the development of the city-state of Florence down to the 16th century. *H—Peter Smith.*

STUARD, SUSAN M. (ed.). *Women in Medieval Society* (1976). An excellent representative collection of essays on the role of women in the Middle Ages. *H & P—U of Pa Pr.*

Modern (1500–1900) Other than American

ALBRECHT-CARRIÉ, RENÉ b. 1904. *A Diplomatic History of Europe Since the Congress of Vienna* (rev. ed. 1973). An excellent one-volume treatment, with useful maps and bibliography. *P—Har-Row.*

ALLEN, HARRY CRANBROOK b. 1917. *Conflict and Concord* (1960). Traces Anglo-American relations from 1783 to 1952 from the British point of view. *o.p.*

ASHLEY, MAURICE PERCY b. 1907. *The Golden Century* (1969). A well-written account of the 17th century, skillfully blending political and cultural forces to interpret the significance of a remarkable age. *o.p.*

BAINTON, RONALD H. b. 1894. *The Age of the Reformation* (1956). A clear, concise summary with excerpts from the primary materials of the period. *H—Peter Smith; P—Van Nos Reinhold.*

The Berkshire Studies in European History. A first-rate series of popularizations by distinguished specialists. These short and clearly written studies include such outstanding works as *The Renaissance* by WALLACE K. FERGUSON and *The Age of Metternich* by ARTHUR J. MAY. *P—HR&W.*

BRINTON, CRANE 1898-1968. *The Anatomy of Revolution* (1950). This provocative book provides a comparative study of the English, American, French, and Russian revolutions. *H—Peter Smith; P—Random.*

CLOUGH, SHEPARD BANCROFT b. 1901. *European Economic History* (2nd ed. 1968). A lucid and well-organized survey of the economic development of Western civilization. *H—McGraw.*

DAVIDOFF, LEONORE. *The Best Circles* (1973). One of the best accounts of the role of women in Victorian society. *H—Rowman.*

ELLIOTT, JOHN HUXTABLE b. 1930. *The Old World and the New, 1492–1650* (1970). A concise and useful introduction to a vast subject. *H & P—Cambridge U Pr.*

GAY, PETER b. 1923. *The Enlightenment* (1966-69). A comprehensive and provocative survey of the critical philosophical movement of the 18th century. *H—Knopf 2 vols.*

GRIMM, HAROLD J. b. 1901. *The Reformation Era, 1500–1650* (rev. ed. 1973). A clear and careful survey of a complex era in modern history. *H—Macmillan.*

HERR, RICHARD b. 1922. *Spain* (1971). A competent survey from the beginnings but with emphasis on the last two centuries. *P—P-H.*

The Norton History of Modern Europe. An excellent series of thorough and well-balanced volumes with extensive bibliographies. Individual titles include *The Foundations of Early Modern Europe, 1460– 1559* by EUGENE F. RICE, Jr.; *The Age of Religious Wars, 1559– 1689* by RICHARD S. DUNN; *Kings and Philosophers, 1689– 1789* by LEONARD KRIEGER; and *The Age of Revolution and Reaction, 1789–1850* by CHARLES BREUNIG. *P—Norton.*

PALMER, ROBERT ROSWELL b. 1909. *Twelve Who Ruled* (1941). A fascinating collective biography of the members of the Committee of Public Safety in France. *P—Atheneum.*

———. *The World of the French Revolution* (1972). An illuminating account clearly showing interrelationships among the various revolutionary movements of the 18th century. *P—Har-Row.*

PARRY, JOHN HORACE b. 1914. *Trade and Dominion* (1972). A well-written and stimulating survey of European overseas empires in the 18th century. *H—Praeger.*

PLUMB, JOHN HAROLD b. 1911. *In the Light of History* (1972). A series of delightful essays, most of which deal with aspects of the 18th century. *H—HM; P—Dell.*

RIASANOVSKY, NICHOLAS V. b. 1923. *A History of Russia* (3rd ed. 1977). An excellent, up-to-date survey, emphasizing the periods since 1500. *H—Oxford U Pr.*

Rise of Modern Europe. Various specialists have written reliable and readable interpretations of various periods with detailed bibliographies for those who wish to read further. Representative titles include *Europe and the French Imperium* by GEOFFREY BRUUN: *The World of Humanism* by MYRON P. GILMORE; *A Generation of Materialism, 1871–1900* by CARLTON J. H. HAYES: and *The Triumph of Science and Reason* by FRANK L. NUSSBAUM. *P—Har-Row.*

SIMPSON, LESLEY BYRD b. 1891. *Many Mexicos* (4th ed. 1966). One of the best one-volume surveys of Mexican history from the beginnings. *H & P—U of Cal Pr.*

TAYLOR, ALAN JOHN PERCIVAL b. 1906. *The Habsburg Monarchy, 1800–1918* (rev. 1976). An excellent treatment of a difficult subject. *P—U of Chicago Pr.*

WEDGWOOD, CICELY VERONICA b. 1910. *The King's Peace* (1969) and *The King's War* (1958). Modern reappraisals of the background of the English Civil War and of the war itself written in a flowing narrative style. *P—Macmillan.*

YOUNG, GEORGE M. 1882-1959. *Victorian England* (2nd ed. 1964). A detailed, accurate, appealing portrait of an age. *P—Oxford U Pr.*

Contemporary (since 1900), Other than American

CHURCHILL, SIR WINSTON 1874-1965. *The Second World War* (1948-53). A six-volume personal narrative of the vital and dramatic war years written in forceful, colorful style. *H—HM; P—Bantam.*

EISENHOWER, DWIGHT D. 1890-1969. *Crusade in Europe* (1948). The commander's report to the public on his assignment: clear, concise, judicious, still interesting. *H—DaCapo.*

FAY, SIDNEY BRADSHAW 1876-1967. *Origins of the World War* (rev. ed. 1938). An expert marshaling of the background of World War I, going back as far as 1871. *P—Free Pr.*

KOGON, EUGEN b. 1903. *Theory and Practice of Hell* (1950). A calm, objective description of the Nazi concentration camp system and of a Christian's six years at Buchenwald. *H—Octagon.*

LASH, JOSEPH P. b. 1909. *Roosevelt and Churchill, 1939–1941* (1976). A readable and solidly documented dramatic account of the close—if sometimes difficult—partnership of Roosevelt and Churchill to preserve the freedom of the Western World. An excellent complement and supplement to Rauch (see below). *H—Norton.*

LIE, TRYGVE 1896-1968. *In the Cause of Peace* (1954). The first secretary-general's account of the first difficult seven years of the United Nations. *o.p.*

RAUCH, BASIL b. 1908. *Roosevelt from Munich to Pearl Harbor* (1950). An analysis of the development of the Roosevelt foreign policy before America's entry into World War II, challenging the views of extremists of both right and left. *H—DaCapo.*

SHIRER, WILLIAM b. 1904. *The Challenge of Scandinavia* (1955). A history of the Scandinavian countries (Denmark, Finland, Norway, Sweden) since 1930, emphasizing the high level of social and economic well-being they have achieved. *o.p.*

————. *The Rise and Fall of the Third Reich* (1960). A monumental and highly absorbing account of the rise and fall of Hitler based on personal observation and on the examination of voluminous documents. *H & P—S&S 2 vols.*

SNYDER, LOUIS L. b. 1907 (ed.). *Fifty Major Documents of the Twentieth Century* (1955). An invaluable collection, including the Austro-Hungarian ultimatum to Serbia in 1914, the Munich agreement of 1939, the legislation enfranchising women in Britain and the United States in 1918-1919, the Nuremberg Laws on race, Churchill's "Blood, Toil, Tears, and Sweat" address, the secret Yalta agreement, and the text of the Truman Doctrine. *P—Van Nos Reinhold.*

VINACKE, HAROLD M. b. 1893. *A History of the Far East in Modern Times* (6th ed. 1959). A standard introductory account. *o.p.*

WOLFE, BERTRAM DAVID 1896-1977. *Three Who Made a Revolution* (4th ed. 1964). A biographical history of the men and the forces that brought on the Russian Revolution, focusing on Lenin, Trotsky, and Stalin. *P—Dell.*

The United States

ADAMS, JAMES TRUSLOW 1878-1949. *The Epic of America* (rev. ed. 1933). Stirring pageant of the American spirit and character, stressing the "American dream" of a better life for the common people and ignoring the seamier sides of American history and life. *o.p.*

ALLEN, FREDERICK L. 1890-1954. *Only Yesterday* (1931). The years following World War I, treating the Teapot Dome scandals and the "flaming youth" period with deftness and charm. *H & P—Har-Row.*

BAILEY, HUGH C. b. 1929. *Liberalism in the New South* (1969). A careful study of the work and influence of Southern social reformers and of the Progressive Movement from 1877 to the end of the Wilson administration. *H—U of Miami Pr.*

BAILEY, THOMAS ANDREW b. 1902. *A Diplomatic History of the American People* (8th ed. 1969). A popular, authoritative survey, perhaps not sufficiently critical for many contemporary tastes. *H—P-H.*

BAILYN, BERNARD. *The Ideological Origins of the American Revolution* (1967). Traces the origins of revolutionary ideology and the evolution of the American concepts of democracy and federalism. *H— Harvard U Pr.*

BEARD, CHARLES A. 1874-1948 and MARY BEARD 1876-1958. *Rise of American Civilization* (1949). An outstanding historical analysis of the factors, mainly economic, behind the emergence of contemporary America. *o.p.*

BOORSTIN, DANIEL J. b. 1914. *The Americans: The Democratic Experience* (1973). An excellent example of the "New History," emphasizing the changes, some revolutionary, that occurred in homes, farms, factories, and cities throughout the expanding nation. *H— Random.*

Chronicles of America. Over 50 small volumes, each by a distinguished scholar, each covering a limited aspect of American history with accuracy and unusual readability. *H—US Pubs.*

COMMAGER, HENRY STEELE b. 1902 (ed.). *America in Perspective* (1947). Accounts of the United States made by foreigners after traveling through the country—often illuminating, frequently disturbing. *o.p.*

CRAVEN, AVERY ODELLE b. 1886. *The Coming of the Civil War* (2nd ed. 1957). Readable, scholarly, objective account, developing the thesis that the democratic process "failed in the critical period that culminated in the Civil War." *H & P—U of Chicago Pr.*

CURTI, MERLE b. 1897. *The Growth of American Thought* (3rd ed. 1964). An excellent survey of American social, intellectual, and scientific thought. *H—Har-Row.*

DONALD, DAVID b. 1920. *Charles Sumner and the Coming of the Civil War* (1960). A careful, dispassionate study of one of America's most complex and controversial leaders in the sectional conflict that culminated in the Civil War. *H—Knopf.*

Federalist Papers. See "The 18th Century," page 45.

FILLER, LOUIS b. 1912. *The Muckrakers* (rev. ed. 1975). A vivid and sound account of the contributions of the muckraking journalists in exposing the evils of the trusts and in searching for an improved democracy during the first decades of this century. *P—Pa St U Pr.*

FLEXNER, ELEANOR b. 1909. *Century of Struggle* (1968). More than an account of the women's rights movement in the United States and the enfranchisement of 26 million people, this scholarly, comprehensive volume traces the economic and social history of women in America through 1920. *H—Harvard U Pr; P—Atheneum, Harvard U Pr.*

FRANKLIN, JOHN HOPE b. 1915. *From Slavery to Freedom: A History of Negro Americans* (4th ed. 1974). A scholarly, comprehensive, readable survey of Black slavery in the Western hemisphere from its origins in Africa to the present. *H & P—Knopf.*

GRANT, ULYSSES S. 1822-1885. *Personal Memoirs of U. S. Grant* (1885-86). The Union general and subsequent president writes a straightforward, informed account of the significant events of his time. *H—AMS Pr, Peter Smith (abr.).*

GRANTHAM, DEWEY W. b. 1921. *The Democratic South* (1963). A solid analysis of the forces that have molded the contemporary South. *H—U of Ga Pr; P—Norton.*

HACKER, LOUIS MORTON b. 1899. *The Triumph of American Capitalism* (1940). American history to 1900, focusing on the economic and political forces that shaped the American version of capitalism. *H—Columbia U Pr.*

HEFFNER, RICHARD D. b. 1925 (ed.). *A Documentary History of the United States* (rev. ed. 1956). Contains 25 basic American documents, each with an introduction and some interpretation. Includes not only such standard items as Washington's Farewell Address and Franklin D. Roosevelt's Four Freedoms speech, but also F. J. Turner's classic account of frontier influences, Hoover's views on rugged individualism, and the Marshall Plan. *o.p.*

HENRY, ROBERT S. 1889-1970. *The Story of the Confederacy* (rev. ed. 1957). A distinguished account; the best book with which to begin one's study of the Civil War. *H—Peter Smith.*

History of American Life Series. Under the general editorship of Arthur M. Schlesinger, Jr., this series contains over a dozen balanced, informed studies of limited periods in the economic, social, and cultural past of the United States. Representative titles include *Revolutionary Generation, 1763–1790* by EVARTS B. GREENE; *Irrepressible Conflict, 1850–1865* by ARTHUR C. COLE; *Emergence of Modern America, 1865–1878* by ALLAN NEVINS; and *Age of the Great Depression, 1929–1941* by DIXON WECTER. *H—Macmillan.*

HOFSTADTER, RICHARD 1916-1970. *Anti-Intellectualism in American Life* (1963). A stimulating but often depressing study of the reaction of Americans to the intellectual currents of their history. This book offers a corrective to some of the rosier accounts of American history. *H—Knopf; P—Random.*

JENSEN, MERRILL b. 1905. *The New Nation* (1950). A careful analysis of the United States during the formative years of the Confederation, 1781 to 1789. *P—Random.*

MILLER, JOHN C. b. 1907. *Crisis in Freedom: The Alien and Sedition Acts* (1964). A carefully documented and dramatic account of the threat the Federalists posed to human liberty in their efforts to perpetuate themselves in power. *P—Little.*

New American Nation Series. Edited by Henry Steele Commager and Richard B. Morris, this series of over 40 volumes attempts to synthesize the new and traditional history in studies covering the background and development of the American Nation from the discovery and exploration to the post-World War II era. The best volumes in the series include *The Coming of the Revolution, 1763–1775* by LAWRENCE HENRY GIPSON; *The Era of Theodore Roosevelt and the Birth of Modern America, 1900–1912* by GEORGE E. MOWRY; and *Woodrow Wilson and the Progressive Era, 1910–1917* by ARTHUR S. LINK. *H & P—Har-Row.*

PANCAKE, JOHN S. b. 1920. *1777: The Year of the Hangman* (1977). A sound, dramatic account of the American Revolution from the march of the redcoats on Lexington and Concord in April 1775 to the surrender of Burgoyne and the attempt to pen up the British in Philadelphia in 1777. *H—U of Ala Pr.*

PERKINS, DEXTER b. 1889. *History of the Monroe Doctrine* (rev. ed. 1963). The definitive account of the policy that has done so much to shape inter-American relations. *H & P—Little.*

PHILLIPS, ULRICH BONNELL 1877-1934. *Life and Labor in the Old South* (1929). An informed analysis of the forces that molded the antebellum South and an interesting account of the relations between races. *H & P—Little.*

The Rivers of America. Edited by Carl Carmer, this series of more than 50 volumes on rivers—from the Allegheny to the Yazoo—gives the history and folklore of the total area through which the title river flows. The best of these constitute superb history writing. *H—HR&W.*

WEBB, WALTER PRESCOTT 1888-1963. *The Great Plains* (1957). An original scholarly interpretation of the Great Plains by a distinguished authority, showing the importance of the horse, the six-shooter, the wire fence, and the windmill in the successful settlement of a huge land area. *P—G&D.*

WILLIAMS, T. HARRY b. 1909. *Lincoln and the Radicals* (1941). A dramatic and authoritative account of the efforts of radicals to dominate the Lincoln administration. *P—U of Wis Pr.*

WOOD, GORDON S. *The Creation of the American Republic, 1776–1787* (1969). Argues the thesis that Americans of the Revolutionary generation developed new concepts of politics that took it out of the classical and medieval traditions, and advanced the concept that sovereignty resides in the people and in the need for a system of checks and balances that would keep it there. *H—U of NC Pr.*

21. Politics

James T. Crown

Politics may be simply defined as the study of the theory and practice of government and statecraft. Political scientists attempt to systematize and refine political observations and perceptions.

Contributions to the understanding of politics are made by many writers other than scholars. Politics provided the stuff of tragedy and comedy for Sophocles and Aristophanes as well as for Shakespeare and Shaw because it displays the highest aspirations and the deepest depravity, presents a being aspiring to perfectibility but at times kin to a devil. New developments in politics have inspired thrillers whose final chapters have yet to be written—in part by readers, who must help determine whether in the world of tomorrow humankind can survive or will even want to. Many thoughtful people read these books even though they seem like absurd exaggerations. Why? Why do people gather together in more and more homes, cafés, libraries, bookshops, and classrooms, not to plot the overthrow of governments but to find out more about them? The probable answer is that in this supposed age of alienation and disenchantment with government, people are not withdrawing from thought but rather are questioning most of the age-old assumptions about government.

Many readers today seek better answers to old questions which once intrigued mainly philosophers—thinkers such as Plato, Aristotle, Machiavelli, and Marx. They want to probe the fundamental political problems: Why do we have states? Who should rule and to what ends? How can power be obtained and maintained? What is the proper line separating state control and individual freedom? Can and should the government be an instrument for social change? How far should the state carry out the wishes of the people? The study of political theory ponders these questions, among others. Readers interested in these questions may wish to examine works indicated in the first section of the book list.

Readers turning to the next section, The Legal Order, may wish to explore the constitutional framework of the state, to probe the more practical aspects of justice and injustice as it operates in the courts and on the streets, to free their minds from glib generalizations about "equality before the law" or the "neutrality of courts," which common experience tells them are not literally true. Some may wish to read to determine whether the law might meet their career wishes.

How government really works and how we get it to work the way we want it to is the province of the Practical Politics section. Among the questions dealt with in works in this section is who gets what, when, how, and why? Most of the authors believe they are describing and analyzing the actual, helping the reader dispel oversimplified theories or unreal aspirations.

The section International Relations examines both theoretically and practically the relations of sovereign states with one another, analyzing not only the alarming degree to which anarchy and the rule that "might makes right" often prevail in these relations, but also studying certain restraints on loose political association that might provide hope for a livable future. Essential to an understanding of international relations, the study of comparative government provides insights into why various societies have evolved and how they have developed distinctively different patterns of government and with what consequences. This study helps save us from a national fault of parochialism.

Theory

ARISTOTLE. *Nicomachaen Ethics* and *Politics*. See "Greece," page 6.

BOUC, ALAIN. *Mao Tse-tung: A Guide to His Thought* (1977). Khrushchev said that the statements of Mao were shocking, sometimes because of their simplicity, sometimes because of their complexity. A perceptive French journalist helps to sort out the probable meanings. Bouc argues that Mao's concept of "serve the people" is a useful substitute for passive individualism in organizing society. *H—St Martin.*

BOWIE, NORMAN E. b. 1942 and ROBERT L. SIMON. *The Individual and the Political Order* (1977). A sophisticated introduction to social and political philosophy, analyzing classic and modern concepts of liberty, justice, and individual rights. *P—P-H.*

CARSTEN, F. L. b. 1911. *The Rise of Fascism* (1967). Traces the rise mainly of European fascism. *H & P—U of Cal Pr.*

DOLBEARE, KENNETH M. b. 1930 and PATRICIA DOLBEARE. *American Ideologies* (3rd ed. 1976). Engagingly attempts to categorize and explain rational and less rational competing political beliefs likely to remain at issue in coming decades. *P—Rand.*

HOBBES. *Leviathan*. See "Philosophy," page 182.

KIRK, RUSSELL b. 1918. *The Conservative Mind* (1953). A distinguished

American conservative explains why he respects the past and authority and why he is cautious about rapid government reforms. *o.p.*

MACHIAVELLI. *The Prince*. See "The Renaissance and Reformation," page 27.

MARX. *Economic and Philosophical Manuscripts*. See "Philosophy," page 183.

MENDEL, ARTHUR P. b. 1927 (ed.). *Essential Works of Marxism* (1961). Contains some of the most fundamental Marxist writings, including the *Communist Manifesto*, Lenin's *State and Revolution*, and Stalin's *Foundations of Leninism*. The editor provides useful critiques of the documents and of Soviet practice. *P—Bantam*.

ORWELL. *1984*. See "20th-Century British Novels," page 106.

PLATO. *The Republic*. See "Greece," page 7.

SIBLEY, MULFORD Q. b. 1912 (ed.). *Quiet Battle* (1969). A contributor to the theory of nonviolent resistance collects and comments on both classic and modern arguments and analyzes the relation of these theories to the "rule of law." *P—Beacon Pr.*

STUPAK, RONALD J. b. 1934 et al. *Understanding Political Science* (1977). A clear and absorbing introduction to how scholars of political theory, methodology, international relations, comparative government, and American politics go about their work and how they evaluate it. *P—Alfred Pub.*

WOODCOCK, GEORGE b. 1912. *Anarchism: A History of Libertarian Ideas and Movements* (1962). An often fascinating presentation of the main intellectual and sentimental arguments, and sometimes of the lives and fortunes, of advocates of anarchism, which denies the legitimacy of any government. The study of anarchism makes a good beginning for the consideration of the basic question in politics: why do we have government? *H—Peter Smith; P—NAL.*

The Legal Order

ABRAHAM, HENRY J. b. 1921. *Judicial Process* (3rd rev. ed. 1975). The best introduction to what courts are all about and to what is and what isn't important. A convincing corrective for many parochial attitudes toward law, and a good book to read before becoming immersed in cases. *H & P—Oxford U Pr.*

COFFEY, ALAN b. 1931 et al. *Human Relations: Law Enforcement in a Changing Community* (2nd ed. 1975). The basics of law enforcement at the local level, stressing the problems involved and the means for improving justice, especially for minorities. Solution-oriented, interesting, and readable. *H—P-H.*

CORWIN, EDWARD S. 1878-1963. *The Constitution and What It Means Today* (rev. ed. 1974). Harold W. Chase and Craig R. Ducat skillfully update this classic analysis of what the Constitution means in terms of court and other actions that have given it life and sometimes changed it drastically. *H & P—Princeton U Pr.*

LEWIS, ANTHONY b. 1927. *Gideon's Trumpet* (1964). A "three cheers for democracy" introduction to civil liberties that accurately and fascinatingly shows how an individual from the lowest socio-economic status finds justice through the amazingly complex, fault-ridden United States judicial system. Reads like a novel. *H & P—Random.*

McLAUCHLAN, WILLIAM P. b. 1942. *American Legal Processes* (1977). Stressing civil litigation, the author describes the practical role of the court and what really happens in courtrooms and judges' chambers. Should help the general reader decide whether to use the court system to resolve a conflict and the undergraduate student whether to study law. *H—Wiley.*

SHAPIRO, MARTIN M. b. 1933 and DOUGLAS HOBBES b. 1933. *The Politics of Constitutional Law* (1973). Covers basic cases but also examines noncourtroom institutions and forces—e.g., the opinions of the elite or of special interests—that determine what the law actually means in practice. Shows how implementation is often quite different from legislative or judicial intent. *H—Winthrop.*

THOMAS, WILLIAM R. *The Burger Court and Civil Liberties* (1976). Even the influence of a resigned president can linger on in the courts. The author scrutinizes the important role of Richard Nixon appointees to the Supreme Court, showing both continuities and contrasts between the Burger Court and the previous Warren Court. *P—Kings Court.*

Practical Politics and Government in General

BARKER, LUCIUS b. 1928 and JESSE McCORRY. *Black Americans and the Political System* (1976). Examines most of the basic aspects of government covered in a standard textbook but with the purpose of showing how attitudes, institutions, and processes keep Blacks and other minority groups from full protection of the law. *H & P—Winthrop.*

BARNETT, MARGUERITE ROSS and JAMES A. HEFNER. *Public Policy for the Black Community* (1976). A solution-oriented study to be read in conjunction with the title described above. *H & P—Alfred Pub.*

DODD, LAWRENCE C. and BRUCE I. OPPENHEIMER (eds.). *Congress Reconsidered* (1977). Various experts provide knowledgeable, judicious, and readable assessments of the meaning of changes and continuity in the legislative branch of American government. *H & P—Praeger.*

DOLBEARE, KENNETH M. b. 1930 and MURRAY J. EDELMAN b. 1919. *American Politics: Policies, Power, and Change* (2nd ed. 1974). A basic text, recommended as good reading because it skillfully ties together various elements of government and politics and inspires readers to think critically and independently. *P—Heath.*

DYE, THOMAS R. b. 1935. *Who's Running America?* (1976). Discusses power structures in much the way professionals on Wall Street do, but with a different purpose: to alert the reader as to how "elite-led" American democracy actually works. *H & P—P-H.*

HAWLEY, WILLIS D. and FREDERIC WIRT b. 1924 (eds.). *The Search for Community Power* (2nd ed. 1974). A first book to read on the problems and pleasures of locating and exploring networks of community power in urban politics. *P—P-H.*

IPPOLITO, DENNIS b. 1942 et al. *Public Opinion and Responsible Democracy* (1976). Gives meaning to the often vapid study of public opinion by showing as clearly as possible how it relates to governing and governability in America. The linkage between elite and mass opinion is clarified. *H—P-H.*

KOENIG, LOUIS b. 1916. *The Chief Executive* (3rd rev. ed. 1975). A well-informed, comprehensive, and interesting examination of the legal, political, and administrative aspects of the presidency, correcting many popular misconceptions. *P—HarBraceJ.*

KYLE, PATRICIA. *Integrating the Neglected Majority* (1976). Examines with zest and imagination the real and potential power of American women, demonstrating both the remarkable capacity of society and government to resist change and some surprising changes the women's movement has achieved. *H—Kings Court.*

O'CONNOR, JAMES. *The Fiscal Crisis of the State* (1973). A trenchant leftist critique of current American government attempting to show why things are not working the way they are supposed to, and why many expected governmental results are impossible to achieve. *H & P—St Martin.*

OWENS, HENRY and CHARLES SCHULTZE b. 1924 (eds.). *Setting Priorities: The Next Ten Years* (1976). Experts (a number of whom have joined the Carter administration) associated with the prestigious Brookings Institute discuss what is most likely to happen in government domestic and international programs in the near future and what might be the alternatives and their costs. *P—Brookings.*

PARKINSON, C. NORTHCOTE b. 1909. *Parkinson's Law and Other Studies in Administration* (1957). A scholar whose law has become a part of our culture explains how all forms of social organization tend to strangle themselves in organizational hypertrophy. Written tongue-in-cheek, this book is a reminder that politics without humor can become monstrous. *P—Ballantine.*

POMPER, GERALD b. 1935 (ed.). *Elections 1976* (1977). Probes the mood of the 1976 elections and suggests what to watch for in terms of possible political realignments during the Carter years. *P—P-H.*

SAFFELL, DAVID C. b. 1941. *Watergate: Its Effects on the American Political System* (1974). Americans ask, "Did Watergate change anything?" The author offers a more focused and judicious answer than those found in the news media. *P—Winthrop.*

International Relations and Comparative Government

BARGHOORN, FREDERICK C. b. 1911. *Detente and the Democratic Movement in the U.S.S.R.* (1976). An author long bitterly critical of the Soviet system and detente presents a survey and analysis that will interest those who believe in the desirability and feasibility of involvement by the American government and people in the internal aspects of Soviety society. Barghoorn is especially interested in the foreign policy recommendations of Soviet dissidents Sakarov, Medvedev, Amalrik, and Solzhenitsyn. *H—Free Press.*

BARNET, RICHARD J. and RONALD E. MÜLLER. *Global Reach* (1975). Successfully and vigorously explains the impact of giant multinational corporations on the third world. Despite some populist excesses, one of the two or three most important books of the 1970s for those who want to know what is really happening in world politics. *H—S&S.*

COHEN, LENARD J. and JANE P. SHAPIRO b. 1938 (eds.). *Communist Systems in Comparative Perspective* (1974). Mainly a comparison of Soviet and East European states in terms of ideology and instruments of government control. Does not fully anticipate the rise of Western Eurocommunism and its reverberations in Eastern Europe. *P—Doubleday.*

FALK, RICHARD b. 1930. *This Endangered Planet* (1972). The most cogent and clearly written argument that global conditions—such as resort to massive violence, population increase, exhaustion of resources, and other environmental concerns—make global politics and government necessary now. *P—Random.*

HALBERSTAM, DAVID b. 1934. *The Best and the Brightest* (1972). How did Vietnam happen? How can a repetition be avoided? This book provides a good starting place in the search for answers. *H—Random; P—Fawcett World.*

HUNTFORD, ROLAND b. 1927. *The New Totalitarians* (1972). Argues that Sweden, which many seek to follow as the model social democracy, is actually a realization of Huxley's *Brave New World. H—Stein & Day.*

IRISH, MARIAN D. b. 1909 and ELKE FRANK b. 1934. *United States Foreign Policy* (1975). A model of clarity, comprehensiveness, and fairness. Equally enlightening for general readers and for those preparing for foreign service exams. *P—HarBraceJ.*

KEOHANE, ROBERT O. b. 1941 and JOSEPH S. NYE b. 1937 (eds.). *Transnational Relations and World Politics* (1972). A seminal series of articles demonstrating that nongovernmental factors such as multinational corporations, labor unions, large foundations, and professional associations are already creating a global politics much less state-oriented than had been thought. Not for beginners. *H & P— Harvard U Pr.*

KIM, C. I. EUGENE b. 1930 and LAWRENCE ZIRING b. 1928. *An Introduction to Asian Politics* (1977). A thorough examination of political institutions, forces, and trends in the area where a majority of the people on earth live. *H—P-H.*

LEVI, WERNER b. 1912. *Law and Politics in the International Society* (1976). The author carefully weighs instances drawn from contemporary affairs where power politics overrides the restraints imposed by international legal norms. *P—Sage.*

MERKL, PETER H. b. 1932. *Comparative Politics* (1967). Emphasizing political culture, socialization, groups, parties, and institutional structures, this advanced text explains how both developed and developing countries can be usefully studied in a comparative manner. *o.p.*

MORGAN, PATRICK M. b. 1940. *Deterrence* (1977). It is widely held that peace between the superpowers is maintained today principally by weapons systems that provide "mutual assured destruction" (M.A.D.). The author weighs the implications of the somewhat amorphous and often misperceived rules of deterrence. *H—Sage.*

MORGENTHAU, HANS J. b. 1904. *Politics among Nations* (5th ed. 1974). Although technology seems to have rendered the jungle view of world affairs obsolete, this impressive work has helped train so many decision-makers that, like Machiavelli's *The Prince*, it must be considered important reading. *H—Knopf.*

PUTNAM, ROBERT D. b. 1941. *Comparative Study of Political Elites* (1976). Putnam shows why and how elites run governments and assesses the consequences. *P—P-H.*

SCHELL, ORVILLE b. 1940. *In the People's Republic* (1977). An unusually perceptive and wise Chinese-speaking American gives readers a remarkable firsthand view of what life is like in selected Chinese communes and factories. *H—Random.*

SCHMITT, DAVID E. b. 1940. *The Dynamics of the Third World* (1974). Examines political and social forces at play in Chile, Mexico, Syria, Nigeria, China, and India, pointing out many contrasts and some similarities in development. *H & P—Winthrop.*

SPIEGEL, STEVEN L. b. 1941 (ed.). *At Issue: Politics in the World Arena* (1973). Useful articles thoughtfully and perceptively treating such issues as the Middle East conflict, southern Africa, the energy crisis and OPEC, terrorism, and arms-control diplomacy. *P—St Martin.*

22. Economics

Jack Minkoff

Economists are continuously compelled by events to consider anew the processes by which human beings live. Depression, war, revolution, and rapid technological change have made the 20th century a living laboratory for economic inquiry. During the quarter century after World War II, economists were supremely confident of the power of their theories to guide nations, both advanced and underdeveloped, on the path of perpetual growth and eventual affluence. The events of the 1970s, however, shattered the congratulatory mien of the profession. Advanced, capitalist nations have suffered both unemployment and inflation. Most underdeveloped nations remain mired in poverty. And now we seem to confront a world of shrinking natural resources, our lofty expectations transformed into a cruel illusion.

The disparity between the assumptions of conventional economic theory and the real world has created a state of intellectual disarray. A growing number of economists argue that power and politics can no longer be disregarded in economic analysis, proposing that the scope of economics revert to its earlier history when it was called political economy.

Although the founding fathers of economics wrote their treatises in the 18th and early 19th centuries, we are struck by the number of uncertainties about seemingly simple economic matters that survive in our age. For example, we still ask: What motivates people to work? Is egalitarianism feasible? Is technology neutral? What determines the distribution of income within and between societies? Is there a limit to economic growth?

How such basic economic questions are answered may well determine the organization and thrust of societies far into the future. As the Soviet-Chinese ideological debate makes apparent, it is these decisions rather than the formal proclamation of a socialist or capitalist system that fixes the character of a nation's economic order.

A good place for the reader to begin sorting out the socio-economic problems now facing the widely heterogeneous community of nations might be the following trio of recent works: John K. Galbraith's *Economics and the Public Purpose*, an analysis of the character of advanced capitalism; Gunnar Myrdal's *The Challenge of World Poverty*, a diagnosis of the socio-economic pathology of the impoverished nations; and Mesarovic and Pestel's *Mankind at the Turning Point*, an examination of the limits to growth facing all humanity.

Of course there are other ways into the subject of economics. A thorough modern textbook such as Samuelson's *Economics* may be a useful point of departure. Or the classics in economic history might provide initial motivation to read further. Certainly, the ideas of the great economists, in their own words or as paraphrased in histories of thought and doctrine, may be studied with benefit and relevance.

BALOGH, THOMAS b. 1905. *The Economics of Poverty* (2nd rev. ed. 1974). Analyzes the present structure of international trade—which, according to Balogh, maintains the disparities between rich and poor states—and argues forcefully for a new world-trading system. *H—Intl Arts & Sci.*

BARAN, PAUL A. 1910-1964 and PAUL M. SWEEZY b. 1910. *Monopoly Capital* (1966). A socialist analysis of modern American economy and society, exposing the not-so-admirable characteristics of advanced capitalism. *P—Monthly Rev.*

BARNET and MÜLLER. *Global Reach.* See "Politics," page 206.

BERLE, ADOLPH A. 1895-1971 and GARDINER C. MEANS b. 1896. *The Modern Corporation and Private Property* (rev. ed. 1968). A thorough study of the ownership and control of huge corporations; a modern classic of economics. *H & P—HarBraceJ.*

BETTELHEIM, CHARLES b. 1913. *Cultural Revolution and Industrial Organization in China* (1974). A sympathetic account of the Chinese attempt to democratize the administration of work by a French Marxist who has found the Soviet system lacking. *P—Monthly Rev.*

BOK, DEREK C. b. 1930 and JOHN T. DUNLOP b. 1914. *Labor and the American Community* (1970). An unadorned, comprehensive survey of the workings of U.S. labor unions and their considerable impact on society. *H & P—S&S.*

BURNS, ARTHUR F. b. 1904 and WESLEY CLAIR MITCHELL 1874-1948. *Measuring Business Cycles* (1946). Mitchell is important for first applying quantitative methods in the social sciences. *H—Columbia U Pr.*

CARR, DONALD E. b. 1903. *Energy and the Earth Machine* (1976). This lively, opinionated, but deeply informed book evaluates our endowment of energy resources, exposes the misguided policies that have brought about the current predicament, and points to a way out. *H—Norton.*

CARR, EDWARD H. b. 1892. *The New Society* (1957). A thoughtful and readable series of essays on the problems created by the trend of modern society away from individualism and competition toward welfare and mass freedom. *P—Beacon Pr.*

CLOUGH. *European Economic History*. See "History," page 196.

COX, OLIVER C. 1901-1974. *Race Relations: Elements and Social Dynamics* (1976). This provocative book by a Black scholar analyzes the socio-economic disabilities suffered by Black Americans from the perspective that their condition is a consequence of the nature of a white-dominated society. *H—Wayne St U Pr.*

DE SCHWEINITZ, KARL, Jr. b. 1920. *Industrialization and Democracy* (1964). Concludes that the industrialization process, under capitalist or socialist auspices, requires harsh discipline and social compulsion, neither of which is congenial to democracy. *H—Free Pr.*

Economic Report of the President (annual, issued each January). An invaluable annual compendium of current information on the functioning of our economy as well as a statement of the economic philosophy of the administration in power. Not bedside reading but required for any informed citizen. *H & P—US Govt Ptg Off.*

ENGLER, ROBERT b. 1922. *The Brotherhood of Oil: Energy Policy and the Public Interest* (1977). Not merely a study of the oil crisis but a stimulating analysis of concentration in the energy industry and its harmful effects on the American and world economy. *H—U of Chicago Pr.*

ESTALL, R. C. and R. OGILVIE BUCHANAN b. 1894. *Industrial Activity and Economic Geography* (3rd ed. 1973). A clear introduction to some of the concepts and process relationships involved in the geography of industry. *H & P—Humanities.*

FRANKLIN, RAYMOND S. b. 1930. *American Capitalism: Two Visions* (1977). A readily accessible exposition of the neo-Marxian framework of analysis combined with a critique of the American economy and conventional economic theory. *P—Random.*

FRIEDMAN, MILTON b. 1912. *Capitalism and Freedom* (1963). The foremost spokesman of the conservative "Chicago school" of economics, and a Nobel laureate, argues that freedom relies on capitalism because this system, when functioning satisfactorily, promotes competition and disperses power. *H & P—U of Chicago Pr.*

_____ and WALTER W. HELLER b. 1915. *Monetary vs. Fiscal Policy* (1969). An elegant and witty debate between high priests of the contending schools on a fundamental controversy dividing the profession. *H & P—Norton.*

GALBRAITH, JOHN KENNETH b. 1908. *The Affluent Society* (3rd rev. ed. 1976). A modern classic that endures as a stimulating corrective to conventional thinking about the operation and goals of our economy. *H—HM; P—HM, NAL.*

_____. *Economics and the Public Purpose* (1973). With serious intent and humor the author dissects the interrelationship between the ills of American society and the power held by the corporate elite, presenting his prescription for restoring social health. *H—HM; P—HM, NAL.*

HANSEN, ALVIN 1887-1975. *A Guide to Keynes* (1953). A clear, helpful guide to Keynes's *General Theory* (see below). *P—McGraw.*

HAYEK, FRIEDRICH A. b. 1899. *Road to Serfdom* (1944). A luminary of the profession forcefully argues that government intervention in economic activity inevitably leads to tyranny. *H & P—U of Chicago Pr.*

HAZLITT, HENRY b. 1894. *The Failure of the "New Economics"* (1959). A systematic, vigorous, sometimes convincing attack on Keynes's *General Theory* (see below). *H—Arlington Hse.*

HEILBRONER, ROBERT L. b. 1919. *The Worldly Philosophers* (rev. ed. 1972). Lively, highly readable accounts of the great economic thinkers and their doctrines. *H & P—S&S.*

_____. *The Making of Economic Society* (3rd ed. 1975). An absorbing narration of economic history, skillfully weaving together economic theory, technological innovation, and social evolution. *H & P—P-H.*

_____. *The Limits of American Capitalism* (1966). The author attributes American political conservatism to a big-business orientation and anticipates the near-future day when technology and science will demand that scientists replace capitalists as the ruling elite of a planned political economy. *H & P—Har-Row.*

KEYNES, JOHN MAYNARD 1883-1946. *Essays in Biography* (1933). Engaging biographical studies of the Cambridge economists— Malthus, Marshall, Edgeworth—as well as of political figures of the 1920s. *P—Norton.*

_____. *The General Theory of Employment, Interest, and Money* (1936). The most influential economic tract published in the 20th century. Although sparkling in spots, it is written primarily for economists; the general reader may prefer to approach its logic through Hansen's popular interpretation (see above). *H & P—HarBraceJ.*

KREPS, JUANITA b. 1921. *Sex in the Marketplace: American Women at Work* (1971). A brief, meaty book by a distinguished economist and cabinet officer. It sets forth essential data on the economic status of women who work outside the home and reviews proposals intended to reduce sexual inequality. *H & P—Johns Hopkins.*

LODGE, GEORGE C. b. 1927. *The New American Ideology* (1975). A professor at the citadel of free enterprise, the Harvard Business School, concludes that the ideology of *laissez-faire* is outmoded and that circumstances require a new ideology focused on community interdependence and state responsibility. *H—Knopf.*

MALTHUS. *Essay on the Principles of Population.* See "The 18th Century," page 46.

MARSHALL, ALFRED 1842-1924. *Principles of Economics* (1890). A restatement of the whole structure of economic thought in the grand tradition with a view toward economic progress. *H—Folcroft.*

MARX, KARL 1818-1883. *Capital* (1867). More than one hundred years after its publication, this seminal book is still the most incisive critique of capitalism. *H & P—Intl Pub Co 3 vols.*

MELMAN, SEYMOUR b. 1917. *Pentagon Capitalism* (1970). Despite its weaknesses in style and organization, an important statement of the thesis that our economy is dominated by the military-industrial complex and suffers substantially therefrom. *P—McGraw.*

MESAROVIC, MIHAJLO b. 1928 and EDUARD PESTEL b. 1914. *Mankind at the Turning Point* (1974). A restrained but gripping analysis of the environmental, resource, and population constraints pressing in on humankind; considers both the socio-political factors and the quantitative elements that threaten humanity with catastrophe. *H—Dutton; P—Dutton, NAL.*

MILLER, HERMAN P. b. 1921. *Rich Man, Poor Man* (1971). The U.S. Census statistics of income distribution and income inequality since World War II are brought vividly and understandably to life. *H—T Y Crowell; P—Apollo Eds.*

MOUSSA, PIERRE b. 1922. *The Underprivileged Nations* (1963). A thoughtful primer on economic growth and underdeveloped countries; lacks the holistic design of Myrdal (see below). *H—Peter Smith.*

MYRDAL, GUNNAR b. 1898. *The Challenge of World Poverty* (1970). Examining the interplay of economic, sociological, and political factors, an eminent social scientist offers the clearest insight into the plight of the world's poor countries. A work of passionate indignation occasionally marred by a pontifical tone. *H—Pantheon; P—Random.*

NETZER, DICK b. 1928. *Economics and Urban Problems: Diagnoses and Prescriptions* (2nd ed. 1974). The continuing disintegration of city life in the United States makes this concise and clearly written introduction to urban problems timely and necessary. *H—Basic.*

NOVE, ALEC b. 1915. *The Soviet Economy* (2nd rev. ed. 1969). A good introduction to the structure, problems, and concepts of the Soviet economic system, written for the lay reader. *H & P—Praeger.*

OKUN, ARTHUR M. b. 1928. *Equality and Efficiency: The Big Trade-off* (1975). An articulate exposition, by a prominent Keynesian theorist and counselor, of the current economic reasoning that advocates the sacrifice of equity to growth. *H & P—Brookings.*

PASSELL, PETER b. 1944 and LEONARD ROSS. *The Retreat from Riches: Affluence and Its Enemies* (1972). A spirited attack on the zero growth school of thought. These optimists see the market system blessing us with continuous growth and spreading affluence. *P—Viking Pr.*

PECHMAN, JOSEPH A. b. 1918 and BENJAMIN A. OKNER b. 1936. *Who Bears the Tax Burden?* (1974). A concise examination of the tax system of the United States, suggesting that, as common opinion has suspected, rich and poor alike pay about the same proportion of their income in taxes. *H & P—Brookings.*

ROBINSON, JOAN b. 1903. *Economic Heresies* (1971). An attack on the current Keynesian orthodoxy by a renowned Cambridge economist who argues that the philosophical underpinnings and the doctrinal assumptions of economics often reveal an ideological bias hard to reconcile with scientific objectivity. *H & P—Basic.*

ROLFE, SIDNEY E. b. 1921 and JAMES L. BURTLE b. 1919. *The Great Wheel: The World Monetary System* (1973). Removes the veil of mystery from international money matters. Explains how the system functions, the reasons for its collapse in 1971, and the instability inherent in subsequent arrangements. *H—Quadrangle; P—McGraw.*

SAMUELSON, PAUL A. b. 1915. *Economics: An Introductory Analy-*

sis (10th ed. 1976). The leading elementary text ever since its first edition in 1948. *H—McGraw.*

SCHUMACHER, E. F. 1911-1977. *Small Is Beautiful: Economics as if People Mattered* (new ed. 1975). Drawing upon Asian and Western thought, the author contends that modern large-scale technology is destructive of the human spirit and civilization and calls for the creation of an economy on a more human scale. *H & P—Har-Row.*

SCHUMPETER, JOSEPH A. 1883-1950. *Capitalism, Socialism, and Democracy* (3rd ed. 1950). An economist-philosopher examines two competing economies, forecasting the supplanting of capitalism by socialism though preferring the former. *P—Har-Row.*

SHONFIELD, ANDREW b. 1917. *Modern Capitalism: The Changing Balance of Public and Private Power* (1965). A review of the economic methods and institutions of modern capitalism, which the author finds characterized by social welfare, public management, steadily rising income, and intellectual incoherence. *P—Oxford U Pr.*

SILK, LEONARD b. 1918. *The Economists* (1976). A fascinating survey for the layreader of the ideas of five of the most prominent economists active today—Boulding, Friedman, Galbraith, Leontief, and Samuelson—that lays bare the discipline's current anarchy. *H—Basic.*

SMITH. *The Wealth of Nations.* See "18th Century," page 46.

SOULE, GEORGE HENRY 1887-1970. *Ideas of the Great Economists* (1952). Concise, deft treatment of the panorama of economic thought from the Greeks to Keynes. *P—NAL.*

SOWELL, THOMAS b. 1930. *Race and Economics* (1975). A radically different perspective from that of Cox (see above). This gracefully written historical analysis of the comparative status of ethnic groups in the United States, authored by a Black economist, concludes that a change in personal attitudes is the key to the economic improvement of minorities. *H & P—McKay.*

TAYLOR, OVERTON H. b. 1897. *Economics and Liberalism* (1955). Philosophical, thought-provoking essays on the foundations and limitations of classical liberalism. *H—Harvard U Pr.*

TOBIN, JAMES b. 1918. *The New Economics: One Decade Older* (1974). A leading exponent of the "New Economics" reviews modern Keynesian principles and the record of economic policy implementation since the 1960s and judges the craft essentially sound. *H—Princeton U Pr.*

TUSSING, A. DALE b. 1935. *Poverty and a Dual Economy* (1975). A provocative analysis of the extent of poverty, the causes of poverty, the programs intended to cope with poverty, and the reasons why they have failed. *H & P—St Martin.*

VEBLEN, THORSTEIN 1859-1929. *The Theory of the Leisure Class* (1899). Barbed, pungent, classic study of the "conspicuous consumption" of the rich and near rich. *H—HM; P—Funk & W, NAL.*

_____. *The Portable Veblen* (1948). Edited by Max Lerner, this volume contains the first half of *Theory* and generous selections from Veblen's other writings. *H & P—Viking Pr.*

23. Anthropology

Elizabeth Weatherford

Anthropology is the comparative study of human beings and their societies. Although we are one biologically unique species, we exhibit a dramatic diversity of physical and behavioral characteristics. Among human beings, unlike other animal species, physical variations in the environment play a relatively minor part in their most important adaptation—to the mores of their culture. The study of humankind, therefore, demands a whole interrelated collection of specialized sciences, some historical, some documentary, some biological, and some sociological.

Anthropology embraces four specializations: archaeology, which tries to reconstruct the history of ancient societies by examining their material remains; linguistics, which studies the growth and structure of one of humanity's most distinct behavior devices, language; physical anthropology, which examines human biological diversity and physical evolution and, through comparative studies with other primates (e.g., chimpanzees), relates the human potential for forming a culture to these physiological data; and, finally, cultural anthropology, which focuses on the organization of all human societies and on the beliefs and practices of those who comprise them.

Cultural anthropology is of the most interest and value to the general reader because through the study of unfamiliar cultures one often comes to a better understanding of one's own. It has been discovered that what may seem unusual practices or beliefs are really only logical alternative ways in which different peoples have tried to answer universal questions and solve real problems: how to relate to unseen forces, to insure good harvests, to cure illness, to establish relationships with neighboring peoples, and the like. Anthropological studies of many different societies have contributed countless examples for analysis and comparison, enabling the development of theories about how and why a society takes its form. One influential theory contends that such apparently diverse practices within a culture as the language, the mythology, the structure of the family, and the pattern of government are, in fact, profoundly interrelated.

Typically, an anthropologist's research is conducted through participation in and observation of one culture's activities, ideas, and social relations over a one- or two-year period. The anthropologist often returns to that society to continue analyzing and recording life patterns. From this fieldwork the observer-participant writes an ethnography of that society. Most early studies by anthropologists were of very small societies, often unknown to nonspecialists; many of these groups lacked writing and had very simple technologies. During recent decades, however, anthropologists have turned to larger and more complex societies, partly because of their interest in how small, self-contained societies are being affected by contact with technology and the industrialized world. The fate of tribal peoples whose domains have come under the jurisdiction of state governments, the changes wrought by the movement of peasant farmers to cities, and the possibilities for healing people by utilizing the best of both traditional folk knowledge and modern medicine are a few of the topics currently being studied. Some anthropologists are critically examining long-held assumptions of the discipline as a result of the observed effects of modernization on both the ecological and social relationships of the peoples studied.

Because of its interest in a total society, anthropology enables those who study it to perceive human history from many perspectives. On the one hand, it observes and is critical of the assimilation processes that are altering drastically the rural peoples of the world. On the other, by its recognition of the reasonableness of the immense variety of human responses to a social demand, it allows us to weigh parochial concepts and to participate in human experiences that transcend time and place.

BERREMAN, GERALD b. 1930 et al. *Anthropology Today* (1971). Comprehensive and beautifully illustrated survey of the ideas and practice of anthropology. *H—CRM Bks.*

BOAS. *Primitive Art.* See "Fine Arts and Design," page 170.

BRACE, C. F. b. 1930 and ASHLEY MONTAGU b. 1905. *Man's Evolution* (1965). Clear presentation of the human fossil record and human evolution in the light of contemporary theory. *H—Macmillan.*

DEETZ, JAMES b. 1930. *Invitation to Archeology* (1967). Brief introduction to the principles, methods, and problems of the present-day archaeologist. *H & P—Natural Hist.*

DIAMOND, STANLEY b. 1922. *In Search of the Primitive* (1974). Brilliant essays critical of the discipline of anthropology and the civilization that produced it, stressing the complexity of the contact between modern investigators and the traditional peoples being studied. *H & P— Transaction Bks.*

DORSON, RICHARD M. b. 1916. *Folklore and Folklife* (1972). Essays that introduce the reader to the broad outlines of folklore studies. *H—U of Chicago Pr.*

EAMES, EDWIN b. 1930 and JUDITH GRANICH GOODE. *Anthropology of Cities* (1977). Introduces urban anthropology by examining ideas, current research, and what anthropology may add to the study of cities. *P—P-H.*

EIMERL, SAREL and IRVEN DEVORE b. 1934. *The Primates* (1965). Well-illustrated survey of the order of beings to which monkeys, apes, and humans belong. *H—Silver.*

EVANS-PRITCHARD, EDWARD E. b. 1902. *Witchcraft, Oracles, and Magic among the Azande* (1937). An absorbing study dealing with one aspect of Zande thought when the Zande, a Central African people, were under Anglo-Egyptian rule in the 1930s. *H & P—Oxford U Pr.*

FORDE, C. DARYLL b. 1902. *Habitat, Economy, and Society* (1963). Considers the broad features of 16 non-European societies in terms of their economic pattern, relationship to the physical environment, and social organization—that of food gatherers, cultivators, or pastoral nomads. *o.p.*

FRIEDLANDER, JUDITH b. 1944. *Being Indian in Hueyapan* (1975). Sensitively written account of an Indian village in central Mexico and a commentary on the discrepancy between the actual life of the villagers and the national ideology about that life. *H & P—St Martin.*

GARN, STANLEY M. b. 1922. *Human Races* (3rd ed. 1971). A compressed and comprehensible exposition of the whole subject of race from a biological viewpoint by a physical anthropologist. *H—C C Thomas.*

GEERTZ, CLIFFORD b. 1926. *The Interpretation of Cultures* (1973). Demonstrates one possible interpretation of the nature of society—that it is a system of symbols shared by its individual members. Draws examples from fieldwork in Indonesia, including Java and Bali. *H—Basic.*

GRIAULE, MARCEL 1898-1956. *Conversations with Ogotemmeli* (1965). Offers a unique and firsthand account of the myth, religion, and philosophy of the Dogon of Mali as recounted by an elderly wise man. *P—Oxford U Pr.*

HALL, EDWARD T. b. 1914. *The Hidden Dimension* (1966). Examines the implications of the use of space for personal and business relations and in cross-cultural interactions. *H & P—Doubleday.*

HARNER, MICHAEL b. 1929 (ed.). *Hallucinogens and Shamanism* (1973). Essays on the shamanistic practices of many cultures. *H & P—Oxford U Pr.*

HEIDER, KARL b. 1935. *Ethnographic Film* (1976). First full-length history of ethnographic film, examining the development of methodology from the work of Robert Flaherty to the present. *H—U of Tex Pr.*

HOEBEL, E. A. b. 1906. *The Law of Primitive Man* (1954). An introduction to the methods of legal control in traditional societies. *P—Atheneum.*

HYMES, DELL b. 1927. *Reinventing Anthropology* (1973). Provocative essays that analyze the implications of anthropological research for the people being studied and for those doing the study. *H—Pantheon; P—Random.*

LEVI-STRAUSS, CLAUDE b. 1908. *Tristes Tropiques* (1955). An account by a distinguished French anthropologist of his experiences doing fieldwork in Brazil. By setting his observations into context and by drawing extensive parallels and comparisons, he creates a provocative and highly readable book. *H & P—Atheneum.*

LEWIS, I. M. b. 1930. *Ecstatic Religions* (1971). Wide-ranging sociological study of possession cults in shamanistic regions of Africa, Arctic Asia, and South America that also analyzes the relationship of such cults to marginal groups. *H—Peter Smith; P—Penguin.*

LURIE, NANCY O. b. 1924. *Mountain Wolf Woman* (1961). The autobiography of a Winnebago woman told to and annotated by her adopted kinswoman. *H—U of Mich Pr.*

MALINOWSKI, BRONISLAW 1884-1942. *Argonauts of the Western Pacific* (1961). Classic monograph on the Trobriand Islanders, discussing among other things their system of ritualized exchange. The author was one of the founders of field research. *P—Dutton.*

MAUSS, MARCEL 1872-1950. *The Gift* (1967). The first systematic study of how the exchange of gifts is a transaction basic to all human relationships between individuals and groups. *P—Norton.*

MEAD, MARGARET b. 1901. *Sex and Temperament in Three Primitive Societies* (1935). A series of studies concerned with the cultural definition of sex roles in three societies in New Guinea. *H—Peter Smith; P—Morrow.*

MONTAGU, ASHLEY b. 1905. *Frontiers of Anthropology* (1974). A documentary history of anthropology based on writings of such firsthand culture observers as Christopher Columbus, Charles Darwin, and 20th-century anthropologists. *H & P—Putnam.*

————. *Man's Most Dangerous Myth: The Fallacy of Race* (1974). Clarifies the concept of race by elaborating how Western culture stresses a social idea of race that is very different from the biological idea. *H & P—Oxford U Pr.*

MOONEY, JAMES 1861-1921. *The Ghost Dance Religion* (1896). Firsthand account of a revivalist cult that swept through many native American tribes west of the Mississippi at the end of the 19th century. *H & P—U of Chicago Pr.*

OAKLEY, KENNETH P. b. 1911. *Man the Toolmaker* (5th ed. 1976). Presents early human implements of wood, bone, shell, stone, and metal—evidence for the evolution of human culture. *P—British Bk Ctr, U of Chicago Pr.*

OTTEN, CHARLOTTE b. 1915. *Anthropology and Art* (1971). Readings in cross-cultural esthetics and the relationship between art and culture. *P—U of Tex Pr.*

RADIN, PAUL 1883-1959. *The Trickster* (1956). Studies of one of the earliest and most universal mythic figures through an examination of the Winnebago cycle of trickster myths. *P—Schocken.*

REITER, RAYNA R. b. 1946 (ed.). *Toward an Anthropology of Women* (1976). Essays concerned with reevaluating women's roles in societies through an examination of the origin of sex differences, the use of women as symbols, and the function of economic power and work in women's lives and social status. *H & P—Monthly Review.*

ROSALDO, MICHELLE b. 1944 and LOUISE LAMPHERE b. 1940 (eds.). *Woman, Culture, and Society* (1974). Sixteen anthropologists reporting on values, prestige systems, and survival strategies of women in various cultures. *H & P—Stanford U Pr.*

ROTHENBERG, JEROME b. 1931. *Technicians of the Sacred* (1969). Translations annotated by a contemporary poet make up this rather unusual treatment of the poetries of traditional and ancient cultures. *P—Doubleday.*

SAPIR, EDWARD 1884-1930. *Language* (1921). A basic and classic treatment of one of the most characteristic of human behaviors—its sounds, grammatical processes and concepts, kinds of structures, and changes in the course of history. *P—HarBraceJ.*

TALAYESVA, DON C. b. 1890. *Sun Chief* (1942). Ed. by Leo W. Simmons. A Hopi describes his daily life and world view. *H & P—Yale U Pr.*

TAX, SOL b. 1907 (ed.). *Horizons of Anthropology* (1964). Twenty-one classic essays on various topics of interest that comprise anthropology. *P—Aldine.*

TURNBULL, COLIN b. 1924. *The Forest People* (1961). A lively and readable account of the Bambuti (Pygmies) of the Ituri Forest of the Congo. *H & P—S&S.*

_____. *The Mountain People* (1972). A disturbing account of the slow death and dehumanization of the Ik, a small group of hunters living in the mountains separating Uganda, the Sudan, and Kenya, following their removal from their native lands. *H & P—S&S.*

VAN GENNEP, ARNOLD 1873-1957. *The Rites of Passage* (1909). The first work to note that there are regular and significant rituals in most cultures to mark the transitional stages in life—birth, puberty, marriage, and death. *H & P—U of Chicago Pr.*

WAGLEY, CHARLES b. 1913 and MARVIN HARRIS b. 1927. *Minorities in the New World* (1958). Authoritative account of racial and ethnic minorities—Black, Indian, white—in Latin America and Anglo-America. *H & P—Columbia U Pr.*

WAX, ROSALIE b. 1911. *Doing Fieldwork* (1971). The fieldwork method is described and discussed in terms of the author's own experiences in three different situations. *H & P—U of Chicago Pr.*

WHITTEN, NORMAN E. b. 1937 and JOHN F. SZWED b. 1936 (eds.). *Afro-American Anthropology* (1970). Twenty-two articles dealing with New World African cultures, including analyses of music, socioeconomic adaptations, and the definition of Black culture. *H & P—Free Pr.*

WILSON, MONICA b. 1908. *Good Company* (1963). A study of the Nyakyusa of southern Tanzania, whose unusual social system is based not on family but on villages of people of the same age. *P—Beacon Pr.*

WISSLER, CLARK 1870-1947. *Material Culture of the Blackfoot Indians* (1910). Long, illustrated essay that views Blackfoot cultural history between 1808 and 1910, exploring various parts of their material life, such as food preparation, quill and bead work, and tepee manufacture. *H—AMS Pr.*

WOLF, ERIC b. 1923. *Sons of the Shaking Earth* (1959). Remarkable history of the valley of Mexico, location of the earliest domestication of corn, and much later home of the Aztecs and their descendants. *H & P—U of Chicago Pr.*

WORTH, SOL 1922-1977 and JOHN ADAIR b. 1913. *Through Navajo Eyes* (1973). Investigation of the question: How do people structure their reality through film? The authors document the Navajo Film Project and explore the film communication and anthropological problems underlying their work. *H & P—Ind U Pr.*

24. Sociology

William Ray Arney

The sociologist's concern is to observe, describe, and explain organized human behavior. The object of study is the social world that emerges from human interaction. All basic social institutions—religious, political, economic, educational, familial—are of interest to the sociologist. How do institutions arise? How are they related to one another? How do they influence behavior? How and why does the social world change? Such questions are of sociological importance. But beyond these common interests there are substantial differences within the field.

Sociologists differ concerning the way behavior should be observed. Some argue that everyday face-to-face interaction is the only appropriate method of sociological study. Others are interested in macrosocial behavior—factual accounts of group actions. Still others carry on their "observation" via questionnaires, telephone interviews, or by other standard means of collecting data on social behavior.

Schemes for description and explanation are equally diverse. It is impossible in this brief essay to describe the varied theoretical perspectives used by sociologists. But the critical reader should be aware that theoretical differences in the discipline are often indicative of underlying political differences among proponents of different perspectives. For example, functionalism, a dominant theoretical perspective in American sociology, tries to assess the ways in which various social institutions and varying kinds of behavior contribute to the smooth, orderly operation of society. From this orientation a problem arises if order is disrupted, if something is "dysfunctional." Functionalism rests on a commitment to political stability. On the other hand, Marxism suggests that the fundamental restructuring of society is a prerequisite to the solution of enduring social problems such as economic inequality, racism, and the oppression of women.

The political character of sociology is also demonstrated by recent changes in the ways sociologists are supported. To a greater degree than ever before, government relies on sociological analyses of the problems of urban areas, the effects of education, the impact on population, the implications of social disorder, and so on. Both public and private agencies have moved away from supporting research through grants to contracting for specified, specialized studies by sociologists. Many sociologists have thus become active in the policymaking process, but at the same time the profession has become more closely tied to and reliant on those with clear political commitments and motivations.

Despite extensive government and business ties, sociology remains an intellectually vigorous discipline. There is considerable room for intradisciplinary dissent and debate concerning the way social behavior is to be studied and the ends to which such study should be directed. Edward Wilson's *Sociobiology* has renewed interest in and discussion about the biological bases of behavior. Books such as those by Braverman, Bowles and Gintis, Piven and Cloward, and Freire question the entire conceptual framework from which we have tried to understand such common social institutions as education, public relief, and the division of labor in society. Ernest Becker and Noam Chomsky challenge the assumptions and practices on which a century of sociology has rested.

So as one reads sociology it should be remembered that there is no agreement on disciplinary content or method. The profession at present provides an intellectual battleground. Read with an open and critical mind.

ALINSKY, SAUL D. 1909-1972. *Rules for Radicals* (1971). A proposal and practical primer for the radical organization of the middle classes. Outcome: a humanistic revolution. *P—Random.*

ARIÈS, PHILIPPE b. 1914. *Centuries of Childhood: A Social History of Family Life* (1962). A sensitive study of the emergence of the notion of childhood. *P—Random.*

BEAUVOIR, SIMONE DE b. 1908. *The Second Sex* (1953). The fountainhead of the international women's movement. In this controversial treatise, touching with encyclopedic erudition upon every aspect of women's lives, the existentialist thinker demands that women claim their identities and reject millennia of socio-psychic restraints imposed by men. *H—Knopf; P—Random.*

BECKER, ERNEST. *The Structure of Evil: An Essay on the Unification of the Sciences of Man* (1968). The analytical split between fact and value—so crucial to scientific endeavor—has permitted development of a social science of domination and control. A provocative and challenging thesis. *H—Braziller; P—Free Pr.*

BENDIX, REINHARD b. 1916 and SEYMOUR MARTIN LIPSET b. 1922 (eds.). *Class, Status, and Power* (rev. ed. 1966). A compilation of classic papers on stratification. *H—Free Pr.*

BERGER, PETER L. b. 1929 and THOMAS LUCKMAN b. 1927. *The Social Construction of Reality: A Treatise in the Sociology of Knowledge* (1966). Basic work outlining the way people construct their social world—institutions, authority, roles, etc.—and how that world is transmitted from generation to generation. *H—Irvington; P—Doubleday.*

BLAU, PETER M. b. 1915 and O. DUDLEY DUNCAN b. 1912. *The American Occupational Structure* (1967). The major empirical study of social mobility in the United States. *H—Wiley.*

BOWLES, SAMUEL and HERBERT GINTIS b. 1940. *Schooling in Capitalist America: Educational Reform and the Contradictions of Economic Life* (1976). Encyclopedic, scholarly analysis of extant data on the history, structure, and function of education in society. *H—Basic.*

BRAVERMAN, HARRY b. 1920. *Labor and Monopoly Capital: The Degradation of Work in the Twentieth Century* (1975). An intelligent analysis of the transformation of work under modern monopoly capitalism. An insightful critique of the technological determinism of earlier literature on occupations. *H & P—Monthly Rev.*

CHOMSKY, NOAM b. 1928. *Reflections on Language* (1975). Thoughts on the nature of the human mind by a noted linguist. Challenges some of the basic assumptions of social science. *H & P—Pantheon.*

DAHRENDORF, RALF. *Essays in the Theory of Society* (1968). Dahrendorf gave impetus to a school of thought that views conflict as central to the study of social and political processes. *H & P—Stanford U Pr.*

DURKHEIM, EMILE 1858-1917. *Suicide* (trans. 1951). The classic study of the correlates of suicide, still a model for contemporary empirical research. *H & P—Free Pr.*

_____. *The Elementary Forms of the Religious Life* (trans. 1961). A seminal contribution to the study of religion, the great symbolic stabilizer of society. *H & P—Free Pr.*

ETZIONI, AMITAI b. 1929. *The Active Society: A Theory of Societal and Political Processes* (1968). Argues that the "post-modern" society of alienation and inauthenticity must be changed to an "active society," one that is responsive to basic human needs. Etzioni is among today's most active professionals in social policy formulation and implementation. *H & P—Free Pr.*

FIRESTONE, SHULAMITH b. 1945. *The Dialect of Sex: The Case for Feminist Revolution* (1970). A major statement of radical feminist theory. Firestone sees the biological relationship of women to men as the root of many social evils such as racism and gross economic inequality. Contains proposals for fundamental social reform. *P—Bantam, Morrow.*

FREIRE, PAULO b. 1921. *Pedagogy of the Oppressed* (1971). An indictment of present pedagogical methods with recommendations for change. The author has used his techniques to raise political consciousness among peasant laborers in South America. *P—Seaburg.*

FRIEDAN, BETTY b. 1921. *The Feminine Mystique* (2nd ed. 1974). A
1963 bestseller that changed lives. A prime mover of feminism, Friedan
drew attention to the post-World War II malaise of women: pushed by
a consumer- and advertising-oriented society into the prescribed utopia
of marriage/motherhood/suburban house tending, guilt-ridden if they
sought identity or expression except through husbands, children, and
homes. *H—Norton; P—Dell.*

GEERTZ, CLIFFORD b. 1926. *The Interpretation of Cultures* (1973).
Excellent, enjoyable essays on the importance of the concept of culture.
H—Basic.

GIDDENS, ANTHONY. *Capitalism and Modern Social Theory: An
Analysis of the Writing of Marx, Durkheim, and Max Weber*
(1971). An erudite exposition and comparison of the thought of three
grand masters of social theory. *H & P—Cambridge U Pr.*

GOFFMAN, ERVING b. 1922. *The Presentation of Self in Everyday
Life* (1958). Everyday social behavior viewed as drama, with people
as the actors and their social space as the stage. *H—Overbrook Pr;
P—Doubleday.*

GOULDNER, ALVIN W. b. 1920. *The Coming Crisis of Western
Sociology* (1970). Contends that the functionalism of Parsons (see
below) cannot deal with change and that Marxism can. A crisis will
arise when sociologists must use a theoretical perspective that stands
in opposition to the class interests of those who control the agencies that
support academics. *H—Basic; P—Avon.*

HABERMAS, JÜRGEN. *Toward a Rational Society: Student Protest,
Science, and Politics* (trans. 1971). Theoretically integrated essays,
expressing a radical view of diverse topics. *P—Beacon Pr.*

HARRINGTON, MICHAEL b. 1928. *The Other America* (1964). An early,
important statement on poverty in America and a politically influential
book. *H—Macmillan; P—Penguin.*

HOMANS, GEORGE C. b. 1910. *Social Behavior: Its Elementary
Forms* (rev. ed. 1974). The structure and function of small groups. A
basic treatment of social exchange. *H—HarBraceJ.*

HOROWITZ, IRVING LOUIS b. 1929. *Three Worlds of Development:
The Theory and Practice of International Stratification* (1966).
Analysis of class structure applied to nations. *H & P—Oxford U Pr.*

INKELES, ALEX b. 1920. *What Is Sociology?* (1965). Straightforward
exposition of the nature of the discipline and the profession. *H & P—
P-H.*

JENCKS, CHRISTOPHER b. 1936. et al. *Inequality: A Reassessment
of the Effects of Family and Schooling in America* (1972). Extensive statistical analyses lead to the conclusion that schooling does
little to relieve overall inequality. Controversial social policies are
discussed. *H—Basic; P—Har-Row.*

KUHN, THOMAS S. b. 1922. *The Structure of Scientific Revolutions*
(2nd ed. 1970). Important discussion of changes in scientific theory,
method, and fact. *H & P—U of Chicago Pr.*

LAZARSFELD, PAUL F. 1901-1976. *Qualitative Analysis: Historical
and Critical Essays* (1971). A collection of papers by a grand master

of sociological method. Also contains three essays on Lazarsfeld's work. *P—Allyn.*

LENSKI, GERHARD b. 1924. *Power and Privilege* (1966). Theory of stratification based on change from subsistence to surplus-producing economies. *H—McGraw.*

MEAD, GEORGE HERBERT 1863-1931. *Mind, Self, and Society from the Standpoint of a Social Behaviorist* (1934). A person is a product of society. Mead discusses socialization and the way rationality and creativity emerge through social interaction. *H & P—U of Chicago Pr.*

MEADOWS, DONNELLA H. et al. *The Limits to Growth: A Report for the Club of Rome's Project on the Predicament of Mankind* (2nd ed. 1974). A readable report on computer simulations of the interaction of world population, natural resources, and economy. This book aroused considerable controversy in many academic disciplines. *H & P— Universe.*

MERTON, ROBERT K. b. 1910. *Social Theory and Social Structure* (enlarged ed. 1968). Classical essays on social structure. Contains arguments for the development of "middle range" theories—those that are concerned with social phenomena on less than a sweeping scale. *H— Free Pr.*

_____ and ROBERT A. NISBET b. 1913 (eds.). *Contemporary Social Problems* (4th ed. 1976). Excellent collection of papers on a range of social problems: inequality, aging, minorities, group relations, sex roles, population, terrorism, crime, etc. *H—HarBraceJ.*

MILGRAM, STANLEY b. 1933. *Obedience to Authority: An Experimental View* (1974). Compelling report of the controversial research program showing that people obey authority even when their obedience will inflict pain and suffering on others. *H & P—Har-Row.*

MILLETT, KATE b. 1934. *Sexual Politics* (1970). The first synthesis of the early writing of the current women's movement. Views male dominance of women as socially conditioned and ideologically supported. *P—Avon.*

MILLS, C. WRIGHT 1916-1962. *The Power Elite* (1956). Argues that the United States is controlled by a small, interlocking group of people from the military, politics, and business. *H & P—Oxford U Pr.*

_____. *The Sociological Imagination* (1959). An important early critique of American sociology. Excellent essays by an original, radical thinker. *H & P—Oxford U Pr.*

MYRDAL, GUNNAR b. 1898 et al. *Asian Drama: An Inquiry Into the Poverty of Nations* (1968). Mammoth study of the social and political roots of poverty in Southeast Asia. Politically significant scholarship of the highest order. *P—Pantheon 3 vols.*

PADOVER, SAUL K. b. 1905 (ed.). *The Karl Marx Library* (1971). A well-edited set of topical volumes containing the writings of one of the world's most influential thinkers. *H & P—McGraw 6 vols.*

PARSONS, TALCOTT b. 1902. *The System of Modern Societies* (1971). Parsons' work has shaped much of American sociology. Here, in a readable book, he develops a theory of social evolution and attempts to account for modern European and American history under his scheme. *P—P-H.*

PIVEN, FRANCES FOX b. 1932 and RICHARD A. CLOWARD b. 1926. *Regulating the Poor: The Functions of Public Relief* (1971). Views public relief as a device used by the haves to control the have-nots in times of potential political instability. *H—Pantheon; P—Random.*

REISMAN, DAVID b. 1909 et al. *The Lonely Crowd* (1950). The changing social character of the American people from "inner directed" to "other directed." *H & P—Yale U Pr.*

THOMLINSON, RALPH b. 1925. *Population Dynamics: Causes and Consequences of World Demographic Change* (2nd ed. 1976). A balanced mixture of historical and contemporary material on population. A solid introduction to population problems. *H—Random.*

WALLACE, WALTER L. b. 1927. *Sociological Theory: An Introduction* (1969). A splendid overview of contemporary sociological theory. Explains and gives examples of eleven "isms" that inform the discipline. *H—Aldine; P—Irvington.*

WALLERSTEIN, IMMANUEL b. 1930. *The Modern World System: Capitalist Agriculture and the Origins of the European World Economy in the Sixteenth Century* (1974). Encyclopedic review of secondary historical sources that traces the emergence of a European world economy in the 16th century. The first of four projected volumes. *H—Acad Pr.*

WEBER, MAX 1864-1920. *The Protestant Ethic and the Spirit of Capitalism* (1930). One of the great sociological insights: the linkage of Protestant ideology to the emergence of industrial society. *H & P—Scribner.*

WILSON, EDWARD O. b. 1929. *Sociobiology: The New Synthesis* (1975). Extraordinarily controversial book suggesting that attention be directed to the biological bases of social behavior. Denounced by some as a rationalization of stereotypes and the status quo and an attempt to resurrect racist and sexist biological determinism; hailed by others as a serious "fundamental intellectual challenge" to contemporary sociology. *H—Harvard U Pr.*

25. Communications and Language

Mark Schulman

Many teachers and scholars working in the broad area of communications and language suffer at times from professional anxieties, if not from an outright identity crisis. The reason is that communications is an emerging discipline that borrows freely from many other established disciplines. It is kindred to anthropology, linguistics, psychology, and sociology in the social sciences; to literature, speech, and theatre in the humanities; to human biology, engineering, and mathematics in the sciences—and draws freely from all of them as well as from the less readily definable disciplines of journalism, film, and broadcasting. Although the diversity of attitudes and approaches often confuses and occasionally confounds, it stimulates intellectual excitement as well as spirited, constructive interdisciplinary debate.

In this brief essay, "communications and language" cannot be defined with finality. About "language," near precision is possible: the aspect of human endeavor that separates people from other animals—the systematic oral/aural and written use of symbols which, through their logical order and cultural acceptance, allows communication within social communities. The language reading list that follows includes some of the classics on the subject, such as those by Sapir, Robert Hall, and Hayakawa, as well as some recent significant contributions, such as books by Farb on sociolinguistics, Newman on the demise of standard English, and Williams on the impact on meaning of cultural change. Works on specialized contemporary themes are here too: Dillard on Black English, Miller and Swift on sexism and language, and Edward Hall on nonverbal communication.

Defining communications poses far greater difficulty. One useful distinction often made is between "communication" and "communications." Communication refers to the primary process of social interaction through the sending and receiving of messages. Communications, on the other hand, encompasses the secondary techniques (or means) of that process, those dependent on technological invention and operation. Thus, while every society communicates (not a few scholars argue that communication *is* culture), some societies have more sophisticated (but not necessarily more efficient, accurate, or humane) communications than others. Even so, this distinction blurs in usage, with the two words often used interchangeably.

In general, the communications book list covers both technique and process. Social processes are strongly represented, and books with nontechnical explanations are often preferred to more scholarly but more difficult studies. Some books listed focus on basic processes (Schramm). Others consider the media that form these processes: DeFleur and McLuhan on general theories of mass communications; Casty and Sobel on the scope and impact of the media industries; Rosen and Sklar on film; Dorfman and Mattelart on comics; Maddox and Smith on new technologies; and Friendly, Newcomb, Skornia, and Tuchman on television.

Any book list on communications must embrace what some view, falsely, as peripheral areas: advertising, the support system and (some say) reason for the existence of the commercial media (Ewen and Schwartz); the mass culture molded by the mass media (Rosenberg and White); and the consciousness of people subjected to a constant barrage of unidirectional messages (Cirino and Schiller). The most important contemporary thinking in communications is in these peripheral areas; unfortunately, the book industry (itself a mass medium) also produces the most trash in these areas.

The future of communication and language studies is unclear, though expansion seems reasonably certain. It is clear that the most productive and interesting work attempts to analyze the relationship of communication to individual consciousness and to cultural patterns in society. Once the results of the research and thinking in this area are in (and they are just beginning to appear [see Enzensberger]), they will clarify further what communications means and alter substantially future lists of good reading.

The books in the following list have been selected with care; if you want to read beyond the list, proceed with caution.

Communications

ARONSON, JAMES b. 1915. *Deadline for the Media: Today's Challenges to Press, TV and Radio* (1972). A longtime journalist for both the establishment and radical or alternative press, Aronson outlines the crucial issues facing the American press in the last quarter of the century. *H & P—Bobbs.*

BROWN, LES b. 1928. *Television: The Business Behind the Box* (1971). A lively, revealing insider's analysis of a typical year in the television business, written when Brown was the television editor of *Variety*. *H—HarBraceJ.*

CARPENTER, EDMUND b. 1922. *Oh, What a Blow That Phantom Gave Me!* (1973). A McLuhanophilic anthropologist zooms through many different cultures to analyze (with as much depth as possible at that breathtaking pace) "how media change people and people change media." *H—HR&W; P—Bantam.*

CASTY, ALAN b. 1929 (ed.). *Mass Media and Mass Man* (2nd ed. 1968). One of the better anthologies, carefully selected and precisely arranged, detailing the effects of mass media on cultural values and the dissemination of information. *H—Peter Smith; P—HR&W.*

CIRINO, ROBERT. *Don't Blame the People* (1972). Subtitled "How the News Media Use Bias, Distortion and Censorship to Manipulate Public Opinion," the book details just that in page after page of fascinating documentation. *P—Random.*

DEFLEUR, MELVIN L. b. 1923 and SANDRA BALL-ROKEACH. *Theories of Mass Communication* (3rd ed. 1975). The updated classic study of the various issues and perspectives in mainstream mass communication theory. *P—McKay.*

DORFMAN, ARIEL b. 1942 and ARMAND MATTELART b. 1936. *How to Read Donald Duck: Imperialist Ideology in the Disney Comic* (1975). Fascinating, provocative documentation, by two Chilean scholars now in exile, of the role of Walt Disney comics in the cultural penetration of the third world. *P—Int General.*

ENZENBERGER, HANS MAGNUS b. 1929. *The Consciousness Industry: On Literature, Politics, and the Media* (1974). Difficult but readable treatment of various aspects of consciousness, including two chapters specifically on the media. Translated from the German. *H—Seabury.*

EWEN, STUART. *Captains of Consciousness: Advertising and the Social Roots of the Consumer Culture* (1976). Seeking the roots of mass culture, Ewen discovers them in the emergence of mass consumption and modern advertising. *H & P—McGraw.*

FRIENDLY, ALFRED W. b. 1915. *Due to Circumstances Beyond Our Control . . .* (1967). Insightful and entertaining anecdotal personal account of the author's years as president of CBS News. *P—Random.*

JOHNSON, NICHOLAS b. 1934. *How to Talk Back to Your Television Set* (1970). Already a classic of its genre, this book by the maverick former Federal Communications Commission member tells the reader with delightful clarity how TV is, how it got that way, and what can be done about it. *H—Little.*

KAYE, EVELYN b. 1937. *The Family Guide to Children's Television: What to Watch, What to Miss, What to Change, and How to Do It* (1974). The title says it all about this exciting book—the best of the lot in dealing with the crucial relationship of TV to children. *H & P—Pantheon.*

McLUHAN, MARSHALL b. 1911. *Understanding Media: The Extensions of Man* (1964). A very large percentage of this book is nonsense, a small percentage brilliant insight. *H—McGraw; P—McGraw, NAL.*

MADDOX, BRENDA. *Beyond Babel: New Directions in Communications* (1974). A guide to the future, fashioned by changes and advances in communication technology. A nontechnical and useful source for general readers. *P—Beacon Pr.*

NEWCOMB, HORACE (ed.). *Television: The Critical View* (1976). Wide-ranging and coherently organized anthology of essays helping to establish how television fits into American culture. *P—Oxford U Pr.*

ROSEN, MARJORIE. *Popcorn Venus: Women, Movies, and the American Dream* (1974). Lively if uneven account of the image of women in Hollywood films, from the very beginning. *P—Avon.*

ROSENBERG, BERNARD b. 1923 and DAVID MANNING WHITE b. 1917 (eds.). *Mass Culture Revisited* (1971). Large collection of valuable reprints, notable for its inclusion of important excerpts and authors. This is an update of the editors' original book, *Mass Culture. H—Van Nos Reinhold.*

SCHILLER, HERBERT I. b. 1919. *The Mind Managers* (1973). Like this author's other works, this book breaks new ground in organizing the data on communications. Essential reading for those who want to understand how the knowledge industry manipulates consciousness. *H & P—Beacon Pr.*

SCHRAMM, WILBUR b. 1907. *Men, Messages and Media: A Look at Human Communication* (1973). A basic text by one of the top authorities in the field, summarizing the mainstream approach to communication theory. *P—Har-Row.*

SCHWARTZ, TONY. *The Responsive Chord* (1973). As an attempt to piece together bits of knowledge about how the electronic media do what they do, this is an influential addition to mass communications theory. *H & P—Doubleday.*

SKLAR, ROBERT b. 1936. *Movie-Made America: A Cultural History of American Movies* (1975). Thought-provoking survey of the role of films in shaping 20th-century American culture. *H & P—Random.*

SKORNIA, HARRY J. b. 1910. *Television and Society: An Inquest and Agenda for Improvement* (1965). A classic study of television and its role in American society. Includes specific recommendations as a call to action. *P—McGraw.*

SMITH, RALPH LEE b. 1927. *The Wired Nation: Cable TV—The Electronic Communications Highway* (1972). Though some aspects have changed since the publication of this book, it remains the definitive short, perceptive analysis of the cable television situation. *P—Har-Row.*

SOBEL, ROBERT b. 1931. *The Manipulators: America in the Media Age* (1976). A well-written story of the growth and rise to dominance of the five entertainment and information industries in the United States: newspapers, radios, movies, television, and higher education. *H—Doubleday.*

TUCHMAN, GAYE (ed.). *The TV Establishment: Programming for Profit and Power* (1974). A sophisticated collection of critical analyses—the best of its kind—dissecting television. *H & P—P-H.*

TUNSTALL, JEREMY. *The Media Are American* (1977). Incisive, cogent, sometimes disturbing study of the effects of the spread of "Americanized media" throughout the global communications system. *H—Columbia U Pr.*

WELLS, ALAN b. 1940 (ed.). *Mass Media and Society* (2nd ed. 1975). Collection of uneven but important essays on the sociology of media. *H & P—Mayfield Pub.*

Language

ANDERSON, WALLACE L. b. 1917 and NORMAN C. STAGEBERG b. 1905 (eds.). *Introductory Readings on Language* (4th ed. 1975). Selected readings in nontechnical language in such areas as the nature of language, word meanings and changes, logic, metaphor, semantics, dialects, structural grammar, and usage. *P—HR&W.*

CHASE, STUART b. 1888 and MARIAN T. CHASE. *The Power of Words* (1954). A popular and highly simplified account of many topics in semantics and communication. Part II considers applications of concepts in semantics. *H—HarBraceJ.*

CHOMSKY. *Reflections on Language.* See "Sociology," page 223.

CLEATOR, P. E. b. 1908. *Lost Languages* (1959). The story of the decipherment of writings in lost languages—such as Egyptian, Persian, and Hittite—and what we learn from these writings about the people who produced them. *o.p.*

DILLARD, J. L. b. 1924. *Black English: Its History and Usage in the United States* (1972). A strong and convincing argument detailing the validity and structure of Black nonstandard English as an important dialect in the United States. *H—Random.*

FARB, PETER b. 1929. *Word Play: What Happens When People Talk* (1973). The nontechnical explication of the tenets of socio-linguistics, or, says Farb, "the remarkable ability of human beings to play upon one another with their speech." *H—Knopf; P—Bantam.*

HALL, EDWARD T. b. 1914. *The Silent Language* (1959). The interrelatedness of patterns in culture and language, and the differences in these patterns among various ethnic groups. Original, and free from anthropological jargon. *P—Doubleday.*

HALL, ROBERT A., Jr. b. 1911. *Linguistics and Your Language* (1960). Basic concepts of language and linguistics explained for everyone with clarity and vigor by a top-flight linguist. *P—Doubleday.*

HAYAKAWA, S. I. b. 1906. *Language in Thought and Action* (3rd ed. 1972). Fascinating semantic study of human interaction through communication, stressing the need for cooperation. *H & P—HarBraceJ.*

MILLER, CASEY and KATE SWIFT. *Words and Women: New Language in New Times* (1976). One of the first and best of several recent books dealing with sexism and language. *H—Doubleday.*

MUELLER, CLAUS b. 1941. *The Politics of Communication: A Study in the Political Sociology of Language, Socialization, and Legitimation* (1973). In some ways this is a difficult book, but it merits careful study for its well-documented analysis of the relationship between information control and political systems. *H & P—Oxford U Pr.*

NEWMAN, EDWIN b. 1919. *Strictly Speaking: Will America Be the Death of English?* (1974). One of the best of the American-English-is-destroying-*real*-English school—because it is erudite, witty, and fun. *H—Bobbs; P—Warner Bks.*

SAPIR. *Language.* See "Anthropology," page 219.

WILLIAMS, RAYMOND b. 1921. *Keywords: A Vocabulary of Culture and Society* (1976). Intellectually stimulating discussion of meaning in relation to cultural change, through the semantic definition of 155 key words in English. *H & P—Oxford U Pr.*

26. Psychology

Paul C. Obler

One of the most characteristic and influential accomplishments of the last half century of the present scientific age is the development of a science of human behavior. What was known in the pre-scientific past was from introspection, random observation, and homely reasoning. Such knowledge was frequently projected—often with profundity—into philosophy, the arts, and religion. But only when theory could be checked against facts—systematized facts—could the scientific study of mental activity and personality (a genuine psychology) be born. This genuine psychology builds upon physiology, and it extends its investigations into the borderlands of philosophy, sociology, anthropology, politics, and even economics. Human beings are physiological creatures of sensation, perception, memory, thought, and emotion; but they are also social beings with habits of love and hate, work and play, creation and destruction, worship and art. Psychology's tremendous range of concern today has resulted in a bewildering variety of conflicting theories or schools, specialized fields, and professional activities.

The literature of psychology is equally various, and much of it is published in paperbound editions. The newcomer needs to pick a way very carefully among the genuine classics, the useful guides, the esoteric and statistics-laden monographs, and the over-simplified potboilers dispensing "psychology to the millions." The list of books recommended here is divided into four sections that cover the matter of psychology—with some overlappings, of course. The reader should begin by sampling books from each section in turn.

Those in the first section provide a general view of the subject, including its historical development and the contributions of its great pioneering figures, the founders of the early "schools." Section two presents the general theories of the nature of human beings as developed by various schools—structuralism, functionalism, psychoanalysis, behaviorism, gestalt, and existentialism. Each school tends to be more interested in some problems than in others. Gestalt psychology, for instance, focuses on perception, whereas psychoanalysis is especially concerned with unconscious motivation. Some theoretical issues are the subject of polemics: behaviorists and existentialists would seem to differ in their views of the basic nature of people; and in counseling psychology, the transactionalists, primal screamers, ESTs, or others claim superior therapeutic efficacy. But most psychologists today are not rigid adherents of any one school; rather they are eclectics who use theories and methods of a particular school because they are interested in certain problems.

Readers can begin to learn about modern psychology by discovering what psychologists are interested in and what they do to satisfy those interests. Sections three and four contain books about significant general and applied fields of psychological interest. That there is overlap should not be disturbing; psychology is a fast-growing and dynamic enterprise. Often the procedures of its specialists will seem only remotely connected: what has an interest in glands as reacting mechanisms to do with the psychology of occupational adjustment or of rote learning? But if readers will remember that psychology is by definition the science of human behavior, they will appreciate both the diversity of its activities and its common theme—that nothing natural to human behavior should be foreign to human beings. This is a modern application of the simple but profoundly difficult ancient admonition, "Know thyself."

General Psychology

CRM, INC. *Psychosources: A Psychology Resource Catalog* (1972). Ed. by Evelyn Shapiro. A montage of starting places and controversies focusing on key issues in contemporary psychology. Though far from definitive, the book directs the reader to original sources. *P—Bantam.*

DREVER, JAMES 1873-1950 and HARVEY WALLERSTEIN. *A Dictionary of Psychology* (rev. ed. 1976). An inexpensive collection of almost 5,000 generally excellent definitions. *H—Gannon; P—Penguin.*

EYSENCK, H. J. b. 1916. *Uses and Abuses of Psychology* (7th ed. 1962). Controversial in its evaluations but freighted with useful information on intelligence testing, psychotherapy, the roots of prejudice, abnormal behavior, and social attitudes. *P—Penguin.*

HAHN, JOHN F. b. 1924 and SANFORD LOPATER. *Psychology: The Basic Principles* (1976). A manageable presentation of behavior and heredity; learning and conditioning; memory, forgetting, and performance; motivation; emotion; sensation and perception; imagery and cognition; abilities and aptitudes; personality; social psychology. This review ends with a section on the history, methods, and goals of modern psychology. *P—Littlefield.*

HAVEMANN, ERNEST b. 1912. *The Age of Psychology* (1957). This little book, based on the author's articles for *Life* magazine, is useful to anyone coming to the field fresh. *P—S&S.*

LANDE, NATHANIEL. *Mindstyles/Lifestyles* (1976). Wide-ranging but necessarily superficial look at today's changing lifestyles in the context of leading psychotherapies, traditional and avant garde; a discussion of such practices as those at Esalen and of EST encounters. *P—Price Stern.*

SARGENT, S. STANSFELD b. 1906 and KENNETH R. STAFFORD b. 1922. *Basic Teachings of the Great Psychologists* (1965). Each of the 17 chapters in this excellent introduction deals with an important aspect of human behavior, and the key names associated with the subject are assimilated into the chapter. *P—Doubleday.*

Psychological Theories

ADLER, ALFRED 1870-1937. *The Science of Living* (1969). Pithy introduction to the thought of this great pioneer, particularly to his concepts of life-style and inferiority feelings. *P—Doubleday.*

ASSAGIOLI, ROBERTO b. 1893. *Psychosynthesis* (1971). Significant attempt at a unified understanding of personality, drawing terms and theoretical emphases from many sources. Invaluable for techniques of self-assessment, and a must for those interested in counseling. *P— Viking Pr.*

BECKER, ERNEST. *The Denial of Death* (1973). This Pulitzer prize-winning work utilizes insights from theology and cultural anthropology to create a new science of human behavior. *H & P—Free Pr.*

BERNE, ERIC 1910-1970. *Games People Play* (1970). The basic handbook of transactional analysis; the theory helps the individual to autonomous action beyond the various games. *H—Grove; P—Ballantine, Grove.*

BRY, ADELAIDE b. 1920. *A Primer of Behavioral Psychology* (1975). Sketches the contributions of early workers, then focuses on contemporary behaviorists—Wolpe, Skinner, Eysenck. *P—NAL.*

FREUD, SIGMUND 1859-1939. *A General Introduction to Psychoanalysis* (1920). These 28 introductory lectures should be the reader's first encounter with Freud. *H—Liveright; P—PB, S&S.*

———. *A General Selection from the Works* (1957). Ed. by John Rickman. Groups Freud's writings under convenient headings and moves from the earliest to the latest materials. *H—Liveright; P—Doubleday.*

HALL, CALVIN b. 1909. *A Primer of Freudian Psychology* (1954). This little book offers a lucid, nontechnical account of Freud's influential theories and is intended especially for the reader beginning the study of psychology. *P—NAL.*

JAMES, WILLIAM 1842-1910. *Psychology: The Briefer Course* (1962). Ed. by Gordon Allport. Short of studying James's pioneering but long *Principles of Psychology*, the reader gets a good introduction through this book. *P—Macmillan.*

JONES. *The Life and Work of Sigmund Freud.* See "Biography," page 151.

JUNG, C. G. 1875-1961. *Modern Man in Search of a Soul* (1933). The basic introduction to Jung's analysis of the contemporary psyche. *P— HarBraceJ.*

KOHLER, WOLFGANG 1887-1967. *Gestalt Psychology* (1947). This challenge to the behaviorists is the fundamental text of the gestaltists and required reading for any serious student. *P—NAL.*

LAING, R. D. b. 1927. *The Divided Self* (1969). Brilliant, revolutionary work that defies conventional notions of madness. *H—Pantheon; P—Penguin.*

MASLOW, ABRAHAM H. b. 1908. *Toward a Psychology of Being* (2nd ed. 1968). An exciting, wise book in which Maslow, by using the peak experiences of psychologically healthy people as a foundation, evolves a scientifically based psychology in which growth and self-actualization become possible. *H & P—Van Nos Reinhold.*

MAY, ROLLO b. 1909 (ed.). *Existential Psychology* (2nd ed. 1961). Contends that no human being can be explained in terms of any of the usual psychological methodologies that focus on the *why* and *how* of a problem. *P—Random.*

MOUSTAKAS, CLARK. *Creativity and Conformity* (1967). Eloquent plea for confrontation, encounter, and honesty of self as the only means by which the individual can relate to others beyond the everyday forms. *P—Van Nos Reinhold.*

MULLAHY, PATRICK b. 1912. *Oedipus: Myth and Complex* (1948). Analyzes the Sophocles play and gives a concise review of the development of psychoanalytic theory from the late 19th century to Horney, Sullivan, and Fromm. *o.p.*

ORNSTEIN, ROBERT E. (ed.). *The Nature of Human Consciousness* (1973). Defining psychology as the "science of consciousness," Ornstein presents an interesting collection of essays in which esoteric psychologies (Zen, meditation) are blended with the latest work. *H—Viking Pr; P—W H Freeman.*

PERLS, FRITZ 1894-1970. *Gestalt Therapy Verbatim* (1976). Transcripts of actual therapy sessions with Perls's explanatory comments inserted. *P—Bantam.*

RANK, OTTO 1884-1939. *Beyond Psychology* (1941). Students of psychology with a sophisticated interest in the social sciences as well will find fascinating this study arguing that the supernatural world view, as projected in religion and reflected in the arts, gives meaning to the brute facts of biological and social existence. *H—Gannon; P—Dover.*

SKINNER, B. F. b. 1904. *About Behaviorism* (1974). The most authoritative introduction to the philosophy of the "science of human behavior" by its chief contemporary spokesman. Tackles 20 common misconceptions about behaviorism and argues for a more thoroughgoing practice of this influential psychology. *H—Knopf; P—Random.*

WATSON, JOHN B. 1878-1958. *Behaviorism* (rev. ed. 1958). Should be read along with Skinner for an earlier version of a psychology that attempts to bridge the distance between animal and human behavior study. *P—Norton.*

WATTS, ALAN 1915-1973. *Psychotherapy East and West* (1975). A unique contribution that does much to dispel Western notions about the deeper insights derived from unconventional therapies. *P—Random.*

General Fields

ACKERMAN, NATHAN b. 1908. *The Psychodynamics of Family Life* (1958). A classic by the leader of the view that disturbed individuals always belong to disturbed families; moves toward formulating an integrated family therapy. *H & P—Basic.*

BACHRACH, ARTHUR J. b. 1923. *Psychological Research* (3rd ed. 1972). A clear presentation of both the formal principles of the scientific methods as they relate to psychology and of the enjoyment and challenge of doing research. *P—Random.*

BIRNEY, ROBERT C. b. 1925 and RICHARD C. TEEVAN b. 1919 (eds.). *Measuring Human Motivation* (1962). Essays on contemporary methods of measurement. *P—Van Nos Reinhold.*

CANDLAND, DOUGLAS K. b. 1934 (ed.). *Emotion: Bodily Change* (1962). A good set of selections introducing the enduring problem in psychology—what is emotion and how can it be measured? *o.p.*

DULANY, DONELSON E., Jr. b. 1928 et al. *Contributions to Modern Psychology* (2nd ed. 1963). Provides detailed accounts of experiments and observations upon which most general discussions of the broad field are based; covers intelligence, perception, learning and memory, thinking, development. *P—Oxford U Pr.*

ELLIS, HENRY C. b. 1927. *Fundamentals of Human Learning and Cognition* (1972). Concise introduction to this important field. *H & P—Wm C Brown.*

ERIKSON, ERIK H. b. 1902. *Childhood and Society* (rev. ed. 1964). Original contribution on the social significance of childhood. Describes also Erikson's theory of the eight stages of human development. *H & P—Norton.*

FARNHAM, MARYNIA F. b. 1899. *The Adolescent* (1962). Scholarly, up-to-date information on adolescent psychology written on a mature but nontechnical level. *P—Macmillan.*

FROMM, ERICH b. 1900. *Man for Himself* (1947). A leading current thinker argues persuasively for his own semi-Freudian interpretation of human nature. *H—HR&W; P—Fawcett World.*

HORNEY, KAREN 1885-1952. *Feminine Psychology* (1973). Ed. by Harold Kelman. Nonpolemical, wise study by a pioneer in this field. *H & P—Norton.*

KESSEN, WILLIAM b. 1925 (ed.). *The Child* (1965). Readings in the history of child psychology, including early essays by Locke and Rousseau as well as Piaget's classic *Growth of Thought. P—Wiley.*

LAZARUS, RICHARD S. b. 1922 and E. M. OPTON, Jr. b. 1936 (eds.) *Personality* (2nd ed. 1971). Includes seminal articles by Allport, Rogers, and Cattell dealing with four main issues relating to personality: description, development, dynamics, and determinants. *H—Peter Smith; P—P-H.*

LINTON, RALPH 1893-1953. *The Cultural Background of Personality* (1945). Most later studies of culture and personality have been built on Linton's pioneer work. *P—P-H.*

MENNINGER, KARL b. 1893 et al. *The Vital Balance: The Life Process in Mental Health and Illness* (1967). Early attempt at a holistic, humanistic, and less technical view of mental illness; attacks the professional urge to classify and sees many persons as "obliged to make awkward and expensive maneuvers to maintain themselves." *P—Viking Pr.*

RAPAPORT, DAVID 1911-1960. *Emotions and Memory* (rev. ed. 1972). A solid work, integrating material from different languages and frames of reference, on the role of emotions in remembering and forgetting. *H & P—Intl Univs Pr.*

SULLIVAN, HARRY STACK 1892-1949. *The Psychiatric Interview* (1954). Illuminating on what is involved; required for those interested in counseling. *H & P—Norton.*

VERNON, M. D. b. 1901. *The Psychology of Perception* (1962). A nontechnical outline of the psychological processes involved in our visual perception of things around us—shape, color, movement, space relationships. *o.p.*

WALLACE, ANTHONY F. D. b. 1923. *Culture and Personality* (2nd ed. 1970). A book for initiated readers, explaining the culture-and-personality system and giving a thorough review and cogent critique of current work in this interesting field. *P—Random.*

WHITING, JOHN W. M. b. 1908 and IRVIN L. CHILD b. 1915. *Child Training and Personality* (1953). A provocative study of the extent to which and the ways in which the personality processes in individuals determine the integration of their culture. *P—Yale U Pr.*

Applied Fields

BLOCK, N. J. b. 1942 and GERALD DWORKIN b. 1937. *The IQ Controversy* (1976). Refreshing discussion about whether intelligence has a genetic component; the complex ethical, political, and sociological issues stemming from the problem are considered. *H & P—Pantheon.*

BROWN, BARBARA b. 1917. *New Mind, New Body. Bio-Feedback* (1974). The leading researcher in this new field discusses the remarkable possibilities of bio-feedback training. *H—Har-Row; P—Bantam.*

BROWN, JAMES A. b. 1911. *The Social Psychology of Industry* (1954). A lively account of challenging issues paramount in industrial relations. *H—Gannon; P—Penguin.*

GROF, STANISLAV b. 1931. *Realms of the Human Unconscious* (1976). Summarizes the author's LSD research over 17 years. Explores the use of LSD in treatment of schizophrenia and for easing the experience of dying. *H—Viking Pr; P—Dutton.*

HARPER, ROBERT b. 1915. *The New Psychotherapies* (1975). An introduction to family and group therapies. *P—P-H.*

KOVEL, JOEL b. 1936. *A Complete Guide to Therapy* (1976). Describes the many available therapies, suggesting the advantages and disadvantages of each. *H—Pantheon.*

MASTERS, ROBERT E. L. and JEAN HOUSTON. *The Varieties of Psychedelic Experience* (1967). Probably the sanest and soundest book on the psychedelic experience, arguing that drugs are no panacea for mental ills but have beneficial uses under controlled supervision. *P—Dell.*

MEARNS, HUGHES 1875-1965. *Creative Power* (2nd rev. ed. 1959). The author's early experiments in tapping the creative springs of children through the arts caused a minor revolution in our nation's schools. *H—Peter Smith; P—Dover.*

PROGOFF, IRA. *At a Journal Workshop* (1975). A transpsychological approach to psychological problems; invaluable tool for persons interested in self-help. *H—Dialogue Hse.*

27. Biological Sciences

Daniel McKinley

Biology is the story of all life on earth—past, present, and future. Any narrower definition fails to convey its majestic sweep in time and space. And biology is a human matter, for neither ours nor any other species can be comprehended apart from the total world in which it has evolved and lives. Thus, even such huge undertakings as classification of plants and animals or descriptions of their anatomy or physiology (upon which some individual biologists necessarily focus their attention) are but small facets of a subject so many-sided and so rich in beauty and fascination that no educated person can neglect it.

There is no separate literature of biology; nor are its facts restricted to a small number of minds, isolated in laboratories. The knowledge of biology belongs to all human beings, for the realities of science are the realities of life itself. No one can understand the problems that concern us today without first understanding the forces that have made us what we are, physically and mentally.

For most people, biology deals primarily with living creatures of the living earth. Pleasure in color, form, and movement; awareness of the amazing diversity of life, and enjoyment of natural beauty— these are part of our heritage as a living species. Thus, the first systematic acquaintance with biology ought to come through nature—in fields and forests and on the shore. For those who wish to observe nature firsthand, the best introductions are in the Peterson *Field Guide Series*, now in over twenty volumes (*H & P—HM*). Later, to amplify and verify, one should explore biology in the laboratory and prepare for its analysis at molecular and atomic levels. Some of the most gifted and imaginative biologists not only first approached their subject through sensory impression and emotional response but also returned to nature as a wellspring of confirmation of the old and as inspiration for new approaches. Many memorable writings— even when addressed primarily to the intellect—are rooted in emotional reaction to that life stream. Great nature writers such as Hudson and Thoreau have valid places in one's reading in biology; and every biologist's feelings of concern and satisfaction are reinforced when sharing the well-honed biological insights of poets such as Wordsworth, Coleridge, Clare, and Hopkins. For both poets and biologists there is tonic discipline in having felt, tasted, smelled, and listened in a world of plants, animals, and seasons not programmed for us.

As the frontiers of science expand, there is inevitable specialization. All mental faculties of individuals or groups are brought to bear upon a single aspect of some problem. Thus, some biologists fix their attention upon certain groups or parts of organisms: mycology (molds and mushrooms), virology (viruses), or neurology (nervous systems); and others concentrate upon biological structure or process: anatomy (internal parts), physiology (body chemistry), or genetics (inheritance). But a countertendency today leads even radically distinct specialists to work in cooperation. Oceanographic expeditions commonly include biologists with various specialties as well as chemists, physicists, geologists, and meteorologists—so diverse are the problems presented by just one aspect of earth's surface. Biologists also share discoveries of other sciences. Physicists have found that radioactive elements in fossils disintegrate at a rate that can be determined accurately, thus providing a tool that has quickly revolutionized our conceptions of the age of our planet and permitting a far more accurate approach than ever before to the problem of human evolution. Chemists and geneticists, by joining forces, are perhaps solving the riddle of the gene—the actual means by which it transmits and produces hereditary characteristics—and in the process generating new mysteries for research.

There are many levels of good reading in biology. The great minds in biology, as in other disciplines, walk in small companies. If they live long enough, they see solved a few of the looming problems they uncover. Some of the classics in biology are good reading only for good biologists: e.g., Paul A. Weiss's *Developmental Biology*, Harold F. Blum's *Time's Arrow and Evolution*, and D'Arcy Wentworth Thompson's *On Form and Function*. Such books clearly rebut the contention of novices that in science anything over ten years old is worthless. Seminal biologists of stature, the original thinkers, must often inform the lay understanding through interpreters, leaving critics to sort out what is good biology as well as good reading.

In the 20th century, much biological thought has been deliberately focused on ecology, the study of the relation of living creatures to their environment. Awareness of ecological relationships is—or ought to be—the basis of modern conservation programs, for it is futile to try to preserve any species unless the kind of environment it requires is also preserved.

If we have been slow to apply concepts of ecology generally, we have been even tardier in thinking ecologically about the human species (see the following chapter, "Ecosophy and the Environ-

ment"). Yet the welfare of our species as part of a varied fabric
of experience—perhaps even its survival—depends on our learning
to live in harmony with other species and with the same forces that
control all life.

The varied roles of separate species or organisms in understanding ourselves are complex. To simplify these is to simplify the
result. Whereas a peacock's tail is made to be seen, at least by
peafowls, some of the most elaborately beautiful animals never see
each other and may not even be seen. Consider the perfect symmetry
of shape and pattern and the jewellike brilliance of color of a small
nemertean worm that lives all its adult life in the darkness of the
mantle cavity of a burrowing seashore clam. Seen under the microscope, the little worm is a joy to the eye and a solace to the mind.
Yet its perfection was made for neither.

A close reading of such classic works as Elizabeth Sewell's *The
Orphic Voice* shows clearly how biology shares very deep roots with
other disciplines. Furthermore, great ideas in biology instruct even
when ambiguous—consider Arthur O. Lovejoy's study of the
Platonic Great Chain of Being, which almost stifled early biology
but later led to a firm intuitive grasp of the holistic roles of organisms in ecological communities.

Any of the books listed below can lead to ever wider views of the
richness and diversity of biological thought and writing. In them
and in the works they lead to, the reader can explore the marvels of
biology as measured thus far by human intellect.

ARDREY, ROBERT b. 1908. *African Genesis* (1961). Lively speculation
    on the evolution of the human species, with forays into the study of
    human fossils and comparative behavior. *H—Atheneum; P—Dell.*

ASIMOV, ISAAC b. 1920. *The Wellsprings of Life* (1960). Popular and
    informed summary of knowledge about the origin and development of
    life. *P—NAL.*

BATES, MARSTON b. 1906. *The Forest and the Sea* (1960). A fascinat-
    ing introduction to animal ecology by a master of prose and a first-
    rate field biologist. *P—Random.*

BATESON, GREGORY b. 1904. *Steps to an Ecology of Mind* (1972).
    Essays by a keenly alert anthropologist on the tangled contributions
    of skin-in and skin-out biology to the finished product that we call
    mind, describing expertly the interplay of freedom and determinism.
    P—Ballantine.

BEEBE, WILLIAM 1877-1962. *Jungle Peace* (1918). One of many good
    books by a gifted naturalist and a master of brisk reporting. *o.p.*

BODSWORTH, FRED b. 1918. *Last of the Curlews* (1955). With sustained
    drama and a keen observation of nature, the author tells the story of the
    decline and final destruction of the "last" of an extinct species. *P—
    Dodd.*

CARSON, RACHEL 1907-1964. *The Sea Around Us* (1951). A sensitive,
    gracefully written account of the origin, history, and dynamics of the
    sea written by the very first editor of this chapter on Biological
    Sciences. *H—Oxford U Pr; P—NAL.*

COLLIS, JOHN STEWART b. 1900. *The Triumph of the Tree* (1954). Trees discussed as among the world's most ancient and successful organisms and as fellow beings in human history and mythology. *o.p.*

COMFORT, ALEX b. 1920. *The Nature of Human Nature* (1967). The dimensions of human behavior leads the reader into the biology of many matters in this penetrating and erudite portrait. *H—Har-Row.*

CORNER, E. J. H. b. 1906. *The Life of Plants* (1964). A first-rate botanist discusses plants in their natural habitats and not just their cells in a glass dish, their tissues on a glass slide, or as imprisoned individuals out of context in glass houses. *o.p.*

CRICK, FRANCIS b. 1916. *Of Molecules and Men* (1966). A vigorous account from a Nobel laureate and one of the great performers in the drama of molecular biology. *P—U of Wash Pr.*

CUTRIGHT, PAUL RUSSELL b. 1897. *The Great Naturalists Explore South America* (facs. ed. 1940). Not only good reading but an exciting account of how naturalists invaded a continent without laying it to waste. *H—Bks for Libs.*

DARWIN, CHARLES 1809-1882. *The Voyage of the Beagle* (1839). A better book for the nonbiologist to learn about Darwin's excellence as a biologist and great observer than *The Origin of Species* (1859) or *The Descent of Man* (1871), although the latter are more influential works. *H—Har-Row (abr.); P—Dutton, Natural Hist.*

DESMOND, ADRIAN J. b. 1947. *The Hot-blooded Dinosaurs* (1976). How little we know about the past can be gathered by reading this exciting book that claims that many cherished beliefs about the now dead dinosaurs may prove untrue. *H—Dial: P—Warner Bks.*

DETHIER, VINCENT G. b. 1915. *To Know a Fly* (1963). Makes the study of the housefly a humorous, personal, and fascinating adventure. *P—Holden-Day.*

DORST, JEAN b. 1924. *Before Nature Dies* (1970). Easily the best biological review of world conservation. Not just a plea for preservation but a firmly informed account of what earth's biology is all about and how it got into its present bind. *H—HM; P—Penguin.*

DUBOS, RENÉ J. b. 1901. *So Human an Animal* (1968). A good sample of the many books by a distinguished bacterial ecologist and philosophical biologist with a penchant for putting human failings (organic and cultural) into an evolutionary framework. *H & P—Scribner.*

EISELEY, LOREN C. 1907-1977. *The Immense Journey* (1957). A powerful, imaginative exploration of evolutionary events that led to our natural world and its molding of the human species. *P—Random.*

ELTON, CHARLES S. b. 1900. *The Ecology of Animals* (3rd ed. 1966). This lucid little textbook merits inclusion because its author is a founder of modern ecology and observes closely and writes well. *P—Halsted Pr.*

EVANS, HOWARD ENSIGN b. 1919. *Life on a Little-known Planet* (1968). That earth remains a "little-known planet" is not the fault of such assiduous watchers of small fry as Evans, an expert on solitary wasps. *H—Dutton; P—Dell.*

FRASER DARLING, SIR FRANK b. 1903. *A Naturalist on Rona* (1939). The author began his career as one of the ablest bird and mammal watchers. His contributions to conservation have been great and are here reported in prose that is a delight to read. *H—Kraus Repr.*

GARSTANG, WALTER. *Larval Forms and Other Zoological Verses* (1962). Remarkable for the varied forms attempted and for the author's success in putting into verse some very difficult zoological matter. *o.p.*

GOODALL, JANE (BARONESS VAN LAWICK-GOODALL) b. 1934. *In the Shadow of Man* (1971). Notable account of chimpanzee watching by the acute observer who did much to make natural observations of the great apes a reality. *H—HM; P—Dell.*

HARDIN, GARRETT b. 1915. *Nature and Man's Fate* (1959). By a tireless, versatile interpreter of the significance of biology, this book delineates areas of great concern to the human species. *P—NAL.*

HARDY, SIR ALISTER b. 1896. *The Open Sea* (2nd ed. 1971). Beautifully illustrated and written account of plankton, fish, and fisheries. *H—HM.*

HOCKING, BRIAN b. 1914. *Biology or Oblivion* (rev. ed. 1972). Provides a versatile quiver of arrows to shoot at anyone who underestimates the import of biology and the urgency of the issues it deals with. *H & P— Schenkman.*

———. *Six-legged Science* (rev. ed. 1971). Both an instructive and entertaining account of insects. *H & P—Schenkman.*

HOWELLS, WILLIAM W. b. 1908. *Mankind in the Making* (rev. ed. 1967). A keenly interesting account of human fossils and of other species that led to our species. *H—Doubleday.*

HUDSON, WILLIAM H. 1841-1922. *The Naturalist in La Plata* (1892). Unforgettable account of Argentine natural history, told with the love of truth and detail well known to those who have read Hudson's *Green Mansions* (1904) and the autobiographical *Far Away and Long Ago* (1918). *H—AMS Pr, Folcroft.*

HUTCHINSON, GEORGE EVELYN b. 1903. *The Itinerant Ivory Tower* (1953). Apt scholarly reflections on biology and other subjects that are a credit to the author's science and to Western culture. *H—R West.*

HUXLEY, SIR JULIAN 1887-1975. *Man in the Modern World* (1948). Thirteen essays by a distinguished biologist provide a good sampling from a man who wrote prolifically and clearly on ecology and evolution. *o.p.*

KAVALER, LUCY b. 1929. *Mushrooms, Molds, and Miracles* (1965). The mythology, natural history, and human importance of fungi, fascinatingly told. *H—British Am Bks, John Day.*

KRUTCH, JOSEPH WOOD 1893-1970. *The Twelve Seasons* (1949). Many have written well about the country year but few have done so with a more deliberate dedication to the biological in nature than this literary critic and professor of English. *H—Bks for Libs.*

———. (ed.). *Great American Nature Writing* (1950). An influential proponent of the significance of biology in our lives, Krutch introduces this collection with a superb essay on the role of nature in literature. *o.p.*

LA BARRE, WESTON b. 1911. *The Human Animal* (1954). Speculations by a social anthropologist who knows both people and biology. *H & P— U of Chicago Pr.*

LEOPOLD, ALDO 1886-1948. *A Sand County Almanac* (1949). Essays by one of the greatest prose stylists among ecologists, conservationists, and naturalists. A founder of modern wildlife conservation, Leopold wrote a text, *Game Management* (1933), that is both good reading and a persuasive account of what must yet be done. *H—Oxford U Pr; P—Ballantine, Oxford U Pr.*

Life Nature Library. A beautifully illustrated series of some 25 volumes on various areas of biology and groups of organisms. Each is by a recognized expert; some, like RUTH MOORE's *Evolution* (1962) and E. CLARK HOWELLS' *Early Man* (1965), are among the best short accounts of their subjects. *H—Silver, Time-Life.*

LORENZ, KONRAD Z. b. 1903. *King Solomon's Ring* (1952). A delightful guide to understanding and investigating animal behavior, by a Nobel laureate. *H—T Y Crowell; P—Apollo Eds.*

———. *On Aggression* (1966). Aggression is presented as an essential part of the social life of animals. Its place and control among people is persuasively argued by a leading ethnologist. *H—HarBraceJ; P— Bantam, HarBraceJ.*

MEEUSE, B. J. D. b. 1916. *The Story of Pollination* (1961). Accords plants exciting lives and useful roles in nature without dragging in either personification or autobiography. *H—Ronald.*

MONOD, JACQUES 1910-1976. *Chance and Necessity: An Essay on the Natural Philosophy of Modern Biology* (1971). A popular account that offers important reflections on an important subject. *H— Knopf; P—Random.*

OLBY. *The Path to the Double Helix*. See "Physical Sciences and Mathematics," page 255.

PRUITT, WILLIAM O., Jr. b. 1922. *Animals of the North* (1967). An effective combination of narrative and ecology written by a biologist whose firsthand knowledge is fully integrated with his philosophical grasp of community biology. *H—Har-Row.*

SANDERSON, IVAN T. 1911-1973. *Animal Treasure* (1937). Even small adventures read interestingly in Sanderson's clear prose, and his illustrations of intriguing creatures are superlative. *P—Pyramid Pubns.*

SCHALLER, GEORGE B. b. 1933. *The Year of the Gorilla* (1964). One of the most insightful of modern studies of the great apes; full of pleasant writing, appealing drawings, peaceful beasts, and devoted reporters. *H & P—U of Chicago Pr.*

SETON, ERNEST THOMPSON 1860-1946. *Ernest Thompson Seton's America* (1954). A small sample of an incredible life's work, edited by Farida Wiley. Seton was one of a select group of grand masters with one foot solidly implanted in the literary world and the other in the wilderness. *P—Devin.*

SEWELL, ELIZABETH b. 1919. *The Orphic Voice* (1960). The myth of Orpheus provides illuminating connections between biology and poetry in an elegant treatise, both in the history of ideas and of meaning, centered on the theme that nature is a language and that poetry has a natural history. *P—Har-Row.*

SHEPARD, PAUL b. 1925. *The Tender Carnivore and the Sacred Game* (1973). Scholarly speculations about humankind as a hunting species and about the influence of hunting on our evolution, social development, and future. *o.p.*

SIMPSON, GEORGE GAYLORD b. 1902. *The Meaning of Evolution* (rev. ed. 1967). Understandable to most educated readers, yet comprehensive and detailed enough to be useful to general biologists, this book is a fair example of Simpson's dedication to informing non-scientists about the significance of his work. *H & P—Yale U Pr.*

SMITH, HOMER 1895-1956. *Kamongo* (rev. ed. 1949). An absorbing dialogue on evolution between a young biologist and a priest during a prolonged chance meeting. *P—Viking Pr.*

STEINBECK, JOHN 1902-1968 and E. F. RICKETTS. *The Sea of Cortez* (1941). This travelog-autobiography contains good biology and gives insight into the minds and motives of biologists. *H—Viking Pr.*

THOREAU. *Walden.* See "Biography," page 154.

WATTS, MAY THEILGAARD b. 1893. *Reading the Landscape* (1957). Ranks high among books interpreting the ecological history of the countryside; love for learning and the land shines through. *H—Macmillan.*

WIGGLESWORTH, VINCENT BRIAN b. 1899. *The Life of Insects* (1964). The largest group of animals, described by a versatile and experienced entomologist. *o.p.*

WILSON. *Sociobiology.* See "Sociology," page 226.

ZINSSER, HANS 1878-1940. *Rats, Lice, and History* (1935). A masterly account of the role of mammals, insects, and disease in human social evolution. No reader in biology should miss it. *H—Little.*

28. Ecosophy and the Environment

Paul Shepard

Those Western thinkers of the past two centuries who did not share the Faustian urge to dominate and exploit planet Earth and all its plant and animal inhabitants were generally considered eccentric and ignored. In recent decades, however, increasing knowledge about the depletion of natural resources, the near-extinction of some mammal, bird, and fish species, and the widespread pollution of air and water has compelled awareness of the counterproductive results of efforts to control and master the environment. Our faith in linear progress rooted in a scientific technology and our arrogant humanism—a faith that long blinded people to their arbitrary destruction of the environment—has been agonizingly shattered.

In recent years we have tried to atone for our ecological sins with frenetic zeal. We have analyzed the decay in the quality of life, identified numerous problems, and have sought solutions piecemeal through uncoordinated social programs and expedient political decisions. This approach is not working and offers little hope. At an even more fundamental level must come a deeply felt and widespread revolution in how we view the environment and humanity's relationship to it.

This necessary new social and philosophical approach to ecology has resulted, among other effects, in the coining of a new term, *ecosophy*, which is being used with increasing frequency. Ecosophy affirms or implies that the sensibility arising from an ecological perspective may permeate any branch of human thought, indeed may profoundly affect one's world view or philosophy of life. It seems useful to separate ecology—that branch of biology dealing with the science of ecosystems—from what Aldo Leopold called "the upshot"—that is, the many and varied consequences of an unecological orientation. It is also necessary, though less obvious, not to equate environmentalism, conservation, or bio-politics with the organic holism of integrated ecological thought.

Ecosophy implies a way of experiencing—of perceiving, valuing, and attitude-forming—in which one's philosophy is attuned to ecological reality. Paramount in that reality is the interdependence of living things and their organization with the nonliving into what have been called "evolutionary tracking systems." Implicit also in this new natural philosophy is recognition that thought and culture—that is, mind in all its forms and manifestations—are parts of such systems. The Norwegian philosopher Arne Naess makes a useful distinction between ecosophy and ecological philosophy, characterizing the latter as an aspect of the formal discipline of philosophy and the former as a mode of knowing and being.

The objective in this chapter is to identify books that go beyond ecology or political advocacy. Their writers locate wisdom in the ecological illumination of human affairs, a wisdom transcending the alarms it triggers or the techniques it fosters in the use of the earth. The writers come from different disciplines and backgrounds but all share the sense that the way in which we affirm the priority of nature is central to our humanity as well as to the preservation of a livable world.

APPLETON, JAY b. 1919. *The Experience of Landscape* (1975). An unusual synthesis of several disciplines—biology, psychology, esthetics—as a means of exploring and explaining our preferences for particular places. *H—Wiley.*

CARSON, RACHEL 1907-1964. *Silent Spring* (1962). A landmark book in ecosophy that precipitated the revolution in environmental sensibility of the 1960s and 1970s. A beautifully written, carefully documented condemnation of the indiscriminate use of chemical pesticides. *H—HM; P—Fawcett World.*

COBB, EDITH b. 1905. *The Ecology of Imagination in Childhood* (1977). An exquisite and imaginative study of the child's relationship to nature, identifying with sensitivity the needs of the developing child for specific experience with the nonhuman. *H—Columbia U Pr.*

COMMONER, BARRY b. 1917. *The Closing Circle* (1971). Close to a definitive study of ecology and its relationship to modern industrial civilization. A primer for those interested in the options open in the struggle for a livable world. *H—Knopf; P—Bantam.*

DALY, HERMAN b. 1938. *Toward a Steady-State Economics* (1973). A shattering analysis of the way in which environmental destruction has resulted from assumptions of perpetual growth made by traditional economics and a refutation of those assumptions. *H & P—W H Freeman.*

DELORIA, VINE b. 1933. *Planetary Man* (1977). A modern version of the American Indian philosophy about living in harmony with the earth by an author with a wide grasp of the complexities of the contemporary world. *H—Har-Row.*

EHRLICH, PAUL R. b. 1932 and ANNE H. EHRLICH. *Population, Resources, Environment: Issues in Human Ecology* (1972). A basic source book on the relationship of human numbers to planetary resources. The Ehrlichs' position—that of activist biologists—sometimes conflicts with, sometimes complements, the views of Commoner (see above). *H—W H Freeman.*

GLACKEN, CLARENCE b. 1909. *Tracers on the Rhodian Shore* (1973). A scholarly treatise that traces historically and intellectually the Western view of the relationship of humankind and nature from pre-biblical times to the present. *H & P—U of Cal Pr.*

HARDIN, GARRETT b. 1915. *Exploring New Ethics for Survival: The Voyage of the Spaceship Beagle* (1973). This fictional account of an emigrant group in a spaceship satirizes the competing interests, rationalizations, and equivocations of spaceship Earth. Alternating with installments of the tale are factual and interpretive chapters about mankind's ecological situation. *H—Viking Pr; P—Penguin.*

HIGHTOWER, JIM. *Hard Tomatoes, Hard Times* (1973). Dissects the agribusiness from bad food through ravaged lands to pollution, destroying the myth that federal bureaucracies administer our natural resources in the public interest. *H & P—Schenkman.*

KOZLOVSKY, DANIEL b. 1937. *An Ecological and Evolutionary Ethic* (1974). Reflections about the different impacts evolutionary and ecological ideas have on our culture. *H—P-H.*

LEISS, WILLIAM b. 1939. *The Limits to Satisfaction* (1976). Argues that peoples' impact on the resources of the planet is more affected by what they think they want than by actual physical needs, and contends that we can comfortably adapt to fewer wants. *H & P—U of Toronto Pr.*

LEOPOLD. *A Sand County Almanac.* See "Biological Sciences," page 245.

LORENZ, KONRAD Z. b. 1903. *Behind the Mirror* (1977). A Nobel laureate applies ethology (fieldstudy of animal behavior) to the capacities and habits of human beings as thinking animals. *H—HarBraceJ.*

McHARG, IAN b. 1920. *Design with Nature* (1971). A watershed approach to modern design and planning by an outspoken, creative landscape architect; a thoroughly articulated theory of ecology in land use on a large scale. *H & P—Natural Hist.*

MARGALEF, RAMON. *Perspectives in Ecological Theory* (1968). A second reader for those who have mastered the basic principles of ecology. *H & P—U of Chicago Pr.*

MEADOWS, DENNIS b. 1942 et al. *Dynamics of Growth in a Finite World* (1974). A systems analysis approach to the global use of the physical world; expanded deliberations by the authors of the controversial *Limits to Growth.* *H—Wright-Allen.*

OPHULS, WILLIAM. *Ecology and the Politics of Scarcity* (1977). Ophuls argues that the only way that the socially catastrophic effects of anticipated chronic scarcity can be avoided is for all our institutions and customs to come to terms with a steady-state, no growth society. *P—Freeman.*

Parabola (150 Fifth Ave., New York, N.Y.). A graceful journal centering in the function and structure of myth. Many articles are multidisciplinary and concern the relationships between people and nature.

SCHUMACHER. *Small Is Beautiful*. See "Economics," page 214.

SEARS, PAUL B. b. 1891. *The Living Landscape* (1966). A beautifully written description of the earth as a living entity, demonstrating its ecological integration. *P—Basic.*

SEWELL. *The Orphic Voice*. See "Biological Sciences," page 245.

SHEPARD, PAUL b. 1925. *Thinking Animals* (1978). Investigates the use of animals as instruments of thought, not only in a literary sense but as essential elements in the development of identity in children. *H— Viking Pr.*

SLATER, PHILIP b. 1927. *Earthwalk* (1974). A ranging, radical criticism of the ecological arrogance of modern society. Slater sees solutions to many of our dilemmas because they have been "fostered, not invented or legislated." *H—Doubleday; P—Bantam, Doubleday.*

SNYDER, GARY b. 1930. *Earth House Hold* (1969). Essays, poems, and sketches about wilderness, Buddhism, and the primitive by a Pulitzer Prize winner. Snyder never neglects people as the center of his concerns, yet never without reference to the natural as essential to human life. *P—New Directions.*

WATT, KENNETH b. 1929. *The Titanic Effect* (1974). An approach to economic myopia and its crippling effects on human ecology—a concern Watt, an ecologist, shares with Herman Daly, an economist (see above). *H—Dutton.*

WILSON. *Sociobiology*. See "Sociology," page 226.

29. Physical Sciences and Mathematics

Herman Y. Krinsky

One distinction of the human species is its continuous curiosity about the internal and external manifestations of the universe: we have always felt a need to know, understand, and explain the workings of the physical world. In an effort to comprehend, we have invented science, mathematics, and religion.

In prehistoric times, however, sheer survival seems to have been the driving force, the need to know was purely operational—how to make fire, tools, hunting and fighting implements. As society became more complex and living less marginal, the knowledge required increased in complexity. To measure land, to irrigate, to develop and maintain commerce, to predict the seasons, humankind had to invent mathematical systems and evolve the specialist. Given a friendly environment, a measure of security, and some leisure—particularly in ancient Greece—thinkers replaced the operational (the *how*) with the explanatory (the *why*). The way was now clear for abstract conjecture.

As physical science and mathematics gradually replaced superstition and mystery with rational explanations—that is, by the 16th and 17th centuries—thinking became bolder. Perhaps it was possible to understand the physical events and phenomena occurring in the universe, from the microscopic to the cosmic, in terms of a few basic concepts. This is where we have been, and this is where we still are. We have long since reached the stage at which no one can begin to encompass all of human understanding, when knowledge is so vast that specialists invariably have gaps in their specialties.

The 20th century has been a period of self-sustaining revolution in mathematics and all the sciences. We have landed on the moon—not once but several times. We have surveyed the surface of Mars. We have reduced the huge computer complexes of the 1950s to desk-top devices. From the enunciation of the quantum theory in 1900 to the Pulsars, Quasars, Quarks, and Charm, old foundations have crumbled and new theories been developed with confusing speed. In this rapid profusion of change (many still living today have been heated by coal, oil, and atomic generated electricity; have traveled by horse cart, train, automobile, and jet; and have written with quill, fountain pen, ballpoint, and computer punch card), the need to know and understand is more urgent than ever.

Many see our time as one of continuing scientific specialization and mathematical speculation. The scientist is a person with very special interests who communicates in mathematics, jargon, and distinctive prose. Although the quantitative details are often beyond the grasp of most intelligent amateurs, the qualitative aspects of these new concepts are not. Indeed, the thinking person as well as the scientist has a need to recognize the complex moral, philosophical, sociological, psychological, and political implications that accompany scientific and technological advance.

The highly selective list of books below is mainly nontechnical; those books that require some technical or mathematical knowledge have been so identified. The magazine *Scientific American* will keep the reader up to date with developments in science and technology. And such TV series as "Nova" and "The Ascent of Man" do an excellent job of keeping the intelligent citizen informed.

ARMITAGE. *The World of Copernicus*. See "Biography," page 148.

BARNETT, LINCOLN K. b. 1909. *The Universe and Dr. Einstein* (rev. ed. 1957). One of the soundest and clearest expositions of relativity and quantum theory. *P—Bantam.*

BEDINI, SILVIO A. b. 1917. *Thinkers and Tinkers* (1975). This American bicentennial product covers the history of American science, invention, and technical ingenuity from the time of discovery to Independence. *H—Scribner.*

BORN, MAX 1882-1970. *The Restless Universe* (rev. ed. 1957). A Nobel laureate guides the intelligent reader step-by-step through the maze of molecules, atoms, subatomic particules, and nuclear physics. Has delightful illustrations in the form of flip-over "animated sequences." *H—Peter Smith; P—Dover.*

————. *The Born-Einstein Letters* (1970). This epic correspondence of two great physicists between 1916 and 1955 has often been quoted by other greats of the Quantum Era. The insights and philosophical implications are devastating, but some letters are incomprehensible to the lay reader. *H—Walker & Co.*

BRONOWSKI, JACOB 1908-1974. *The Ascent of Man* (1974). A stunning and monumental work that runs from the beginnings to today. This clear, fresh, lucid book should be read and reread; the TV series based on it seen and reseen. *H & P—Little.*

CALDER, NIGEL b. 1931. *The Restless Earth: A Report on the New Geology* (1972). A lucid, well-illustrated survey for the nonspecialist of theories concerning the earth's crust (plate tectonics, continental drift, formation of mountains and ocean basins) and the origin and evolution of life. *H—Viking Pr; P—Penguin.*

CARTER, GEORGE F. b. 1912. *Man and the Land* (3rd ed. 1975). In a stimulating style the author explains the role of humanity's perception as a dynamic factor in the evaluation and use of the earth. *H—HR&W.*

CONANT, JAMES B. b. 1893 et al. *Harvard Case Histories in Experimental Science* (1957). Designed to give the general reader a feel for the tactics and strategy of scientific investigation. *H—Harvard U Pr 2 vols.*

CRONEIS, CAREY G. b. 1901 and WILLIAM C. KRUMBEIN b. 1902. *Down to Earth* (1961). A lively, absorbing introduction to geology, explaining the origin of humans, their place in nature, and the interrelationships of geology, physics, biology, and mathematics. *P—U of Chicago Pr.*

DANTZIG, TOBIAS 1884-1956. *Number: The Language of Science* (4th rev. ed. 1954). Long considered one of the most successful presentations of mathematics for the nonprofessional, this book was described by Einstein as the "most interesting book on the evolution of mathematics which has ever fallen into my hands." *P—Free Pr.*

EINSTEIN, ALBERT 1879-1955. *Relativity: The Special and General Theory* (1920). Authoritative, nontechnical analysis by the founder of the theory. *H—Peter Smith; P—Crown.*

FARRINGTON. *Greek Science.* See "Greece," page 8.

FRANK. *Einstein.* See "Biography," page 150.

GAMOW, GEORGE 1904-1968. *One, Two, Three . . . Infinity* (rev. ed. 1961). A distinguished physicist, who leads the field in interpreting science to the lay person, writes a splendid introduction to the facts and speculations of modern mathematics and science. *P—Bantam, Viking Pr.*

_____. *The Creation of the Universe* (rev. ed. 1961). Explains the origin and evolution of the universe in clear language. *H—Viking Pr.*

_____. *Gravity* (1962). Relates the contributions of Galileo, Newton, Einstein, and others to our understanding of one of the greatest enigmas—the nature of gravity. *P—Doubleday.*

_____. *A Planet Called Earth* (1963). A clear, illuminating coverage of the earth's geological and biological history. *o.p.*

_____. *Mr. Tompkins in Paperback* (1966). Modern physics as dreamed by Mr. Tompkins. Thoroughly delightful and solidly informative. *H & P—Cambridge U Pr.*

_____. *Thirty Years That Shook Physics* (1966). Quantum theory explained with a minimum of mathematics and a maximum of clarity; contains many anecdotes, photographs, and biographical sketches. *P—Doubleday.*

GARDNER, MARTIN b. 1914. *Fads and Fallacies in the Name of Science* (2nd ed. 1957). The story of pseudoscientists, cults, and human gullibility fascinatingly recounted. *P—Dover.*

_____. (ed.). *Great Essays in Science* (1957). A brilliant collection of 31 varied essays, each both solid and readable. *P—WSP.*

_____. *The Ambidextrous Universe* (1965). A nontechnical analysis of symmetry and asymmetry in the universe. *o.p.*

_____ and A. RAVIELLI b. 1916. *Relativity for the Million* (1962). Well-illustrated, witty, popular treatment of a difficult scientific concept. *H—Macmillan.*

GOODMAN, NATHAN G. 1899-1971 (ed.). *The Ingenious Dr. Franklin* (1956). A short and engaging collection of Franklin's scientific letters reissued for the bicentennial. *H & P—U of Pa Pr.*

GREENBERGER, MARTIN b. 1931 (ed.). *Computers and the World of the Future* (1962). The impact of computers on human endeavor as seen by Norbert Wiener, C. P. Snow, and many others. *P—MIT Pr.*

HARE, F. KENNETH b. 1919. *The Restless Atmosphere* (4th ed. 1966). Highly readable and thoroughly informative introduction to climates. *o.p.*

HEISENBERG, WERNER b. 1901. *Philosophical Problems of Nuclear Science* (1952). A history of atomic concepts from ancient Greece to the present, and a description of the aims of modern physics by the founder of the Uncertainty Principle. *o.p.*

_____. *Physics and Beyond* (1971). Heisenberg provides further insights into the giants of modern physics: Sommerfeld, Pauli, Bohr, Einstein, and Planck. He also explains what it was for him to be a German in Germany during World War II. *H & P—Har-Row.*

HOFFMANN, BANESH b. 1906 and HELEN DUKAS. *Albert Einstein* (1972). A touching and poignant biography for the general reader by one of Einstein's collaborators and his secretary. *P—NAL.*

IHDE, AARON J. b. 1909. *The Development of Modern Chemistry* (1964). A comprehensive history of chemistry—well-illustrated and with extensive and informative appendixes. Some knowledge of chemistry is needed. *H—Har-Row.*

JEANS, JAMES 1877-1946. *The Universe Around Us* (4th ed. 1944). Relegating mathematics to footnotes, this great astronomer relates physics, chemistry, and geology to astronomy. *H & P—Cambridge U Pr.*

KISCH, BRUNO 1890-1966. *Scales and Weights* (rev. ed. 1976). The history, methodology, and equipment are presented for an area that is often taken for granted. *H—Yale U Pr.*

LANGENBERG, D. N. b. 1932 and B. N. TAYLOR b. 1936 (eds.). *Precision Measurements and Fundamental Constants* (1970). A collection of papers given at the 1970 International Conference of the National Bureau of Standards, summarizing the consistent, basic constants of present-day science. Requires some mathematical sophistication. *P— US Govt Ptg Off.*

McCULLOUGH, DAVID b. 1933. *The Great Bridge* (1972). Recounts fascinatingly the engineering and the social impact of the world's greatest, though not longest, bridge, the Brooklyn. *H—S&S; P—Avon.*

MENDELSSOHN, KURT A. G. b. 1906. *The Quest for Absolute Zero* (1966). An engaging historical account of the approach to absolute zero. Nonmathematical, this book clearly treats one of the physical limits. *o.p.*

MOORE. *Niels Bohr.* See "Biography," page 152.

NAGEL, ERNEST b. 1901 and JAMES R. NEWMAN b. 1907. *Gödel's Proof* (1958). A small book introducing one of the most revolutionary mathematical concepts of the 20th century. Though not highly technical, this book must be read with paper and pencil. *H & P—NYU Pr.*

NEWMAN, JAMES R. b. 1907 (ed.). *The World of Mathematics* (1956). A four-volume anthology of mathematical literature from the Greeks to modern times, compiled for both amateur and expert. *H & P—S&S.*

OLBY, ROBERT b. 1933. *The Path to the Double Helix* (1974). The absorbing history of how the structure of DNA was discovered and of how these discoveries led to the monumental work of Watson and Crick. *H—U of Wash Pr.*

OPPENHEIMER, J. ROBERT 1904-1967. *Science and the Common Understanding* (1966). The significance of science today is explained by one who actively applied moral principles in his work. *P—S&S.*

POINCARÉ, JULES HENRI 1854-1912. *Science and Method* (1914). Describes the basic methodology and psychology of scientific discovery and analyzes the nature of experimentation, theory, and the human mind as they are applied to the acquisition of organized knowledge.

RAPPORT, SAMUEL b. 1903 and HELEN WRIGHT b. 1914. *The Crust of the Earth* (1955). An excellent lay person's introduction to geological science, discussing the formation of the earth, its age and history, the search for knowledge about early human life, and such topics. *o.p.*

READ, JOHN 1884-1963. *Prelude to Chemistry* (1966). A truly delightful trip through the pseudoscience of alchemy. *P—MIT Pr.*

REID, CONSTANCE b. 1918. *A Long Way from Euclid* (1963). This well-written book on higher mathematics requires only a recollection of high school geometry. *H—T Y Crowell.*

RULE, WILFRED P. et al. *FORTRAN IV Programming* (1973). If you have a high school background, this manual will take you by the hand and lead you through the intricacies of a major computer language, FORTRAN IV, anticipating and answering your questions. *P—Prindle.*

RUSSELL, BERTRAND 1872-1970. *The ABC of Relativity* (3rd rev. ed. 1969). A popular account of the meaning and significance of relativity by a great mathematician and equally great philosopher. *P—Humanities, NAL.*

SCHRÖDINGER, ERWIN 1887-1961. *Science, Theory and Man* (1957). Nine essays on people and the changing world, introducing the reader to the philosophical outlook of one of the founders of the new science. *o.p.*

Scientific American, Editors of. This first-rate magazine publishes yearly articles-in-depth on timely subjects. Recent books include *The Ocean* (1969), *The Biosphere* (1970), *Energy and Power* (1971), *Communication* (1972), *Life and Death and Medicine* (1973), *The Human Population* (1974), *The Solar System* (1975), and *Food and Agriculture* (1976). *H & P—W H Freeman.*

SHAMOS, MORRIS H. b. 1917 (ed.). *Great Experiments in Physics* (1959). Original papers are presented with copious marginal notes. The contributions range from Galileo to Einstein, and some technical knowledge is necessary. *o.p.*

SHIPMAN, HENRY L. b. 1948. *Black Holes, Quasars, and the Universe* (1976). A brilliant, well-written, not-too-technical discussion of the "hottest" subjects in cosmology. *H & P—HM.*

SHKLOVSKII, I. S. b. 1916 and CARL SAGAN b. 1934. *Intelligent Life in the Universe* (1966). A remarkable collaboration between a Soviet and an American astronomer. Some technical knowledge is essential. *P—Dell.*

SLOANE, N. J. b. 1939. *A Handbook of Integer Sequences* (1974). A delightful book for the number buff. *H—Acad Pr.*

STEIN, SHERMAN K. *Mathematics: The Man-Made Universe* (3rd ed. 1975). Requiring no mathematics beyond high school algebra, Stein develops ideas in number theory, topology, set theory, and other areas. *H—W H Freeman.*

THOMAS, WILLIAM L., Jr. b. 1920 (ed.). *Man's Role in the Changing Face of the Earth* (1956). Scholars from many disciplines contribute to the discussion of this controversial and dynamic theme. *H—U of Chicago Pr.*

TIETZE, HEINRICH b. 1880. *Famous Problems of Mathematics* (1965). For the reader with some higher mathematics. The angle is not trisected, the circle remains unsquared, and Fermat's Last Problem is still unsolved, but the imagination is whetted. *H—Graylock.*

ULAM, STANISLAW M. b. 1909. *Adventures of a Mathematician* (1976). The autobiography of a prodigy of our day, full of entertaining anecdotes about giants such as von Neumann, Fermi, Gamow, and others. *H—Scribner.*

WHITEHEAD, ALFRED NORTH 1861-1947. *Science and the Modern World* (1925). A distinguished modern philosopher and mathematician provides a sweeping, path-breaking, difficult interpretation of the universe in terms of events, organisms-in-process. *P—Free Pr.*

WIENER, NORBERT 1894-1964. *Cybernetics* (2nd ed. 1961). One of the most original and influential books of this century, opening the door to the computer age. *H & P—MIT Pr.*

––––––. *God and Golem, Inc.* (1964). Explores at the amateur's level, the ethical and religious problems growing out of the human development of machines. *H & P—MIT Pr.*

YUKAWA, HIDEKI b. 1907. *Creativity and Intuition* (1973). A Japanese scientist presents a nontechnical view of Western science. The distinctive approach and cultural orientation are revealing and edifying. *H—Kodansha.*

Science Fiction

Much good reading and some good science and provocative social thought can be found in science fiction. This edition of *Good Reading* omits a selective list of science fiction titles not because we undervalue either their general worth or their academic legitimacy (many colleges have already introduced a course in science fiction into the curriculum), but because the books rated as best are hard to determine.

Science-fiction reading buffs may well be the best source for books to start with. Or you might consult *Anatomy of Wonder: Science Fiction* (1976, Bowker), a critically annotated guide to some 1,400 of the best adult and juvenile science-fiction titles.

Without recommending best titles (which are much in dispute), we do recommend that you encounter at least the following novelists (who are recognized as masters of the genre). Each has written at least one science fiction masterpiece (and a few have written two or more) that is either good literature or sound science or usually both. If you choose to read science fiction, do not miss Isaac Asimov, Ray Bradbury, John Brunner, Arthur C. Clarke, Robert A. Heinlein, Aldous Huxley, Ursula McGuin, Walter Miller, Larry Niven and Jerry Pournelle, Kurt Vonnegut, and H. G. Wells (one of the fathers of the genre).

Special Section

30. Reference Books

Donald A. Sears

Any book becomes a reference book when we use it to answer a specific question of fact or idea—that is, when we refer to it for an answer. *Good Reading*, for example, with its essays and annotated book lists, is a reference guide to good reading: it answers questions about what is interesting and worthwhile to read in a broad spectrum of subject fields. Another way to define a reference book is to say that it is one we dip into for a particular purpose and not one that we read clear through. We are not likely to read all of *Who's Who* or *Books in Print* or the *Encyclopaedia Britannica* (though many readers, their research in encyclopedic works completed, are often intrigued by and browse lengthily in adjacent and quite unrelated articles). Each of these books serves its purpose when we consult it for specific information; each is an example of a basic reference book.

Most people have in their homes at least a few reference books— a dictionary, a *World Almanac*, an atlas, one or more cookbooks, or a garden or houseplant encyclopedia. But few can afford to own all that they might wish to use. For most reference books we go to the reference collection of a library. And even though a large library will not possess all the reference works in existence, every library will have a varied and useful collection that is generally found in a special section or room.

The great advantage of a reference book is that it serves as a shortcut. By being familiar with reference tools we can find the answer we seek with little waste of time. We might have to scan through several histories of the Civil War before finding the exact date of a particular battle, but a dictionary of dates will yield the information in seconds. Insofar as the library is the treasury of knowledge, reference books are the keys to that treasure. There is an answer to every conceivable *factual* question if one but knows where to look.

Though well over a hundred major reference titles are included in the following pages, they are only a small—though representative and suggestive—sampling of the great bibliographical and other reference guides that are available.

Bibliographies and General Indexes

Nearly every library has the *Cumulative Book Index* (Wilson), *Books in Print* (Bowker), *Subject Guide to Books in Print* (Bowker), and *Paperbound Books in Print* (Bowker). These volumes bring reasonably up to date (with information about publisher, price, date, edition, etc.) the staggering array of books published. Information about a wanted book can usually be found under any of three entries: (1) author's name, (2) title of the book, and (3) subjects with which the book deals. Larger libraries have sets of the National Union Catalog of the Library of Congress, which lists works in all languages published throughout the world.

Libraries also have files of publications that analyze, usually under authors and subjects, the contents of magazines. Material on any subject can thus be found in files of thousands of volumes of periodicals. Representative analyses are *Poole's Index* (19th-century periodicals), *Readers' Guide to Periodical Literature*, *Popular Periodical Index*, *Social Sciences Index*, *Humanities Index*, and *P.A.I.S.* (*Public Affairs Information Service*). The *New York Times Index* (1913 to date) is issued semimonthly and serves both as a guide to that newspaper and, indirectly, as a guide to articles appearing in other newspapers on approximately the same date. Additionally, there are many indexes for special fields: art, bibliography, business, education, music, technology, etc. An example is the annual *MLA International Bibliography of Books and Articles on the Modern Languages and Literatures*.

Abstracts (summaries of published works) are another kind of helpful analysis of the literature of a given subject: *Biological Abstracts*, *Chemical Abstracts*, *Historical Abstracts*, *MLA Abstracts of Articles in Scholarly Journals*, and *Psychological Abstracts* are five of many such publications.

The *Essay and General Literature Index* (1900 to date), a subject analysis of thousands of collective works, cites component parts of selected compilations. Almost any published short literary work can be found through special indexes: *Granger's Index to Poetry* (Columbia U Pr), *Play Index* (Wilson), *Fiction Catalog* (Wilson), *Short Story Index* (Wilson), and *Song Index* (Shoe String).

Full and helpful lists of all sorts of reference books on every subject are *Guide to Reference Books* (ALA) and *How and Where to Look It Up* (McGraw). Bibliographies have been cumulated annually since 1937 in *Bibliographic Index* (Wilson).

For self-help in library orientation and use of reference material, a handy manual is *New Library Key* (Wilson).

Encyclopedias

Standard, frequently revised general encyclopedias with helpful index volumes are *Encyclopedia Americana* (30 vols. 1977 Grolier Inc), *Encyclopaedia Britannica* (30 vols. 1977 Ency Brit Ed) and *World Book Encyclopedia* (22 vols. 1977 Field Ent). Each is kept up to date by annual yearbooks. The best single-volume work for an individual's desk is *The New Columbia Encyclopedia* (1975 Lippincott).

Fact Books

One or more of several small single volumes, each including an amazing collection of information, can be very helpful near one's desk. Annually revised titles include *World Almanac* (H—Doubleday; P—Newspaper Ent), *Yearbook of the United Nations* (Intl Pubns Serv), *Guinness Book of World Records* (H—Sterling; P—Bantam), *Statistical Abstract of the United States* (US Govt Ptg Off), and *U.S. Book of Facts, Statistics and Information* (PB).

Atlases

Of major scope is *The Times Atlas of the World* (H—Quadrangle). Good and not too cumbersome general volumes are *National Geographic Atlas of the World* (Natl Geog), *Cosmopolitan World Atlas* (Rand), and *Advanced Atlas of Modern Geography* (McGraw). A specialized volume is *Historical Atlas of the World* (B&N). Two useful paperbound atlases for the modest home library are *Regional Atlas* (Rand) and *Historical Atlas of the World* (Rand).

Allied to atlases are such books as *The Columbia-Lippincott Gazetteer of the World* (Columbia U Pr) and *American Place-Names* (Oxford U Pr).

Dictionaries

Outstanding comprehensive authorities are the *Oxford English Dictionary* (13 vols. and suppl. Oxford U Pr), *Dictionary of American English on Historical Principles* (4 vols. U of Chicago Pr), and *Webster's Third New International Dictionary* (Merriam). Smaller desk dictionaries include *American Heritage Dictionary of the English Language* (HM), *Funk and Wagnalls Standard College Dictionary* (Funk & W), *Webster's New World Dictionary* (Collins-World), and (recommended) *Webster's New Collegiate Dictionary* (1976 Merriam).

Other useful books in this category include *Dictionary of Modern English Usage* (Oxford U Pr), *Dictionary of American Slang* (T Y Crowell), *Webster's Dictionary of Synonyms* (Merriam), and *Roget's International Thesaurus* (T Y Crowell).

Many abridged versions of Roget are published as paperbounds. Standard for etymologists is *Origins: A Short Etymological Dictionary of Modern English* (Macmillan). There are also dictionaries for every major and most minor foreign languages. A useful volume for the foreign traveler is the paperbound *New College Multilingual Dictionary* (Bantam), which contains 4,591 basic words in English, French, Spanish, Italian, German, Russian, and Portuguese.

Literature

Cassell's Encyclopaedia of World Literature (Morrow), the *Columbia Dictionary of Modern European Literature* (Columbia U Pr), *Crowell's Handbook of Classical Literature* (T Y Crowell), and *Oxford Companion to French Literature* (Oxford U Pr) are helpful in providing information about foreign-language books and authors.

The *Cambridge History of English Literature* (Cambridge U Pr), *Literary History of the United States* (Macmillan), and the *Reader's Encyclopedia of American Literature* (T Y Crowell) are historical reference works. More critical articles may be found in *Encyclopedia of Poetry and Poetics* (Princeton U Pr). For its field, there is the *McGraw-Hill Encyclopedia of World Drama* (McGraw).

In addition, general books, so miscellaneous and widely varied in the information they include as to be miniature encyclopedias, include the series of **Oxford Companions** (Oxford U Pr), *Brewer's Dictionary of Phrase and Fable* (Har-Row), *Great Treasury of Western Thought* (Bowker), and *Reader's Adviser* (3 vols. Bowker).

Who said it? Books of quotations arranged by authors or subjects, with copious indexes of key words, will give the answer. Among a great many, the following four are particularly helpful: *Bartlett's Familiar Quotations* (Little), *New Dictionary of Quotations* (Knopf), *Oxford Dictionary of Quotations* (Oxford U Pr), and *Home Book of Quotations* (Dodd).

Poems can often be located in anthologies, a particularly useful set of which is published by Oxford U Pr. Also useful is *Granger's Index to Poetry* and its supplement (Columbia U Pr).

Critical opinion may be located through such tools as *Book Review Digest* (Wilson), *Book Review Index* (Gale), or *Current Book Review Citations* (Wilson).

Biography

Who's Who in America (Marquis) is a biennial biographical directory, in outline form, of prominent living Americans, supplemented by regional volumes and *Who's Who of American Women*. *Who's Who* (St Martin) is an annual publication, mainly listing Britons. *International Who's Who* (Intl Pubns Serv) covers all countries. *Current Biography* (Wilson) is a monthly publication, annually cumulated, with profiles and portraits of prominent people of various nationalities.

Dictionary of American Biography (Scribner) contains authoritative and detailed biographies of Americans no longer living; based on it is the handy *Concise Dictionary of American Biography* (Scribner). *Dictionary of National Biography* (Oxford U Pr) is the corresponding British set. Also historical is *Notable American Women* (Harvard U Pr). *New Century Cyclopedia of Names* (P-H) and *Webster's Biographical Dictionary* (Merriam) are widely inclusive but have only brief entries.

Biographical reference books abound for nearly every area of human effort, from art to zoology. The following series of Wilson books deal only with authors: *American Authors, 1600–1900; British Authors before 1800; British Authors of the Nineteenth Century; Twentieth Century Authors; European Authors, 1000–1900;* and *World Authors: 1950–1970.* The *Contemporary Writers Series* (St Martin) has separate volumes on dramatists, novelists, and poets. *Biography Index* (Wilson)—annually and triennially cumulated from quarterly publications—locates biographical material in current books and periodicals. Special volumes feature outline biographies of those in particular professions: e.g., *Directory of American Scholars* (Bowker).

Extremely useful is *Biographical Dictionaries Master Index* (Gale), a guide to more than 725,000 listings in over 50 current who's whos and other works of collected biographies.

Art and Music

For the fine arts the best recent reference tool is *Encyclopedia of World Art* (15 vols. McGraw). Extremely useful also is *McGraw-Hill Dictionary of Art* (5 vols.). Reasonably recent smaller publications include *Architectural and Building Trades Dictionary* (Am Tech), *Contemporary Artists* (St Martin), *Dictionary of Antiques and Decorative Arts* (Scribner), and *Dictionary of Architecture* (Overlook Pr).

In music the standard monumental work is *Grove's Dictionary of Music and Musicians* (10 vols. plus suppl. St Martin). Less inclusive but useful general compendiums include *Harvard Dictionary of Music* (Harvard U Pr), *New College Encyclopedia of Music* (Norton), *Oxford Companion to Music* (Oxford U Pr), and *International Cyclopedia of Music and Musicians* (Dodd). For information about opera, see *Complete Opera Book* (Putnam); for modern music, *Popular American Composers* (Wilson).

Philosophy, Psychology, and Religion

Still useful, though old, are *Dictionary of Philosophy and Psychology* (Peter Smith) and *Encyclopaedia of Religion and Ethics* (Scribner). Briefer but more recent is the *Dictionary of*

Philosophy (Littlefield). Most recent and most detailed is the *Encyclopedia of Philosophy* (8 vols. Macmillan).

The *Harvard List of Books in Psychology* (Harvard U Pr) is an up-to-date bibliography. Also useful is *American Handbook of Psychiatry* (Basic). Small paperbound dictionaries of psychology are published by Citadel Pr, Dell, and Penguin.

Old but standard for biography and history is *The Jewish Encyclopedia* (Gordon Pr); newer is *Encyclopaedia Judaica* (Macmillan). *The New Catholic Encyclopedia* (McGraw) replaces a 50-year-old version. Useful shorter works are *Harper's Bible Dictionary* (Har-Row) and the *Interpreter's Dictionary of the Bible* (Abingdon).

History

A helpful bibliography of historical materials is the *Harvard Guide to American History* (Harvard U Pr). Useful also are *Dictionary of Dates* (Greenwood and Hafner) and *Encyclopedia of World History* (HM). Limited to our own history is *Encyclopedia of American History* (Har-Row). Lengthy reference histories are *Cambridge Ancient History* (17 vols.), *Cambridge Medieval History* (8 vols.), and *Cambridge Modern History* (14 vols.), all by Cambridge U Pr. For quick reference to world events since 1940 there are the annual volumes of *Facts on File*.

Social Sciences

For this area there is an 18-volume publication, *International Encyclopedia of the Social Sciences* (Macmillan). *Business Periodicals Index* (Wilson) indexes major business and trade periodicals.

Useful volumes for economics include *Dictionary of Economics* (B&N), *Oxford Economic Atlas of the World* (Oxford U Pr), and *Historical Statistics of the United States, Colonial Times to 1957* (US Govt Ptg Off).

For political science and government, worldwide, there are *Encyclopedia of Modern World Politics* (HR&W), *Yearbook of the United Nations* (Intl Pubns Serv), and *Political Handbook and Atlas of the World* (Har-Row). These books are helpful for state and local government: *Book of the States* (Am Hist Res), *Municipal Year Book* (Int City Mgt), and *New Dictionary of American Politics* (B&N).

For sociology, see *Dictionary of Sociology and Related Sciences* (Littlefield).

Science

Good representative general works are *Scientific Encyclopedia* (Van Nos Reinhold), *Harper Encyclopedia of Science* (Har-Row), and *Dictionary of Scientific Terms* (Van Nos Reinhold).

Useful for astronomy are *Guide to the Sky* (Cambridge U Pr), *Guide to the Stars* (Philos Lib), and *Space Encyclopedia* (Dutton).

Botany is served by *Glossary of Botanic Terms* (Hafner), *Hortus Second* (Macmillan), and *Flowering Plants and Ferns* (Cambridge U Pr).

Chemistry is covered by a wide range of encyclopedias and dictionaries, including *Dictionary of Applied Chemistry* (Wiley), *Chemical Encyclopedia* (Van Nos Reinhold), *Encyclopedia of Chemistry* (Van Nos Reinhold), and *Concise Chemical and Technical Dictionary* (Chem Pub).

Those seeking information on physical and mental health can consult *Dorland's Illustrated Medical Dictionary* (Saunders) and *Psychiatric Dictionary* (Oxford U Pr).

For recent developments in science and technology, *Applied Science and Technology Index* and the new *General Science Index* (both Wilson) are subject indexes to periodicals in the fields of applied and pure sciences.

Miscellaneous

As a sample of the wide range of reference works, the following is a selection of titles that have demonstrated their worth: (1) For the foreign traveler: frequently revised Baedeker guides to individual countries (various publishers) and **Fodor's Modern Guide Series** (McKay); (2) For the sports enthusiast: *Encyclopedia of Sports* (A S Barnes); (3) For the writer: *MLA Handbook for Writers of Research Papers, Theses, and Dissertations* (Modern Lang), *A Manual of Style* (U of Chicago Pr), the annual *Writer's Market* (Writer's Digest), and *Literary Market Place* (Bowker); (4) For the job seeker: *Current Career and Occupational Literature* (Wilson); (5) For the socially perplexed: *New Complete Book of Etiquette* (Doubleday) or *Everyday Etiquette* (Bantam); (6) For the committee member: *Robert's Rules of Order* (Pyramid Pubns, Revell, Scott F).

Often libraries contain many source books that readers can use but that they might not expect libraries to have: out-of-town and international telephone directories; hotel guides; medical and legal directories; museum directories; etc.

Professional librarians at schools, colleges, universities, and public libraries are trained and experienced in aiding readers and researchers to find their way around in the vast array of reference books. Consult them: they are always eager to help.

Author, Title, and
Subject Index
to the
Good Reading Book Lists